PRAGMATISM

ISBN 0-915145-37-5 (pbk)
Previously published by
New American Library as 451-MW 1006-150

PRAGMATISM

THE CLASSIC WRITINGS

Edited, with Introduction and commentary, by H. S. Thayer

Charles Sanders Peirce
William James
Clarence Irving Lewis
John Dewey
George Herbert Mead

HACKETT PUBLISHING COMPANY
Indianapolis / Cambridge

Acknowledgments

For permission to use copyrighted material I am grateful to the following:

The American Psychological Association, for George Herbert Mead, "Social Consciousness and the Consciousness of Meaning," *Psychological Bulletin*, VII (1910), pp. 397–405.

The Belknap Press of Harvard University Press for "Definition of Pragmatic and Pragmatism," "The Architectonic Construction of Pragmatism," and "Historical Affinities and Genesis." Reprinted by permission of the publishers from Charles Hartshorne & Paul Weiss, editors, *Collected Papers of Charles Sanders Peirce*, Vol. V, 1934, 1962, Cambridge, Mass.: Harvard University Press, Copyright by the President and Fellows of Harvard College.

Roberta L. Dewey, for John Dewey, "The Construction of Good" in *The Quest for Certainty*; "The Development of American Pragmatism," "The Practical Character of Reality" and "The Unit of Behavior" in *Philosophy and Civilization*; "The Pattern of Inquiry" in *Logic: The Theory of Inquiry*.

Holt, Rinehart and Winston, Inc., for John Dewey, "The Pattern of Inquiry." From *Logic: The Theory of Inquiry* by John Dewey (New York, 1938). Copyright 1938, by Holt, Rinehart and Winston, Inc. Copyright © 1966 by Roberta L. Dewey. Reprinted by permission of Holt, Rinehart and Winston, Inc.

The Editors of *The Journal of Philosophy*, for C. I. Lewis, "A Pragmatic Conception of the A Priori," *The Journal of Philosophy*, XX (1923); and George Herbert Mead, "The Social Self," *The Journal of Philosophy, Psychology, and Scientific Methods*, X (1913).

The New York Times Company, for "Pragmatism—What It Is—By Prof. William James," an interview with William James by Edwin Bjorkman, *The New York Times* (Nov. 3, 1907). Copyright © 1907 by The New York Times Company. Reprinted by permission.

G. P. Putnam's Sons, for John Dewey, "The Development of American Pragmatism" and "The Practical Character of Reality" and "The Unit of Behavior." Reprinted by permission of G. P. Putnam's Sons from *Philosophy and Civilization* by John Dewey (New York, 1931). Copyright 1931 by John Dewey: renewed 1958 by Roberta L. Dewey.

(The following page constitutes an extension of this copyright page.)

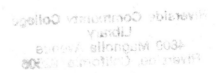

I also thank Paul R. Reynolds, Inc., Mr. John James, and Alexander R. James for their helpful cooperation concerning the material from William James included in the present volume.

Second Printing 1987

Cover design by Laszlo J. Balogh

For further information, please address
HACKETT PUBLISHING COMPANY, INC.
P.O. Box 44937
Indianapolis, IN 46204

Library of Congress Cataloging in Publication Data
Main entry under title:

Pragmatism, the classic writings.

Reprint. Originally published: New York:
New American Library, 1970.
Bibliography: p.
1. Pragmatism—Addresses, essays, lectures.
I. Thayer, H. S. (Horace Standish), 1923–
B832.P77   1982   144'.3   82-2944
ISBN 0-915145-38-3   AACR2
ISBN 0-915145-37-5 (pbk.)

PREFACE

In this book I have attempted to present the basic, most suggestive, and certainly some of the best writings of the major philosophers of American pragmatism. With one exception, the materials here represented consist of whole papers or whole chapters from books. While skillful editorial excision of the irrelevant, redundant, and awkward and the judicious repiecing of a man's writings is to be applauded, in the case of philosophy (and poetry) this task is also precarious and often treacherous. The superimposition of an editor's standards of relevancy and felicity over a philosopher's prose is guided by what are ultimately philosophic convictions and taste. And matters philosophical are always to some extent unsettled and debatable. Even the most balanced of editorial sensibilities can inadvertently go wrong. Hence, in this book, the complete statement of the philosopher's argument has been preserved in its entirety. The one exception is James' great two-volume *Principles of Psychology*, for which considerable selectivity was necessary.*

In thus presenting the classic writings of pragmatism, I am obliged to explain that by "classic" is meant the original and formative expressions of this philosophy articulated by its most eminent spokesmen. There is a considerable literature of substantial and valuable work by other pragmatists and sympathizers—European as well as American—that well deserves attention but could not be included here. In addition, there are some very important contemporary developments and applications of pragmatism, but these can scarcely be classified as "classic" in the above sense. It should also be observed that while each of the philosophers here—Peirce, James, Dewey, Mead, and Lewis—went on to elaborate distinct and comprehensive philosophies, these other doctrines are not to be looked for in these pages. But what remains to form the substance of this book has an originality and largeness of vision while preserving a sense of relevance and fidelity to the complexities of its human subject matter. And these are marks of genius in philosophy. Pragmatism was a new essaying of Human Nature and the

---

* Also the first three paragraphs of Dewey's "The Practical Character of Reality" (selection XIV), which are now dated.

Understanding, to use old captions for it; it was a theory of the reflective and experimental operations of intelligence in conduct responsive to needs and directed to rendering future experience increasingly malleable to human growth and satisfactions. The concentration of analysis was on the possibilities of human action in a contingent and changeful world and on the functions of thought and language as ways of discovering the world and more clearly discerning the goods attainable in it, as well as making any enjoyment of these more luminous and complete. So it is that the pragmatists achieved an authenticity of aim and expression in the practice of a venerable vocation the pursuit of which is knowledge but of a kind whose existence is its own justification.

This book is dedicated to two able philosophical pragmatists, longtime friends who met at Carroll College Academy in Waukesha, 1902, and who were once colleagues in the University of Wisconsin, 1919–1922: M. C. Otto and V. T. Thayer. The book has also benefited from rethinking after intervals occupied with the concerns of Hewitt, Alexandrea, and Jonathan.

Finally, I want to thank Professor Robert Paul Wolff for suggesting this project to me.

H. S. Thayer

CONTENTS

INTRODUCTION

Pragmatism was the most influential philosophy in America during the first quarter of the present century. Its influence was also felt in Europe, although sinuously, and its doctrines were given rather different philosophic expression by English, French, and German thinkers. Viewed against other intellectual currents of American life, pragmatism stands out as a movement that not only affected academic philosophy but had a profound impact upon the study of law, education, political and social theory, religion, and the arts.

It is primarily as a movement rather than by any one doctrine that pragmatism is best understood. The movement is no longer active, having largely succeeded in its critical and positive aims. Contrary to general opinion fashionable a few years ago, however, pragmatism now seems to have a future as a suggestive body of ideas with a wealth of materials, insights, and analyses pertinent to and often anticipating current advances in philosophy. There are signs of a rediscovery and further exploration of this legacy. Still, the best argument for a philosophy lies in that philosophy itself. This is one of two reasons for the present volume; the other, less contentious and perhaps more inviting, is to make available in convenient form a substantial presentation of the most characteristic and important statements from its major spokesmen of this influential modern philosophy: the classic writings of pragmatism.

Each of the philosophers of pragmatism—Peirce, James, Dewey, Mead, and Lewis—was thoroughly trained and absorbed in Anglo-European philosophy and literature. It used to be said by its critics that pragmatism was a peculiarly American turn of thought, a glorification of *ac-*

tion and the *useful,* an idealization of American Big Business. The idiom and circumstances in which this philosophy initially found expression was, surely, American. But no justification for these familiar characterizations can be found in the writings of the pragmatists (as the reader of this book may discern for himself). Furthermore, the roots of American pragmatism and its technical formulation are deeply lodged in the historical course of European philosophy. We will be helped to an understanding of the motivating ideas, the problems as they were felt, and the sense of urgency about them that initiated the development of pragmatism and occupied its founders by a brief look at that history.

"The sun is new each day," said Heraclitus, the philosopher of change, although perhaps privately acknowledging that not everything under the sun is new, for even our way of ascertaining this truth is not new every day. If there is a fixed and salient fact about life, however, it is that we change. And surely the predominant characteristic of modern history is the rapidity of social and intellectual change that has occurred since the transformation of medieval European civilization in the twelfth and thirteenth centuries.

Now change is a condition of tension, as Heraclitus also saw. In the thirteenth century this tension of the old and the new, of advance and resistance, is amply revealed in religion, politics, and the arts; philosophically the tension is centered in the conflicting roles of reason and faith, in an incipient rational and natural science straining within and against a venerable Christian theology.

The relation of reason and revealed truth or, more generally, the relation of knowledge and value had been explored and variously developed by many Hellenistic philosophers and by the Church fathers. Defenses of reason and of faith continued to be developed in successive generations throughout the middle ages with, as might be expected, extremist positions being taken on both sides. A major resolution of this conflict was developed by St. Thomas in the thirteenth century. But with the emergence of modern science in the sixteenth and seventeenth centuries the problem of finding some satisfactory relation between scientific reason and established religious and moral values became more acute. For the new science not only presented a radical departure from earlier conceptions of the kind of universe we live in—thus envisaging nature as an immense mathematical structure of restless particles and bodies, in contrast to the tidy hierarchy of species and beings of medieval cosmology—that science was also a vital source of technology. The social and economic expansion of Western Europe from the thirteenth century on was both a cause and effect of accelerated scientific technology. Expansion in intellectual and geographical dimensions as well as of the productivity and powers of industrial society, resulted in new kinds of experience, discoveries, novelties, and perplexities that challenged the imagination and for the understanding of which the placid tradition of classical and medieval wisdom appeared to offer no evident solution or relevant insight.

All of this had its most serious impact on the inherited moral tradition, the established patterns of belief and conduct of European culture. It was, of course, the Church that first and foremost clarified, directed, and sustained the moral heritage. In the Church and through the genius of St. Augustine there was effected a complex assimilation of Greek philosophy and humanism, Christian doctrine, and Roman ideals of practical and imperial power. This synthesis was always unstable, always subject to the pressure of historical experience, and its elements all too readily breaking out into the diverse currents of scepticism, mysticism, or rationalism. Worldly preoccupations and other worldly aims were ever sources of conflict within the Church. So too was the dualism between a supernatural realm of religious values and revealed truth and the growing body of scientific knowledge. In due course and almost inevitably, the Church was rent by spiritual division, revolution, and reformation within and, gradually losing its hold on science, was occasionally to war against scientific reason when threatened by ideas "contrary to the true sense and authority of Holy Scriptures." *

As modern philosophy emerged from the medieval and Renaissance background, it thus came endowed less with a clear sense of direction than with problems. Two of these are of concern to us here. The first was a problem of formulating an adequate explanation of scientific knowledge;

---

* The language of the Inquisition in sentencing Galileo. See J. J. Fahie, *Galileo, His Life and Work* (London, 1903), p. 313.

the second was that of providing an account of man's moral experience the genuineness of which would be in some way reconcilable and compatible with natural science—neither discrediting nor discredited by the latter.

As to the first problem, there was no doubt about the *fact* of scientific knowledge. The problem lay rather in accounting for this fact. How was the new world of science to be rendered intelligible in the vocabulary and concepts of the philosophic past, how adapt the older instruments of interpretation to new conditions? More disturbing, however, was the prevailing agreement among scientists and philosophers that the world of science was not accessible through ordinary modes of experience. The new knowledge encouraged its own dualism, a cleavage between experience and nature. If the mechanical world of bodies is the cause of all or some of our sensations and ideas, if these latter are often inaccurate and misleading "resemblances" of their outer causes, if our sense of touch, taste and color really have no objective counterparts in nature, how do we acquire knowledge of the world? If all that we know is our own ideas, as the effects of bodies acting on us, how do we achieve knowledge of those causes?

Descartes (1596–1650) was the first philosopher to advance a theory of knowledge designed to resolve the aforementioned problems. He attempted to demonstrate that some of our conceptions are known with certainty to be true. The focus is on the workings of the Mind; drawing upon the subtle and richly suggestive philosophy of Augustinian Platonism, Descartes finds the mind to be a "treasure house" of ideas. Some of these are self-authenticating, and their truth is recognized by an inner illumination, an intuitive light of reason. Thus the thinker can know with certainty that he exists, that God exists, that the scientific world exists. Moreover, God's goodness guarantees the truth of all our clear and distinct conceptions; and among these are the truths of mathematics and natural science. Science then, for Descartes, rests upon indubitable first principles, a conviction that the pragmatists were to reject critically as will be seen in this book. But such was the way Descartes tried to solve the problem of clarifying and defending the legitimacy of his own and Galilean physics.

Descartes' efforts were not, however, regarded as fully successful by his contemporaries or by most later philosophers. Still, to have stated these problems clearly, and wrestled with them, is one reason why Descartes is referred to as the father of modern philosophy. It remained for Locke to attempt another explanation of scientific knowledge—this time Newtonian science—and the relation of science to morality and religion.

Locke's focus, like Descartes', was on the mind, the Understanding. But Locke was in certain crucial respects less successful than Descartes in his analysis of knowledge; and he had his critics, not the least of them Leibniz, Berkeley, and Hume. In introducing his work to his readers, Locke paid tribute to Boyle, "the incomparable Mr. Newton," and some other scientists "of that strain." * Newtonian science, as embodied in *Philosophiae Naturalis Principia Mathematica* of 1686, was the triumph of the age and the paradigm of scientific reason throughout the eighteenth century. But this (and Newton's *Opticks,* 1704) was the mechanical philosophy that Keats among others questioned:

> Do not all charms fly
> At the mere touch of cold philosophy?

> Philosophy will clip an Angel's wings,
> Conquer all mysteries with rule and line†

This science would even "Unweave a rainbow" with its explanations.‡ Approximately a hundred years earlier another lesser poet commented on the threat of excessive Newtonianism—and in his verse is found just the theme of these pages. In a poem, "Essay on Reason" (1735), Walter Harte contended that scientific reason is important, but it has its limits; a "medium" must be kept, there are other values:

> Reason, like virtue, in a medium lies:
> A hair's-breadth more might make us mad, not wise,
> Out-know ev'n knowledge, and out-polish art,
> Till Newton drops down giddy—a Descartes!

William Blake put a different case for "reason." Science was not *reason* but the touch of death to sense, imagination, insight, and truth.

---

* John Locke, *An Essay Concerning Human Understanding* (London, 1690), "Epistle to the Reader."

† Keats, *Lamia,* II, ll. 229–230; 234–235.

‡ *Lamia* II, l. 237. Originally he wrote "Destroy a rainbow."

> Reason and Newton, they are quite two things:
> For so the Swallow & the Sparrow sings.
> Reason says "Miracle"; Newton says "Doubt."
> Aye! that's the way to make all nature out.
> "Doubt, Doubt, & don't believe without experiment." *

Blake was opposed to the method of the new science as well as to its propensity to reduce all subject matters to atoms and mechanical laws, an opposition that expressed the alarm of many thinkers, including Bishop Berkeley: "The End of Epicurean or Newtonian Philosophy . . . is Atheism." For Blake, the holy and life-giving spirit encompasses and transforms the "particles" of science:

> The Atoms of Democritus
> And Newton's particles of Light,
> Are sands upon the Red sea shore
> Where Israel's tents do shine so bright.†

It was finally Kant (1724–1804) who wrought an elaborate and profound interpretation of human reason and experience within which Newtonian science and morality were placed respectively as subject matters of Pure and Practical Reason. Kant thus achieved for the eighteenth century what St. Thomas had worked out for the thirteenth century, a comprehensive adjustment and balance of the interests and claims of knowledge and moral ideals. Kant's revolutionary discovery was that the mind does not passively reflect experience, rather it actively creates the order of scientific and ethical experience; ‡ it

* From *Epigrams, Verses, and Fragments*, beginning "You don't believe—I won't attempt to make ye."

† *Verses and Fragments*, 2nd series (1800–1810). For an excellent study of the reactions of eighteenth-century poetry to Newton's *Opticks* see Marjorie Hope Nicolson, *Newton Demands the Muse* (Princeton, 1946).

‡ The "discovery" had actually been made earlier in the history of philosophy, notably by Platonists. It is echoed by Wordsworth in the end of *The Recluse* and in his Preface to the *Excursion:*

> How exquisitely the individual Mind
> . . . to the external World
> is fitted:—and how exquisitely, too—
> Theme this but little heard of among men—
> The external World is fitted to the Mind;
> And the creation (by no lower name
> Can it be called) which they with blended might
> Accomplish.

Wordsworth's friend, Coleridge, registered this reaction to Newton's "does not derive its laws from, but prescribes them to nature" and it does not receive but postulates the fundamental conditions of moral experience: God, freedom, and immortality. Kant remarked that these postulates, necessary to the meaning of moral experience, lay not within but outside knowledge, and he asserted, "I have therefore found it necessary to deny *knowledge,* in order to make room for *faith.*"

The generation coming after Kant found the analysis of knowledge—the sharp cleavage between science and ethics and the austere, almost Newtonian character of Kant's ethic of the moral law—too rigid and too static and confining as a rendition of the possibilities and creative powers of human experience. Romanticism in effect softened and then extended Kant's conception of the mind prescribing laws to nature; the mind prescribes all sorts of imaginative and suggestive interpretative ideas to all sorts of experience. This is a seeing of things by means of and through symbols, imagination, and myths, for these are the "ideals" of Romantic Idealism. Science is but one of these suggestive ways of interpreting experience. There is also poetry, art, ethics, even religion; each of these are ways by which experience is illuminated and made significant. The knower as an artist giving vision to life, molding and imparting value to experience, was a favorite symbol of the Romantic movement—man, the Self or Ego creatively engaged with the Not-Self, the world of resistance and malleability and ideal possibilities.

Not unnaturally, the exploratory spirit of Romanticism was responsive to history, to the relevance of the past and the development of cultures; it produced evolutionary analyses and doctrines and encouraged the growth of the social sciences. With Hegel, finally, these diverse and energetic intellectual attitudes and accomplishments received their summation and integration into a new rationalism, more inclusive and flexible than the "Reason" of the past. Here, what is rational *is* real; what is real is rational. But the real is also processive and developmental. The uni-

---

Opticks: "Newton was a mere materialist. *Mind,* in his system, is always *passive,—a lazy Looker-on* on an external world. If the mind be not *passive,* if it be indeed made in God's Image, and that, too, in the sublimest sense, the Image of the Creator, there is ground for the suspicion that any system built on the passiveness of the mind must be false, as a system." Letter to Thomas Poole, March 23, 1801.

verse, the Whole of things is a directive process of processes through which the Absolute as Spirit realizes itself. The whole is Hegel's ultimate datum and all-inclusive context within which, or in reference to which, all other subject matters are to be understood. "Truth is the whole," but this means that any one thing is to be understood by its relations to all other things; the whole is the Absolute realizing itself "through the process of its own development." Understanding is included in this Whole; "It is the very nature of understanding to be a process, and being a process it is Rationality."

Once again in the history of philosophy, an assimilation of reason and values, knowledge and ideals of conduct had been advanced. For Hegel, the directive course of history exhibits value *and* reason; indeed, as he saw it, the distinction is false to the full concrete nature of reality. For value and knowledge are both aspects of the real. Furthermore, ethical value is accessible to and understood by the critical rational methods of intelligence at work in science and in all knowledge. This perspective on the method and workings of reason through history as a developmental process of incomplete materials and conflicting forces within which reason is operative as contributing to more stable and understandable structures profoundly influenced later Hegelians including John Dewey. He wrote of Hegel's historical vision:

> in intellectual and practical effect, it lifted the idea of process above that of fixed origins and fixed ends, and presented the social and moral order, as well as the intellectual, as a scene of becoming, and it located reason somewhere within the struggles of life.*

While the vast and impressive restoration of systematic reason by Hegel has continued to be the point of departure—and usually critically so—for all subsequent philosophizing, just the kind of conflict of the old and new ways of thinking, the pattern of intellectual and moral perplexities that we have been thus far surveying, occurred in the middle of the nineteenth century. For not long after Hegel completed his work, twenty-nine years after his death a revolutionary advance in science again challenged the prevailing thought of the time. This was the Darwinian revo-

* *The Influence of Darwin on Philosophy* (New York, 1910), p. 66.

lution that came with the publication of the *Origin of Species* in 1859.

To some, including the young John Dewey, Darwinian theory was regarded as compatible with and an extension of Hegel's doctrines. For some others of a more theological persuasion it was necessary either to reject Darwin or argue that evolution is God, or God's way with the world. These were attractive if not very reliable forms of scientific theism. But Darwinism was also clearly a break from much of the philosophic past. It challenged the idea of a universe created for or directed to some overall final purpose; it shook the long-esteemed belief in a world of fixed structures, of essences—even efficacious Reason—controlling natural developments. The particular conditions and form of change, rather than universal "laws" of growth, became the significant item. And particular changes, variations among and within species, were seen as functions of particular adaptive circumstances and purposes or "struggles." The variability of life in nature, the contingencies of successful and unsuccessful adaptions, appeared to render any philosophic attempt to formulate a complete system of natural phenomena or to legislate the goals of nature vain and pretentious. Chance and design were both features of the world but in neither case deducible from metaphysical principles. Finally, man's life was seen as set within nature and like all other living forms subject to uncertainty, unprivileged although advantageously equipped for survival.

Unlike many of his readers, Darwin was relatively modest in philosophizing over the results of his work. But the careful assemblage of data and the concepts of "struggle for existence" and "natural selection" prompted widespread speculation, not always within the bounds of sobriety or understanding. One tempting thesis was to interpret the history of human institutions, the social structure of a civilization, and its technological arts as forms of struggle and adaptation. Herbert Spencer, for one, had argued (in 1855) that "the process of mental evolution" in all its details is an "adjustment of inner to outer relations"; the operations of the mind "meet" external conditions or "fail," and the organism will then not prosper or survive. It was easy to extend this view over the history of thought, ideas, and ideologies. Philosophies in whole or in part could thus be regarded as products of the evolutionary struggle subject to conditions of survival and success.

To Charles Peirce the major feature of Darwin's accomplishment was the application of the statistical method to biology.* This new scientific advance, cultivating the use of probabilities, was evidence of how "chance begets order." For William James, Darwinism pointed to the instrumental character of thought and that "all our theories are *instrumental,* are mental modes of *adaptation* to reality." † Peirce, James, and Dewey regarded the implications of the Darwinian view of man as clearly affirming the experimental and purposive nature of thought. "The rational meaning of every proposition lies in the future . . ." wrote Peirce, and its meaning "is that form in which the proposition is applicable to human conduct." ‡ The most striking feature of the new theory of pragmatism, Peirce remarked, "was its recognition of an inseparable connection between rational cognition and rational purpose." §

This recognition of the "inseparable connection" was indeed fundamental to pragmatism. It was also the crucial point at which the pragmatists found their answer to the two recurrent philosophical problems whose history we have been sketching here. The theory of thought and of mind as aspects of behavior and understandable in reference to purposeful human conduct—in short, a theory of meaning and action—made it possible to provide an interpretation of scientific knowledge and moral judgment as equally coherent and integral features of deliberative behavior. I have suggested that in responding to these serious problems of understanding knowledge and the relation of knowledge and value, philosophers have drawn upon and utilized the past, not only for suggestions of how to proceed or what to avoid, but for the very language and distinctions necessary to articulating the task before them. The pragmatists were no exception to this. It was to Berkeley and Mill, Kant, Fichte, Schelling and Romantic Idealism, Hegel and Hegelianism that Peirce, James, Dewey, and later pragmatists turned—supported by contemporary advances in psychology, biology, physics and logic—in working out the pragmatic solution to the prob-

* See p. 63, below.
† *Pragmatism* (New York, 1907), p. 194.
‡ See p. 113, below.
§ See p. 103, below. Also see Dewey's discussion of this, p. 24, below.

lem of the split between scientific knowledge and ethical values.

There are two ways of dating the origins of pragmatism. First, there was the "Metaphysical Club," founded by Peirce and James among others in whose meetings at Cambridge the idea of pragmatism was first put forth in "the early seventies." Peirce has described this event (see p. 54), but it is worth noticing that in its initial formation pragmatism was the product of cooperative efforts, the give and take of critical discussion in the Club. The second date is nearly enough the beginning of the written history of pragmatism: in January 1878 two remarkable papers appeared in two periodicals. One paper was by Charles Peirce, the other by William James. The one ("How To Make Our Ideas Clear," see IV, p. 79) addressed itself to the operation of thought and the clarification of meaning; the other ("Spencer's Definition of Mind as Correspondence") developed a theory of the controlling conditions of thought, in contrast to Spencer's mechanical view of mind as a set of inner relations adjusting to outer relations. James wrote:

> What right has one, in a formula embracing professedly the "entire process of mental evolution," to mention only phenomena of cognition and to omit all sentiments, all aesthetic impulses, all religious emotions and personal affections? The ascertainment of outward fact constitutes only one species of mental activity. The genus contains, in addition to purely cognitive judgments . . . an immense number of emotional judgments: judgments of the ideal, judgments that things *should* exist thus and not so. How much of our mental life is occupied with this matter of a better or a worse? *

These initial analyses were deepened and broadened into a general philosophy of psychology and logic, a philosophy of the operation of thought in controlling future experience with knowledge qualified by values, and an empirical methodology of the use of language and the nature of inquiry and judgment. These were the ways in which Dewey, Mead, and Lewis built upon and enlarged the work of Peirce and James. Dewey has well described the general position:

* For more on this paper see pp. 125–26, below.

> Pragmatism . . . presents itself as an extension of histori-
> cal empiricism, but with this fundamental difference, that
> it does not insist upon antecedent phenomena but upon
> consequent phenomena; not upon the precedents but upon
> the possibilities of action. And this change in point of
> view is almost revolutionary in its consequences.*

This was the "revolutionary" view that found a fruitful application in the social sciences, legal theory, the study of
art and education. The consequences of general ideas help
create a future that is "different from what it would have
been if thought had not intervened." The test and justification of ideas lies in their contributary function of shaping
future experience.

> . . . this taking into consideration of the future takes us to
> the conception of a universe whose evolution is not fin-
> ished, of a universe which is still, in James' term, "in the
> making," . . . up to a certain point still plastic.†

This last "metaphysical implication" of pragmatism,
Dewey notes, "confirms the human and moral importance
of thought and of its reflective operation in experience."

Since we have gathered in this book the basic writings
of pragmatism,‡ it is unnecessary here to expound doctrine. The philosophers speak very well for themselves.
John Dewey has set forth an excellent account of the early
development and aims of American pragmatism. It is appropriate, therefore, to preface the philosophical writings
with that essay.

---

* See pp. 32–3, below.

† See p. 33, below.

‡ In the footnotes to the selections that follow, occasional references
and comments by the editor are set in square brackets. The source
of each of the selected writings of Peirce, James, Dewey, Mead, and
Lewis in this volume is briefly identified at the outset. For the complete statement of the sources, see Sources of the Selections, pp.
375–77, below.

I. John Dewey:
The Development of
American Pragmatism[*]

The purpose of this article is to define the principal theories of the philosophical movements known under the names of Pragmatism, Instrumentalism, or Experimentalism. To do this we must trace their historical development; for this method seems to present the simplest way of comprehending these movements, and at the same time avoiding certain current misunderstandings of their doctrines and their aims.

The origin of Pragmatism goes back to Charles Sanders Peirce, the son of one of the most celebrated mathematicians of the United States, and himself very proficient in the science of mathematics; he is one of the founders of the modern symbolic logic of relations. Unfortunately Peirce was not at all a systematic writer and never expounded his ideas in a single system. The pragmatic method which he developed applies only to a very narrow and limited universe of discourse. After William James had extended the scope of the method, Peirce wrote an exposition of the origin of pragmatism as he had first conceived it; it is from this exposition that we take the following passages.

The term "pragmatic," contrary to the opinion of those who regard pragmatism as an exclusively American conception, was suggested to him by the study of Kant. In the *Metaphysic of Morals* Kant established a distinction between *pragmatic* and *practical*. The latter term applies to moral laws which Kant regards as *a priori*, whereas the

[*] From *Philosophy and Civilization* (1931)

former term applies to the rules of art and technique which are based on experience and are applicable to experience. Peirce, who was an empiricist, with the habits of mind, as he put it, of the laboratory, consequently refused to call his system "practicalism," as some of his friends suggested. As a logician he was interested in the art and technique of real thinking, and especially interested, as far as pragmatic method is concerned, in the art of making concepts clear, or of construing adequate and effective definitions in accord with the spirit of scientific method.

Following his own words, for a person "who still thought in Kantian terms most readily, *'praktisch'* and *'pragmatisch'* were as far apart as the two poles; the former belonging in a region of thought where no mind of the experimental type can ever make sure of solid ground under his feet, the latter expressing relation to some definite human purpose. Now quite the most striking feature of the new theory was its recognition of an inseparable connection between rational cognition and rational purpose." *

In alluding to the experimental type of mind, we are brought to the exact meaning given by Peirce to the word "pragmatic." In speaking of an experimentalist as a man whose intelligence is formed in the laboratory, he said: "Whatever assertion you may make to him, he will either understand as meaning that if a given prescription for an experiment ever can be and ever is carried out in act, an experience of a given description will result, or else he will see no sense at all in what you say." And thus Peirce developed the theory that "the rational purport of a word or other expression, lies exclusively in its conceivable bearing upon the conduct of life; so that, since obviously nothing that might not result from experiment can have any direct bearing upon conduct, if one can define accurately all the conceivable experimental phenomena which the affirmation or denial of a concept could imply, one will have therein a complete definition of the concept.†

The essay in which Peirce developed his theory bears the title: *How to Make Our Ideas Clear.*‡ There is a remarkable similarity here to Kant's doctrine. Peirce's effort was to interpret the universality of concepts in the domain

---

* *The Monist*, vol. XV (1905), p. 163. [See p. 103, below.]

† *Ibid.*, p. 162. [See p. 102, below.]

‡ *Popular Science Monthly*, vol. XII (1878), pp. 286–302. [See IV, below.]

of *experience* in the same way in which Kant established the law of practical reason in the domain of the *a priori*. "The rational meaning of every proposition lies in the future. . . . But of the myriads of forms into which a proposition may be translated, what is that one which is to be called its very meaning? It is, according to the pragmatist, that form in which the proposition becomes applicable to human conduct, not in these or those special circumstances, nor when one entertains this or that special design, but that form which is most directly applicable to self-control under every situation, and to every purpose." * So also, "the pragmatist does not make the *summum bonum* to consist in action, but makes it to consist in that process of evolution whereby the existent comes more and more to embody generals . . ." †—in other words—the process whereby the existent becomes, with the aid of action, a body of rational tendencies or of habits generalized as much as possible. These statements of Peirce are quite conclusive with respect to two errors which are commonly committed in regard to the ideas of the founder of pragmatism. It is often said of pragmatism that it makes action the end of life. It is also said of pragmatism that it subordinates thought and rational activity to particular ends of interest and profit. It is true that the theory according to Peirce's conception implies essentially a certain relation to action, to human conduct. But the role of action is that of an intermediary. In order to be able to attribute a meaning to concepts, one must be able to apply them to existence. Now it is by means of action that this application is made possible. And the modification of existence which results from this application constitutes the true meaning of concepts. Pragmatism is, therefore, far from being that glorification of action for its own sake which is regarded as the peculiar characteristic of American life.

It is also to be noted that there is a scale of possible applications of concepts to existence, and hence a diversity of meanings. The greater the extension of the concepts, the more they are freed from the restrictions which limit them to particular cases, the more is it possible for us to attribute the greatest generality of meaning to a term. Thus the theory of Peirce is opposed to every restriction

* *The Monist*, vol. XV, pp. 173–74. [See p. 117, below.]
† *Ibid.*, p. 178. [See p. 113, below.]

of the meaning of a concept to the achievement of a particular end, and still more to a personal aim. It is still more strongly opposed to the idea that reason or thought should be reduced to being a servant of any interest which is pecuniary or narrow. This theory was American in its origin in so far as it insisted on the necessity of human conduct and the fulfillment of some aim in order to clarify thought. But at the same time, it disapproves of those aspects of American life which make action an end in itself, and which conceive ends too narrowly and too "practically." In considering a system of philosophy in its relation to national factors it is necessary to keep in mind not only the aspects of life which are incorporated in the system, but also the aspects against which the system is a protest. There never was a philosopher who has merited the name for the simple reason that he glorified the tendencies and characteristics of his social environment; just as it is also true that there never has been a philosopher who has not seized upon certain aspects of the life of his time and idealized them.

The work commenced by Peirce was continued by William James. In one sense James narrowed the application of Peirce's pragmatic method, but at the same time he extended it. The articles which Peirce wrote in 1878 commanded almost no attention from philosophical circles, which were then under the dominating influence of the neo-kantian idealism of Green, of Caird, and of the Oxford School, excepting those circles in which the Scottish philosophy of common sense maintained its supremacy. In 1898 James inaugurated the new pragmatic movement in an address entitled, "Philosophical Conceptions and Practical Results," later reprinted in the volume, *Collected Essays and Reviews*. Even in this early study one can easily notice the presence of those two tendencies to restrict and at the same time to extend early pragmatism. After having quoted the psychological remark of Peirce that "beliefs are really rules for action, and the whole function of thinking is but one step in the production of habits of action," and that every idea which we frame for ourselves of an object is really an idea of the possible effects of that object, he expressed the opinion that all these principles could be expressed more broadly than Peirce expressed them. "The ultimate test for us of what a truth means is indeed the conduct it dictates or inspires. But it inspires that conduct because it first foretells some particular turn to our experience which shall call for just that conduct from us. And I should prefer to express Peirce's principle by saying that the effective meaning of any philosophic proposition can always be brought down to some particular consequence, in our future practical experience, whether active or passive; the point lying rather in the fact that the experience must be particular, than in the fact that it must be active." * In an essay written in 1908 James repeats this statement and states that whenever he employs the term "the practical," he means by it, "the distinctively concrete, the individual, the particular, and effective as opposed to the abstract, general, and inert—'Pragmata' are things in their plurality—particular consequences can perfectly well be of a theoretic nature." †‡

William James alluded to the development which he gave to Peirce's expression of the principle. In one sense, one can say that he enlarged the bearing of the principle by the substitution or particular consequences for the general rule or method applicable to future experience. But in another sense this substitution limited the application of the principle, since it destroyed the importance attached by Peirce to the greatest possible application of the rule, or the habit of conduct—its extension to universality. That is to say, William James was much more of a nominalist than Peirce.

One can notice an extension of pragmatism in the above passage. James there alludes to the use of a method of determining the meaning of truth. Since truth is a term and has consequently a meaning, this extension is a legitimate application of pragmatic method. But it should be re-

---

* *Collected Essays and Reviews* (New York, 1920), p. 412.

† *The Meaning of Truth* (New York, 1909), pp. 209–210.

‡ In a footnote James gave an example of the errors which are committed in connection with the term "Practical," quoting M. Bourdeau who had written that "Pragmatism is an Anglo Saxon reaction against the intellectualism and rationalism of the Latin mind. . . . It is a philosophy without words, a philosophy of gestures and of facts, which abandons what is general and holds only to what is particular." In his lecture at California, James brought out the idea that his pragmatism was inspired to a considerable extent by the thought of the British philosophers, Locke, Berkeley, Hume, Mill, Bain, and Shadworth Hodgson. But he contrasted this method with German transcendentalism, and particularly with that of Kant. It is especially interesting to notice this difference between Peirce and James: the former attempted to give an experimental, not an *a priori* interpretation of Kant, whereas James tried to develop the point of view of the British thinkers.

marked that here this method serves only to make clear the meaning of the term "truth" and has nothing to do with the truth of a particular judgment. The principal reason which led James to give a new color to pragmatic method was that he was preoccupied with applying the method to determine the meaning of philosophical problems and questions and that, moreover, he chose to submit to examination philosophical notions of a theological or religious nature. He wished to establish a criterion which would enable one to determine whether a given philosophical question has an authentic and vital meaning or whether, on the contrary, it is trivial and purely verbal; and in the former case, what interests are at stake when one accepts and affirms one or the other of ɪo theses in dispute. Peirce was above all a logician; w ereas James was an educator and humanist and wished to force the general public to realize that certain problem , certain philosophical debates, have a real importance ɪor mankind, because the beliefs which they bring into play lead to very different modes of conduct. If this important distinction is not grasped, it is impossible to understand the majority of the ambiguities and errors which belong to the later period of the pragmatic movement.

James took as an example the controversy between theism and materialism. It follows from this principle that if the course of the world is considered as completed, it is equally legitimate to assert that God or matter is its cause. Whether one way or the other, the facts are what they are, and it is they which determine whatever meaning is to be given to their cause. Consequently the name which we can give to this cause is entirely arbitrary. It is entirely different if we take the future into account. God then has the meaning of a power concerned with assuring the final triumph of ideal and spiritual values, and matter becomes a power indifferent to the triumph or defeat of these values. And our life takes a different direction according as we adopt one or the other of these alternatives. In the lectures on pragmatism published in 1907, he applies the same criticism to the philosophical problem of the One and the Many, that is to say of Monism and Pluralism, as well as to other questions. Thus he shows that Monism is equivalent to a rigid universe where everything is fixed and immutably united to others, where indetermination, free choice, novelty, and the unforeseen in experience have no place; a universe which demands the sacrifice of the concrete and complex diversity of things to the simplicity and nobility of an architectural structure. In what concerns our beliefs, Monism demands a rationalistic temperament leading to a fixed and dogmatic attitude. Pluralism, on the other hand, leaves room for contingence, liberty, novelty, and gives complete liberty of action to the empirical method, which can be indefinitely extended. It accepts unity where it finds it, but it does not attempt to force the vast diversity of events and things into a single rational mold.

From the point of view of an educator or of a student or, if you will, of those who are thoroughly interested in these problems, in philosophical discussions and controversies, there is no reason for contesting the value of this application of pragmatic method, but it is no less important to determine the nature of this application. It affords a means of discovering the implications for human life of philosophical conceptions which are often treated as of no importance and of a purely dialectical nature. It furnishes a criterion for determining the vital implications of beliefs which present themselves as alternatives in any theory. Thus as he himself said, "the whole function of philosophy ought to be to find the characteristic influences which you and I would undergo at a determinate moment of our lives, if one or the other formula of the universe were true." However, in saying that the whole function of philosophy has this aim, it seems that he is referring rather to the teaching than to the construction of philosophy. For such a statement implies that the world formulas have already all been made, and that the necessary work of producing them has already been finished, so that there remains only to define the consequences which are reflected in life by the acceptance of one or the other of these formulas as true.

From the point of view of Peirce, the object of philosophy would be rather to give a fixed meaning to the universe by formulas which correspond to our attitudes or our most general habits of response to the environment; and this generality depends on the extension of the applicability of these formulas to specific future events. The *meaning* of concepts of "matter" and of "God" must be fixed before we can even attempt to reach an understanding concerning the *value* of our belief in these concepts.

Materialism would signify that the world demands on our part a single kind of constant and general habits; and God would signify the demand for another type of habits; the difference between materialism and theism would be tantamount to the difference in the habits required to face all the detailed facts of the universe. The world would be one in so far as it would be possible for us to form a single habit of action which would take account of all future existences and would be applicable to them. It would be many in so far as it is necessary for us to form several habits, differing from each other and irreducible to each other, in order to be able to meet the events in the world and control them. In short, Peirce wrote as a logician and James as a humanist.

William James accomplished a new advance in Pragmatism by his theory of the will to believe, or as he himself later called it, the right to believe. The discovery of the fundamental consequences of one or another belief has without fail a certain influence on that belief itself. If a man cherishes novelty, risk, opportunity and a variegated esthetic reality, he will certainly reject any belief in Monism, when he clearly perceives the import of this system. But if, from the very start, he is attracted by esthetic harmony, classic proportions, fixity even to the extent of absolute security, and logical coherence, it is quite natural that he should put faith in Monism. Thus William James took into account those motives of instinctive sympathy which play a greater role in our choice of a philosophic system than do formal reasonings; and he thought that we should be rendering a service to the cause of philosophical sincerity if we would openly recognize the motives which inspire us. He also maintained the thesis that the greater part of philosophic problems and especially those which touch on religious fields are of such a nature that they are not susceptible of decisive evidence one way or the other. Consequently he claimed the right of a man to choose his beliefs not only in the presence of proofs or conclusive facts, but also in the absence of all such proof. Above all when he is forced to choose between one meaning or another, or when by refusing to choose he has a right to assume the risks of faith, his refusal is itself equivalent to a choice. The theory of the will to believe gives rise to misunderstandings and even to ridicule; and therefore it is necessary to understand clearly in what way James used it.

We are always obliged to act in any case; our actions and with them their consequences actually change according to the beliefs which we have chosen. Moreover it may be that, in order to discover the proofs which will ultimately be the intellectual justification of certain beliefs—the belief in freedom, for example, or the belief in God—it is necessary to begin to act in accordance with this belief.

In his lectures on pragmatism, and in his volume of essays bearing the title *The Meaning of Truth,* which appeared in 1909, James extended the use of the pragmatic method to the problem of the nature of truth. So far we have considered the pragmatic method as an instrument in determining the meaning of words and the vital importance of philosophic beliefs. Now and then we have made allusion to the future consequences which are implied. James showed, among other things, that in certain philosophic conceptions, the affirmation of certain beliefs could be justified by means of the nature of their consequences, or by the differences which these beliefs make in existence. But then why not push the argument to the point of maintaining that the meaning of truth in general is determined by its consequences? We must not forget here that James was an empiricist before he was a pragmatist, and repeatedly stated that pragmatism is merely empiricism pushed to its legitimate conclusions. From a general point of view, the pragmatic attitude consists in "looking away from first things, principles, 'categories,' supposed necessities; and of looking towards last things, fruits, consequences, facts." It is only one step further to apply the pragmatic method to the problem of truth. In the natural sciences there is a tendency to identify truth in any particular case with a verification. The verification of a theory, or of a concept, is carried on by the observation of particular facts. Even the most scientific and harmonious physical theory is merely an hypothesis until its implications, deduced by mathematical reasoning or by any other kind of inference, are verified by observed facts. What direction, therefore, must an empirical philosopher take who wishes to arrive at a definition of truth by means of an empirical method? He must, if he wants to apply this method, and without bringing in for the present the pragmatic formula, first find particular cases from which he then generalizes. It is therefore in submitting conceptions to the control of experience, in the process of verifying them, that one finds examples of what is called truth. Therefore any philosopher who applies this empirical method without the least prejudice in favor of pragmatic doctrine, can be led to conclude that truth "means" verification, or if one prefers, that verification, either actual or possible, is the definition of truth.

In combining this conception of empirical method with the theory of pragmatism, we come upon other important philosophical results. The classic theories of truth in terms of the coherence or compatibility of terms, and of the correspondence of an idea with a thing, hereby receive a new interpretation. A merely mental coherence without experimental verification does not enable us to get beyond the realm of hypothesis. If a notion or a theory makes pretense of corresponding to reality or to the facts, this pretense cannot be put to the test and confirmed or refuted except by causing it to pass over into the realm of action and by noting the results which it yields in the form of the concrete observable facts to which this notion or theory leads. If, in acting upon this notion, we are brought to the fact which it implies or which it demands, then this notion is true. A theory corresponds to the facts when it leads to the facts which are its consequences, by the intermediary of experience. And from this consideration the pragmatic generalization is drawn that all knowledge is prospective in its results, except in the case where notions and theories after having been first prospective in their application, have already been tried out and verified. Theoretically, however, even such verifications or truths could not be absolute. They would be based upon practical or moral certainty, but they are always subject to being corrected by unforeseen future consequences or by observed facts which had been disregarded. Every proposition concerning truths is really in the last analysis hypothetical and provisional, although a large number of these propositions have been so frequently verified without failure that we are justified in using them as if they were absolutely true. But, logically, absolute truth is an ideal which cannot be realized, at least not until all the facts have been registered, or as James says "bagged," and until it is no longer possible to make other observations and other experiences.

Pragmatism, thus, presents itself as an extension of historical empiricism, but with this fundamental difference, that it does not insist upon antecedent phenomena but upon consequent phenomena; not upon the precedents but upon the possibilities of action. And this change in point of view is almost revolutionary in its consequences. An empiricism which is content with repeating facts already past has no place for possibility and for liberty. It cannot find room for general conceptions or ideas, at least no more than to consider them as summaries or records. But when we take the point of view of pragmatism we see that general ideas have a very different role to play than that of reporting and registering past experiences. They are the bases for organizing future observations and experiences. Whereas, for empiricism, in a world already constructed and determined, reason or general thought has no other meaning than that of summing up particular cases, in a world where the future is not a mere word, where theories, general notions, rational ideas have consequences for action, reason necessarily has a constructive function. Nevertheless the conceptions of reasoning have only a secondary interest in comparison with the reality of facts, since they must be confronted with concrete observations.*

Pragmatism thus has a metaphysical implication. The doctrine of the value of consequences leads us to take the future into consideration. And this taking into consideration of the future takes us to the conception of a universe whose evolution is not finished, of a universe which is still, in James' term, "in the making," "in the process of becoming," of a universe up to a certain point still plastic.

Consequently reason, or thought, in its more general sense, has a real, though limited, function, a creative, constructive function. If we form general ideas and if we put them in action, consequences are produced which could not be produced otherwise. Under these conditions the world will be different from what it would have been if thought had not intervened. This consideration confirms the human and moral importance of thought and of its reflective operation in experience. It is therefore not true to say that James treated reason, thought, and knowledge

---

* William James said in a happy metaphor, that they must be "cashed in," by producing specific consequences. This expression means that they must be able to lead to concrete facts. But for those who are not familiar with American idioms, James' formula was taken to mean that the consequences themselves of our rational conceptions must be narrowly limited by their pecuniary value. Thus Mr. Bertrand Russell wrote recently that pragmatism is merely a manifestation of American commercialism.

with contempt, or that he regarded them as mere means of gaining personal or even social profits. For him reason has a creative function, limited because specific, which helps to make the world other than it would have been without it. It makes the world really more reasonable; it gives to it an intrinsic value. One will understand the philosophy of James better if one considers it in its totality as a revision of English empiricism, a revision which replaces the value of past experience, of what is already given, by the future, by that which is as yet mere possibility.

These considerations naturally bring us to the movement called instrumentalism. The survey which we have just made of James' philosophy shows that he regarded conceptions and theories purely as instruments which can serve to constitute future facts in a specific manner. But James devoted himself primarily to the moral aspects of this theory, to the support which it gave to "meliorism" and moral idealism, and to the consequences which followed from it concerning the sentimental value and the bearing of various philosophical systems, particularly to its destructive implications for monistic rationalism and for absolutism in all its forms. He never attempted to develop a complete theory of the forms or "structures" and of the logical operations which are founded on this conception. Instrumentalism is an attempt to establish a precise logical theory of concepts, of judgments and inferences in their various forms, by considering primarily how thought functions in the experimental determinations of future consequences. That is to say, it attempts to establish universally recognized distinctions and rules of logic by deriving them from the reconstructive or mediative function ascribed to reason. It aims to constitute a theory of the general forms of conception and reasoning, and not of this or that particular judgment or concept related to its own content, or to its particular implications.

As far as the historical antecedents of instrumentalism are concerned, two factors are particularly important, over and above this matter of experimental verification which we have already mentioned in connection with James. The first of these two factors is psychological, and the second is a critique of the theory of knowledge and of logic which has resulted from the theory proposed by neo-kantian idealism and expounded in the logical writings of such philosophers as Lotze, Bosanquet, and F. H. Bradley. As we have already said, neo-kantian influence was very marked in the United States during the last decade of the nineteenth century. I myself, and those who have collaborated with me in the exposition of instrumentalism, began by being neo-kantians, in the same way that Peirce's point of departure was kantianism and that of James was the empiricism of the British School.

The psychological tendencies which have exerted an influence on instrumentalism are of a biological rather than a physiological nature. They are, more or less, closely related to the important movement whose promoter in psychology has been Doctor John Watson and to which he has given the name of Behaviorism. Briefly, the point of departure of this theory is the conception of the brain as an organ for the coordination of sense stimuli (to which one should add modifications caused by habit, unconscious memory, or what are called today "conditioned reflexes") for the purpose of effecting appropriate motor responses. On the basis of the theory of organic evolution it is maintained that the analysis of intelligence and of its operations should be compatible with the order of known biological facts, concerning the intermediate position occupied by the central nervous system in making possible responses to the environment adequate to the needs of the living organism. It is particularly interesting to note that in the *Studies in Logical Theory* (1903), which was their first declaration, the instrumentalists recognized how much they owed to William James for having forged the instruments which they used, while at the same time, in the course of the studies, the authors constantly declared their belief in a close union of the "normative" principles of logic and the real processes of thought, in so far as these are determined by an objective or biological psychology and not by an introspective psychology of states of consciousness. But it is curious to note that the "instruments" to which allusion is made, are not the considerations which were of the greatest service to James. They precede his pragmatism and it is among some of the pages of his *Principles of Psychology* that one must look for them. This important work (1890) really developed two distinct theses.

The one is a reinterpretation of introspective psychology, in which James denies that sensations, images, and ideas are discrete and in which he replaces them by a continuous stream which he calls "the stream of conscious-

ness." This conception necessitates a consideration of relations as an immediate part of the field of consciousness,
having the same status as qualities. And throughout his
Psychology James gives a philosophical tinge to this conception by using it in criticizing the atomism of Locke and
of Hume as well as the *a priorism* of the synthesis of rational principles by Kant and his successors, among whom
should be mentioned in England, Thomas Hill Green, who
was then at the height of his influence.

The other aspect of his *Principles of Psychology* is of a
biological nature. It shows itself in its full force in the criterion which James established for discovering the existence of mind. "The pursuance of future ends and the
choice of means for their attainment are thus the mark
and criterion of the presence of mentality in a
phenomenon." * The force of this criterion is plainly
shown in the chapter on Attention, and its relation to Interest considered as the force which controls it, and its teleological function of selection and integration; in the
chapter on Discrimination and Comparison (Analysis and
Abstraction), where he discusses the way in which ends to
be attained and the means for attaining them evoke and
control intellectual analysis; and in the chapter on Conception, where he shows that a general idea is a mode of sig-
nifying particular things and not merely an abstraction
from particular cases or a superempirical function—that it
is a teleological instrument. James then develops this idea
in the chapter on reasoning where he says that "the only
meaning of essence is teleological, and that classification and
conception are purely teleological weapons of mind."

One might complete this brief enumeration by mention-
ing also the chapter of James' book in which he discusses
the Nature of Necessary Truths and the Role of Experience, and affirms in opposition to Herbert Spencer, that
many of our most important modes of perception and
conception of the world of sensible objects are not the cumulative products of particular experience, but rather original biological sports, spontaneous variations, which are
maintained because of their applicability to concrete experiences after once having been created. Number, space,
time, resemblance, and other important "categories" could
have been brought into existence, he says, as a conse-

* *The Principals of Psychology* (New York, 1890), vol. I, p. 8.

quence of some particular cerebral instability, but they could by no means have been registered on the mind by outside influence. Many significant and useless concepts also arise in the same manner. But the fundamental categories have been cumulatively extended and reinforced because of their value when applied to concrete instances and things of experience. It is therefore not the origin of a concept, it is its application which becomes the criterion of its value; and here we have the whole of pragmatism in embryo. A phrase of James' very well summarizes its import: "the popular notion that 'Science' is forced on the mind *ab extra,* and that our interests have nothing to do with its constructions, is utterly absurd."

Given the point of view which we have just specified and the interest attaching to a logical theory of conception and judgment, and there results a theory of the following description. The adaptations made by inferior organisms, for example their effective and coordinated responses to stimuli, become teleological in man and therefore give occasion to thought. Reflection is an indirect response to the environment, and the element of indirection can itself become great and very complicated. But it has its origin in biological adaptive behavior and the ultimate function of its cognitive aspect is a prospective control of the conditions of the environment. The function of intelligence is therefore not that of copying the objects of the environment, but rather of taking account of the way in which more effective and more profitable relations with these objects may be established in the future.

How this point of view has been applied to the theory of judgment is too long a story to be told here. We shall confine ourselves here to saying that, in general, the "subject" of a judgment represents that portion of the environment to which a reaction must be made; the predicate represents the possible response or habit or manner in which one should behave towards the environment; the copula represents the organic and concrete act by which the connection is made between the fact and its signification; and finally the conclusion, or the definitive object of judgment, is simply the original situation transformed, a situation which implies a change as well in the original subject (including its mind) as in the environment itself. The new and harmonious unity thus attained verifies the bearing of the data which were at first chosen to serve as subject and of the concepts introduced into the situation during the process as teleological instruments for its elaboration. Until this final unification is attained the perceptual data and the conceptual principles, theories, are merely hypotheses from a logical point of view. Moreover, affirmation and negation are intrinsically alogical: they are acts.

. . . Logic, therefore, leads to a realistic metaphysics in so far as it accepts things and events for what they are independently of thought, and to an idealistic metaphysics in so far as it contends that thought gives birth to distinctive acts which modify future facts and events in such a way as to render them more reasonable, that is to say, more adequate to the ends which we propose for ourselves. This ideal element is more and more accentuated by the inclusion progressively of social factors in human environment over and above natural factors; so that the needs which are fulfilled, the ends which are attained are no longer of a merely biological or particular character, but include also the ends and activities of other members of society.

. . . it should be clear after this rapid survey of the history of pragmatism that American thought continues European thought. We have imported our language, our laws, our institutions, our morals, and our religion from Europe, and we have adapted them to the new conditions of our life. The same is true of our ideas. For long years our philosophical thought was merely an echo of European thought. . . . Since these systems are readaptations they take into consideration the distinctive traits of the environment of American life. But as has already been said, they are not limited to reproducing what is worn and imperfect in this environment. They do not aim to glorify the energy and the love of action which the new conditions of American life exaggerated. They do not reflect the excessive mercantilism of American life. Without doubt all these traits of the environment have not been without a certain influence on American philosophical thought; our philosophy would not be national or spontaneous if it were not subject to this influence. But the fundamental idea which the movements of which we have just spoken have attempted to express is the idea that action and opportunity justify themselves only to the degree in which they render life more reasonable and increase its value. Instrumentalism maintains in opposition to many contrary tendencies in the American environment, that action should be intelligent and reflective, and that thought should occupy a central position in life. That is the reason for our insistence on the teleological phrase of thought and knowledge. If it must be teleological in particular and not merely true in the abstract, that is probably due to the practical element which is found in all the phases of American life. However that may be, what we insist upon above all else is that intelligence be regarded as the only source and sole guarantee of a desirable and happy future. It is beyond doubt that the progressive and unstable character of American life and civilization has facilitated the birth of a philosophy which regards the world as being in continuous formation, where there is still place for indeterminism, for the new, and for a real future. But this idea is not exclusively American, although the conditions of American life have aided this idea in becoming self-conscious. It is also true that Americans tend to underestimate the value of tradition of rationality considered as an achievement of the past. But the world has also given proof of irrationality in the past and this irrationality is incorporated in our beliefs and our institutions. There are bad traditions as there are good ones: it is always important to distinguish. Our neglect of the traditions of the past, with whatever this negligence implies in the way of spiritual impoverishment of our life, has its compensation in the idea that the world is recommencing and being remade under our eyes. The future as well as the past can be a source of interest and consolation and give meaning to the present. Pragmatism and instrumental experimentalism bring into prominence the importance of the individual. It is he who is the carrier of creative thought, the author of action and of its application. Subjectivism is an old story in philosophy; a story which began in Europe and not in America. But American philosophy, in the systems which we have expounded, has given to the subject, to the individual mind, a practical rather than an epistemological function. The individual mind is important because only the individual mind is the organ of modifications in traditions and institutions, the vehicle of experimental creation. One-sided and egoistic individualism in American life has left its imprint on our practices. For better or for worse, depending on the point of view, it has transformed the esthetic and fixed individualism of the old European culture into an active individualism. But the idea of a society of individuals is not foreign to American thought; it penetrates even our current individualism which is unreflective and brutal. And the individual which American thought idealizes is not an individual *per se,* an individual fixed in isolation and set up for himself, but an individual who evolves and develops in a natural and human environment, an individual who can be educated.

If I were asked to give an historical parallel to this movement in American thought I would remind my reader of the French philosophy of the enlightenment. Every one knows that the thinkers who made that moment illustrious were inspired by Bacon, Locke, and Newton; what interested them was the application of scientific method and the conclusions of an experimental theory of knowledge to human affairs, the critique and reconstruction of beliefs and institutions. As Höffding writes, they were animated "by a fervent faith in intelligence, progress, and humanity." And certainly they are not accused today, just because of their educational and social significance, of having sought to subordinate intelligence and science to ordinary utilitarian aims. They merely sought to free intelligence from its impurities and to render it sovereign. One can scarcely say that those who glorify intelligence and reason in the abstract, because of their value for those who find personal satisfaction in their possession, estimate intelligence more truly than those who wish to make it the indispensable guide of intellectual and social life. When an American critic says of instrumentalism that it regards ideas as mere servants which make for success in life, he only reacts, without reflection, to the ordinary verbal associations of the word "instrumental," as many others have reacted in the same manner to the use of the word "practical." . . . This criticism does not hold. It is by no means the production of beliefs useful to morals and society which these systems pursue. It is the formation of a faith in intelligence, as the one and indispensable belief necessary to moral and social life. The more one appreciates the intrinsic esthetic, immediate value of thought and of science, the more one takes into account what intelligence itself adds to the joy and dignity of life, the more one should feel grieved at a situation in which the exercise and joy of reason are limited to a narrow, closed and technical social group and the more one should ask how it is possible to make all men participators in this inestimable wealth.

Charles Sanders Peirce

INTRODUCTION

Charles Sanders Peirce (1839–1914) was born in Cambridge, Massachusetts, the son of Benjamin Peirce, an eminent Harvard mathematician. Charles was an unusually precocious child and was thought so clearly destined for greatness that he was overindulged in ways that may have contributed to his later difficulties with persons in authority and his inability to focus his work into published form. He graduated from Harvard in 1859 with an undistinguished record but later, in 1863, received the first Sc.B. degree in chemistry in Harvard history *summa cum laude*. For a time he was employed by the United States Coast and Geodetic Survey; he carried out important work in astronomy, making measurements of the light of stars. His experiments with pendulums in determining the intensity of gravity won him international notice. The one book he published in his lifetime was *Photometric Researches,* 1878.

Peirce taught at Johns Hopkins from 1879 to 1884; among his students there were John Dewey, Josiah Royce, and Thorstein Veblen. On receiving a modest inheritance in 1887 at the age of forty-eight, Peirce retired to Milford, Pennsylvania. There in isolation but for the company of his wife and occasional friends, he wrote on a variety of philosophical and scientific subjects and attempted to complete his philosophic system of "synechism." His financial position worsened, and his wife was troubled with ill health. The always loyal William James arranged occasional lectures for him in Cambridge, but Peirce never obtained a permanent university position and was compelled to do considerable hack reviewing in order to supplement his inadequate income. His last years were spent in poverty, suffering from cancer and neglected at large, struggling to complete several major works in philosophy and logic.

In addition to being a reflection of analytic practice in science, the experimentalist's procedure in the laboratory, Peirce's pragmatism grew out of his study of the phenomenology of thought and the nature of language. For many years he worked on a general theory of *signs* and, corresponding to this in certain ways, a theory of the categories or "modes of being." For Peirce, the investigation of thought depends upon an understanding of signs and their uses. For

> there is no element whatever of man's consciousness which has not something corresponding to it in the word . . . the word or sign which a man uses *is* the man himself.*

And

> . . . all thought whatsoever is a sign, and is mostly of the nature of language.†

This approach to understanding the nature of thought and mind by means of language was especially worked out by Mead.

Peirce developed a novel and important account of the function of thought, or "inquiry," which he sketched in broad outline and most of which was taken up into Dewey's extensive construction of a theory of inquiry. Peirce depicts the function of thought as a form of behavior initiated by the irritation of doubt and proceeding to some resolution in a state of belief. Belief is a condition of organic stability and issues in habits of action. If and when the habitual modes of action become blocked or disturbed, belief is threatened, and doubt ensues. There are various ways of settling belief and these are discussed in "The Fixation of Belief" (see selection III, below). Of these methods one, the scientific, has an important advantage over the others. It is the only one that allows us to arrive at beliefs which we have any reason to think are true. To believe is to be comfortable, but to be comfortable is not necessarily to have truth. In the absence of critical controls over the other methods of fixing belief—the methods

---

* *Collected Papers* (Cambridge, Mass., 1934), vol. V, paragraph 314.
† *Ibid.*, vol. V, paragraph 421.

of tenacity, authority, and *a priori*—there is no objective criterion for assessing the beliefs thus produced and no critical interest in validation of belief anyway. Peirce's objection to these methods is that truth *is* important, among other reasons because in the long run the practice of these methods leads to dissatisfaction; the social impulse is at root against them. One's own beliefs are easily shaken by the discovery that other persons hold different beliefs. "But here already is a vague concession that there is some *one* thing which a proposition should represent." What we need then is a method that captures the spirit of this social impulse: This method "must be such that the ultimate conclusion of every man shall be the same. Such is the method of science."

The background of Peirce's pragmatism (as he recalled it later) and his most influential statements of the main ideas are to be found in the next selections. The most famous, but not the clearest formulation of his principal thesis is: "Consider what effects, which might conceivably have practical bearings, we conceive the object of our conception to have. Then, our conception of these effects is the whole of our conception of the object." The sense of this becomes evident in the context of "How To Make Our Ideas Clear" (IV, below), where it occurs and also from Dewey's discussion of Peirce (in the preceding essay). It suffices to note here that this "rule" is intended as a procedure for promoting linguistic and conceptual clarity and successful communication when men are wrestling with intellectual problems. Generally speaking, Peirce's pragmatism is a method with two main critical uses: First, and negatively, where disputes and problems seem to admit of no resolution whatever, pragmatism advises that language and concepts are being used in differing and confused ways. In this respect Peirce comments, "Pragmatism solves no real problem. It only shows that supposed problems are not real problems." But the second use of the method supplies a procedure for reconstructing and explicating meanings. The procedure guides us in translating, or replacing, unclear concepts with clear ones. Peirce illustrates this use in considering the concepts of "hard," "weight," "force," and "reality." In each case the procedure takes a *conditional* form. Thus, to say of some object O that it is *hard* means roughly: If under certain conditions, an operation of scratch-testing is performed on O, O will not be scratched. Specification of the experimental conditions, the operation, and the consequences, gives us the meaning or "purport" of the term "hard." Generally, we attain clarity in our use of a term when we can supply a conditional statement for it of this kind. What we understand by a term T consists in a description of certain kinds of operations that *would* produce certain kinds of consequences when the conditions referred to by T are present. Peirce even defined truth this way: A true belief is one that *would* "be agreed to by all who investigate" it. He was not maintaining, as some critics suppose, that we can only know whether a belief is true after it has been investigated by everyone and the last man alive on earth. Rather, we *mean* by "truth" that if a certain operation is performed (viz., continuous inquiry by the community of investigators) assent to the belief in question *would* increase and dissent from it diminish. Thus I can know what I *mean* by saying a belief is true; and although I can never be *certain* that any belief *is* true, I have ways of critically assessing the reliability of beliefs, the best of these being the continued application of scientific method. If we add that true beliefs are those over which assent among investigators "would increase *in the long run*," we can see how the theory of probability and the notion of a *limit* of endless investigation and confirmation play basic roles in Peirce's theory of meaning and of truth. For to say that O is hard is to "predict that no matter how often you try the experiment" of scratching O, it will *always* resist being scratched. Meaning then contains a predictive component and a reference to innumerable confirming instances. This lies behind Peirce's contention that "our idea of any thing is our idea of its sensible effects" (or "conceived effects") and that the meaning of a proposition "lies in the future."

It is readily seen how Peirce's scheme for clarifying meaning anticipated (while it was in certain ways more sophisticated and flexible than) the later programs of operationalism and the verifiability theory of meaning.

A wealth of interesting and significant philosophical consequences flow from the study of this method of pragmatism and its applications. Peirce was led to enlarge upon some of this (thus see the last selection, V) in developing his theory of experimental empiricism; his analysis of the operation of inquiry and belief, of the fallible character of all thought and probablistic nature of verification; and his view of the thoroughly social and moral acquisition and ends of knowledge.

II. Definition and Description of Pragmatism

(i) A DEFINITION OF PRAGMATIC AND PRAGMATISM*

Pragmatic anthropology, according to Kant,† is practical ethics.

Pragmatic horizon is the adaptation of our general knowledge to influencing our morals.

The opinion that metaphysics is to be largely cleared up by the application of the following maxim for attaining clearness of apprehension: "Consider what effects that might conceivably have practical bearings we conceive the object of our conception to have. Then, our conception of these effects is the whole of our conception of the object."

[The doctrine that the whole "meaning" of a conception expresses itself in practical consequences, consequences either in the shape of conduct to be recommended, or in that of experiences to be expected, if the conception be true; which consequences would be different if it were untrue, and must be different from the consequences by which the meaning of other conceptions is in turn expressed. If a second conception should not appear to have other consequences, then it must really be only the first conception under a different name. In methodology it is certain that to trace and compare their respective conse-

* From "Pragmatic and Pragmatism," *Dictionary of Philosophy and Psychology*, ed. by J. M. Baldwin (New York, 1902), vol. II, pp. 321–322.

† *Anthropologie in pragmatischer Hinsicht*, Vorrede.

quences is an admirable way of establishing the differing meanings of different conceptions.] *

This maxim was first proposed by C. S. Peirce in the *Popular Science Monthly* for January, 1878 (xii. 287); † and he explained how it was to be applied to the doctrine of reality. The writer was led to the maxim by reflection upon Kant's *Critic of the Pure Reason.* Substantially the same way of dealing with ontology seems to have been practiced by the Stoics. The writer subsequently saw that the principle might easily be misapplied, so as to sweep away the whole doctrine of incommensurables, and, in fact, the whole Weierstrassian way of regarding the calculus. In 1896 William James published his *Will to Believe,*‡ and later § his *Philosophical Conceptions and Practical Results,* which pushed this method to such extremes as must tend to give us pause. The doctrine appears to assume that the end of man is action—a stoical axiom which to the present writer at the age of sixty does not recommend itself so forcibly as it did at thirty. If it be admitted, on the contrary, that action wants an end, and that that· end must be something of a general description, then the spirit of the maxim itself, which is that we must look to the upshot of our concepts in order rightly to apprehend them, would direct us towards something different from practical facts, namely, to general ideas, as the true interpreters of our thought. Nevertheless, the maxim has approved itself to the writer, after many years of trial, as of great utility in leading to a relatively high grade of clearness of thought. He would venture to suggest that it should always be put into practice with conscientious thoroughness, but that, when that has been done, and not before, a still higher grade of clearness of thought can be attained by remembering that the only ultimate good which the practical facts to which it directs attention can subserve is to further the development of concrete reasonableness; so that the meaning of the concept does not lie in

* This paragraph was contributed by William James.

† [See IV and pp. 88, 110, below.]

‡ *New World,* vol. V (1896), pp. 327–347; reprinted in 1897 in *The Will to Believe, and Other Essays in Popular Philosophy.* [See selection VIII below.]

§ In 1898; *University of California Chronicle;* reprinted in 1920 in *Collected Essays and Reviews,* ed. by R. B. Perry (New York: 1920).

any individual reactions at all, but in the manner in which those reactions contribute to that development. Indeed, in the article of 1878, above referred to, the writer practiced better than he preached; for he applied the stoical maxim most unstoically, in such a sense as to insist upon the reality of the objects of general ideas in their generality.

A widely current opinion during the last quarter of a century has been that reasonableness is not a good in itself, but only for the sake of something else. Whether it be so or not seems to be a synthetical question, not to be settled by an appeal to the principle of contradiction—as if a reason for reasonableness were absurd. Almost everybody will now agree that the ultimate good lies in the evolutionary process in some way. If so, it is not in individual reactions in their segregation, but in something general or continuous. Synechism is founded on the notion that the coalescence, the becoming continuous, the becoming governed by laws, the becoming instinct with general ideas, are but phases of one and the same process of the growth of reasonableness. This is first shown to be true with mathematical exactitude in the field of logic, and is thence inferred to hold good metaphysically. It is not opposed to pragmatism in the manner in which C. S. Peirce applied it but includes that procedure as a step.

(ii) THE ARCHITECTONIC CONSTRUCTION OF PRAGMATISM*

. . . Pragmatism was not a theory which special circumstances had led its authors to entertain. It had been designed and constructed, to use the expression of Kant,† architectonically. Just as a civil engineer, before erecting a bridge, a ship, or a house, will think of the different properties of all materials, and will use no iron, stone, or cement, that has not been subjected to tests; and will put them together in ways minutely considered, so, in constructing the doctrine of pragmatism the properties of all

* From ms. c. 1905.
† See *Kritik der reinen Vernunft*, A832, B860.

indecomposable concepts were examined and the ways in which they could be compounded. Then the purpose of the proposed doctrine having been analyzed, it was constructed out of the appropriate concepts so as to fulfill that purpose. In this way, the truth of it was proved. There are subsidiary confirmations of its truth; but it is believed that there is no other independent way of strictly proving it. . . .

But first, what is its purpose? What is it expected to accomplish? It is expected to bring to an end those prolonged disputes of philosophers which no observations of facts could settle, and yet in which each side claims to prove that the other side is in the wrong. Pragmatism maintains that in those cases the disputants must be at cross-purposes. They either attach different meanings to words, or else one side or the other (or both) uses a word without any definite meaning. What is wanted, therefore, is a method for ascertaining the real meaning of any concept, doctrine, proposition, word, or other sign. The object of a sign is one thing; its meaning is another. Its object is the thing or occasion, however indefinite, to which it is to be applied. Its meaning is the idea which it attaches to that object, whether by way of mere supposition, or as a command, or as an assertion.

Now every simple idea is composed of one of three classes; and a compound idea is in most cases predominantly of one of those classes. Namely, it may, in the first place, be a quality of feeling, which is positively such as it is, and is indescribable; which attaches to one object regardless of every other; and which is *sui generis* and incapable, in its own being, of comparison with any other feeling, because in comparisons it is representations of feelings and not the very feelings themselves that are compared. Or, in the second place, the idea may be that of a single happening or fact, which is attached at once to two objects, as an experience, for example, is attached to the experiencer and to the object experienced. Or, in the third place, it is the idea of a sign or communication conveyed by one person to another (or to himself at a later time) in regard to a certain object well known to both. . . . Now the bottom meaning of a sign cannot be the idea of a sign, since that latter sign must itself have a meaning which would thereby become the meaning of the original sign. We may therefore conclude that the ultimate meaning of any sign consists either in an idea predominantly of feeling or in one predominantly of acting and being acted on. For there ought to be no hesitation in assenting to the view that all those ideas which attach essentially to two objects take their rise from the experience of volition and from the experience of the perception of phenomena which resist direct efforts of the will to annul or modify them.

But pragmatism does not undertake to say in what the meanings of all signs consist, but merely to lay down a method of determining the meanings of intellectual concepts, that is, of those upon which reasonings may turn. Now all reasoning that is not utterly vague, all that ought to figure in a philosophical discussion involves, and turns upon, precise necessary reasoning. Such reasoning is included in the sphere of mathematics, as modern mathematicians conceive their science. "Mathematics," said Benjamin Peirce, as early as 1870, "is the science which draws necessary conclusions"; * and subsequent writers have substantially accepted this definition, limiting it, perhaps, to precise conclusions. The reasoning of mathematics is now well understood. It consists in forming an image of the conditions of the problem, associated with which are certain general permissions to modify the image, as well as certain general assumptions that certain things are impossible. Under the permissions, certain experiments are performed upon the image, and the assumed impossibilities involve their always resulting in the same general way. The superior certainty of the mathematician's results, as compared, for example, with those of the chemist, are due to two circumstances. First, the mathematician's experiments being conducted in the imagination upon objects of his own creation, cost next to nothing; while those of the chemist cost dear. Secondly, the assurance of the mathematician is due to his reasoning only concerning hypothetical conditions, so that his results have the generality of his conditions; while the chemist's experiments relating to what will happen as a matter of fact are always open to the doubt whether unknown conditions may not alter. Thus, the mathematician knows that a column of figures will add up the same, whether it be set down in black ink or in red; because he goes on the assumption that the sum

---

* "Linear Associative Algebra," §1, *American Journal of Mathematics,* vol. IV (1881), pp. 97–229.

of any two numbers of which one is M and the other one more than N will be one more than the sum of M and N; and this assumption says nothing about the color of the ink. The chemist assumes that when he mixes two liquids in a test tube, there will or will not be a precipitate whether the Dowager Empress of China happens to sneeze at the time, because his experience has always been that laboratory experiments are not affected by such distant conditions. Still, the solar system is moving through space at a great rate, and there is a bare possibility that it may just then have entered a region in which sneezing has very surprising force.

Such reasonings and all reasonings turn upon the idea that if one exerts certain kinds of volition, one will undergo in return certain compulsory perceptions. Now this sort of consideration, namely, that certain lines of conduct will entail certain kinds of inevitable experiences is what is called a "practical consideration." Hence is justified the maxim, belief in which constitutes pragmatism; namely,

In order to ascertain the meaning of an intellectual conception one should consider what practical consequences might conceivably result by necessity from the truth of that conception; and the sum of these consequences will constitute the entire meaning of the conception.

Many plausible arguments in favor of this doctrine could easily be adduced; but the only way hitherto discovered of really proving its truth, without in any measure begging the question, is by following the thorny path that we have thus very roughly sketched.

(iii) HISTORICAL AFFINITIES AND GENESIS*

. . . Any philosophical doctrine that should be completely new could hardly fail to prove completely false; but the rivulets at the head of the river of pragmatism are easily traced back to almost any desired antiquity.

Socrates bathed in these waters. Aristotle rejoices when he can find them. They run, where least one would suspect

* From ms. c. 1906.

them, beneath the dry rubbish heaps of Spinoza. Those clean definitions that strew the pages of the *Essay concerning Humane Understanding* (I refuse to reform the spelling) had been washed out in these same pure springs. It was this medium, and not tar water, that gave health and strength to Berkeley's earlier works, his *Theory of Vision* and what remains of his *Principles.* From it the general views of Kant derive such clearness as they have. Auguste Comte made still more—much more—use of this element; as much as he saw his way to using. Unfortunately, however, both he and Kant, in their rather opposite ways, were in the habit of mingling these sparkling waters with a certain mental sedative to which many men are addicted —and the burly business men very likely to their benefit, but which plays sad havoc with the philosophical constitution. I refer to the habit of cherishing contempt for the close study of logic.

So much for the past. The ancestry of pragmatism is respectable enough; but the more conscious adoption of it as *lanterna pedibus* in the discussion of dark questions, and the elaboration of it into a method in aid of philosophic inquiry came, in the first instance, from the humblest *souche* imaginable. It was in the earliest seventies * that a knot of us young men in Old Cambridge, calling ourselves, half ironically, half defiantly, "The Metaphysical Club"—for agnosticism was then riding its high horse, and was frowning superbly upon all metaphysics—used to meet, sometimes in my study, sometimes in that of William James. It may be that some of our old-time confederates would today not care to have such wild-oats-sowings made public, though there was nothing but boiled oats, milk, and sugar in the mess. Mr. Justice Holmes, however, will not, I believe, take it ill that we are proud to remember his membership; nor will Joseph Warner, Esq.† Nicholas St. John Green was one of the most interested fellows, a skillful lawyer and a learned one, a disciple of Jeremy Bentham. His extraordinary power of disrobing warm and breathing truth of the draperies of long worn formulas, was what attracted attention to him everywhere. In particular,

* To judge from the *Letters of William James* (Boston, 1920), vol. 2, p. 233, there was a meeting of this club in the autumn of 1874.
† A friend of William James, who worked with Mr. Justice Holmes on Kent's *Commentaries.*

he often urged the importance of applying Bain's * definition of belief, as "that upon which a man is prepared to act." From this definition, pragmatism is scarce more than a corollary; so that I am disposed to think of him as the grandfather of pragmatism. Chauncey Wright, something of a philosophical celebrity in those days, was never absent from our meetings. I was about to call him our corypheus; but he will better be described as our boxing master whom we—I particularly—used to face to be severely pummeled. He had abandoned a former attachment to Hamiltonianism to take up with the doctrines of Mill, to which and to its cognate agnosticism he was trying to weld the really incongruous ideas of Darwin. John Fiske and, more rarely, Francis Ellingwood Abbot, were sometimes present, lending their countenances to the spirit of our endeavors, while holding aloof from any assent to their success. Wright, James, and I were men of science, rather scrutinizing the doctrines of the metaphysicians on their scientific side than regarding them as very momentous spiritually. The type of our thought was decidedly British. I, alone of our number, had come upon the threshing floor of philosophy through the doorway of Kant, and even my ideas were acquiring the English accent.

Our metaphysical proceedings had all been in winged words (and swift ones, at that, for the most part), until at length, lest the club should be dissolved, without leaving any material souvenir behind, I drew up a little paper expressing some of the opinions that I had been urging all along under the name of pragmatism. This paper was received with such unlooked-for kindness, that I was encouraged, some half dozen years later, on the invitation of the great publisher, Mr. W. H. Appleton, to insert it, somewhat expanded, in the *Popular Science Monthly* for November 1877 and January 1878, not with the warmest possible approval of the Spencerian editor, Dr. Edward Youmans. The same paper appeared the next year in a French redaction in the *Révue Philosophique* (vol. VI, 1878, p. 553; vol. VII, 1879, p. 39). In those medieval times, I dared not in type use an English word to express an idea unrelated to its received meaning. The authority of

---

* Cf. *The Emotions and the Will*, 3d ed. (1875), ch 11, p. 505.

Mr. Principal Campbell* weighed too heavily upon my conscience. I had not yet come to perceive, what is so plain today, that if philosophy is ever to stand in the ranks of the sciences, literary elegance must be sacrificed—like the soldier's old brilliant uniforms—to the stern requirements of efficiency, and the philosophist must be encouraged—yea, and required—to coin new terms to express such new scientific concepts as he may discover, just as his chemical and biological brethren are expected to do. Indeed, in those days, such brotherhood was scorned, alike on the one side and on the other—a lamentable but not surprising state of scientific feeling. As late as 1893, when I might have procured the insertion of the word pragmatism in the *Century Dictionary*, it did not seem to me that its vogue was sufficient to warrant that step.†

* Author of a textbook on rhetoric in use at Harvard College in Peirce's day.

† *Pragmatism*. It is a singular instance of that overmodesty and unyielding self-underestimate on my part of which I am so justly proud as my principal claim to distinction that I should have omitted *pragmatism*, my own offspring, with which the world resounds. See Baldwin's *Dictionary* where is my original definition of 1878 and an exegesis, not very deep, of William James. Pragmatism is a method in philosophy. *Philosophy* is that branch of positive science (i.e., an investigating theoretical science which inquires what is the fact, in contradistinction to pure mathematics which merely seeks to know what follows from certain hypotheses) which makes no observations but contents itself with so much of experience as pours in upon every man during every hour of his waking life. The study of philosophy consists, therefore, in reflection, and *pragmatism* is that method of reflection which is guided by constantly holding in view its purpose and the purpose of the ideas it analyzes, whether these ends be of the nature and uses of action or of thought.

"... the whole subsequent argument has already had its main lines mapped out by our introductory discussion of that *Weltanschauung* which Professor James has called *pragmatism*."—F. C. S. Schiller (in *Personal Idealism*, edited by Henry Cecil Sturt, London and New York, 1902), p. 63.

The passage of Professor James here alluded to is as follows: "... Mr. Charles Sanders Peirce has rendered thought a service by disentangling from the particulars of its application the principle by which these men were instinctively guided, and by singling it out as fundamental and giving to it a Greek name. He calls it the principle of *pragmatism*."—William James, *The Varieties of Religious Experience* (New York, 1902), p. 444.

It will be seen [from the original statement] that *pragmatism* is not a *Weltanschauung* but is a method of reflection having for its purpose to render ideas clear.

Pragmatistic, a., having the character of pragmatism, as a method in philosophy.

Pragmatist, n., in philosophy, one who professes to practice pragmatism. Thus Schiller of Oxford, author of *Riddles of the Sphinx*,

It is now high time to explain what pragmatism is. I must, however, preface the explanation by a statement of what it is not, since many writers, especially of the starry host of Kant's progeny, in spite of pragmatists' declarations, unanimous, reiterated, and most explicit, still remain unable to "catch on" to what we are driving at, and persist in twisting our purpose and purport all awry. I was long enough, myself, within the Kantian fold to comprehend their difficulty; but let it go. Suffice it to say once more that pragmatism is, in itself, no doctrine of metaphysics, no attempt to determine any truth of things. It is merely a method of ascertaining the meanings of hard words and of abstract concepts. All pragmatists of whatsoever stripe will cordially assent to that statement. As to the ulterior and indirect effects of practicing the pragmatistic method, that is quite another affair.

All pragmatists will further agree that their method of ascertaining the meanings of words and concepts is no other than that experimental method by which all the successful sciences (in which number nobody in his senses would include metaphysics) have reached the degrees of certainty that are severally proper to them today; this experimental method being itself nothing but a particular application of an older logical rule, "By their fruits ye shall know them."

Beyond these two propositions to which pragmatists assent *nem. con.*, we find such slight discrepancies between the views of one and another declared adherent as are to be found in every healthy and vigorous school of thought in every department of inquiry. The most prominent of all our school and the most respected, William James, defines pragmatism as the doctrine that the whole "meaning" of a concept expresses itself either in the shape of conduct to be recommended or of experience to be expected. Between this definition and mine there certainly appears to be no slight theoretical divergence, which, for the most part, becomes evanescent in practice; and though we may differ on important questions of philosophy—especially as regards the infinite and the absolute—I am inclined to think that the discrepancies reside in other than the pragmatistic

---

is a pragmatist, although he does not very thoroughly understand the nature of pragmatism.—From Peirce's personal interleaved copy of the *Century Dictionary*, c. 1902.

ingredients of our thought. If pragmatism had never been heard of, I believe the opinion of James on one side, of me on the other would have developed substantially as they have; not withstanding our respective connecting them at present with our conception of that method. The brilliant and marvelously human thinker, Mr. F. C. S. Schiller, who extends to the philosophic world a cup of nectar stimulant in his beautiful *Humanism,* seems to occupy ground of his own, intermediate, as to this question, between those of James and mine.

I understand pragmatism to be a method of ascertaining the meanings, not of all ideas, but only of what I call "intellectual concepts," that is to say, of those upon the structure of which, arguments concerning objective fact may hinge. Had the light which, as things are, excites in us the sensation of blue, always excited the sensation of red, and *vice versa,* however great a difference that might have made in our feelings, it could have made none in the force of any argument. In this respect, the qualities of hard and soft strikingly contrast with those of red and blue; because while red and blue name mere subjective feelings only, hard and soft express the factual behavior of the thing under the pressure of a knife edge. (I use the word "hard" in its strict mineralogical sense, "would resist a knife edge.") My pragmatism, having nothing to do with qualities of feeling, permits me to hold that the predication of such a quality is just what it seems, and has nothing to do with anything else. Hence, could two qualities of feeling everywhere be interchanged, nothing but feelings could be affected. Those qualities have no intrinsic significations beyond themselves. Intellectual concepts, however—the only sign burdens that are properly denominated "concepts"— essentially carry some implication concerning the general behavior either of some conscious being or of some inanimate object, and so convey more, not merely than any feeling, but more, too, than any existential fact, namely, the "would-acts," "would-dos" of habitual behavior; and no agglomeration of actual happenings can ever completely fill up the meaning of a "would-be." But [Pragmatism asserts] that the *total* meaning of the predication of an intellectual concept is contained in an affirmation that, under all conceivable circumstances of a given kind (or under this or that more or less indefinite part of the cases of their fulfillment, should the predication be modal) the subject of the predication would behave in a certain general way—that is, it would be true under given experiential circumstances (or under a more or less definitely stated proportion of them, *taken as they would occur*, that is in the same order of succession, *in experience*).*

* It is in this phrase that I find my sole opportunity of calling attention to the fact that the ratio of frequency with which members of one denumeral collection are found among members of another denumeral, and therefore equal, collection depends upon the order of succession of the members of the latter collection. In order to afford matter for your rumination, my reader, I set down the first members of two endless series, each embracing all integers, and nothing else. The order of succession of the numbers of the first series is that of their occurrence in counting, or (what is the same thing) that of the multitudes they represent. The second series is derived by dividing each member of the first series, first, by 2, and then the final quotient by 3, as often as possible without remainder, and then remultiplying the ultimate quotient by 2 as many times as were the divisions by 3, and the product by 3 as many times as the divisions by 2, and setting down the ultimate product in that place in the second series which in the first series had been occupied by the number originally taken. The consequence will be that the number which, in either series, occupies the $(2^M.3^N.Q)$th place will in the other series occupy, and occupy none other than the $(2^N.3^M.Q)$th place. Here are the first members:

1 . 2 . 3 . 4 . 5 . 6 . 7 . 8 . 9 . 10 . 11 . 12 . 13 . 14 . 15 . 16 . 17 . 18 . 19 . 20 . 21 . 22 . 23 . 24 . 25 . 26 . 27 . 28 . 29 . 30 . 31 . 32 . 33 . 34 . 35 . 36 . 37 . 38 . 39 . 40. etc.

1 . 3 . 2 . 9 . 5 . 6 . 7 . 27 . 4 . 15 . 11 . 18 . 13 . 21 . 10 . 81 . 17 . 12 . 19 . 45 . 14 . 33 . 23 . 54 . 25 . 39 . 8 . 63 . 29 . 30 . 31 . 243 . 22 . 51 . 35 . 36 . 37 . 57 . 26 . 135 . etc.

In the upper series every other number is even; in the lower, only every third. In the upper every third number is divisible by 3; in the lower every second is so. It is obvious that the principle involved must overthrow certain arguments about probabilities. Thus, a quarter of a century ago, a London professor put forth the argument (accompanied by the arrogant references then usual, but now disused from obvious motives, toward an American opponent who did not then think it worthwhile to reply, nor would now, but for the illustration of how the general principle is applicable to Probabilities), that because for every form of question to which the true answer is "Yes," another form of the same question is possible to which the true answer is "No," and conversely; therefore, there is an *a priori* probability equal to ½ that any given proposition is true. He forgot that, in order to make this out, he would have to show that one form of the question occurred just as often as the other, *in the course of experience*. Whether the fact be so or not is open to doubt. One circumstance that seems to point toward its falsity is that there is, in the English language, no word equivalent to the French "oui"—as opposed to "si"—as an answer to the negative

A most pregnant principle, quite undeniably, will this "kernel of pragmatism" prove to be, that the *whole* meaning of an intellectual predicate is that certain kinds of events would happen, once in so often, in the course of experience, under certain kinds of existential conditions—provided it can be proved to be true. But how is this to be done in the teeth of Messrs. Bradley, Taylor, and other high metaphysicians, on the one hand, and of the entire nominalistic nation, with its Wundts, its Haeckels, its Karl Pearsons, and many other regiments, in their divers uniforms, on the other? . . .

---

form of the question. But, however the fact may be, certain it is that no practical underwriter or actuary would, or ought to, allow an argument based on a form of words to make a dollar's difference in the premium to be paid for a policy.

III. The Fixation of Belief*

i.

Few persons care to study logic, because everybody conceives himself to be proficient enough in the art of reasoning already. But I observe that this satisfaction is limited to one's own ratiocination, and does not extend to that of other men.

We come to the full possession of our power of drawing inferences the last of all our faculties, for it is not so much a natural gift as a long and difficult art. The history of its practice would make a grand subject for a book. The medieval schoolman, following the Romans, made logic the earliest of a boy's studies after grammar, as being very easy. So it was as they understood it. Its fundamental principle, according to them, was that all knowledge rests on either authority or reason; but that whatever is deduced by reason depends ultimately on a premise derived from authority. Accordingly, as soon as a boy was perfect in the syllogistic procedure, his intellectual kit of tools was held to be complete.

To Roger Bacon, that remarkable mind who in the middle of the thirteenth century was almost a scientific man, the schoolmen's conception of reasoning appeared only an obstacle to truth. He saw that experience alone teaches anything—a proposition which to us seems easy to understand, because a distinct conception of experience has been handed down to us from former generations; which to him also seemed perfectly clear, because its difficulties had not yet unfolded themselves. Of all kinds of experience, the best, he thought, was interior illumination, which teaches many things about nature which the external senses could never discover, such as the transubstantiation of bread.

Four centuries later, the more celebrated Bacon, in the

* *Popular Science Monthly* (1877).

first book of his, *Novum Organum,* gave his clear account of experience as something which must be opened to verification and reexamination. But, superior as Lord Bacon's conception is to earlier notions, a modern reader who is not in awe of his grandiloquence is chiefly struck by the inadequacy of his view of scientific procedure. That we have only to make some crude experiments, to draw up briefs of the results in certain blank forms, to go through these by rule, checking off everything disproved and setting down the alternatives, and that thus in a few years physical science would be finished up—what an idea! "He wrote on science like a Lord Chancellor," indeed. . . .

The early scientists, Copernicus, Tycho Brahe, Kepler, Galileo, Harvey, and Gilbert, had methods more like those of their modern brethren. Kepler undertook to draw a curve through the places of Mars* and his greatest service to science was in impressing on men's minds that this was the thing to be done if they wished to improve astronomy; that they were not to content themselves with inquiring whether one system of epicycles was better than another but that they were to sit down by the figures and find out what the curve, in truth, was. He accomplished this by his incomparable energy and courage, blundering along in the most inconceivable way (to us), from one irrational hypothesis to another, until, after trying twenty-two of these, he fell, by the mere exhaustion of his invention, upon the orbit which a mind well furnished with the weapons of modern logic would have tried almost at the outset.

In the same way, every work of science great enough to be remembered for a few generations affords some exemplification of the defective state of the art of reasoning of the time when it was written; and each chief step in science has been a lesson in logic. It was so when Lavoisier and his contemporaries took up the study of chemistry. The old chemist's maxim had been *"Lege, lege, lege, labora, ora, et relege."* Lavoisier's method was not to read and pray, not to dream that some long and complicated chemical process would have a certain effect, to put it into practice with dull patience, after its inevitable failure to dream that with some modification it would have another result, and to end by publishing the last dream as a fact: his way was to carry his mind into his laboratory, and to

---

* Not quite so, but as nearly as can be told in a few words.

make of his alembics and cucurbits instruments of thought, giving a new conception of reasoning as something which was to be done with one's eyes open, by manipulating real things instead of words and fancies.

The Darwinian controversy is, in large part, a question of logic. Mr. Darwin proposed to apply the statistical method of biology. The same thing has been done in a widely different branch of science, the theory of gases. Though unable to say what the movement of any particular molecule of gas would be on a certain hypothesis regarding the constitution of this class of bodies, Clausius and Maxwell were yet able, by the application of the doctrine of probabilities to predict that in the long run such and such a proportion of the molecules would, under given circumstances, acquire such and such velocities; that there would take place, every second, such and such a number of collisions, etc.; and from these propositions they were able to deduce certain properties of gases, especially in regard to their heat relations. In like manner, Darwin, while unable to say what the operation of variation and natural selection in every individual case will be, demonstrates that in the long run they will adapt animals to their circumstances. Whether or not existing animal forms are due to such action, or what position the theory ought to take, forms the subject of a discussion in which questions of fact and questions of logic are curiously interlaced.

ii.

The object of reasoning is to find out, from the consideration of what we already know, something else which we do not know. Consequently, reasoning is good if it be such as to give a true conclusion from true premises, and not otherwise. Thus the question of validity is purely one of fact and not of thinking. A being the premises and B being the conclusion, the question is, whether these facts are really so related that if A is B is. If so, the inference is valid; if not, not. It is not in the least the question whether, when the premises are accepted by the mind, we feel an impulse to accept the conclusion also. It is true that we do generally reason correctly by nature. But that is an accident; the true conclusion would remain true if we had no impulse to accept it; and the false one would remain false, though we could not resist the tendency to believe in it.

We are, doubtless, in the main logical animals, but we are not perfectly so. Most of us, for example, are naturally more sanguine and hopeful than logic would justify. We seem to be so constituted that in the absence of any facts to go upon we are happy and self-satisfied; so that the effect of experience is continually to counteract our hopes and aspirations. Yet a lifetime of the application of this corrective does not usually eradicate our sanguine disposition. Where hope is unchecked by any experience, it is likely that our optimism is extravagant. Logicality in regard to practical matters is the most useful quality an animal can possess, and might, therefore, result from the action of natural selection; but outside of these it is probably of more advantage to the animal to have his mind filled with pleasing and encouraging visions, independently of their truth; and thus, upon unpractical subjects, natural selection might occasion a fallacious tendency of thought.

That which determines us, from given premises, to draw one inference rather than another is some habit of mind, whether it be constitutional or acquired. The habit is good or otherwise, according as it produces true conclusions from true premises or not; and an inference is regarded as valid or not, without reference to the truth or falsity of its conclusion specially, but according as the habit which determines it is such as to produce true conclusions in general or not. The particular habit of mind which governs this or that inference may be formulated in a proposition whose truth depends on the validity of the inferences which the habit determines; and such a formula is called a *guiding principle* of inference. Suppose, for example, that we observe that a rotating disk of copper quickly comes to rest when placed between the poles of a magnet, and we infer that this will happen with every disk of copper. The guiding principle is that what is true of one piece of copper is true of another. Such a guiding principle with regard to copper would be much safer than with regard to many other substances—brass, for example.

A book might be written to signalize all the most important of these guiding principles of reasoning. It would probably be, we must confess, of no service to a person whose thought is directed wholly to practical subjects, and whose activity moves along thoroughly beaten paths. The problems which present themselves to such a mind are matters of routine which he has learned once for all to handle in learning his business. But let a man venture into an unfamiliar field, or where his results are not continually checked by experience, and all history shows that the most masculine intellect will ofttimes lose his orientation and waste his efforts in directions which bring him no nearer to his goal, or even carry him entirely astray. He is like a ship on the open sea, with no one on board who understands the rules of navigation. And in such a case some general study of the guiding principles of reasoning would be sure to be found useful.

The subject could hardly be treated, however, without being first limited; since almost any fact may serve as a guiding principle. But it so happens that there exists a division among facts, such that in one class are all those which are absolutely essential as guiding principles, while in the other[s] are all those which have any other interest as objects of research. This division is between those which are necessarily taken for granted in asking whether a certain conclusion follows from certain premises, and those which are not implied in that question. A moment's thought will show that a variety of facts are already assumed when the logical question is first asked. It is implied, for instance, that there are such states of mind as doubt and belief—that a passage from one to the other is possible, the object of thought remaining the same, and that this transition is subject to some rules which all minds are alike bound by. As these are facts which we must already know before we can have any clear conception of reasoning at all, it cannot be supposed to be any longer of much interest to inquire into their truth or falsity. On the other hand, it is easy to believe that those rules of reasoning which are deduced from the very idea of the process are the ones which are the most essential; and, indeed, that so long as it conforms to these it will, at least, not lead to false conclusions from true premises. In point of fact, the importance of what may be deduced from the assumptions involved in the logical question turns out to be greater than might be supposed, and this for reasons which it is difficult to exhibit at the outset. The only one which I shall here mention is that conceptions which are really products of logical reflections, without being readily seen to be so, mingle with our ordinary thoughts, and are frequently the causes of great confusion. This is the case, for example, with the conception of quality. A quality as such is never an object of observation. We can see that a thing is blue or green, but the quality of being blue and the quality of being green are not things which we see; they are products of logical reflections. The truth is that common sense, or thought as it first emerges above the level of the narrowly practical, is deeply inbued with that bad logical quality to which the epitet *metaphysical* is commonly applied; and nothing can clear it up but a severe course of logic.

iii.

We generally know when we wish to ask a question and when we wish to pronounce a judgment, for there is a dissimilarity between the sensation of doubting and that of believing.

But this is not all which distinguishes doubt from belief. There is a practical difference. Our beliefs guide our desires and shape our actions. The Assassins, or followers of the Old Man of the Mountain, used to rush into death at his least command, because they believed that obedience to him would insure everlasting felicity. Had they doubted this, they would not have acted as they did. So it is with every belief, according to its degree. The feeling of believing is a more or less sure indication of there being established in our nature some habit which will determine our actions. Doubt never has such an effect.

Nor must we overlook a third point of difference. Doubt is an uneasy and dissatisfied state from which we struggle to free ourselves and pass into the state of belief; while the latter is a calm and satisfactory state which we do not wish to avoid, or to change to a belief in anything else.* On the contrary, we cling tenaciously, not merely to believing, but to believing just what we do believe.

Thus, both doubt and belief have positive effects upon

---

* I am not speaking of secondary effects occasionally produced by the interference of other impulses.

us, though very different ones. Belief does not make us act at once, but puts us into such a condition that we shall behave in a certain way, when the occasion arises. Doubt has not the least effect of this sort, but stimulates us to action until it is destroyed. This reminds us of the irritation of a nerve and the reflex action produced thereby; while for the analogue of belief, in the nervous system, we must look to what are called nervous associations—for example, to that habit of the nerves in consequence of which the smell of a peach will make the mouth water.

iv.

The irritation of doubt causes a struggle to attain a state of belief. I shall term this struggle *inquiry,* though it must be admitted that this is sometimes not a very apt designation.

The irritation of doubt is the only immediate motive for the struggle to attain belief. It is certainly best for us that our beliefs should be such as may truly guide our actions so as to satisfy our desires; and this reflection will make us reject any belief which does not seem to have been so formed as to insure this result. But it will only do so by creating a doubt in the place of that belief. With the doubt, therefore, the struggle begins, and with the cessation of doubt it ends. Hence, the sole object of inquiry is the settlement of opinion. We may fancy that this is not enough for us, and that we seek not merely an opinion, but a true opinion. But put this fancy to the test and it proves groundless; for as soon as a firm belief is reached we are entirely satisfied, whether the belief be false or true. And it is clear that nothing out of the sphere of our knowledge can be our object, for nothing which does not affect the mind can be a motive for a mental effort. The most that can be maintained is that we seek for a belief that we shall *think* to be true. But we think each one of our beliefs to be true, and, indeed, it is mere tautology to say so.

That the settlement of opinion is the sole end of inquiry is a very important proposition. It sweeps away, at once, various vague and erroneous conceptions of proof. A few of these may be noticed here.

1. Some philosophers have imagined that to start an inquiry it was only necessary to utter or question or set it down on paper, and have even recommended us to begin our studies with questioning everything! But the mere putting of a proposition into the interrogative form does not stimulate the mind to any struggle after belief. There must be a real and living doubt, and without all this, discussion is idle.

2. It is a very common idea that a demonstration must rest on some ultimate and absolutely indubitable propositions. These, according to one school, are first principles of a general nature; according to another, are first sensations. But, in point of fact, an inquiry, to have that completely satisfactory result called demonstration, has only to start with propositions perfectly free from all actual doubt. If the premises are not in fact doubted at all, they cannot be more satisfactory than they are.

3. Some people seem to love to argue a point after all the world is fully convinced of it. But no further advance can be made. When doubt ceases, mental action on the subject comes to an end; and, if it did go on, it would be without a purpose. . . .

v.

If the settlement of opinion is the sole object of inquiry, and if belief is of the nature of a habit, why should we not attain the desired end, by taking any answer to a question, which we may fancy, and constantly reiterating it to ourselves, dwelling on all which may conduce to that belief, and learning to turn with contempt and hatred from anything which might disturb it? This simple and direct method is really pursued by many men. I remember once being entreated not to read a certain newspaper lest it might change my opinion upon free trade. "Lest I might be entrapped by its fallacies and misstatements" was the form of expression. "You are not," my friend said, "a special student of political economy. You might, therefore, easily be deceived by fallacious arguments upon the subject. You might, then, if you read this paper, be led to believe in protection. But you admit that free trade is the true doctrine; and you do not wish to believe what is not true." I have often known this system to be deliberately adopted. Still oftener, the instinctive dislike of an undecided state of mind, exaggerated into a vague dread of doubt, makes men cling spasmodically to the views they already take. The man feels that if he only holds to his belief without wavering, it will be entirely satisfactory. Nor can it be denied that a steady and immovable faith yields great peace of mind. It may, indeed, give rise to inconveniences, as if a man should resolutely continue to believe that fire would not burn him, or that he would be eternally damned if he received his *ingesta* otherwise than through a stomach pump. But then the man who adopts this method will not allow that its inconveniences are greater than its advantages. He will say, "I hold steadfastly to the truth and the truth is always wholesome." And in many cases it may very well be that the pleasure he derives from his calm faith overbalances any inconveniences resulting from its deceptive character. Thus, if it be true that death is annihilation, then the man who believes that he will certainly go straight to heaven when he dies, provided he will have fulfilled certain simple observances in this life, has a cheap pleasure which will not be followed by the least disappointment. A similar consideration seems to have weight with many persons in religious topics, for we frequently hear it said, "Oh, I could not believe so-and-so, because I should be wretched if I did." When an ostrich buries its head in the sand as danger approaches, it very likely takes the happiest course. It hides the danger, and then calmly says there is no danger; and, if it feels perfectly sure there is none, why should it raise its head to see? A man may go through life, systematically keeping out of view all that might cause a change in his opinions, and if he only succeeds—basing his method, as he does, on two fundamental psychological laws—I do not see what can be said against his doing so. It would be an egotistical impertinence to object that his procedure is irrational, for that only amounts to saying that his method of settling belief is not ours. He does not propose to himself to be rational, and indeed, will often talk with scorn of man's weak and illusive reason. So let him think as he pleases.

But this method of fixing belief, which may be called

the method of tenacity, will be unable to hold its ground in practice. The social impulse is against it. The man who adopts it will find that other men think differently from him, and it will be apt to occur to him in some saner moment that their opinions are quite as good as his own, and this will shake his confidence in his belief. This conception, that another man's thought or sentiment may be equivalent to one's own, is a distinctly new step, and a highly important one. It arises from an impulse too strong in man to be suppressed, without danger of destroying the human species. Unless we make ourselves hermits, we shall necessarily influence each other's opinions; so that the problem becomes how to fix belief, not in the individual merely, but in the community.

Let the will of the state act, then, instead of that of the individual. Let an institution be created which shall have for its object to keep correct doctrines before the attention of the people, to reiterate them perpetually, and to teach them to the young; having at the same time power to prevent contrary doctrines from being taught, advocated, or expressed. Let all possible causes of a change of mind be removed from men's apprehensions. Let them be kept ignorant, lest they should learn of some reason to think otherwise than they do. Let their passions be enlisted, so that they may regard private and unusual opinions with hatred and horror. Then, let all men who reject the established belief be terrified into silence. Let the people turn out and tar and feather such men, or let inquisitions be made into the manner of thinking of suspected persons, and, when they are found guilty of forbidden beliefs, let them be subjected to some signal punishment. When complete agreement could not otherwise be reached, a general massacre of all who have not thought in a certain way has proved a very effective means of settling opinion in a country. If the power to do this be wanting, let a list of opinions be drawn up, to which no man of the least independence of thought can assent, and let the faithful be required to accept all these propositions, in order to segregate them as radically as possible from the influence of the rest of the world.

This method has, from the earliest times, been one of the chief means of upholding correct theological and political doctrines, and of preserving their universal or catholic character. In Rome, especially, it has been practiced from the days of Numa Pompilius to those of Pius Nonus. This is the most perfect example in history; but wherever there is a priesthood—and no religion has been without one—this method has been more or less made use of. Wherever there is aristocracy, or a guild, or any association of a class of men whose interests depend or are supposed to depend on certain propositions, there will be inevitably found some traces of this natural product of social feeling. Cruelties always accompany this system; and when it is consistently carried out, they become atrocities of the most horrible kind in the eyes of any rational man. Nor should this occasion surprise, for the officer of a society does not feel justified in surrendering the interests of that society for the sake of mercy, as he might of his own private interests. It is natural, therefore, that sympathy and fellowship should thus produce a most ruthless power.

In judging this method of fixing belief, which may be called the method of authority, we must, in the first place, allow its immeasurable mental and moral superiority to the method of tenacity. Its success is proportionally greater; and in fact it has over and over again worked the most majestic results. The mere structures of stone which it has caused to be put together—in Siam, for example, in Egypt, and in Europe—have many of them a sublimity hardly more than rivaled by the greatest works of nature. And, except the geological epochs, there are no periods of time so vast as those which are measured by some of these organized faiths. If we scrutinize the matter closely, we shall find that there has not been one of their creeds which has remained always the same; yet the change is so slow as to be imperceptible during one person's life, so that individual belief remains sensibly fixed. For the mass of mankind, then, there is perhaps no better method than this. If it is their highest impulse to be intellectual slaves, then slaves they ought to remain.

But no institution can undertake to regulate opinions upon every subject. Only the most important ones can be attended to, and on the rest men's minds must be left to the action of natural causes. This imperfection will be no source of weakness so long as men are in such a state of culture that one opinion does not influence another—that is, so long as they cannot put two and two together. But in the most priest-ridden states some individuals will be found who are raised above that condition. These men possess a wider sort of social feeling; they see that men in other countries and in other ages have held to very different doctrines from those which they themselves have been brought up to believe; and they cannot help seeing that it is the mere accident of their having been taught as they have, and of their having been surrounded with the manners and associations they have, that has caused them to believe as they do and not far differently. And their candor cannot resist the reflection that there is no reason to rate their own views at a higher value than those of other nations and other centuries; and this gives rise to doubts in their minds.

They will further perceive that such doubts as these must exist in their minds with reference to every belief which seems to be determined by the caprice either of themselves or of those who originated the popular opinions. The willful adherence to a belief, and the arbitrary forcing of it upon others, must, therefore, both be given up and a new method of settling opinions must be adopted, which shall not only produce an impulse to believe, but shall also decide what proposition it is which is to be believed. Let the action of natural preferences be unimpeded, then, and under their influence let men conversing together and regarding matters in different lights, gradually develop beliefs in harmony with natural causes. This method resembles that by which conceptions of art have been brought to maturity. The most perfect example of it is to be found in the history of metaphysical philosophy. Systems of this sort have not usually rested upon observed facts, at least not in any great degree. They have been chiefly adopted because their fundamental propositions seemed "agreeable to reason." This is an apt expression; it does not mean that which agrees with experience, but that which we find ourselves inclined to believe. Plato, for example, finds it agreeable to reason that the distances of the celestial spheres from one another should be proportional to the different lengths of strings which produce harmonious chords. Many philosophers have been led to their main conclusions by considerations like this; but this is the lowest and least developed form which the method takes, for it is clear that another man might find Kepler's theory, that the celestial spheres are proportional to the inscribed and circumscribed spheres of the different regular solids, more agreeable to *his* reason. But the shock of opinions will soon lead men to rest on preferences of a far more universal nature. Take, for example, the doctrine that man only acts selfishly—that is, from the consideration that acting in one way will afford him more pleasure than acting in another. This rests on no fact in the world, but it has a wide acceptance as being the only reasonable theory.

This method is far more intellectual and respectable from the point of view of reason than either of the others which we have noticed. But its failure has been the most manifest. It makes of inquiry something similar to the development of taste; but taste, unfortunately, is always more or less a matter of fashion, and accordingly, metaphysicians have never come to any fixed agreement, but the pendulum has swung backward and forward between a more material and a more spiritual philosophy, from the earliest times to the latest. And so from this, which has been called the *a priori* method, we are driven, in Lord Bacon's phrase, to a true induction. We have examined into this *a priori* method as something which promised to deliver our opinions from their accidental and capricious element. But development, while it is a process which eliminates the effect of some casual circumstances, only magnifies that of others. This method, therefore, does not differ in a very essential way from that of authority. The government may not have lifted its finger to influence my convictions; I may have been left outwardly quite free to choose, we will say, between monogamy and polygamy, and appealing to my conscience only, I may have concluded that the latter practice is in itself licentious. But when I come to see that the chief obstacle to the spread of Christianity among a people of as high culture as Hindus has been a conviction of the immorality of our way of treating women, I cannot help seeing that, though governments do not interfere, sentiments in their development will be very greatly determined by accidental causes. Now there are some people, among whom I must suppose that my reader is to be found, who, when they see that any belief of theirs is determined by any circumstance extraneous to the facts, will from that moment not merely admit in words that that belief is doubtful but will experience a real doubt of it, so that it ceases in some degree at least to be a belief.

To satisfy our doubts, therefore, it is necessary that a method should be found by which our beliefs may be caused by nothing human, but by some external permanency—by something upon which our thinking has no effect. Some mystics imagine that they have such a method in a private inspiration from on high. But that is only a form of the method of tenacity, in which the conception of truth as something public is not yet developed. Our external permanency would not be external, in our sense, if it was restricted in its influence to one individual. It must be something which affects, or might affect, every man. And, though these affections are necessarily as various as are individual conditions, yet the method must be such that the ultimate conclusion of every man shall be the same, or would be the same if inquiry were sufficiently persisted in. Such is the method of science. Its fundamental hypothesis, restated in more familiar language, is this: There are real things, whose characters are entirely independent of our opinions about them; those realities affect our senses according to regular laws, and, though our sensations are as different as our relations to the objects, yet, by taking advantage of the laws of perception, we can ascertain by reasoning how things really are, and any man, if he have sufficient experience and reason enough about it, will be led to the one true conclusion. The new conception here involved is that of reality. It may be asked how I know that there are any realities. If this hypothesis is the sole support of my method of inquiry, my method of inquiry must not be used to support my hypothesis. The reply is this: 1 If investigation cannot be regarded as proving that there are real things, it at least does not lead to a contrary conclusion; but the method and the conception on which it is based remain ever in harmony. No doubts of the method, therefore, necessarily arise from its practice, as is the case with all the others. 2 The feeling which gives rise to any method of fixing belief is a dissatisfaction at two repugnant propositions. But here already is a vague concession that there is some *one* thing to which a proposition should conform. Nobody, therefore, can really doubt that there are realities, or, if he did, doubt would not be a source of dissatisfaction. The hypothesis, therefore, is one which every mind admits. So that the social impulse does not cause me to doubt it. 3 Everybody uses the scientific method about a great many things, and only ceases to use it when he does not know how to apply it. 4 Experience of the method has not led me to doubt it, but, on the contrary, scientific investigation has had the most wonderful triumphs in the way of settling opinion. These afford the explanation of my not doubting the method or the hypothesis which it supposes; and not having any doubt, nor believing that anybody else whom I could influence has, it would be the merest babble for me to say more about it. If there be anybody with a living doubt upon the subject, let him consider it.

To describe the method of scientific investigation is the object of this series of papers. At present I have only room to notice some points of contrast between it and other methods of fixing belief.

This is the only one of the four methods which presents any distinction of a right and a wrong way. If I adopt the method of tenacity and shut myself out from all influences, whatever I think necessary to doing this is necessary according to that method. So with the method of authority: the state may try to put down heresy by means which, from a scientific point of view, seem very ill calculated to accomplish its purposes; but the only test *on that method* is what the state thinks, so that it cannot pursue the method wrongly. So with the *a priori* method. The very essence of it is to think as one is inclined to think. All metaphysicians will be sure to do that, however they may be inclined to judge each other to be perversely wrong. The Hegelian system recognizes every natural tendency of thought as logical, although it is certain to be abolished by counter-tendencies. Hegel thinks there is a regular system in the succession of these tendencies, in consequence of which, after drifting one way and the other for a long time, opinion will at last go right. And it is true that metaphysicians get the right ideas at last; Hegel's system of Nature represents tolerably the science of his day; and one may be sure that whatever scientific investigation has put out of doubt will presently receive *a priori* demonstration on the part of the metaphysicians. But with the scientific method the case is different. I may start with known and observed facts to proceed to the unknown; and yet the rules which I follow in doing so may not be such as investigation would approve. The test of whether I am truly following the method is not an immediate appeal to my feelings and purposes, but, on the contrary, itself involves the application of the method. Hence it is that bad reasoning as well as good reasoning is possible; and this fact is the foundation of the practical side of logic.

It is not to be supposed that the first three methods of settling opinion present no advantage whatever over the scientific method. On the contrary, each has some peculiar convenience of its own. The *a priori* method is distinguished for its comfortable conclusions. It is the nature of the process to adopt whatever belief we are inclined to, and there are certain flatteries to one's vanities which we all believe by nature, until we are awakened from our pleasing dream by rough facts. The method of authority will always govern the mass of mankind; and those who wield the various forms of organized force in the state will never be convinced that dangerous reasoning ought not to be suppressed in some way. If liberty of speech is to be untrammeled from the grosser forms of constraint, then uniformity of opinion will be secure by a moral terrorism to which the respectability of society will give its thorough approval. Following the method of authority is the path of peace. Certain nonconformities are permitted; certain others (considered unsafe) are forbidden. These are different in different countries and in different ages; but, wherever you are let it be known that you seriously hold a tabooed belief, and you may be perfectly sure of being treated with a cruelty no less brutal but more refined than hunting you like a wolf. Thus, the greatest intellectual benefactors of mankind have never dared, and dare not now, to utter the whole of their thought; and thus a shade of *prima facie* doubt is cast upon every proposition which is considered essential to the security of society. Singularly enough, the persecution does not all come from without; but a man torments himself and is oftentimes most distressed at finding himself believing propositions which he has been brought up to regard with aversion. The peaceful and sympathetic man will, therefore, find it hard to resist the temptation to submit his opinions to authority. But most of all I admire the method of tenacity for its strength, simplicity, and directness. Men who pursue it are distinguished for their decision of character, which becomes very easy with such a mental rule. They do not waste time in trying to make up their minds to what they want, but, fastening like lightning upon whatever alternative comes first, they hold to it to the end, whatever happens, without an instant's irresolution. This is one of the splendid qualities which generally accompany brilliant, unlasting success. It is impossible not to envy the man who can dismiss reason, although we know how it must turn out at last.

Such are the advantages which the other methods of settling opinions have over scientific investigation. A man should consider well of them; and then he should consider that, after all, he wishes his opinions to coincide with the fact, and that there is no reason why the results of those first three methods should do so. To bring about this effect is the prerogative of the method of science. Upon such considerations he has to make his choice—a choice which is far more than the adoption of any intellectual opinion, which is one of the ruling decisions of his life, to which when once made he is bound to adhere. The force of habit will sometimes cause a man to hold on to old beliefs after he is in a condition to see that they have no sound basis. But reflection upon the state of the case will overcome these habits, and he ought to allow reflection full weight. People sometimes shrink from doing this, having an idea that beliefs are wholesome which they cannot help feeling rest on nothing. But let such persons suppose an analogous though different case from their own. Let them ask themselves what they would say to a reformed Mussulman who should hesitate to give up his old notions in regard to the relations of the sexes; or to a reformed Catholic who should still shrink from the Bible. Would they not say that these persons ought to consider the matter fully, and clearly understand the new doctrine, and then ought to embrace it in its entirety? But, above all, let it be considered that what is more wholesome than any particular belief is integrity of belief; and that to avoid looking into the support of any belief from a fear that it may turn out rotten is quite as immoral as it is disadvantageous. The person who confesses that there is such a thing as truth, which is distinguished from falsehood simply by this, that if acted on it should, on full consideration, carry us to the point we aim at and not astray, and then, though convinced of this, dares not know the truth and seeks to avoid it, is in a sorry state of mind indeed.

Yes, the other methods do have their merits: a clear logical conscience does cost something—just as all that we cherish, costs us dear. But, we should not desire it to be otherwise. The genius of a man's logical method should be loved and reverenced as his bride, whom he has chosen from all the world. He need not condemn the others; on the contrary, he may honor them deeply, and in doing so he only honors her the more. But she is the one that he has chosen, and he knows that he was right in making that choice. And having made it, he will work and fight for her, and will not complain that there are blows to take, hoping that there may be as many and as hard to give, and will strive to be the worthy knight and champion of her from the blaze of whose splendors he draws his inspiration and his courage.

IV. How To Make Our Ideas Clear*

i.

Whoever has looked into a modern treatise on logic of the common sort, will doubtless remember the two distinctions between *clear* and *obscure* conceptions, and between *distinct* and *confused* conceptions. They have lain in the books now for nigh two centuries, unimproved and unmodified, and are generally reckoned by logicians as among the gems of their doctrine.

A clear idea is defined as one which is so apprehended that it will be recognized wherever it is met with, and so that no other will be mistaken for it. If it fails of this clearness, it is said to be obscure.

This is rather a neat bit of philosophical terminology; yet, since it is clearness that they were defining, I wish the logicians had made their definition a little more plain. Never to fail to recognize an idea, and under no circumstances to mistake another for it, let it come in how recondite a form it may, would indeed imply such prodigious force and clearness of intellect as is seldom met with in this world. On the other hand, merely to have such an acquaintance with the idea as to have become familiar with it, and to have lost all hesitancy in recognizing it in ordinary cases, hardly seems to deserve the name of clearness of apprehension, since after all it only amounts to a subjective feeling of mastery which may be entirely mistaken. I take it, however, that when the logicians speak of "clearness," they mean nothing more than such a familiarity with an idea, since they regard the quality as but a small merit, which needs to be supplemented by another, which they call *distinctness*.

* *Popular Science Monthly* (1878).

A distinct idea is defined as one which contains nothing which is not clear. This is technical language; by the *contents* of an idea logicians understand whatever is contained in its definition. So that an idea is *distinctly* apprehended, according to them, when we can give a precise definition of it, in abstract terms. Here the professional logicians leave the subject; and I would not have troubled the reader with what they have to say if it were not such a striking example of how they have been slumbering through ages of intellectual activity, listlessly disregarding the enginery of modern thought, and never dreaming of applying its lessons to the improvement of logic. It is easy to show that the doctrine that familiar use and abstract distinctness make the perfection of apprehension, has its only true place in philosophies which have long been extinct; and it is now time to formulate the method of attaining to a more perfect clearness of thought, such as we see and admire in the thinkers of our own time.

When Descartes set about the reconstruction of philosophy, his first step was to (theoretically) permit skepticism and to discard the practice of the schoolmen of looking to authority as the ultimate source of truth. That done, he sought a more natural fountain of true principles, and professed to find it in the human mind; thus passing, in the directest way, from the method of authority to that of *a priority*, as described in my first paper. Self-consciousness was to furnish us with our fundamental truths, and to decide what was agreeable to reason. But since, evidently, not all ideas are true, he was led to note, as the first condition of infallibility, that they must be clear. The distinction between an idea *seeming* clear and really being so, never occurred to him. Trusting to introspection, as he did, even for a knowledge of external things, why should he question its testimony in respect to the contents of our own minds? But then I suppose, seeing men, who seemed to be quite clear and positive, holding opposite opinions upon fundamental principles, he was further led to say that clearness of ideas is not sufficient, but that they need also to be distinct, i.e., to have nothing unclear about them. What he probably meant by this (for he did not explain himself with precision) was that they must sustain the test of dialectical examination; that they must not only seem clear at the outset, but that discussion must never be able to bring to light points of obscurity connected with them.

Such was the distinction of Descartes, and one sees that it was precisely on the level of his philosophy. It was somewhat developed by Leibniz. This great and singular genius was as remarkable for what he failed to see as for what he saw. That a piece of mechanism could not do work perpetually without being fed with power in some form, was a thing perfectly apparent to him; yet he did not understand that the machinery of the mind can only transform knowledge, but never originate it, unless it be fed with facts of observation. He thus missed the most essential point of the Cartesian philosophy, which is, that to accept propositions which seem perfectly evident to us is a thing which, whether it be logical or illogical, we cannot help doing. Instead of regarding the matter in this way, he sought to reduce the first principles of science to formulas which cannot be denied without self-contradiction and was apparently unaware of the great difference between his position and that of Descartes. So he reverted to the old formalities of logic, and, above all, abstract definitions played a great part in his philosophy. It was quite natural, therefore, that on observing that the method of Descartes labored under the difficulty that we may seem to ourselves to have clear apprehensions of ideas which in truth are very hazy, no better remedy occurred to him than to require an abstract definition of every important term. Accordingly, in adopting the distinction of *clear* and *distinct* notions, he described the latter quality as the clear apprehension of everything contained in the definition; and the books have ever since copied his words. There is no danger that his chimerical scheme will ever again be overvalued. Nothing new can ever be learned by analyzing definitions. Nevertheless, our existing beliefs can be set in order by this process, and order is an essential element of intellectual economy, as of every other. It may be acknowledged, therefore, that the books are right in making familiarity with a notion the first step toward clearness of apprehension, and the defining of it the second. But in omitting all mention of any higher perspicuity of thought, they simply mirror a philosophy which was exploded a hundred years ago. That much-admired "ornament of logic"—the doctrine of clearness and distinctness—may be pretty enough, but it is high time to relegate to our cabinet of curiosities the antique *bijou,* and to wear about us something better adapted to modern uses.

The very first lesson that we have a right to demand that logic shall teach us is how to make our ideas clear; and a most important one it is, depreciated only by minds who stand in need of it. To know what we think, to be masters of our own meaning, will make a solid foundation for great and weighty thought. It is most easily learned by those whose ideas are meager and restricted; and far happier they than such as wallow helplessly in a rich mud of conceptions. A nation, it is true, may, in the course of generations, overcome the disadvantage of an excessive wealth of language and its natural concomitant, a vast, unfathomable deep of ideas. We may see it in history, slowly perfecting its literary forms, sloughing at length its metaphysics, and, by virtue of the untirable patience which is often a compensation, attaining great excellence in every branch of mental acquirement. The page of history is not yet unrolled which is to tell us whether such a people will or will not in the long run prevail over one whose ideas (like the words of their language) are few, but which possesses a wonderful mastery over those which it has. For an individual, however, there can be no question that a few clear ideas are worth more than many confused ones. A young man would hardly be persuaded to sacrifice the greater part of his thoughts to save the rest; and the muddled head is the least apt to see the necessity of such a sacrifice. Him we can usually only commiserate, as a person with a congenital defect. Time will help him, but intellectual maturity with regard to clearness comes rather late, an unfortunate arrangement of nature, inasmuch as clearness is of less use to a man settled in life, whose errors have in great measure had their effect, than it would be to one whose path lies before him. It is terrible to see how a single unclear idea, a single formula without meaning, lurking in a young man's head, will sometimes act like an obstruction of inert matter in an artery, hindering the nutrition of the brain, and condemning its victim to pine away in the fullness of his intellectual vigor and in the midst of intellectual plenty. Many a man has cherished for years as his hobby some vague shadow of an idea, too meaningless to be positively false; he has, nevertheless, passionately loved it, has made it his companion by day and by night, and has given to it his strength and his life, leaving all other occupations for its sake, and in short has lived with it and for it, until it has become, as it were, flesh of his flesh and bone of his bone; and then he has waked up some bright morning to find it gone, clean vanished away like the beautiful Melusina of the fable, and the essence of his life gone with it. I have myself known such a man; and who can tell how many histories of circle squarers, metaphysicians, astrologers, and what not may not be told in the old German story?

ii.

The principles set forth in the first of these papers lead, at once, to a method of reaching a clearness of thought of a far higher grade than the "distinctness" of the logicians. We have there found that the action of thought is excited by the irritation of doubt, and ceases when belief is attained; so that the production of belief is the sole function of thought. All these words, however, are too strong for my purpose. It is as if I had described the phenomena as they appear under a mental microscope. Doubt and Belief, as the words are commonly employed, relate to religious or other grave discussions. But here I use them to designate the starting of any question, no matter how small or how great, and the resolution of it. If, for instance, in a horsecar, I pull out my purse and find a five-cent nickel and five coppers, I decide, while my hand is going to the purse, in which way I will pay my fare. To call such a question Doubt, and my decision Belief, is certainly to use words very disproportionate to the occasion. To speak of such a doubt as causing an irritation which needs to be appeased, suggests a temper which is uncomfortable to the verge of insanity. Yet, looking at the matter minutely, it must be admitted that, if there is the least hesitation as to whether I shall pay the five coppers or the nickel (as there will be sure to be, unless I act from some previously contracted habit in the matter), though irritation is too strong a word, yet I am excited to such small mental activity as may be necessary to deciding how I shall act. Most frequently doubts arise from some indecision, however momentary, in our action. Sometimes it is not so. I have, for example, to wait in a railway station, and to pass the time I read the advertisements on the walls, I compare the advantages of different trains and different routes which I never expect to take, merely fancying myself to be in a state of hesitancy, because I am bored with having nothing to trouble me. Feigned hesitancy, whether feigned for mere amusement or with a lofty purpose, plays a great part in the production of scientific inquiry. However the doubt may originate, it stimulates the mind to an activity which may be slight or energetic, calm or turbulent. Images pass rapidly through consciousness, one incessantly melting into another, until at last, when all is over—it may be in a fraction of a second, in an hour, or after long years—we find ourselves decided as to how we should act under such circumstances as those which occasioned our hesitation. In other words, we have attained belief.

In this process we observe two sorts of elements of consciousness, the distinction between which may best be made clear by means of an illustration. In a piece of music there are the separate notes, and there is the air. A single tone may be prolonged for an hour or a day, and it exists as perfectly in each second of that time as in the whole taken together; so that, as long as it is sounding, it might be present to a sense from which everything in the past was as completely absent as the future itself. But it is different with the air, the performance of which occupies a certain time, during the portions of which only portions of it are played. It consists in an orderliness in the succession of sounds which strike the ear at different times; and to perceive it there must be some continuity of consciousness which makes the events of a lapse of time present to us. We certainly only perceive the air by hearing the separate notes; yet we cannnot be said to directly hear it, for we hear only what is present at the instant, and an orderliness of succession cannot exist in an instant. These two sorts of objects, what we are *immediately* conscious of and what we are *mediately* conscious of, are found in all consciousness. Some elements (the sensations) are completely present at every instant so long as they last, while others (like thought) are actions having beginning, middle, and end and consist in a congruence in the succession of sensations which flow through the mind. They cannot be immediately present to us, but must cover some portion of the past or future. Thought is a thread of melody running through the succession of our sensations.

We may add that just as a piece of music may be written in parts, each part having its own air, so various systems of relationship of succession subsist together between the same sensations. These different systems are distinguished by having different motives, ideas, or functions. Thought is only one such system; for its sole motive, idea, and function is to produce belief, and whatever does not concern that purpose belongs to some other system of relations. The action of thinking may incidentally have other results. It may serve to amuse us, for example, and among *dilettanti* it is not rare to find those who have so perverted thought to the purposes of pleasure that it seems to vex them to think that the questions upon which they delight to exercise it may ever get finally settled; and a positive discovery which takes a favorite subject out of the arena of literary debate is met with ill-concealed dislike. This disposition is the very debauchery of thought. But the soul and meaning of thought, abstracted from the other elements which accompany it, though it may be voluntarily thwarted, can never be made to direct itself toward anything but the production of belief. Thought in action has for its only possible motive the attainment of thought at rest; and whatever does not refer to belief is no part of the thought itself.

And what, then, is belief? It is the demicadence which closes a musical phrase in the symphony of our intellectual life. We have seen that it has just three properties: first, it is something that we are aware of; second, it appeases the irritation of doubt; and, third, it involves the establishment in our nature of a rule of action, or, say for short, a *habit*. As it appeases the irritation of doubt, which is the motive for thinking, thought relaxes, and comes to rest for a moment when belief is reached. But, since belief is a rule for action, the application of which involves further doubt and further thought, at the same time that it is a stopping place, it is also a new starting place for thought. That is why I have permitted myself to call it thought at rest, although thought is essentially an action. The *final* upshot of thinking is the exercise of volition, and of this thought no longer forms a part; but belief is only a stadium of mental action, an effect upon our nature due to thought, which will influence future thinking.

The essence of belief is the establishment of a habit, and different beliefs are distinguished by the different modes of action to which they give rise. If beliefs do not differ in this respect, if they appease the same doubt by producing the same rule of action, then no mere differences in the manner of consciousness of them can make them different beliefs, any more than playing a tune in different keys is drawn between beliefs which differ only in their mode of expression—the wrangling which ensues is real enough, however. To believe that any objects are arranged . . . as in Fig. 1, and to believe that they are ar-

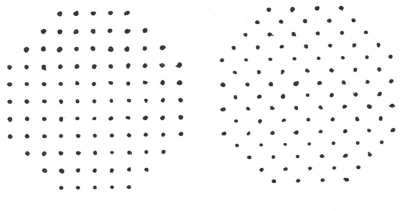

Fig. 1.   *Fig. 2.*

ranged as in Fig. 2, are one and the same belief; yet it is conceivable that a man should assert one proposition and deny the other. Such false distinctions do as much harm as the confusion of beliefs really different, and are among the pitfalls of which we ought constantly to beware, especially when we are upon metaphysical ground. One singular deception of this sort, which often occurs, is to mistake the sensation produced by our own unclearness of thought for a character of the object we are thinking. Instead of perceiving that the obscurity is purely subjective, we fancy that we contemplate a quality of the object which is essentially mysterious; and if our conception be afterward presented to us in a clear form we do not recognize it as the same, owing to the absence of the feeling of unintelligibility. So long as this deception lasts, it obviously puts an impassable barrier in the way of perspicuous thinking; so that it equally interests the opponents of rational thought to perpetuate it, and its adherents to guard against it.

Another such deception is to mistake a mere difference in the grammatical construction of two words for a distinction between the ideas they express. In this pedantic age when the general mob of writers attend so much more to words than to things, this error is common enough. When I just said that thought is an *action,* and that it consists in a *relation,* although a person performs an action but not a relation, which can only be the result of an action, yet there was no inconsistency in what I said, but only a grammatical vagueness.

From all these sophisms we shall be perfectly safe so long as we reflect that the whole function of thought is to produce habits of action; and that whatever there is connected with a thought, but irrelevant to its purpose, is an accretion to it, but no part of it. If there be a unity among our sensations which has no reference to how we shall act on a given occasion, as when we listen to a piece of music, why, we do not call that thinking. To develop its meaning, we have, therefore, simply to determine what habits it involves. Now, the identity of a habit depends on how it might lead us to act, not merely under such circumstances as are likely to arise, but under such as might possibly occur, no matter how improbable they may be. What the habit is depends on *when* and *how* it causes us to act. As for the *when,* every stimulus to action is derived from perception; as for the *how,* every purpose of action is to produce some sensible result. Thus, we come down to what is tangible and practical as the root of every real distinction of thought, no matter how subtle it may be; and there is no distinction of meaning so fine as to consist in anything but a possible difference of practice.

To see what this principle leads to, consider in the light of it such a doctrine as that of transubstantiation. The Protestant churches generally hold that the elements of the sacrament are flesh and blood only in a tropical sense; they nourish our souls as meat and the juice of it would our bodies. But the Catholics maintain that they are literally just that, meat and blood, although they possess all the sensible qualities of wafer cakes and diluted wine. But we can have no conception of wine except what may enter into a belief, either—

1. That this, that, or the other, is wine; or,
2. That wine possesses certain properties.

Such beliefs are nothing but self-notifications that we should, upon occasion, act in regard to such things as we believe to be wine according to the qualities which we be-

lieve wine to possess. The occasion of such action would
be some sensible perception, the motive of it to produce
some sensible result. Thus our action has exclusive reference to what affects the senses, our habit has the same
bearing as our action, our belief the same as our habit, our
conception the same as our belief; and we can consequently mean nothing by wine but what has certain effects,
direct or indirect, upon our senses; and to talk of something as having all the sensible characters of wine, yet
being in reality blood, is senseless jargon. Now, it is not
my object to pursue the theological question; and having
used it as a logical example I drop it, without caring to
anticipate the theologian's reply. I only desire to point
out how impossible it is that we should have an idea in
our minds which relates to anything but conceived sensible
effects of things. Our idea of anything *is* our idea of its
sensible effects; and if we fancy that we have any other we
deceive ourselves, and mistake a mere sensation accompanying the thought for a part of the thought itself. It is absurd to say that thought has any meaning unrelated to its
only function. It is foolish for Catholics and Protestants to
fancy themselves in disagreement about the elements of
the sacrament, if they agree in regard to all their sensible
effects, here or hereafter.

It appears, then, that the rule for attaining the third
grade of clearness of apprehension is as follows: consider
what effects which might conceivably have practical bearings we conceive the object of our conception to have.
Then, our conception of these effects is the whole of our
conception of the object.

iii.

Let us illustrate this rule by some examples; and, to begin
with the simplest one possible, let us ask what we mean by
calling a thing *hard*. Evidently that it will not be scratched
by many other substances. The whole conception of this
quality, as of every other, lies in its conceived effects.
There is absolutely no difference between a hard thing and
a soft thing so long as they are not brought to the test.
Suppose, then, that a diamond could be crystallized in the

midst of a cushion of soft cotton, and should remain there until it was finally burned up. Would it be false to say that that diamond was soft? This seems a foolish question, and would be so, in fact, except in the realm of logic. There such questions are often of the greatest utility as serving to bring logical principles into sharper relief than real discussions ever could. In studying logic we must not put them aside with hasty answers, but must consider them with attentive care, in order to make out the principles involved. We may, in the present case, modify our question, and ask what prevents us from saying that all hard bodies remain perfectly soft until they are touched, when their hardness increases with the pressure until they are scratched. Reflection will show that the reply is this: there would be no *falsity* in such modes of speech. They would involve a modification of our present usage of speech with regard to the words "hard" and "soft," but not of their meanings. For they represent no fact to be different from what it is; only they involve arrangements of facts which would be exceedingly maladroit. This leads us to remark that the question of what would occur under circumstances which do not actually arise is not a question of fact, but only of the most perspicuous arrangement of them.* For example,

---

* In "Issues of Pragmaticism," *The Monist,* vol. XV (1905), pp. 481–99, Peirce qualified this argument, and in so doing moved to a new stage of thought in the direction of (philosophic) realism. This later reflection was, roughly, that if we mean by the hardness of a diamond that it *"will* not be scratched" then, in the case imagined, since the diamond will never be scratched, the issue of its hardness is merely "usage of speech" and not a *"real* fact." But, Peirce then argues, if we mean by the diamond's hardness that it *"would* not be scratched," this commits us to the existence of traits that are realizable whether they are immediately observed and tested or not. This was a move away from the idea that the meaning of a term (e.g., "hard") *is* the method of its verification (e.g., scratch testing). Peirce also points out that the assignment of *hardness* to the diamond is not an "isolated fact." There are other associated and observed properties of the diamond:

> From some of these properties hardness is believed to be inseparable. For like it they bespeak the high polemerization of the molecule. But however this may be, how can the hardness of all other diamonds fail to bespeak *some* real relation among the diamonds without which a piece of carbon would not be a diamond? Is it not a monstrous perversion of the word and concept *real* to say that the accident of the nonarrival of the corundum prevented the hardness of the diamond from having the *reality* which it otherwise, with little doubt, would have had?

the question of free will and fate in its simplest form, stripped of verbiage, is something like this: I have done something of which I am ashamed; could I, by an effort of the will, have resisted the temptation, and done otherwise? The philosophical reply is that this is not a question of fact, but only of the arrangement of facts. Arranging them so as to exhibit what is particularly pertinent to my question—namely, that I ought to blame myself for having done wrong—it is perfectly true to say that, if I had willed to do otherwise than I did, I should have done otherwise. On the other hand, arranging the facts so as to exhibit another important consideration, it is equally true that when a temptation has once been allowed to work, it will, if it has a certain force, produce its effect, let me struggle how I may. There is no objection to a contradiction in what would result from a false supposition. The *reductio ad absurdum* consists in showing that contradictory results would follow from a hypothesis which is consequently judged to be false. Many questions are involved in the free-will discussion, and I am far from desiring to say that both sides are equally right. On the contrary, I am of opinion that one side denies important facts, and that the other does not. But what I do say is that the above single question was the origin of the whole doubt; that, had it not been for this question, the controversy would never have arisen; and that this question is perfectly solved in the manner which I have indicated.

Let us next seek a clear idea of Weight. This is another very easy case. To say that a body is heavy means simply that, in the absence of opposing force, it will fall. This (neglecting certain specifications of how it will fall, etc.,

---

At the same time, we must dismiss the idea that the occult state of things (be it a relation among atoms or something else), which constitutes the reality of a diamond's hardness, can possibly consist in anything but in the truth of a general conditional proposition. For to what else does the entire teaching of chemistry relate except to the "behavior" of different possible kinds of material substance? And in what does that behavior consist except that if a substance of a certain kind should be exposed to an agency of a certain kind, a certain kind of sensible result *would* ensue, according to our experiences hitherto. As for the pragmaticist, it is precisely his position that nothing else than this can be so much as *meant* by saying that an object possesses a character. He is therefore obliged to subscribe to the doctrine of a real Modality, including real Necessity and real Possibility.

which exist in the mind of the physicist who uses the word) is evidently the whole conception of weight. It is a fair question whether some particular facts may not *account* for gravity; but what we mean by the force itself is completely involved in its effects.

This leads us to undertake an account of the idea of Force in general. This is the great conception which, developed in the early part of the seventeenth century from the rude idea of a cause, and, constantly improved upon since, has shown us how to explain all the changes of motion which bodies experience, and how to think about all physical phenomena; which has given birth to modern science, and changed the face of the globe; and which, aside from its more special uses, has played a principal part in directing the course of modern thought, and in furthering modern social development. It is, therefore, worth some pains to comprehend it. According to our rule, we must begin by asking what is the immediate use of thinking about force; and the answer is that we thus account for changes of motion. If bodies were left to themselves, without the intervention of forces, every motion would continue unchanged both in velocity and in direction. Furthermore, change of motion never takes place abruptly; if its direction is changed, it is always through a curve without angles; if its velocity alters, it is by degrees. The gradual changes which are constantly taking place are conceived by geometers to be compounded together according to the rules of the parallelogram of forces. If the reader does not already know what this is, he will find it, I hope, to his advantage to endeavor to follow the following explanation; but if mathematics are insupportable to him, pray let him skip three paragraphs rather than that we should part company here.

A *path* is a line whose beginning and end are distinguished. Two paths are considered to be equivalent, which, beginning at the same point, lead to the same point. Thus the two paths, *A–B–C–D–E* and *A–F–G–H–E* [Fig. 3], are equivalent. Paths which do *not* begin at the same point are considered to be equivalent, provided that, on moving either of them without turning it, but keeping it always parallel to its original position when its beginning coincides with that of the other path, the ends also coincide. Paths are considered as geometrically added together, when one begins where the other ends; thus the path $A-E$ is conceived to be a sum of $A-B$, $B-C$, $C-D$, and $D-E$. In the parallelogram of Fig. 4 the diagonal $A-C$ is the sum of $A-B$ and $B-C$; or, since $A-D$ is geometrically equivalent to $B-C$, $A-C$ is the geometrical sum of $A-B$ and $A-D$.

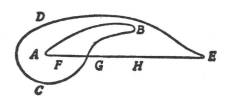

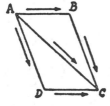

Fig. 3.   *Fig. 4.*

All this is purely conventional. It simply amounts to this: that we choose to call paths having the relations I have described equal or added. But, though it is a convention, it is a convention with a good reason. The rule for geometrical addition may be applied not only to paths, but to any other things which can be represented by paths. Now, as a path is determined by the varying direction and distance of the point which moves over it from the starting point, it follows that anything which from its beginning to its end is determined by a varying direction and a varying magnitude is capable of being represented by a line. Accordingly, *velocities* may be represented by lines, for they have only directions and rates. The same thing is true of *accelerations,* or changes of velocities. This is evident enough in the case of velocities; and it becomes evident for accelerations if we consider that precisely what velocities are to positions—namely, states of change of them—that accelerations are to velocities.

The so-called "parallelogram of forces" is simply a rule for compounding accelerations. The rule is, to represent the accelerations by paths, and then to geometrically add the paths. The geometers, however, not only use the "parallelogram of forces" to compound different accelerations, but also to resolve one acceleration into a sum of several. Let $A-B$ [Fig. 5] be the path which represents a certain acceleration—say, such a change in the motion of a body that at the end of one second the body will, under the influence of that change, be in a position different from

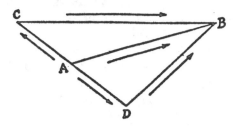

Fig. 5.

what it would have had if its motion had continued un-changed such that a path equivalent to *A–B* would lead from the latter position to the former. This acceleration may be considered as the sum of the accelerations repre-sented by *A–C* and *C–B*. It may also be considered as the sum of the very different accelerations represented by *A–D* and *C–B*. It may also be considered as the sum of the very different accelerations represented by *A–D* and *D–B,* where *A–D* is almost the opposite of *A–C*. And it is clear that there is an immense variety of ways in which *A–B* might be resolved into the sum of two accelerations.

After this tedious explanation, which I hope, in view of the extraordinary interest of the conception of force, may not have exhausted the reader's patience, we are prepared at last to state the grand fact which this conception em-bodies. This fact is that if the actual changes of motion which the different particles of bodies experience are each resolved in its appropriate way, each component accelera-tion is precisely such as is prescribed by a certain law of Nature, according to which bodies in the relative positions which the bodies in question actually have at the mo-ment,* always receive certain accelerations, which, being compounded by geometrical addition, give the acceleration which the body actually experiences.

This is the only fact which the idea of force represents, and whoever will take the trouble clearly to apprehend what this fact is perfectly comprehends what force is. Whether we ought to say that a force *is* an acceleration, or that it *causes* an acceleration, is a mere question of pro-priety of language, which has no more to do with our real meaning than the difference between the French idiom *"Il*

---

* Possibly the velocities also have to be taken into account.

fait froid" and its English equivalent *"It is cold."* Yet it is surprising to see how this simple affair has muddled men's minds. In how many profound treatises is not force spoken of as a "mysterious entity," which seems to be only a way of confessing that the author despairs of ever getting a clear notion of what the word means! In a recent, admired work on *Analytic Mechanics* it is stated that we understand precisely the effect of force, but what force itself is we do not understand! This is simply a self-contradiction. The idea which the word "force" excites in our minds has no other function than to affect our actions, and these actions can have no reference to force otherwise than through its effects. Consequently, if we know what the effects of force are, we are acquainted with every fact which is implied in saying that a force exists, and there is nothing more to know. The truth is, there is some vague notion afloat that a question may mean something which the mind cannot conceive; and when some hair-splitting philosophers have been confronted with the absurdity of such a view, they have invented an empty distinction between positive and negative conceptions, in the attempt to give their nonidea a form not obviously nonsensical. The nullity of it is sufficiently plain from the considerations given a few pages back; and, apart from those considerations, the quibbling character of the distinction must have struck every mind accustomed to real thinking.

iv.

Let us now approach the subject of logic and consider a conception which particularly concerns it, that of *reality*. Taking clearness in the sense of familiarity, no idea could be clearer than this. Every child uses it with perfect confidence, never dreaming that he does not understand it. As for clearness in its second grade, however, it would probably puzzle most men, even among those of a reflective turn of mind, to give an abstract definition of the real. Yet such a definition may perhaps be reached by considering the points of difference between reality and its opposite, fiction. A figment is a product of somebody's imagination; it has such characters as his thought impresses upon it.

That those characters are independent of how you or I think is an external reality. There are, however, phenomena within our own minds, dependent upon our thought, which are at the same time real in the sense that we really think them. But though their characters depend on how we think, they do not depend on what we think those characters to be. Thus, a dream has a real existence as a mental phenomenon if somebody has really dreamt it; that he dreamt so and so does not depend on what anybody thinks was dreamt but is completely independent of all opinion on the subject. On the other hand, considering, not the fact of dreaming, but the thing dreamt, it retains its peculiarities by virtue of no other fact than that it was dreamt to possess them. Thus we may define the real as that whose characters are independent of what anybody may think them to be.

But, however satisfactory such a definition may be found, it would be a great mistake to suppose that it makes the idea of reality perfectly clear. Here, then, let us apply our rules. According to them, reality, like every other quality, consists in the peculiar, sensible effects which things partaking of it produce. The only effect which real things have is to cause belief, for all the sensations which they excite emerge into consciousness in the form of beliefs. The question, therefore, is, how is true belief (or belief in the real) distinguished from false belief (or belief in fiction). Now, as we have seen in the former paper, the idea of truth and falsehood, in their full development, appertain exclusively to the scientific method of settling opinion. A person who arbitrarily chooses the propositions which he will adopt can use the word truth only to emphasize the expression of his determination to hold on to his choice. Of course, the method of tenacity never prevailed exclusively; reason is too natural to men for that. But in the literature of the Dark Ages we find some fine examples of it. When Scotus Erigena is commenting upon a poetical passage in which hellebore is spoken of as having caused the death of Socrates, he does not hesitate to inform the inquiring reader that Helleborus and Socrates were two eminent Greek philosophers, and that the latter having been overcome in argument by the former took the matter to heart and died of it! What sort of an idea of truth could a man have who could adopt and teach, without the qualification of a "perhaps," an opinion taken so entirely at random? The real spirit of Socrates, who I hope would have been delighted to have been "overcome in argument," because he would have learned something by it, is in curious contrast with the naïve idea of the glossist, for whom . . . discussion would seem to have been simply a struggle. When philosophy began to awake from its long slumber, and before theology completely dominated it, the practice seems to have been for each professor to seize upon any philosophical position he found unoccupied and which seemed a strong one, to intrench himself in it, and to sally forth from time to time to give battle to the others. Thus, even the scanty records we possess of those disputes enable us to make out a dozen or more opinions held by different teachers at one time concerning the question of nominalism and realism. Read the opening part of the *Historia Calamitatum* of Abélard, who was certainly as philosophical as any of his contemporaries, and see the spirit of combat which it breathes. For him, the truth is simply his particular stronghold. When the method of authority prevailed, the truth meant little more than the Catholic faith. All the efforts of the scholastic doctors are directed toward harmonizing their faith in Aristotle and their faith in the Church, and one may search their ponderous folios through without finding an argument which goes any further. It is noticeable that where different faiths flourish side by side, renegades are looked upon with contempt even by the party whose belief they adopt; so completely has the idea of loyalty replaced that of truth seeking. Since the time of Descartes, the defect in the conception of truth has been less apparent. Still, it will sometimes strike a scientific man that the philosophers have been less intent on finding out what the facts are than on inquiring what belief is most in harmony with their system. It is hard to convince a follower of the *a priori* method by adducing facts; but show him that an opinion he is defending is inconsistent with what he has laid down elsewhere, and he will be very apt to retract it. These minds do not seem to believe that disputation is ever to cease; they seem to think that the opinion which is natural for one man is not so for another, and that belief will, consequently, never be settled. In contenting themselves with fixing their own opinions by a method which would lead another man to a different result, they betray their feeble hold of the conception of what truth is.

On the other hand, all the followers of science are fully persuaded that the processes of investigation, if only pushed far enough, will give one certain solution to each question to which they can be applied. One man may investigate the velocity of light by studying the transits of Venus and the aberration of the stars; another by the oppositions of Mars and the eclipses of Jupiter's satellites; a third by the method of Fizeau; a fourth by that of Foucault; a fifth by the motions of the curves of Lissajous; a sixth, a seventh, an eighth, and a ninth may follow the different methods of comparing the measures of statical and dynamical electricity. They may at first obtain different results, but, as each perfects his method and his processes, the results will move steadily together toward a destined center. So with all scientific research. Different minds may set out with the most antagonistic views, but the progress of investigation carries them by a force outside of themselves to one and the same conclusion. This activity of thought by which we are carried, not where we wish, but to a foreordained goal, is like the operation of destiny. No modification of the point of view taken, no selection of other facts for study, no natural bent of mind even, can enable a man to escape the predestinate opinion. This great law is embodied in the conception of truth and reality. The opinion which is fated * to be ultimately agreed to by all who investigate is what we mean by the truth, and the object represented in this opinion is the real. That is the way I would explain reality.

But it may be said that this view is directly opposed to the abstract definition which we have given of reality, inasmuch as it makes the characters of the real depend on what is ultimately thought about them. But the answer to this is that, on the one hand, reality is independent, not necessarily of thought in general, but only of what you or I or any finite number of men may think about it; and that, on the other hand, though the object of the final opinion depends on what that opinion is, yet what that

---

* Fate means merely that which is sure to come true, and can nohow be avoided. It is a superstition to suppose that a certain sort of events are ever fated, and it is another to suppose that the word "fate" can never be freed from its superstitious taint. We are all fated to die.

opinion is does not depend on what you or I or any man thinks. Our perversity and that of others may indefinitely postpone the settlement of opinion; it might even conceivably cause an arbitrary proposition to be universally accepted as long as the human race should last. Yet even that would not change the nature of the belief, which alone could be the result of investigation carried sufficiently far; and if, after the extinction of our race, another should arise with faculties and disposition for investigation, that true opinion must be the one which they would ultimately come to. "Truth crushed to earth shall rise again," and the opinion which would finally result from investigation does not depend on how anybody may actually think. But the reality of that which is real does depend on the real fact that investigation is destined to lead, at last, if continued long enough, to a belief in it.

But I may be asked what I have to say to all the minute facts of history, forgotten never to be recovered, to the lost books of the ancients, to the buried secrets.

> Full many a gem of purest ray serene
>   The dark, unfathomed caves of ocean bear;
> Full many a flower is born to blush unseen,
>   And waste its sweetness on the desert air.

Do these things not really exist because they are hopelessly beyond the reach of our knowledge? And then, after the universe is dead (according to the prediction of some scientists), and all life has ceased forever, will not the shock of atoms continue though there will be no mind to know it? To this I reply that, though in no possible state of knowledge can any number be great enough to express the relation between the amount of what rests unknown to the amount of the known, yet it is unphilosophical to suppose that, with regard to any given question (which has any clear meaning), investigation would not bring forth a solution of it, if it were carried far enough. Who would have said, a few years ago, that we could ever know of what substances stars are made whose light may have been longer in reaching us than the human race has existed? Who can be sure of what we shall not know in a few hundred years? Who can guess what would be the result of continuing the pursuit of science for ten thousand years, with the activity of the last hundred? And if it were to go on for a million, or a billion, or any number of years you please, how is it possible to say that there is any question which might not ultimately be solved?

But it may be objected, "Why make so much of these remote considerations, especially when it is your principle that only practical distinctions have a meaning?" Well, I must confess that it makes very little difference whether we say that a stone on the bottom of the ocean, in complete darkness, is brilliant or not—that is to say, that it *probably* makes no difference, remembering always that that stone *may* be fished up tomorrow. But that there are gems at the bottom of the sea, flowers in the untraveled desert, etc., are propositions which, like that about a diamond being hard when it is not pressed, concern much more the arrangement of our language than they do the meaning of our ideas.

It seems to me, however, that we have, by the application of our rule, reached so clear an apprehension of what we mean by reality, and of the fact which the idea rests on, that we should not, perhaps, be making a pretension so presumptuous as it would be singular, if we were to offer a metaphysical theory of existence for universal acceptance among those who employ the scientific method of fixing belief. However, as metaphysics is a subject much more curious than useful, the knowledge of which, like that of a sunken reef, serves chiefly to enable us to keep clear of it, I will not trouble the reader with any more Ontology at this moment. I have already been led much further into that path than I should have desired; and I have given the reader such a dose of mathematics, psychology, and all that is most abstruse, that I fear he may already have left me, and that what I am now writing is for the compositor and proofreader exclusively. I trusted to the importance of the subject. There is no royal road to logic, and really valuable ideas can only be had at the price of close attention. But I know that in the matter of ideas the public prefer the cheap and nasty; and in my next paper I am going to return to the easily intelligible, and not wander from it again. The reader who has been at the pains of wading through this paper shall be rewarded in the next one by seeing how beautifully what has been developed in this tedious way can be applied to the ascertainment of the rules of scientific reasoning.

We have, hitherto, not crossed the threshold of scientific logic. It is certainly important to know how to make our ideas clear, but they may be ever so clear without being true. How to make them so, we have next to study. How to give birth to those vital and procreative ideas which multiply into a thousand forms and diffuse themselves everywhere, advancing civilization and making the dignity of man, is an art not yet reduced to rules, but of the secret of which the history of science affords some hints.

V. What Pragmatism Is*

The writer of this article has been led by much experience to believe that every physicist, and every chemist, and, in short, every master in any department of experimental science, has had his mind molded by his life in the laboratory to a degree that is little suspected. The experimentalist himself can hardly be fully aware of it, for the reason that the men whose intellects he really knows about are much like himself in this respect. With intellects of widely different training from his own, whose education has largely been a thing learned out of books, he will never become inwardly intimate, be he on ever so familiar terms with them; for he and they are as oil and water, and though they be shaken up together, it remarkable how quickly they will go their several mental ways, without having gained more than a faint flavor from the association. Were those other men only to take skillful soundings of the experimentalist's mind—which is just what they are unqualified to do, for the most part—they would soon discover that, excepting perhaps upon topics where his mind is trammeled by personal feeling or by his bringing up, his disposition is to think of everything just as everything is thought of in the laboratory, that is, as a question of experimentation. Of course, no living man possesses in their fullness all the attributes characteristic of his type: it is not the typical doctor whom you will see every day driven in buggy or coupe, nor is it the typical pedagogue that will be met with in the first schoolroom you enter. But when you have found, or ideally constructed upon a basis of observation, the typical experimentalist, you will find that whatever assertion you may make to him, he will either understand as meaning that if a given prescription for an experiment ever can be and ever is carried out in act, an

* *The Monist* (1905).

experience of a given description will result, or else he will see no sense at all in what you say. If you talk to him as Mr. Balfour talked not long ago to the British Association saying that "the physicist . . . seeks for something deeper than the laws connecting possible objects of experience," that "his object is a physical reality" unrevealed in experiments, and that the existence of such nonexperiential reality "is the unalterable faith of science," to all such ontological meaning, you will find the experimentalist mind to be color-blind. What adds to that confidence in this, which the writer owes to his conversations with experimentalists, is that he himself may almost be said to have inhabited a laboratory from the age of six until long past maturity; and having all his life associated mostly with experimentalists, it has always been with a confident sense of understanding them and of being understood by them.

That laboratory life did not prevent the writer (who here and in what follows simply exemplifies the experimentalist type) from becoming interested in methods of thinking; and when he came to read metaphysics, although much of it seemed to him loosely reasoned and determined by accidental prepossessions, yet in the writings of some philosophers, especially Kant, Berkeley, and Spinoza, he sometimes came upon strains of thought that recalled the ways of thinking of the laboratory, so that he felt he might trust to them; all of which has been true of other laboratory men.

Endeavoring, as a man of that type naturally would, to formulate what he so approved, he framed the theory that a *conception*, that is, the rational purport of a word or other expression, lies exclusively in its conceivable bearing upon the conduct of life; so that, since obviously nothing that might not result from experiment can have any direct bearing upon conduct, if one can define accurately all the conceivable experimental phenomena which the affirmation or denial of a concept could imply, one will have therein a complete definition of the concept, and *there is absolutely nothing more in it*. For this doctrine he invented the name *pragmatism*. Some of his friends wished him to call it *practicism* or *practicalism* (perhaps on the ground that *praktikós* is better Greek than *pragmatikós*). But for one who had learned philosophy out of Kant, as the writer, along with nineteen out of every twenty experimentalists who have turned to philosophy, had done, and who still thought in Kantian terms most readily, *praktisch* and *pragmatisch* were as far apart as the two poles, the former belonging in a region of thought where no mind of the experimentalist type can ever make sure of solid ground under his feet, the latter expressing relation to some definite human purpose. Now quite the most striking feature of the new theory was its recognition of an inseparable connection between rational cognition and rational purpose; and that consideration it was which determined the preference for the name *pragmatism*.

Concerning the matter of philosophical nomenclature, there are a few plain considerations which the writer has for many years longed to submit to the deliberate judgment of those few fellow students of philosophy who deplore the present state of that study, and who are intent upon rescuing it therefrom and bringing it to a condition like that of the natural sciences, where investigators, instead of condemning each the work of most of the others as misdirected from beginning to end, cooperate, stand upon one another's shoulders, and multiply incontestable results; where every observation is repeated, and isolated observations go for little; where every hypothesis that merits attention is subjected to severe but fair examination, and only after the predictions to which it leads have been remarkably borne out by experience is trusted at all, and even then only provisionally; where a radically false step is rarely taken, even the most faulty of those theories which gain wide credence being true in their main experimental predictions. To those students, it is submitted that no study can become scientific in the sense described until it provides itself with a suitable technical nomenclature, whose every term has a single definite meaning universally accepted among students of the subject, and whose vocables have no such sweetness or charms as might tempt loose writers to abuse them—which is a virtue of scientific nomenclature too little appreciated. It is submitted that the experience of those sciences which have conquered the greatest difficulties of terminology, which are unquestionably the taxonomic sciences, chemistry, mineralogy, botany, zoology, has conclusively shown that the only way in which the requisite unanimity and requisite ruptures with individual habits and preferences can be brought about is so to shape the canons of terminology that they shall gain the support of *moral principle* and of every man's sense of decency; and that, in particular (under defined restrictions), the general feeling shall be that he who introduces a new conception into philosophy is under an obligation to invent acceptable terms to express it, and that when he has done so, the duty of his fellow students is to accept those terms, and to resent any wresting of them from their original meanings, as not only a gross discourtesy to him to whom philosophy was indebted for each conception, but also as an injury to philosophy itself; and furthermore, that once a conception has been supplied with suitable and sufficient words for its expression, no other *technical* terms denoting the same things, considered in the same relations, should be countenanced. Should this suggestion find favor, it might be deemed needful that the philosophians in congress assembled should adopt, after due deliberation, convenient canons to limit the application of the principle. Thus, just as is done in chemistry, it might be wise to assign fixed meanings to certain prefixes and suffixes. For example, it might be agreed, perhaps, that the prefix *prope-* should mark a broad and rather indefinite extension of the meaning of the term to which it was prefixed; the name of a doctrine would naturally end in *-ism*, while *-icism* might mark a more strictly defined acception of that doctrine, etc. Then again, just as in biology no account is taken of terms antedating Linnæus, so in philosophy it might be found best not to go back of the scholastic terminology. To illustrate another sort of limitation, it has probably never happened that any philosopher has attempted to give a general name to his own doctrine without that name's soon acquiring in common philosophical usage a signification much broader than was originally intended. Thus, special systems go by the names Kantianism, Benthamism, Comteanism, Spencerianism, etc., while transcendentalism, utilitarianism, positivism, evolutionism, synthetic philosophy, etc., have irrevocably and very conveniently been elevated to broader governments.

After awaiting in vain, for a good many years, some particularly opportune conjuncture of circumstances that might serve to recommend his notions of the ethics of terminology, the writer has now, at last, dragged them in over head and shoulders, on an occasion when he has no specific proposal to offer nor any feeling but satisfaction at the course usage has run without any canons or resolutions of a congress. His word "pragmatism" has gained general recognition in a generalized sense that seems to argue power of growth and vitality. The famed psychologist, James, first took it up, seeing that his "radical empiricism" substantially answered to the writer's definition of pragmatism, albeit with a certain difference in the point of view. Next, the admirably clear and brilliant thinker, Mr. Ferdinand C. S. Schiller, casting about for a more attractive name for the "anthropomorphism" of his *Riddle of the Sphinx*, lit, in that most remarkable paper of his on "Axioms as Postulates," upon the same designation "pragmatism," which in its original sense was in generic agreement with his own doctrine, for which he has since found the more appropriate specification "humanism," while he still retains "pragmatism" in a somewhat wider sense. So far all went happily. But at present, the word begins to be met with occasionally in the literary journals, where it gets abused in the merciless way that words have to expect when they fall into literary clutches. Sometimes the manners of the British had effloresced in scolding at the word as ill-chosen—ill-chosen, that is, to express some meaning that it was rather designed to exclude. So then, the writer, finding his bantling "pragmatism" so promoted, feels that it is time to kiss his child good-bye and relinquish it to its higher destiny; while to serve the precise purpose of expressing the original definition, he begs to announce the birth of the word "pragmaticism," which is ugly enough to be safe from kidnappers.*

Much as the writer has gained from the perusal of what other pragmatists have written, he still thinks there is a decisive advantage in his original conception of the doctrine. From this original form every truth that follows from any of the other forms can be deduced, while some errors can be avoided into which other pragmatists have fallen. The original view appears, too, to be a more compact and unitary conception than the others. But its capital merit, in

---

* To show how recent the general use of the word "pragmatism" is, the writer may mention that, to the best of his belief, he never used it in copy for the press before today, except by particular request, in *Baldwin's Dictionary*. Toward the end of 1890, when this part of the *Century Dictionary* appeared, he did not deem that the word had sufficient status to appear in that work. But he has used it continually in philosophical conversation since, perhaps, the midseventies.

the writer's eyes, is that it more readily connects itself with a critical proof of its truth. Quite in accord with the logical order of investigation, it usually happens that one first forms an hypothesis that seems more and more reasonable the further one examines into it, but that only a good deal later gets crowned with an adequate proof. The present writer, having had the pragmatist theory under consideration for many years longer than most of its adherents, would naturally have given more attention to the proof to it. At any rate, in endeavoring to explain pragmatism, he may be excused for confining himself to that form of it that he knows best. In the present article there will be space only to explain just what this doctrine (which, in such hands as it has now fallen into, may probably play a pretty prominent part in the philosophical discussions of the next coming years) really consists in. Should the exposition be found to interest readers of *The Monist,* they would certainly be much more interested in a second article which would give some samples of the manifold applications of pragmaticism (assuming it to be true) to the solution of problems of different kinds. After that, readers might be prepared to take an interest in a proof that the doctrine is true—a proof which seems to the writer to leave no reasonable doubt on the subject, and to be the one contribution of value that he has to make to philosophy. For it would essentially involve the establishment of the truth of synechism.*

The bare definition of pragmaticism could convey no

* [Peirce defined "synechism" as "that tendency of philosophical thought which insists upon the idea of continuity as of prime importance in philosophy and, in particular, upon the necessity of hypotheses involving true continuity . . . The general motive is to avoid the hypothesis that this or that is inexplicable . . . Continuity is nothing but perfect generality of a law of relationship." Baldwin, *Dictionary of Philosophy and Psychology* (New York, 1902), vol. II, p. 657; *Collected Papers* (Cambridge, Mass., 1934), vol. VI., p. 117. *Synechism* is from the Greek: *syn* = with, together; *echein* = have, hold. Peirce viewed the idea of continuity as a principle of feeling, or continuum of general ideas; a principle of analysis and hypothesis; a trait of subject matters. His paper "The Law of Mind," *The Monist,* vol. II (1892), pp. 533–559, *Collected Papers,* vol. VI., pp. 86–113, is a basic statement of the doctrine. Peirce concludes this paper saying that *Synechism* explains many facts that otherwise remain inexplicable and involves first, "logical realism;" second, objective idealism; third, tychism (objective chance) "with its consequent thoroughgoing evolutionism." See also Peirce's description of *Synechism* in the final paragraph of selection II, (i) above.]

satisfactory comprehension of it to the most apprehensive of minds. but requires the commentary to be given below. Moreover, this definition takes no notice of one or two other doctrines without the previous acceptance (or virtual acceptance) of which pragmaticism itself would be a nullity. They are included as a part of the pragmatism of Schiller, but the present writer prefers not to mingle different propositions. The preliminary propositions had better be stated forthwith.

The difficulty in doing this is that no formal list of them has ever been made. They might all be included under the vague maxim, "Dismiss make-believes." Philosophers of very diverse stripes propose that philosophy shall take its start from one or another state of mind in which no man, least of all a beginner in philosophy, actually is. One proposes that you shall begin by doubting everything, and says that there is only one thing that you cannot doubt, as if doubting were "as easy as lying." Another proposes that we should begin by observing "the first impressions of sense," forgetting that our very percepts are the results of cognitive elaboration. But in truth, there is but one state of mind from which you can "set out," namely, the very state of mind in which you actually find yourself at the time you do "set out"—a state in which you are laden with an immense mass of cognition already formed, of which you cannot divest yourself if you would; and who knows whether, if you could, you would not have made all knowledge impossible to yourself? Do you call it *doubting* to write down on a piece of paper that you doubt? If so, doubt has nothing to do with any serious business. But do not make believe; if pedantry has not eaten all the reality out of you, recognize, as you must, that there is much that you do not doubt, in the least. Now that which you do not at all doubt, you must and do regard as infallible, absolute truth. Here breaks in Mr. Make-Believe: "What! Do you mean to say that one is to believe what is not true, or that what a man does not doubt is *ipso facto* true?" No, but unless he can make a thing white and black at once, *he* has to regard what he does not doubt as absolutely true. Now you, *per hypothesiu*, are that man. "But you tell me there are scores of things I do not doubt. I really cannot persuade myself that there is not some one of them about which I am mistaken." You are adducing one of your make-believe facts, which, even if it were established, would only go to show that doubt had a *limen,* that is, is only called into being by a certain finite stimulus. You only puzzle yourself by talking of this metaphysical "truth" and metaphysical "falsity," that you know nothing about. All you have any dealings with are your doubts and beliefs,* with the course of life that forces new beliefs upon you and gives you power to doubt old beliefs. If your terms "truth" and "falsity" are taken in such senses as to be definable in terms of doubt and belief and the course of experience (as for example they would be if you were to define the "truth" as that to a belief in which belief would tend if it were to tend indefinitely toward absolute fixity), well and good: in that case, you are only talking about doubt and belief. But if by truth and falsity you mean something not definable in terms of doubt and belief in any way, then you are talking of entities of whose existence you can know nothing, and which Ockham's razor would clean shave off. Your problems would be greatly simplified if, instead of saying that you want to know the "Truth," you were simply to say that you want to attain a state of belief unassailable by doubt.

Belief is not a momentary mode of consciousness; it is a habit of mind essentially enduring for some time, and mostly (at least) unconscious; and like other habits, it is (until it meets with some surprise that begins its dissolution) perfectly self-satisfied. Doubt is of an altogether contrary genus. It is not a habit, but the privation of a habit. Now a privation of a habit, in order to be anything at all, must be a condition of erratic activity that in some way must get superseded by a habit.

Among the things which the reader, as a rational person, does not doubt is that he not merely has habits, but also can exert a measure of self-control over his future actions; which means, however, *not* that he can impart to them any arbitarily assignable character, but, on the contrary, that a process of self-preparation will tend to impart to action (when the occasion for it shall arise) one fixed character, which is indicated and perhaps roughly measured by the absence (or slightness) of the feeling of self-reproach, which subsequent reflection will induce. Now,

---

* It is necessary to say that "belief" is throughout used merely as the name of the contrary to doubt, without regard to grades of certainty or to the nature of the proposition held for true, i.e., "believed."

this subsequent reflection is part of the self-preparation for action on the next occasion. Consequently, there is a tendency, as action is repeated again and again, for the action to approximate indefinitely toward the perfection of that fixed character, which would be marked by entire absence of self-reproach. The more closely this is approached, the less room for self-control there will be; and where no self-control is possible there will be no self-reproach.

These phenomena seem to be the fundamental characteristics which distinguish a rational being. Blame, in every case, appears to be a modification, often accomplished by a transference, or "projection," of the primary feeling of self-reproach. Accordingly, we never blame anybody for what had been beyond his power of previous self-control. Now, thinking is a species of conduct which is largely subject to self-control. In all their features (which there is no room to describe here), logical self-control is a perfect mirror of ethical self-control—unless it be rather a species under that genus. In accordance with this, what you cannot in the least help believing is not, justly speaking, wrong belief. In other words, for you it is the absolute truth. True, it is conceivable that what you cannot help believing today, you might find you thoroughly disbelieve tomorrow. But then there is a certain distinction between things you "cannot" do, merely in the sense that nothing stimulates you to the great effort and endeavors that would be required, and things you cannot do because in their own nature they are insusceptible of being put into practice. In every stage of your excogitations, there is something of which you can only say, "I cannot think otherwise," and your experientially based hypothesis is that the impossibility is of the second kind.

There is no reason why "thought," in what has just been said, should be taken in that narrow sense in which silence and darkness are favorable to thought. It should rather be understood as covering all rational life, so that an experiment shall be an operation of thought. Of course, that ultimate state of habit to which the action of self-control ultimately tends, where no room is left for further self-control, is, in the case of thought, the state of fixed belief, or perfect knowledge.

Two things here are all-important to assure oneself of and to remember. The first is that a person is not absolutely an individual. His thoughts are what he is "saying to himself," that is, is saying to that other self that is just coming into life in the flow of time. When one reasons, it is that critical self that one is trying to persuade; and all thought whatsoever is a sign, and is mostly of the nature of language. The second thing to remember is that the man's circle of society (however widely or narrowly this phrase may be understood) is a sort of loosely compacted person, in some respects of higher rank than the person of an individual organism. It is these two things alone that render it possible for you—but only in the abstract, and in a Pickwickian sense—to distinguish between absolute truth and what you do not doubt.

Let us now hasten to the exposition of pragmaticism itself. Here it will be convenient to imagine that somebody to whom the doctrine is new, but of rather preternatural perspicacity, asks questions of a pragmaticist. Everything that might give a dramatic illusion must be stripped off, so that the result will be a sort of cross between a dialogue and a catechism, but a good deal more like the latter—something rather painfully reminiscent of Mangnall's *Historical Questions*.

Questioner: I am astounded at your definition of your pragmatism, because only last year I was assured by a person above all suspicion of warping the truth—himself a pragmatist—that your doctrine precisely was "that a conception is to be tested by its practical effects." You must surely, then, have entirely changed your definition very recently.

Pragmatist: If you will turn to Vols. VI and VII of the *Revue Philosophique,* or to the *Popular Science Monthly* for November 1877 and January 1878, you will be able to judge for yourself whether the interpretation you mention was not then clearly excluded. The exact wording of the English enunciation (changing only the first person into the second) was: "Consider what effects that might conceivably have practical bearing you conceive the object of your conception to have. Then your conception of those effects is the WHOLE of your conception of the object."

Questioner: Well, what reason have you for asserting that this is so?

Pragmatist: That is what I specially desire to tell you. But the question had better be postponed until you clearly understand what those reasons profess to prove.

Questioner: What, then, is the *raison d'être* of the doctrine? What advantage is expected from it?

Pragmatist: It will serve to show that almost every proposition of ontological metaphysics is either meaningless gibberish—one word being defined by other words, and they by still others, without any real conception ever being reached—or else is downright absurd; so that all such rubbish being swept away, what will remain of philosophy will be a series of problems capable of investigation by the observational methods of the true sciences—the truth about which can be reached without those interminable misunderstandings and disputes which have made the highest of the positive sciences a mere amusement for idle intellects, a sort of chess—idle pleasure its purpose, and reading out of a book its method. In this regard, pragmaticism is a species of prope-positivism. But what distinguishes it from other species is, first, its retention of a purified philosophy; secondly, its full acceptance of the main body of our instinctive beliefs; and thirdly, its strenuous insistence upon the truth of scholastic realism (or a close approximation to that, well stated by the late Dr. Francis Ellingwood Abbot in the Introduction to his *Scientific Theism*). So, instead of merely jeering at metaphysics, like other prope-positivists, whether by long-drawn-out parodies or otherwise, the pragmaticist extracts from it a precious essence, which will serve to give life and light to cosmology and physics. At the same time, the moral applications of the doctrine are positive and potent; and there are many other uses of it not easily classed. On another occasion, instances may be given to show that it really has these effects.

Questioner: I hardly need to be convinced that your doctrine would wipe out our metaphysics. Is it not as obvious that it must wipe out every proposition of science and everything that bears on the conduct of life? For you say that the only meaning that, for you, any assertion bears is that a certain experiment has resulted in a certain way: nothing else but an experiment enters into the meaning. Tell me, then, how can an experiment, in itself, reveal anything more than that something once happened to an individual object and that subsequently some other individual event occurred?

Pragmatist: That question is, indeed, to the purpose—the purpose being to correct any misapprehensions of pragmaticism. You speak of an experiment in itself, emphasizing *in itself*. You evidently think of each experiment as isolated from every other. It has not, for example, occurred to you, one might venture to surmise, that every connected series of experiments constitutes a single collective experiment. What are the essential ingredients of an experiment? First, of course, an experimenter of flesh and blood. Secondly, a verifiable hypothesis. This is a proposition* relating to the universe environing the experimenter, or to some well-known part of it and affirming or denying of this only some experimental possibility or impossibility. The third indispensable ingredient is a sincere doubt in the experimenter's mind as to the truth of that hypothesis. Passing over several ingredients on which we need not dwell, the purpose, the plan, and the resolve, we come to the act of choice by which the experimenter singles out certain identifiable objects to be operated upon. The next is the external (or quasi-external) ACT by which he modifies those objects. Next, comes the subsequent *reaction* of the world upon the experimenter in a perception; and finally, his recognition of the teaching of the experiment. While the two chief parts of the event itself are the action and the reaction, yet the unity of essence of the experiment lies in its purpose and plan, the ingredients passed over in the enumeration.

Another thing: in representing the pragmaticist as making rational meaning to consist in an experiment (which you speak of as an event in the past), you strikingly fail to catch his attitude of mind. Indeed, it is not in an experiment, but in *experimental phenomena*, that rational meaning is said to consist. When an experimentalist speaks of a *phenomenon*, such as "Hall's phenomenon," "Zeemann's phenomenon" and its modification, "Michelson's phenomenon," or "the chessboard phenomenon," he does not mean any particular event that did happen to somebody in the dead past, but what *surely will* happen to everybody in the

---

* The writer, like most English logicians, invariably uses the word *proposition* not as the Germans define their equivalent, *Satz*, as the language-expression of a judgment (*Urtheil*), but as that which is related to any assertion, whether mental and self-addressed or outwardly expressed, just as any possibility is related to its actualization. The difficulty of the, at best, difficult problem of the essential nature of a Proposition has been increased, for the Germans, by their *Urtheil*, confounding, under one designation, the mental *assertion* with the *assertable*.

living future who shall fulfill certain conditions. The phenomenon consists in the fact that when an experimentalist shall come to *act* according to a certain scheme that he has in mind, then will something else happen, and shatter the doubts of skeptics, like the celestial fire upon the altar of Elijah.

And do not overlook the fact that the pragmaticist maxim says nothing of single experiments or of single experimental phenomena (for what is conditionally true *in futuro* can hardly be singular), but only speaks of *general kinds* of experimental phenomena. Its adherent does not shrink from speaking of general objects as real, since whatever is true represents a real. Now the laws of nature are true.

The rational meaning of every proposition lies in the future. How so? The meaning of a proposition is itself a proposition. Indeed, it is no other than the very proposition of which it is the meaning: it is a translation of it. But of the myriads of forms into which a proposition may be translated, what is that one which is to be called its very meaning? It is, according to the pragmaticist, that form in which the proposition becomes applicable to human conduct, not in these or those special circumstances, nor when one entertains this or that special design, but that form which is most directly applicable to self-control under every situation, and to every purpose. This is why he locates the meaning in future time; for future conduct is the only conduct that is subject to self-control. But in order that that form of the proposition which is to be taken as its meaning should be applicable to every situation and to every purpose upon which the proposition has any bearing, it must be simply the general description of all the experimental phenomena which the assertion of the proposition virtually predicts. For an experimental phenomenon is the fact asserted by the proposition that action of a certain description will have a certain kind of experimental result; and experimental results are the only results that can effect human conduct. No doubt, some unchanging idea may come to influence a man more than it had done; but only because some experience equivalent to an experiment has brought its truth home to him more intimately than before. Whenever a man acts purposively, he acts under a belief in some experimental phenomenon. Consequently, the sum of the experimental phenomena that a proposition implies makes up its entire bearing upon human conduct. Your question, then, of how a pragmaticist can attribute any meaning to any assertion other than that of a single occurrence is substantially answered.

Questioner: I see that pragmaticism is a thoroughgoing phenomenalism. Only why should you limit yourself to the phenomena of experimental science rather than embrace all observational science? Experiment, after all, is an uncommunicative informant. It never expiates*: it only answers "yes" or "no"; or rather it usually snaps out "No!" or, at best, only utters an inarticulate grunt for the negation of its "no." The typical experimentalist is not much of an observer. It is the student of natural history to whom nature opens the treasury of her confidence, while she treats the cross-examining experimentalist with the reserve he merits. Why should your phenomenalism sound the meager jew's-harp of experiment rather than the glorious organ of observation?

Pragmaticist: Because pragmaticism is not definable as "thoroughgoing phenomenalism," although the latter doctrine may be a kind of pragmatism. The *richness* of phenomena lies in their sensuous quality. Pragmaticism does not intend to define the phenomenal equivalents of words and general ideas, but, on the contrary, eliminates their sential element, and endeavors to define the rational purport, and this it finds in the purposive bearing of the word or proposition in question.

Questioner: Well, if you choose so to make Doing the Be-all and the End-all of human life, why do you not make meaning to consist simply in doing? Doing has to be done at a certain time upon a certain object. Individual objects and single events cover all reality, as everybody knows, and as a practicalist ought to be the first to insist. Yet, your meaning, as you have described it, is *general*. Thus, it is of the nature of a mere word and not a reality. You say yourself that your meaning of a proposition is only same proposition in another dress. But a practical man's meaning in the very thing he means. What do you make to be the meaning of "George Washington"?

Pragmaticist: Forcibly put! A good half dozen of your points must certainly be admitted. It must be admitted, in the first place, that if pragmaticism really made Doing to

* [This is probably a misprint for "expatiates."]

be the Be-all and the End-all of life, that would be its death. For to say that we live for the mere sake of action, as action, regardless of the thought it carries out, would be to say that there is no such thing as rational purport. Secondly, in must be admitted that every proposition professes to be true of a certain real, individual object, often the environing universe. Thirdly, it must be admitted that pragmaticism fails to furnish any translation or meaning of a proper name, or other designation of an individual object. Fourthly, the pragmaticistic meaning is undoubtedly general; and it is equally indisputable that the general is of the nature of a word or sign. Fifthly, it must be admitted that the very meaning of a word of significant object ought to be the very essence of reality of what it signifies. But when those admissions have been unreservedly made, if you find the pragmaticist still constrained most earnestly to deny the force of your objection, you ought to infer that there is some consideration that has escaped you. Putting the admissions together, you will perceive that the pragmaticist grants that a proper name (although it is not customary to say that it has a *meaning*) has a certain denotative function peculiar, in each case, to that name and its equivalents; and that he grants that every assertion contains such a denotative or pointing-out function. In its peculiar individuality, the pragmaticist excludes this from the rational purport of the assertion, although *the like* of it, being common to all assertions, and so, being general and not individual, may enter into the pragmaticistic purport. Whatever exists, *ex-sists,* that is, really acts upon other existents, so obtains a self-identity, and is definitely individual. As to the general, it will be a help to thought to notice that there are two ways of being general. A statue of a soldier on some village monument, in his overcoat and with his musket, is for each of a hundred families the image of its uncle, its sacrifice to the Union. That statue, then, though it is itself single, represents any one man of whom a certain predicate may be true. It is *objectively* general. The word "soldier," whether spoken or written, is general in the same way; while the name "George Washington" is not so. But each of these two terms remains one and the same noun, whether it be spoken or written, and whenever and wherever it be spoken or written. This noun is not an existent thing: it is a *type,* or *form,* to which objects, both those that are externally existent and those which are imagined, may *conform,* but which none of them can exactly be. This is subjective generality. The pragmaticistic purport is general in both ways.

As to reality, one finds it defined in various ways; but if that principle of terminological ethics that was proposed be accepted, the equivocal language will soon disappear. For *realis* and *realitas* are not ancient words. They were invented to be terms of philosophy in the thirteenth century, and the meaning they were intended to express is perfectly clear. That is *real* which has such and such characters, whether anybody thinks it to have those characters or not. At any rate, that is the sense in which the pragmaticist uses the word. Now, just as conduct controlled by ethical reason tends toward fixing certain habits of conduct, the nature of which (as, to illustrate the meaning, peaceable habits and not quarrelsome habits) does not depend upon any accidental circumstances, and *in that sense* may be said to be *destined;* so thought, controlled by a rational experimental logic tends to the fixation of certain opinions, equally destined, the nature of which will be the same in the end, however the perversity of thought of whole generations may cause the postponement of the ultimate fixation. If this be so, as every man of us virtually assumes that it is, in regard to each matter the truth of which he seriously discusses, then, according to the adopted definition of "real," the state of things which will be believed in that ultimate opinion is real. But, for the most part, such opinions will be general. Consequently, *some* general objects are real. (Of course, nobody ever thought that *all* generals were real; but the scholastics used to assume that generals were real when they had hardly any, or quite no, experiential evidence to support their assumption; and their fault lay just there, and not in holding that generals could be real.) One is struck with the inexactitude of thought even of analysts of power, when they touch upon modes of being. One will meet, for example, the virtual assumption that what is relative to thought cannot be real. But why not, exactly? *Red* is relative to sight, but the fact that this or that is in that relation to vision what we call being red is not *itself* relative to sight; it is a real fact.

Not only may generals be real, but they may also be *physically efficient,* not in every metaphysical sense, but in the common-sense acception in which human purposes are physically efficient. Aside from metaphysical nonsense, no sane man doubts that if I feel the air in my study to be stuffy, that thought may cause the window to be opened. My thought, be it granted, was an individual event. But what determined it to take the particular determination it did, was in part the general fact that stuffy air is unwholesome, and in part other *Forms,* concerning which Dr. Carus has caused so many men to reflect to advantage—or rather, *by* which, and the general truth concerning which Dr. Carus's mind was determined to the forcible enunciation of so much truth. For truths, on the average, have a greater tendency to get believed than falsities have. Were it otherwise, considering that there are myriads of false hypotheses to account for any given phenomenon, against one sole true one (or if you will have it so, against every true one), the first step toward genuine knowledge must have been next door to a miracle. So, then, when my window was opened, because of the truth that stuffy air is *malsain,* a physical effort was brought into existence by the efficiency of a general and nonexistent truth. This has a droll sound because it is unfamiliar; but exact analysis is with it and not against it; and it has besides, the immense advantage of not blinding us to great facts—such as that the ideas "justice" and "truth" are, notwithstanding the iniquity of the world, the mightiest of the forces that move it. Generality is, indeed, an indispensable ingredient of reality; for mere individual existence or actuality without any regularity whatever is a nullity. Chaos is pure nothing.

That which any true proposition asserts is *real,* in the sense of being as it is regardless of what you or I may think about it. Let this proposition be a general conditional proposition as to the future, and it is a real general such as is calculated really to influence human conduct; and such the pragmaticist holds to be the rational purport of every concept.

Accordingly, the pragmaticist does not make the *summum bonum* to consist in action, but makes it to consist in that process of evolution whereby the existent comes more and more to embody those generals which were just now said to be *destined,* which is what we strive to express in calling them *reasonable.* In its higher stages, evolution takes place more and more largely through self-control, and this gives the pragmaticist a sort of justification for making the rational purport to be general.

There is much more in elucidation of pragmaticism that might be said to advantage were it not for the dread of fatiguing the reader. It might, for example, have been well to show clearly that the pragmaticist does not attribute any different essential mode of being to an event in the future from that which he would attribute to a similar event in the past, but only that the practical attitude of the thinker toward the two is different. It would also have been well to show that the pragmaticist does not make Forms to be the *only* realities in the world, any more than he makes the reasonable purport of a word to be the only kind of meaning there is. These things are, however, implicitly involved in what has been said. There is only one remark concerning the pragmaticist's conception of the relation of his formula to the first principles of logic which need detain the reader.

Aristotle's definition of universal predication,* which is usually designated (like a papal bull or writ of court, from its opening words), as the *Dictum de omni,* may be translated as follows: "We call a predication (be it affirmative or negative), *universal,* when, and only when, there is nothing among the existent individuals to which the subject affirmatively belongs, but to which the predicate will not likewise be referred (affirmatively or negatively, according as the universal predication is affirmative or negative)." . . .† The important words "existent individuals" have been introduced into the translation (which English idiom would not here permit to be literal); but it is plain that "existent individuals" were what Aristotle meant. The other departures from literalness only serve to give modern English forms of expression. Now, it is well known that propositions in formal logic go in pairs, the two of one pair being convertible into another by the interchange of the ideas of antecedent and consequent, subject and predicate, etc. The parallelism extends so far that it is often assumed to be perfect; but it is not quite so. The proper mate of this sort to the *Dictum de omni* is the following definition of affirmative predication: We call a predication *affirmative* (be it universal or particular) when, and only when, there is nothing among the sensational effects that belong universally to the predicate which will not be (universally or particularly, according as the

---

* *Prior Analytics,* I.1. 24b, 28–30.
† [Peirce quotes the Greek text, which has been deleted here.]

affirmative predication is universal or particular) said to belong to the subject. Now, this is substantially the essential proposition of pragmaticism. Of course, its parallelism to the *Dictum de omni* will only be admitted by a person who admits the truth of pragmaticism.

Suffer me to add one word more on this point. For if one cares at all to know what the pragmaticist theory consists in, one must understand that there is no other part of it to which the pragmaticist attaches quite as much importance as he does to the recognition in his doctrine of the utter inadequacy of action or volition or even of resolve or actual purpose, as materials out of which to construct a conditional purpose or the concept of conditional purpose. Had a purposed article concerning the principle of continuity and synthetizing the ideas of the other articles of a series in the early volumes of *The Monist* ever been written, it would have appeared how, with thorough consistency, that theory involved the recognition that continuity is an indispensable element of reality, and that continuity is simply what generality becomes in the logic of relatives, and thus, like generality, and more than generality, is an affair of thought, and is the essence of thought. Yet even in its truncated condition, an extraintelligent reader might discern that the theory of those cosmological articles made reality to consist in something more than feeling and action could supply, inasmuch as the primeval chaos, where those two elements were present, was explicitly shown to be pure nothing. Now, the motive for alluding to that theory just here is that in this way one can put in a strong light a position which the pragmaticist holds and must hold, whether that cosmological theory be ultimately sustained or exploded, namely, that the third category—the category of thought, representation, triadic relation, mediation, genuine thirdness, thirdness as such—is an essential ingredient of reality, yet does not by itself constitute reality, since this category (which in that cosmology appears as the element of habit) can have no concrete being without action, as a separate object on which to work its government, just as action cannot exist without the immediate being of feeling on which to act. The truth is that pragmaticism is closely allied to the Hegelian absolute idealism, from which, however, it is sundered by its vigorous denial that the third category (which Hegel degrades to a mere state of thinking) suffices to make the world, or is even so much as self-sufficient. Had Hegel, instead of regarding the first two stages with his smile of contempt, held on to them as independent or distinct elements of the triune Reality, pragmaticists might have looked up to him as the great vindicator of their truth. (Of course, the external trappings of his doctrine are only here and there of much significance.) For pragmaticism belongs essentially to the triadic class of philosophical doctrines, and is much more essentially so than Hegelianism is. (Indeed, in one passage, at least, Hegel alludes to the triadic form of his exposition as to a mere fashion of dress.)

C. S. PEIRCE

Milford, Pa., September, 1904

POSTSCRIPT. During the last five months, I have met with references to several objections to the above opinions, but not having been able to obtain the text of these objections, I do not think I ought to attempt to answer them. If gentlemen who attack either pragmatism in general or the variety of it which I entertain would only send me copies of what they write, more important readers they could easily find, but they could find none who would examine their arguments with a more grateful avidity for truth not yet apprehended, nor any who would be more sensible of their courtesy.

Feb. 9, 1905

C.S.P.

William James

INTRODUCTION

William James (1842-1910) was born in New York City and educated in England and intermittently in Europe and the United States. One of his brothers was Henry James, the novelist. For a time William aspired to be an artist, but in 1861 he entered Lawrence Scientific School and in 1863 Harvard Medical School. For a year he traveled with Louis Agassiz on a naturalist's expedition to the Amazon basin. He studied medicine in Germany and in 1869 received his M.D. from Harvard. In the years of 1869–1870, he experienced severe depression—one instance of this horror is described in *The Varieties of Religious Experience,* in the chapter on the "Sick Soul" disguised as the report of a "French Correspondent."

In 1873 James was appointed Instructor in Anatomy and Physiology at Harvard and in 1885 Professor of Philosophy, although between 1889 and 1897 his title was Professor of Psychology. His interests in literature and philosophy had always been extensive and his work in psychology often branched out into philosophical and distinctly ethical considerations. In 1890 the major achievement, which has become a classic in psychology and philosophy, the *Principles of Psychology,* was published, and in 1897 his *Will to Believe* and *Other Essays in Popular Philosophy* appeared. *The Varieties of Religious Experience,* being the Gifford Lectures in Edinburgh, was published in 1901–1902, and *Pragmatism: A New Name for Some Old Ways of Thinking* in 1907. James' accomplishments in these books made him a world figure. In the last ten years of his life he suffered from ill health, and his energies were taxed by the demands made upon him as a popular speaker and renowned man of letters.

William James made pragmatism famous in a lecture of 1898. Then and many times thereafter he continued to give Peirce the credit for inventing this philosophy. But it was through James' exposition that pragmatism was received and understood by the world at large.

Peirce and James were lifelong friends and naturally influenced one another. It is often said that James took up the leading ideas of Peirce's pragmatism but, by making them popular, also reduced them to a subjective and loosely knit version of meaning and truth and justification of religious belief. It is true that Peirce sometimes complained about what James, Schiller, Papini, and others were making out of pragmatism; and he was led eventually to baptize his own doctrine as *pragmaticism*, a name ugly enough, as he said, to be safe from kidnappers (see p. 105). But a more scrupulous study of the historical facts will, I think, tell another and more interesting story. While there were undoubted differences between James and Peirce concerning the content and application of pragmatism, far from borrowing or debasing Peirce's ideas, James deliberately and carefully worked out a largely independent and alternative version of pragmatism. His characteristic generosity in crediting others with his ideas has obscured some of this history. Further, the ease with which some of James' pronouncements on pragmatism *seem* to lend themselves to devastating refutation, has encouraged the tendency to regard his writings on the subject as not quite respectable. A serious critique of James' pragmatism has yet to be undertaken. I venture to suggest that it would reveal a far more subtle and comprehensive development of philosophic ideas than has hitherto been supposed.

One main difference between Peirce and James was that while Peirce sought meaning—and the explication of ideas —in general schema and formulae of (possible) action, James focused upon the function of ideas in experience, upon the distinct contributions that ideas or beliefs make in specific human actions. Peirce was a realist (calling himself a "scholastic realist") while James was more of a nominalist, as Dewey has remarked (see p. 27). Peirce recognized this difference. James, he wrote,

> in defining pragmatism, speaks of it as referring ideas to *experiences*, meaning evidently the sensational side of ex-

perience, while I regard *concepts* as affairs of habit or disposition, and of how we should react.*

The difference is even reflected in their respective understandings of the word "pragmatism." Peirce (as we have seen in "What Pragmatism Is" in V, and as Dewey points out, p. 24) was using the term in Kantian fashion as *pragmatisch,* referring to experimental and purposive action; James invoked the Greek, not Kant, in explaining that *pragma* means "action," "practice" (see p. 210).

James was led to view pragmatism not only as a method of clarifying ideas and a theory of *meaning* but also a theory of truth. Further, it is clear that in his early writings he regarded the essential statement of pragmatism to be descriptive of the actual process of much of our thinking. Thus the logical content of pragmatism had a psychological basis as well; and this is one reason why James' pragmatism is a part of a general theory of thought and action. In one of his earliest writings (1878), which presages much of his later doctrine, James commented critically on the influential Spencerian theory of the mind as passively corresponding to external objects.

I, for my part, cannot escape the consideration, forced upon me at every turn, that the knower is not simply a mirror floating with no foothold anywhere, and passively reflecting an order that he comes upon and finds simply existing. The knower is an actor, and coefficient of the truth on one side, whilst on the other he registers the truth which he helps to create. Mental interests, hypotheses, postulates, so far as they are bases for human action—action which to a great extent transforms the world—help to *make* the truth which they declare. In other words, there belongs to mind, from its birth upward, a spontaneity, a vote. It is in the game, and not a mere looker-on; and its judgments of the *should-be,* its ideals, cannot be peeled off from the body of the *cogitandum* as if they were excrences, or meant, at most, survival. We know so little about the ultimate nature of things, or of ourselves, that it would be sheer folly dogmatically to say that an ideal rational order may not be real. The only objective criterion of reality is coerciveness, in the long run, over thought. Objective facts, Spencer's outward relations, are real only because they coerce sensation. Any interest which should be coercive on the same massive scale

* In a letter to Christine Ladd-Franklin quoted in the *Journal of Philosophy, Psychology and Scientific Methods*, vol. XII (1916), p. 718.

would be *eodem jure* real. By its very essence, the reality of a thought is proportionate to the way it grasps us. Its intensity, its seriousness—its interest, in a word—taking these qualities, not at any given instant, but as shown by the total upshot of experience. If judgments of the *should-be* are fated to grasp us in this way, they are what "correspond." *

The mind is teleological, argued James. "The theorizing faculty . . . functions exclusively for the sake of ends." Emotional and practical interests "are the real *a priori* elements in cognition." They shape the process of thinking and our ways of interpreting experience, subject always to the coercive pressure of sensation. In all this, James was liberating the theory of mind from the narrow, static confines of traditional philosophic empiricism which had lost all contact with the actual functioning of thought, the "luxuriant foliage of ideal interests," the mutable and purposeful character of mental activity.

In his *Principles of Psychology*, James' teleological interpretation of mind and the instrumental nature of conception and reasoning was fully elaborated. James attacked the inadequate associationist empiricist school of Herbart in Germany, Hume, the Mills, and Bain in Britain —in which all mental activity is treated as atomistic successions of ideas, "a psychology without a soul"—as well as the Idealistic metaphysical or "spiritualistic" school according to which the faculties of the Soul are "irreducible," "absolute" properties of a "spiritual" Self. He described his own position as "strictly positivistic," keeping psychology based as a natural science on physiology and biology. "Thoughts and feelings" are empirically correlated with definite conditions of the brain. Wherever possible physiological explanations take the place of mentalistic hypotheses.

James' conception of psychology, its real subject matter and method, is central to all of his other philosophic work. It is the point of departure for his study of religious experience and belief, his view of scientific knowledge, his analyses of the nature of value, meaning, and truth. In this James is able to encompass what, to some thinkers, was

---

* "Remarks on Spencer's Definition of Mind as Correspondence" *Journal of Speculative Philosophy* vol. XII (1878), pp. 1–18. Reprinted in *Collected Essays and Reviews* (New York, 1920), pp. 43–68. The above passage is from pp. 67–68.

inimical: an exceedingly sensitive, open, and liberal view of the operations and flights of our thinking, with a biological, evolutionary, and bodily (or physically) centered explanation of all our mental activity.

James' functional approach to psychological subject matters is evident in his manner of identifying mental phenomena. Rather than his appealing to some given datum of introspection or self-evident presence of a spiritual agent, he writes:

> The pursuance of future ends and the choice of means for their attainment are thus the mark and criterion of the presence of mentality in a phenomenon.*

Actions which are "done for an end, and show a choice of means" are expressions of mind. Discrimination and detailed description of the ways in which this exercise of purposeful actions takes place within the physiological and bodily equipment we have inherited and the social adaptions and modifications made in their expression leads James to discuss the nature of habits, the stream of thought, the concept of the self, will, knowledge, and emotion as forms of mentality.

One way in which James stated the principle of pragmatism was: "to interpret each notion by tracing its respective practical consequences" and "the effective meaning of any philosophic proposition can always be brought down to some particular consequence in our future practical experience." Ideas or beliefs that have no distinguishably different consequences or effects then differ only verbally. This process of "bringing down" assertions, claims, or beliefs to specific *differences* they make in experience constitutes their "significance" or "meaning" for James. In this he was reflecting a practice in science. If we wish to determine the meaning of a hypothesis we may ask: What difference does the hypothesis make for our experiments or understanding of the phenomena under study? Notice, that the same kind of question is often put: What difference would our *acceptance* of the hypothesis make? Or, even: What difference would the hypothesis make *if* it were true? Thus considerations of meaning and of truth can coalesce in practice; getting at the meaning is asking

* *The Principles of Psychology* (New York, 1890), vol. I, p. 8. See Dewey's comments above, p. 36, on the "biological nature" of this criterion.

what the consequences would be if the idea were true. James was responsive to these coalescences in various kinds of practical deliberations; this is why the meanings of "meaning" and of "truth" are often associated and overlapping in his expositions of them.

James' use of this principle is evident above in his criterion of "mentality in a phenomenon." There James attempts to state the specific and practical *difference* that the presence of mind makes in observable behavior. The same approach is taken in defining religious experience. James asks in effect: What distinct *difference* does the occurrence of religious experience (and belief) contribute to ordinary experience? This way of "bringing down" the meaning of ideas by determining the *differences* they make for conduct has its background in James' training in medicine and physiology.

> It is a good rule in physiology, when we are studying the meaning of an organ, to ask after its most peculiar and characteristic performance, and to seek its office in that one of its functions which no other organ can possibly exert.*

Beliefs, ideas, and theories are not exactly organs; but they are like organs in being *instruments* of action in certain experiential contexts. And it is their "performance" that delineates, for James, their value, that is, their meaning and truth.

James was thus led to develop a pragmatic conception of *truth,* in which "functional possibilities" and the "workings" of a statement constitute its truth. This he distinguished from a "static" sense in which statements are simply attributed truth or falsehood. On the former interpretation truth ascriptions have a reference not only to a statement, but to a statement and its role in a context of behavior of a specific kind. The reference, says James, is to "something determinate, and some sort of adaption to it." This theory of the "working" and "functional" reference of *truth* permitted the equating of the *true* and the *useful* and *good*. Ideas are true (or useful) or *become* so "in so far as they help us to get in satisfactory relation with other parts of our experience." "Truth," says James, "is *one species of good . . . whatever proves itself to be*

---

* *The Varieties of Religious Experience* (New York, 1902), p. 45.

good in the way of belief . . ." * There were many objections raised to the theory: Some ideas may be true but not useful, and some may be useful but not true: some statements may be useful (thus true) for some persons but not useful (thus false) for others. How can the same statement be both true and false? If ideas become true through verification, so that truth is verification, we waive the law of excluded middle (viz., that every statement is either true or false) and enter a logical limbo in which we cannot account for statements that are true or false but unconfirmable (e.g., "Napolean dreamt of his mother on the night of his third birthday") nor how the meaning of a statement before it is made true differs from the meaning after it is made true.

There are difficulties in James' theory as it is expounded in the selections that follow. The theory never received a rigorous and detailed formulation. But the above objections seem most effective for a defective reason: They trade upon some shifting between certain traditional and "static" notions of truth and James' more novel usage. Even James vacillated, for it is not easy to keep old terminology geared to new distinctions. And the theory is more complicated than James' easy style suggested. Thus that the "same" statement can be useful and true for some persons, useless and false for others, points (perhaps) to the need for distinctions between the "same" linguistic forms but in different contexts of their function and application, as admitting differences of meaning and truth. But how this can be accomplished without serious loss of efficiency and controls over the language of truth ascriptions remains to be investigated.

James' theory of truth and of meaning is related to this argument in *The Will to Believe.* His general view comes to this: When for a person P, a belief B (say, that God exists, or the universe exhibits rational purpose) answers a compelling need of P to interpret the world in a certain way, the "good" supplied by B in the life of P, the difference B makes in P's life, justifies B. But this justification of belief is possible only when the choice of B or not-B is "live," "forced," and "momentous"; the evidence for or against B is equal; and the effect of B is a "vital benefit" to P. These qualifications work against the charge

* See p. 223, below.

that James was engaged in a general defense of religious belief. Moral interests and moral language can be found in almost every important passage of James' writing on pragmatism. Philosophy is an education in and critical analysis of proposed and possible forms of human belief and conduct:

> The whole function of philosophy ought to be to find out what definite difference it will make to you and me, at definite instants of our life, if this world-formula or that world-formula be the true one.*

Here again, in stressing the notion of the "definite difference . . . at definite instants of our life," James was applying his pragmatism. Philosophy is a "bringing down" of the meaning and truth of formulae to the differences they make in actual or projected behavior.

We have seen that James' pragmatism moves into and through many kinds of subject matters. An uninterrupted continuity of aim and resources is preserved, however, since James was a spokesman for the equal claims of the singularity and of the protean forms of experience, of the variegated whole of experience, and of a philosophy that answers to the whole of our nature. In this James stood out among modern philosophers. As Bergson remarked: "In the eyes of William James, the whole man counts." James proposed his pragmatism as a way of providing a methodical and unified clarification of experience for the achievement of a diversity of possible goods.

* See p. 212, below.

VI. An Interview:
   Pragmatism—What It Is

In 1907 the *New York Times* published an interview with William James by Edwin Bjorkman. In the course of an enthusiastic description of his visit with James in Cambridge, Bjorkman suggested the desirability of a clarifying description of pragmatism for a nonacademic audience. James, he reports, "went to his desk and wrote down this statement." James' statement is a remarkably succinct and clear description of his mature thinking about pragmatism and is an excellent introduction to the selections that follow. As far as I know, the full statement has never reappeared in the literature.*

This is the full statement excepting the first two paragraphs and some sentences near the close which are of less relevant interest.

PRAGMATISM and TRUTH

It is true that pragmatic writers have laid more stress than any previous philosophers on human action. But nothing could be more ludicrous than to call this their primary interest, or to explain it by their belief that purely theoretic knowledge of reality, and truth as such, are unattainable. Pragmatism's primary interest is in its doctrine

---

* Extensive excerpts of the statement taken from James' manuscript are given in R. B. Perry, *The Thought and Character of William James* (Boston, 1936), vol. II, pp. 478-80. This has been reprinted in *The Writings of William James,* John J. McDermott, ed. (New York, 1968).

of truth. All pragmatist writers make this the center of their speculations; not one of them is skeptical, not one doubts our ultimate ability to penetrate theoretically into the very core of reality. They only ask what we mean by truth, and they find the answer more intricate than previous philosophers, with their relatively simple minds in this matter, had suspected.

Instead of being a practical substitute for philosophy, good for engineers, doctors, sewage experts, and vigorous untaught minds in general to feed upon, pragmatism has proved so oversubtle that even academic critics have failed to catch its question, to say nothing of their misunderstandings of its answer. Whatever propositions of [or] beliefs may, in point of fact, prove true, it says, the truth of them consists in certain definable relations between them and the reality of which they make report. Both they and the reality belong to the same universe; the beliefs have to do with the reality, and the pragmatic question is: What exactly do you now mean when you say "have to do"? and in particular when you say "have to do truly"?

SECOND ACT of PRAGMATISM

Philosophers have generally been satisfied with the word "agreement" here; but pragmatists have seen that this word covers many different concrete possibilities which, with great subtlety, they have partly analyzed out. There are all sorts of ways of having to do with a thing. To know it, we must mean *that* thing and not another thing; we must be able to portray or copy its inherent nature; and we must know innumerable things *about* it and its relations to other things. To know it rightly, moreover, we must not go astray among all these many ways of knowing it, but select the way that fits in with our momentary interest, be the latter practical or theoretical, and select the way that will *work*. The same thing will thus come to be defined quite differently at different times, yet each time truly enough. Thus the first vague notion of "agreement" with reality becomes specified into that of innumerable ways in which our thoughts may *fit* reality, ways in which the mind's activities cooperate on equal terms with the reality in producing the fit resultant truth.

It is this perception, that truth is a resultant and that minds and realities work together in producing it, that has launched the pragmatist writers on the second act of their career. Reality as such is not truth, and the mind as such is not a mere mirror. Mind *engenders* truth *upon* reality; and as our systems of truth are themselves part of reality (and indeed for us its most important parts), we may say that reality in its largest sense does grow by human thinking. Hence arises the idea that our minds are not here simply to copy a reality that is already complete. They are here to complete it, to add its importance by their own remodeling of it, to decant its contents over, so to speak, into a more significant shape.

In point of fact, the *use* of most of our thinking is to help us to *change* the world. We must for this know definitely *what* we have to change; and thus theoretic truth must at all times come before practical application. But the pragmatist writers have shown that what we here call theoretic truth is itself full of human contradictions. It will be as irrelevant unless it fits the momentary purpose in hand, as our ideas will be irrelevant when they do not fit the reality—the two factors must fit each other. And moreover it turns out that the theoretic truth upon which men base their practice today is itself a resultant of previous human practice, based in turn upon still more previous truth, and so on in indefinite regress, so that we may think of all truth whatever as containing so much human practice *funded*—the word practice here being meant to cover all ways which men may select of handling or attending to the primary reality.

Thus we seem set free to use our theoretical as well as our practical faculties—practical here in the narrower sense—to get the world into a better shape, and all with a good conscience. The only restriction is that the world resists some lines of attack on our part and opens herself to others, so that we must go with the grain of her willingness, to play fairly. Hence the *sursum corda* of pragmatism's message. . . .

CONFUSION WORSE THAN BABEL

There never was such confusion. The tower of Babel was monotony in comparison. The fault has lain on both sides. Dewey is obscure; Schiller bumptious and hasty; James's doctrine of radical empiricism, which has nothing to do with pragmatism and sounds idealistic, has been confounded with his pragmatism; pragmatism itself covers two or three distinct theories; the critics have opened fire before the pragmatists had got their word out; every one has spoken at once, and the upshot has made one despair of men's intelligence. But little by little the mud will settle to the bottom. . . . We shall soon find ourselves at home in the pragmatic view and temper, and will then say that it was not worth so much hubbub.

VII. Selections From
*The Principles of Psychology**

(i) HABIT

When we look at living creatures from an outward point of view, one of the first things that strike us is that they are bundles of habits. In wild animals, the usual round of daily behavior seems a necessity implanted at birth; in animals domesticated, and especially in man, it seems, to a great extent, to be the result of education. The habits to which there is an innate tendency are called instincts; some of those due to education would by most persons be called acts of reason. It thus appears that habit covers a very large part of life, and that one engaged in studying the objective manifestations of mind is bound at the very outset to define clearly just what its limits are.

The moment one tries to define what habit is, one is led to the fundamental properties of matter. The laws of Nature are nothing but the immutable habits which the different elementary sorts of matter follow in their actions and reactions upon each other. In the organic world, however, the habits are more variable than this. Even instincts vary from one individual to another of a kind; and are modified in the same individual, as we shall later see, to suit the exigencies of the case. The habits of an elementary particle of matter cannot change (on the principles of the atomistic philosophy), because the particle is itself an unchangeable thing; but those of a compound mass of matter can change, because they are in the last instance due to the structure of the compound, and either outward forces or inward tensions can, from one hour to another,

* For the specific sources for the following nine selections from James' *The Principles of Psychology* (1890) see p. 376 below.

turn that structure into something different from what it was. That is, they can do so if the body be plastic enough to maintain its integrity, and be not disrupted when its structure yields. The change of structure here spoken of need not involve the outward shape; it may be invisible and molecular, as when a bar of iron becomes magnetic or crystalline through the action of certain outward causes, or india-rubber becomes friable, or plaster "sets." All these changes are rather slow; the material in question opposes a certain resistance to the modifying cause, which it takes time to overcome, but the gradual yielding wherof often saves the material from being disintegrated altogether. When the structure has yielded, the same inertia becomes a condition of its comparative permanence in the new form, and of the new habits the body then manifests. *Plasticity,* then, in the wide sense of the word, means the possession of a structure weak enough to yield to an influence, but strong enough not to yield all at once. Each relatively stable phase of equilibrium in such a structure is marked by what we may call a new set of habits. Organic matter, especially nervous tissue, seems endowed with a very extraordinary degree of plasticity of this sort; so that we may without hesitation lay down as our first proposition the following, that *the phenomena of habit in living beings are due to the plasticity* of the organic materials of which their bodies are composed.* . .

Can we now form a notion of what the inward physical changes may be like, in organs whose habits have thus struck into new paths? In other words, can we say just what mechanical facts the expression "change of habit" covers when it is applied to a nervous system? Certainly we cannot in anything like a minute or definite way. But our usual scientific custom of interpreting hidden molecular events after the analogy of visible massive ones enables us to frame easily an abstract and general scheme of processes which the physical changes in question *may* be like. And when once the possibility of *some* kind of mechanical interpretation is established, Mechanical Science, in her present mood, will not hesitate to set her brand of ownership upon the matter, feeling sure that it is only a question

---

* In the sense above explained, which applies to inner structure as well as to outer form.

of time when the exact mechanical explanation of the case shall be found out.

If habits are due to the plasticity of materials to outward agents, we can immediately see to what outward influences, if to any, the brain matter is plastic. Not to mechanical pressures, not to thermal changes, not to any of the forces to which all the other organs of our body are exposed; for nature has carefully shut up our brain and spinal cord in bony boxes, where no influences of this sort can get at them. She has floated them in fluid so that only the severest shocks can give them a concussion, and blanketed and wrapped them about in an altogether exceptional way. The only impressions that can be made upon them are through the blood, on the one hand and through the sensory nerve roots, on the other; and it is to the infinitely attenuated currents that pour in through these latter channels that the hemispherical cortex shows itself to be so peculiarly susceptible. The currents, once in, must find a way out. In getting out they leave their traces in the paths which they take. The only thing they *can* do, in short, is to deepen old paths or to make new ones; and the whole plasticity of the brain sums itself up in two words when we call it an organ in which currents pouring in from the sense organs make with extreme facility paths which do not easily disappear. For, of course, a simple habit, like every other nervous event—the habit of snuffling, for example, or of putting one's hands into one's pockets, or of biting one's nails—is, mechanically, nothing but a reflex discharge; and its anatomical substratum must be a path in the system. The most complex habits, as we shall presently see more fully, are, from the same point of view, nothing but *concatenated* discharges in the nerve centers, due to the presence here of systems of reflex paths, so organized as to wake each other up successively —the impression produced by one muscular contraction serving as a stimulus to provoke the next, until a final impression inhibits the process and closes the chain. The only difficult mechanical problem is to explain the formation *de novo* of a simple reflex or path in a preexisting nervous system. Here, as in so many other cases, it is only the *premier pas qui coûte*. For the entire nervous system *is* nothing but a system of paths between a sensory *terminus a quo* and a muscular, glandular, or other *terminus ad quem*. A path once traversed by a nerve current might be expected to follow the law of most of the paths we know, and to be scooped out and made more permeable than before; * and this ought to be repeated with each new passage of the current. Whatever obstructions may have kept it at first from being a path should then, little by little, and more and more, be swept out of the way, until at last it might become a natural drainage channel. This is what happens where either solids or liquids pass over a path; there seems no reason why it should not happen where the thing that passes is a mere wave of rearrangement in matter that does not displace itself, but merely changes chemically or turns itself round in place, or vibrates across the line. The most plausible views of the nerve current make it out to be the passage of some such wave of rearrangement as this. If only a part of the matter of the path were to "rearrange" itself, the neighboring parts remaining inert, it is easy to see how their inertness might oppose a friction which it would take many waves of rearrangement to break down and overcome. If we call the path itself the "organ," and the wave of rearrangement the "function," then it is obviously a case for repeating the celebrated French formula of *"La fonction fait l'organe."*

So nothing is easier than to imagine how, when a current once has traversed a path, it should traverse it more readily still a second time. But what made it ever traverse it the first time?† In answering this question we can only fall back on our general conception of a nervous system as a mass of matter whose parts, constantly kept in states of different tension, are as constantly tending to equalize their states. The equalization between any two points occurs through whatever path may at the moment be most pervious. But, as a given point of the system may belong, actually or potentially, to many different paths, and, as the play of nutrition is subject to accidental changes, *blocks* may from time to time occur, and make currents shoot through unwonted lines. Such an unwonted line would be

---

* Some paths, to be sure, are banked up by bodies moving through them under too great pressure, and made impervious. These special cases we disregard.

† We cannot say *the will,* for, though many, perhaps most, human habits were once voluntary actions, no action, as we shall see in a later chapter, can be *primarily* such. While an habitual action may once have been voluntary, the voluntary action must before that, at least once, have been impulsive or reflex. It is this very first occurrence of all that we consider in the text.

a new-created path, which if traversed repeatedly, would become the beginning of a new reflex arc. All this is vague to the last degree, and amounts to little more than saying that a new path may be formed by the sort of *chances* that in nervous material are likely to occur. But, vague as it is, it is really the last word of our wisdom in the matter . . .

This brings us by a very natural transition to the *ethical implications of the law of habit*. They are numerous and momentous. Dr. Carpenter, from whose "Mental Physiology" we have quoted, has so prominently enforced the principle that our organs grow to the way in which they have been exercised, and dwelt upon its consequences, that his book almost deserves to be called a work of edification, on this account alone. We need make no apology, then, for tracing a few of these consequences ourselves:

"Habit a second nature! Habit is ten times nature," the Duke of Wellington is said to have exclaimed; and the degree to which this is true no one can probably appreciate as well as one who is a veteran soldier himself. The daily drill and the years of discipline end by fashioning a man completely over again as to most of the possibilities of his conduct.

> There is a story, which is credible enough, though it may not be true, of a practical joker, who, seeing a discharged veteran carrying home his dinner, suddenly called out, "Attention!" whereupon the man instantly brought his hands down, and lost his mutton and potatoes in the gutter. The drill had been thorough, and its effects had become embodied in the man's nervous structure*

Riderless cavalry horses, at many a battle, have been seen to come together and go through their customary evolutions at the sound of the bugle call. . . .

The great thing, then, in all education, is to *make our nervous system our ally instead of our enemy*. It is to fund and capitalize our acquisitions, and live at ease upon the interest of the fund. *For this we must make automatic and habitual, as early as possible, as many useful actions as we can,* and guard against the growing into ways that are likely to be disadvantageous to us, as we should guard against the plague. The more of the details of our daily life we can hand over to the effortless custody of automatism, the more our higher powers of mind will be set free

---

* Huxley's *Elementary Lessons in Physiology,* lesson xii.

for their own proper work. There is no more miserable human being than one in whom nothing is habitual but indecision, and for whom the lighting of every cigar, the drinking of every cup, the time of rising and going to bed every day, and the beginning of every bit of work, are subjects of express volitional deliberation. Full half the time of such a man goes to the deciding, or regretting, of matters which ought to be so ingrained in him as practically not to exist for his consciousness at all. If there be such daily duties not yet ingrained in any one of my readers, let him begin this very hour to set the matter right. . . .

(ii) TWO KINDS of KNOWLEDGE: KNOWLEDGE of ACQUAINTANCE and KNOWLEDGE-ABOUT

There are two kinds of knowledge broadly and practically distinguishable: we may call them respectively *knowledge of acquaintance* and *knowledge-about*. Most languages express the distinction; thus, γνῶναι, εἰδέναι; *noscere, scire; kennen, wissen; connaître, savoir.** I am acquainted with many people and things, which I know very little about, except their presence in the places where I have met them. I know the color blue when I see it, and the flavor of a pear when I taste it; I know an inch when I move my finger through it; a second of time, when I feel it pass; an effort of attention when I make it; a difference between two things when I notice it; but *about* the inner nature of these facts or what makes them what they are, I can say nothing at all. I cannot impart acquaintance with them to any one who has not already made it himself. I cannot *describe* them, make a blind man guess what blue is like, define to a child a syllogism, or tell a philosopher in just what respect distance is just what it is, and differs from other forms of relation. At most, I can say to my friends, Go to certain places and act in certain ways, and these objects will probably come. All the elementary na-

---

* Cf. John Grote, *Exploratio Philosophica*, p. 60; H. Helmholtz, Popular Scientific Lectures, London, p. 308–309.

tures of the world, its highest genera, the simple qualities of matter and mind, together with the kinds of relation that subsist between them, must either not be known at all, or known in this dumb way of acquaintance without *knowledge-about*. In minds able to speak at all there is, it is true, *some* knowledge about everything. Things can at least be classed, and the times of their appearance told. But in general, the less we analyze a thing, and the fewer of its relations we perceive, the less we know about it and the more our familiarity with it is of the acquaintance-type. The two kinds of knowledge are, therefore, as the human mind practically exerts them, relative terms. That is, the same thought of a thing may be called knowledge-about it in comparison with a simpler thought, or acquaintance with it in comparison with a thought of it that is more articulate and explicit still.

The grammatical sentence expresses this. Its "subject" stands for an object of acquaintance which, by the addition of the predicate, is to get something known about it. We may already know a good deal, when we hear the subject named—its name may have rich connotations. But, know we much or little then, we know more still when the sentence is done. We can relapse at will into a mere condition of acquaintance with an object by scattering our attention and staring at it in a vacuous trancelike way. We can ascend to knowledge *about* it by rallying our wits and proceeding to notice and analyze and think. What we are only acquainted with is only *present* to our minds; we *have* it, or the idea of it. But when we know about it, we do more than merely have it; we seem, as we think over its relations, to subject it to a sort of *treatment* and to *operate* upon it with our thought. The words *feeling* and *thought* give voice to the antithesis. Through feelings we become acquainted with things, but only by our thoughts do we know about them. Feelings are the germ and starting point of cognition, thoughts the developed tree. The minimum of grammatical subject, of objective presence, of reality known about, the mere beginning of knowledge, must be named by the word that says the least. Such a word is the interjection, as *lo! there! voilà!* or the article or demonstrative pronoun introducing the sentence, as *the, it, that*. In Chapter XII we shall see a little deeper into what this distinction, between the mere mental having or feeling of an object and the thinking of it, portends.

The mental states usually distinguished as feelings are the *emotions,* and the *sensations* we get from skin, muscle, viscus, eye, ear, nose, and palate. The "thoughts," as recognized in popular parlance, are the *conceptions* and *judgments.* When we treat of these mental states in particular we shall have to say a word about the cognitive function and value of each. It may perhaps be well to notice now that our senses only give us acquaintance with facts of body, and that of the mental states of other persons we only have conceptual knowledge. Of our own past states of mind we take cognizance in a peculiar way. They are "objects of memory," and appear to us endowed with a sort of warmth and intimacy that makes the perception of them seem more like a process of sensation than like a thought.

(iii) THE STREAM of THOUGHT[*]

Consciousness, then, does not appear to itself chopped up in bits. Such words as "chain" or "train" do not describe it fitly as it presents itself in the first instance. It is nothing jointed; it flows. A "river" or a "stream" are the metaphors by which it is most naturally described. *In talking of it hereafter, let us call it the stream of thought, of consciousness, or of subjective life.*

But now there appears, even within the limits of the same self, and between thoughts all of which alike have this same sense of belonging together, a kind of jointing and separateness among the parts, of which this statement seems to take no account. I refer to the breaks that are produced by sudden *contrasts in the quality* of the successive segments of the stream of thought. If the words

* [Two years after the appearance of *The Principles of Psychology* (New York, 1890), James published a rewritten and much abridged version of this work: *Psychology, Briefer Course* (New York: Henry Holt and Co., 1892), which evidences some interesting changes in James' philosophic thought. Among these the present chapter from the *Principles,* "The Stream of Thought," becomes retitled "The Stream of Consciousness" in the *"Briefer* Course," Ch. XI. Generally in this chapter where James had earlier used "thought" he replaced by it "state" and "consciousness."]

"chain" and "train" had no natural fitness in them, how came such words to be used at all? Does not a loud explosion rend the consciousness upon which it abruptly breaks, in twain? Does not ever sudden shock, appearance of a new object, or change in a sensation, create a real interruption, sensibly felt as such, which cuts the conscious stream across at the moment at which it appears? Do not such interruptions smite us every hour of our lives, and have we the right, in their presence, still to call our consciousness a continuous stream?

This objection is based partly on a confusion and partly on a superficial introspective view.

The confusion is between the thoughts themselves, taken as subjective facts, and the things of which they are aware. It is natural to make this confusion, but easy to avoid it when once put on one's guard. The things are discrete and discontinuous; they do pass before us in a train or chain, making often explosive appearances and rending each other in twain. But their comings and goings and contrasts no more break the flow of the thought that thinks them than they break the time and the space in which they lie. A silence may be broken by a thunder clap, and we may be so stunned and confused for a moment by the shock as to give no instant account to ourselves of what has happened. But that very confusion is a mental state, and a state that passes us straight over from the silence to the sound. The transition between the thought of one object and the thought of another is no more a break in the *thought* than a joint in a bamboo is a break in the wood. It is a part of the *consciousness* as much as the joint is a part of the *bamboo*.

The superficial introspective view is the overlooking, even when the things are contrasted with each other most violently, of the large amount of affinity that may still remain between the thoughts by whose means they are cognized. Into the awareness of the thunder itself the awareness of the previous silence creeps and continues; for what we hear when the thunder crashes is not thunder *pure*, but thunder-breaking-upon-silence-and-contrasting-with-it.* Our feeling of the same objective thunder, coming in this way, is quite different from what it would be were the

---

* Cf. Brentano, *Psychologie*, vol. I. pp. 219–220. Altogether this chapter of Brentano's on the Unity of Consciousness is as good as anything with which I am acquainted.

thunder a continuation of previous thunder. The thunder itself we believe to abolish and exclude the silence; but the *feeling* of the thunder is also a feeling of the silence as just gone; and it would be difficult to find in the actual concrete consciousness of man a feeling so limited to the present as not to have an inkling of anything that went before. Here, again, language works against our perception of the truth. We name our thoughts simply, each after its thing, as if each knew its own thing and nothing else. What each really knows is clearly the thing it is named for, with dimly perhaps a thousand other things. It ought to be named after all of them, but it never is. Some of them are always things known a moment ago more clearly; others are things to be known more clearly a moment hence.* Our own bodily position, attitude, however inattentive, invariably accompanies the knowledge of whatever else we know. We think; and as we think we feel our bodily selves as the

---

* Honor to whom honor is due! The most explicit acknowledgment I have anywhere found of all this is in a buried and forgotten paper by the Rev. James Wills, on "Accidental Association," in the *Transactions of the Royal Irish Academy,* vol. xxi, part i (1846). Mr. Wills writes:

> At every instant of conscious thought there is a certain sum of perceptions, or reflections, or both together, present, and together constituting one whole state of apprehension. Of this some definite portion may be far more distinct than all the rest; and the rest be in consequence proportionally vague, even to the limit of obliteration. But still, within this limit, the most dim shade of perception enters into, and in some infinitesimal degree modifies, the whole existing state. This state will thus be in some way modified by any sensation or emotion, or act of distinct attention, that may give prominence to any part of it; so that the actual result is capable of the utmost variation, according to the person or the occasion. . . . To any portion of the entire scope here described there may be a special direction of the attention, and this special direction is recognized as strictly what is *recognized* as the idea present to the mind. This idea is evidently not commensurate with the entire state of apprehension, and much perplexity has arisen from not observing this fact. However deeply we may suppose the attention to be engaged by any thought, any considerable alteration of the surrounding phenomena would still be perceived; the most abstruse demonstration in this room would not prevent a listener, however absorbed, from noticing the sudden extinction of the lights. Our mental states have always an *essential unity*, such that each state of apprehension, however variously compounded, is a single whole, of which every component is, therefore, strictly apprehended (so far as it is apprehended) as a part. Such is the elementary basis from which all our intellectual operations commence.

seat of the thinking. If the thinking be *our* thinking, it must be suffused through all its parts with that peculiar warmth and intimacy that make it come as ours. Whether the warmth and intimacy be anything more than the feeling of the same old body always there, is a matter for the next chapter to decide. *Whatever* the content of the ego may be, it is habitually felt *with* everything else by us humans, and must form a *liaison* between all the things of which we become successively aware.*

On this gradualness in the changes of our mental content the principles of nerve action can throw some more light. When studying in Chapter III, the summation of nervous activities, we saw that no state of the brain can be supposed instantly to die away. If a new state comes, the inertia of the old state will still be there and modify the result accordingly. Of course we cannot tell, in our ignorance, what in each instance the modifications ought to be. The commonest modifications in sense perception are known as the phenomena of contrast. In esthetics they are the feelings of delight or displeasure which certain particular orders in a series of impressions give. In thought, strictly and narrowly so called, they are unquestionably that consciousness of the *whence* and the *whither* that always accompanies its flows. If recently the brain tract a was vividly excited, and then b, and now vividly c, the total present consciousness is not produced simply by c's excitement, but also by the dying vibrations of a and b as well. If we want to represent the brain process we must write it thus: c—three different processes coexisting,

$$b$$
$$a$$

and correlated with them a thought which is no one of the three thoughts which they would have produced had each of them occurred alone. But whatever this fourth thought may exactly be, it seems impossible that it should not be something *like* each of the three other thoughts whose tracts are concerned in its production, though in a fast-waning phase.

It all goes back to what we said in another connection only a few pages ago. As the total neurosis changes, so does the total psychosis change. But as the changes of neu-

* Compare the charming passage in Taine on Intelligence (New York, ed.), vol. I., pp. 83–84.

rosis are never absolutely discontinuous, so must the successive psychoses shade gradually into each other, although their *rate* of change may be much faster at one moment than at the next.

This difference in the rate of change lies at the basis of a difference of subjective states of which we ought immediately to speak. When the rate is slow we are aware of the object of our thought in a comparatively restful and stable way. When rapid, we are aware of a passage, a relation, a transition *from* it, or *between* it and something else. As we take, in fact, a general view of the wonderful stream of our consciousness, what strikes us first is this different pace of its parts. Like a bird's life, it seems to be made of an alternation of flights and perchings. The rhythm of language expresses this, where every thought is expressed in a sentence, and every sentence closed by a period. The resting places are usually occupied by sensorial imaginations of some sort, whose peculiarity is that they can be held before the mind for an indefinite time, and contemplated without changing; the places of flight are filled with thoughts of relations, static or dynamic, that for the most part obtain between the matters contemplated in the periods of comparative rest.

Let us call the resting places the "substantive parts," and the places of flight the "transitive parts," of the stream of thought. It then appears that the main end of our thinking is at all times the attainment of some other substantive part than the one from which we have just been dislodged. And we may say that the main use of the transitive parts is to lead us from one substantive conclusion to another. . . .

FEELINGS OF TENDENCY

So much for the transitive states. But there are other unnamed states or qualities of states that are just as important and just as cognitive as they, and just as much unrecognized by the traditional sensationalist and intellectualist philosophies of mind. The first fails to find them at all, the second finds their *cognitive function,* but denies that anything in the way of *feeling* has a share in bringing it about. Examples will make clear what these inarticulate psychoses, due to waxing and waning excitements of the brain, are like.*

Suppose three successive persons say to us: "Wait!" "Hark!" "Look!" Our consciousness is thrown into three quite different attitudes of expectancy, although no definite object is before it in any one of the three cases. Leaving out different actual bodily attitudes, and leaving out the reverberating images of the three words, which are of course diverse, probably no one will deny the existence of a residual conscious affection, a sense of the direction from which an impression is about to come, although no positive impression is yet there. Meanwhile we have no names for the psychoses in question but the names hark, look, and wait.

Suppose we try to recall a forgotten name. The state of our consciousness is peculiar. There is a gap therein; but no mere gap. It is a gap that is intensely active. A sort of wraith of the name is in it, beckoning us in a given direction, making us at moments tingle with the sense of our closeness, and then letting us sink back without the longed-for term. If wrong names are proposed to us, this singularly definite gap acts immediately so as to negate them. They do not fit into its mold. And the gap of one word does not feel like the gap of another, all empty of content as both might seem necessarily to be when de-

* M. Paulhan (*Revue Philosophique*, xx, pp. 455–6), after speaking of the faint mental images of objects and emotions, says:

> We find other vaguer states still, upon which attention seldom rests, except in persons who by nature or profession are addicted to internal observation. It is even difficult to name them precisely, for they are little known and not classed; but we may cite as an example of them that peculiar impression which we feel when, strongly preoccupied by a certain subject, we nevertheless are engaged with, and have our attention almost completely absorbed by, matters quite disconnected therewithal. We do not then exactly think of the object of our preoccupation; we do not represent it in a clear manner; and yet our mind is not as it would be without this preoccupation. Its object, absent from consciousness, is nevertheless represented there by a peculiar unmistakable impression, which often persists long and is a strong feeling, although so obscure for our intelligence. A mental sign of the kind is the unfavorable disposition left in our mind toward an individual by painful incidents erewhile experienced and now perhaps forgotten. The sign remains, but is not understood; its definite meaning is lost (p. 458).

scribed as gaps. When I vainly try to recall the name of Spalding, my consciousness is far removed from what it is when I vainly try to recall the name of Bowles. Here some ingenious persons will say: "How *can* the two consciousnesses be different when the terms which might make them different are not there? All that is there, so long as the effort to recall is vain, is the bare effort itself. How should that differ in the two cases? You are making it seem to differ by prematurely filling it out with the different names, although these, by the hypothesis, have not yet come. Stick to the two efforts as they are, without naming them after facts not yet existent, and you'll be quite unable to designate any point in which they differ." Designate, truly enough. We can only designate the difference by borrowing the names of objects not yet in the mind. Which is to say that our psychological vocabulary is wholly inadequate to name the differences that exist, even such strong differences as these. But namelessness is compatible with existence. . . .

Let us use the words *psychic overtone, suffusion,* or *fringe,* to designate the influence of a faint brain process upon our thought, as it makes it aware of relations and objects but dimly received.*

If we than consider the *cognitive function* of different states of mind, we may feel assured that the difference between those that are mere "acquaintance," and those that are "knowledges-*about*" [see ii, above] is reducible almost entirely to the absence or presence of psychic fringes or overtones. Knowledge *about* a thing is knowledge of its relations. Acquaintance with it is limitation to the bare

---

* Cf. also S. Stricker: *Vorlesungen über allg. u. exp. Pathologie* (1879), pp. 462–463 501, 547; *Romanes: Origin of Human Faculty,* p. 82. It is so hard to make one's self clear that I may advert to a misunderstanding of my views by the late Prof. Thomas Maguire of Dublin (Lectures on Philosophy, 1885), p. 200. This author considers that by the "fringe" I mean some sort of psychic material by which sensations in themselves separate are made to cohere together, and wittily says that I ought to "see that uniting sensations by their 'fringe' is more vague than to construct the universe out of oysters by platting their beards." But the fringe, as I use the word, means nothing like this; it is part of the *object cognized,—* substantive *qualities* and *things* appearing to the mind in a *fringe of relations.* Some parts—the transitive parts—of our stream of thought cognize the elations rather than the things; but both the transitive and the substantive parts form one continuous stream, with no discrete "sensations" in it such as Prof. Maguire supposes, and supposes me to suppose, to be there.

impression which it makes. Of most of its relations we are only aware in the penumbral nascent way of a "fringe" of unarticulated affinities about it. And, before passing to the next topic in order, I must say a little of this sense of affinity, as itself one of the most interesting features of the subjective stream.

In all our voluntary thinking there is some topic or subject about which all the members of the thought revolve. Half the time this topic is a problem, a gap we cannot yet fill with a definite picture, word, or phrase, but which, in the manner described some time back, influences us in an intensely active and determinate psychic way. Whatever may be the images and phrases that pass before us, we feel their relation to this aching gap. To fill it up is our thought's destiny. Some bring us nearer to that consummation. Some the gap negates as quite irrelevant. Each swims in a felt fringe of relations of which the aforesaid gap is the term. Or instead of a definite gap we may merely carry a mood of interest about with us. Then, however vague the mood, it will still act in the same way, throwing a mantle of felt affinity over such representations, entering the mind, as suit it, and tingeing with the feeling of tediousness or discord all those with which it has no concern.

Relation, then, to our topic or interest is constantly felt in the fringe, and particularly the relation of harmony and discord, of furtherance or hindrance of the topic. When the sense of furtherance is there, we are "all right"; with the sense of hindrance we are dissatisfied and perplexed, and cast about us for other thoughts. Now *any* thought the quality of whose fringe lets us feel ourselves "all right," is an acceptable member of our thinking, whatever kind of thought it may otherwise be. Provided we only feel it to have a place in the scheme of relations in which the interesting topic also lies, that is quite sufficient to make of it a relevant and appropriate portion of our train of ideas.

For the important thing about a train of thought is its conclusion. That is the *meaning*, or, as we say, the topic of the thought. That is what abides when all its other members have faded from memory. Usually this conclusion is a word or phrase or particular image, or practical attitude or resolve, whether rising to answer a problem or fill a preexisting gap that worried us, or whether accidentally stumbled on in revery. In either case it stands out from the other segments of the stream by reason of the peculiar interest attaching to it. This interest *arrests* it, makes a sort of crisis of it when it comes, induces attention upon it and makes us treat it in a substantive way.

The parts of the stream that precede these substantive conclusions are but the means of the latter's attainment. And, provided the same conclusion be reached, the means may be as mutable as we like, for the "meaning" of the stream of thought will be the same. What difference does it make what the means are? *"Qu'importe le flacon, pourvu qu'on ait l'ivresse?"* The relative unimportance of the means appears from the fact that when the conclusion is there, we have always forgotten most of the steps preceding its attainment. When we have uttered a proposition, we are rarely able a moment afterwards to recall our exact words, though we can express it in different words easily enough. The practical upshot of a book we read remains with us, though we may not recall one of its sentences.

The only paradox would seem to lie in supposing that the fringe of felt affinity and discord can be the same in two heterogeneous sets of images. Take a train of words passing through the mind and leading to a certain conclusion on the one hand, and on the other hand an almost wordless set of tactile, visual and other fancies leading to the same conclusion. Can the halo, fringe, or scheme in which we feel the words to lie be the same as that in which we feel the images to lie? Does not the discrepancy of terms involve a discrepancy of felt relations among them?

If the terms be taken *quâ* mere sensations, it assuredly does. For instance, the words may rhyme with each other —the visual images can have no such affinity as *that*. But *quâ* thoughts, *quâ* sensations *understood,* the words have contracted by long association fringes of mutual repugnance or affinity with each other and with the conclusion, which run exactly parallel with like fringes in the visual, tactile and other ideas. The most important element of these fringes is, I repeat, the mere feeling of harmony or discord of a right or wrong direction in the thought. . . .

(iv) THE SELF

To have a self that I can *care for,* nature must first present me with some *object* interesting enough to make me instinctively wish to appropriate it for its *own* sake, and out of it to manufacture one of those material, social, or spiritual selves, which we have already passed in review. We shall find that all the facts of rivalry and substitution that have so struck us, all the shiftings and expansions and contractions of the sphere of what shall be considered me and mine, are but results of the fact that certain *things* appeal to primitive and instinctive impulses of our nature, and that we follow their destinies with an excitement that owes nothing to a reflective source. These objects our consciousness treats as the primordial constituents of its Me. Whatever other objects, whether by association with the fate of these, or in any other way, come to be followed with the same sort of interest, form our remoter and more secondary self. *The words* ME, *then, and* SELF, *so far as they arouse feeling and connote emotional worth, are* OBJECTIVE *designations, meaning* ALL THE THINGS *which have the power to produce in a stream of consciousness excitement of a certain peculiar sort.* Let us try to justify this proposition in detail.

The most palpable selfishness of man is his bodily selfishness; and his most palpable self is the body to which that selfishness relates. Now I say that he identifies himself with this body because he loves *it,* and that he does not love it because he finds it to be identified with himself. . . .

My own body and what ministers to its needs are thus the primitive object, instinctively determined, of my egoistic interests. Other objects may become interesting derivatively through association with any of these things, either as means or as habitual concomitants; *and so in a thousand ways the primitive sphere of the egoistic emotions may enlarge* and change its boundaries.

This sort of interest is really the *meaning of the word* "*my.*" Whatever has it is *eo ipso* a part of me. My child,

my friend dies, and where he goes I feel that part of myself now is and evermore shall be:

> For this losing is true dying;
> This is lordly man's down-lying;
> This his slow but sure reclining,
> Star by star his world resigning.

The fact remains, however, that certain special sorts of
things tend primordially to possess this interest, and form
the *natural* me. But all these things are *objects*, properly so
called, to the subject which does the thinking.* And this
latter fact upsets at once the dictum of the old-fashioned
sensationalist psychology, that altruistic passions and interests are contradictory to the nature of things, and that if
they appear anywhere to exist, it must be as secondary
products, resolvable at bottom into cases of selfishness,
taught by experience a hypocritical disguise. If the zoolog-
ical and evolutionary point of view is the true one, there is
no reason why any object whatever *might* not arouse passion and interest as primitively and instinctively as any
other, whether connected or not with the interests of the
me. The phenomenon of passion is in origin and essence
the same, whatever be the target upon which it is dis-
charged; and what the target actually happens to be is
solely a question of fact. I might conceivably be as much
fascinated, and as primitively so, by the care of my neighbor's body as by the care of my own. The only check to
such exuberant altruistic interests is natural selection,
which would weed out such as were very harmful to the
individual or to his tribe. Many such interests, however,
remain unweeded out—the interest in the opposite sex, for
example, which seems in mankind stronger than is called
for by its utilitarian need; and alongside of them remain
interests, like that in alcoholic intoxication, or in musical
sounds, which, for aught we can see, are without any utility whatever. The sympathetic instincts and the egoistic
ones are thus coordinate. They arise, so far as we can tell,
on the same psychologic level. The only difference between them is, that the instincts called egoistic form much
the larger mass. . . .

* Lotze, *Med. Psych.*, pp. 498–501; *Microcosmos*, bk. II. chap. V.
§§ 3, 4.

. . . SUMMARY

To sum up now. The consciousness of Self involves a stream of thought, each part of which as "I" can (1) remember those which went before, and know the things they knew; and (2) emphasize and care paramountly for certain ones among them as *"me,"* and *appropriate to these* the rest. The nucleus of the *"me"* is always the bodily existence felt to be present at the time. Whatever remembered-past-feelings *resemble* this present feeling are deemed to belong to the same *me* with it. Whatever other things are perceived to be *associated* with this feeling are deemed to form part of that me's *experience;* and of them certain ones (which fluctuate more or less) are reckoned to be themselves *constituents* of the me in a larger sense —such are the clothes, the material possessions, the friends, the honors and esteem which the person receives or may receive. This me is an empirical aggregate of things objectively known. The *I* which knows them cannot itself be an aggregate, neither for psychological purposes need it be considered to be an unchanging metaphysical entity like the Soul, or a principle like the pure Ego, viewed as "out of time." It is a *Thought,* at each moment different from that of the last moment, but *appropriative* of the latter, together with all that the latter called its own. All the experiential facts find their place in this description, unencumbered with any hypothesis save that of the existence of passing thoughts or states of mind. The same brain may subserve many conscious selves, either alternate or coexisting; but by what modifications in its action, or whether ultra-cerebral conditions may intervene, are questions which cannot now be answered.

If anyone urge that I assign no *reason* why the successive passing thoughts should inherit each other's possessions, or why they and the brain states should be functions (in the mathematical sense) of each other, I reply that the reason, if there be any, must lie where all real reasons lie, in the total sense or meaning of the world. If there be such a meaning, or any approach to it (as we are bound to trust there is), it alone can make clear to us why such finite human streams of thought are called into existence in such functional dependence upon brains. This is as much as to say that the special natural science of *psychology* must stop with the mere functional formula. *If the passing thought be the directly verifiable existent which no school has hitherto doubted it to be, then that thought is itself the thinker,* and psychology need not look beyond. The only pathway that I can discover for bringing in a more transcendental thinker would be to *deny* that we have any *direct* knowledge of the thought as such. The latter's existence would then be reduced to a postulate, an assertion that there *must be* a *knower* correlative to all this *known;* and the problem *who that knower is* would have become a metaphysical problem. With the question once stated in these terms, the spiritualist and transcendentalist solutions must be considered as *prima facie* on a par with our own psychological one, and discussed impartially. But that carries us beyond the psychological or naturalistic point of view.

(v) NOTE: BODY AS THE CENTER OF SELF

The individualized self, which I believe to be the only thing properly called self, is a part of the content of the world experienced. The world experienced (otherwise called the "field of consciousness") comes at all times with our body as its center, center of vision, center of action, center of interest. Where the body is is "here"; when the body acts is "now"; what the body touches is "this"; all other things are "there" and "then" and "that." These words of emphasized position imply a systematization of things with reference to a focus of action and interest which lies in the body; and the systematization is now so instinctive (was it ever not so?) that no developed or active experience exists for us at all except in that ordered form. So far as "thoughts" and "feelings" can be active, their activity terminates in the activity of the body, and only through first arousing its activities can they begin to change those of the rest of the world. The body is the storm center, the origin of coordinates, the constant place of stress in all that experience-train. Everything circles round it, and is felt from its point of view. The word "I," then, is primarily a noun of position, just like "this" and "here." Activities attached to "this" position have prerogative emphasis, and, if activities have feelings, must be felt in a peculiar way. The word "my" designates the kind of emphasis. I see no inconsistency whatever in defending, on the one hand, "my" activities as unique and opposed to those of outer nature, and, on the other hand, in affirming, after introspection, that they consist in movements in the head. The "my" of them is the emphasis, the feeling of perspective-interest in which they are dyed.

(vi) DISCRIMINATION AND COMPARISON

The truth is that Experience is trained by *both* association and dissociation, and that psychology must be writ *both* in synthetic and in analytic terms. Our original sensible totals are, on the one hand, subdivided by discriminative attention, and, on the other, united with other totals—either through the agency of our own movements, carrying our senses from one part of space to another, or because new objects come successively and replace those by which we were at first impressed. The "simple impression" of Hume, the "simple idea" of Locke are both abstractions, never realized in experience. Experience, from the very first, presents us with concreted objects, vaguely continuous with the rest of the world which envelops them in space and time, and potentially divisible into inward elements and parts. These objects we break asunder and reunite. We must treat them in both ways for our knowledge of them to grow; and it is hard to say, on the whole, which way preponderates. But since the elements with which the traditional associationism performs its constructions—"simple sensations," namely—are all products of discrimination carried to a high pitch, it seems as if we ought to discuss the subject of analytic attention and discrimination first.

The noticing of any *part* whatever of our object is an act of discrimination. . . . I have described the manner in which we often spontaneously lapse into the undiscriminating state, even with regard to objects which we have already learned to distinguish. Such anesthetics as chloroform, nitrous oxide, etc., sometimes bring about transient lapses even more total, in which numerical discrimination especially seems gone; for one sees light and hears sound, but whether one or many lights and sounds is quite impossible to tell. Where the parts of an object have already been discerned, and each made the object of a special discriminative act, we can with difficulty feel the object again in its pristine unity; and so prominent may our consciousness of its composition be, that we may hardly believe that it ever could have appeared undivided. But this is an erroneous view, the undeniable fact being that *any number of impressions, from any number of sensory sources falling simultaneously on a mind* WHICH HAS NOT YET EXPERIENCED THEM SEPARATELY, *will fuse into a single undivided object for that mind.* The law is that all things fuse that *can* fuse, and nothing separates except what must. What makes impressions separate we have to study in this chapter. Although they separate easier if they come in through distinct nerves, yet distinct nerves are not an unconditional ground of their discrimination, as we shall presently see. The baby, assailed by eyes, ears, nose, skin, and entrails at once, feels it all as one great blooming, buzzing confusion; and to the very end of life, our location of all things in one space is due to the fact that the original extents or bignesses of all the sensations which came to our notice at once, coalesced together into one and the same space. There is no other reason than this why "the hand I touch and see coincides spatially with the hand I immediately feel." *

It is true that we may sometimes be tempted to exclaim, when once a lot of hitherto unnoticed details of the object lie before us, "How could we ever have been ignorant of these things and yet have felt the object, or drawn the conclusion, as if it were a *continuum,* a *plenum?* There would have been *gaps*—but we felt no gaps; wherefore we must have seen and heard these details, leaned upon these steps; they must have been operative upon our minds, just as they are now, only *unconsciously,* or at least *inattentively.* Our first unanalyzed sensation was really composed of these elementary sensations, our first rapid conclusion was really based on these intermediate inferences, all the while,

* Montgomery in *Mind,* x., p. 527. Cf. also Lipps: *Grundtatsachen des Seelenlebens,* p. 579 ff.

only we failed to note the fact." But this is nothing but the fatal "psychologist's fallacy" of treating an inferior state of mind as if it must somehow know implicitly all that is explicitly known *about the same topic* by superior states of mind. The thing thought of is unquestionably the same, but it is thought twice over in two absolutely different psychoses—once as an unbroken unit, and again as a sum of discriminated parts. It is not one thought in two editions, but two entirely distinct thoughts of one thing. And each thought is within itself a *continuum*, a *plenum*, needing no contributions from the other to fill up its gaps. As I sit here, I think objects, and I make inferences, which the future is sure to analyze and articulate and riddle with discriminations, showing me many things wherever I now notice one. Nevertheless, my thought feels quite sufficient unto itself for the time being; and ranges from pole to pole, as free, and as unconscious of having overlooked anything, as if it possessed the greatest discriminative enlightenment. We all cease analyzing the world at some point, and notice no more differences. The last units with which we stop are our objective elements of being. Those of a dog are different from those of a Humboldt; those of a practical man from those of a metaphysician. But the dog's and the practical man's thoughts *feel* continuous, though to the Humboldt or the metaphysician they would appear full of gaps and defects. And they *are* continuous, *as thoughts*. It is only *as mirrors of things* that the superior minds find them full of omissions. And when the omitted things are discovered and the unnoticed differences laid bare, it is not that the old *thoughts* split up, but that *new thoughts supersede* them, which make new judgments about the same objective world. . . .

(vii) BELIEF and PERCEPTION of REALITY

BELIEF

Everyone knows the difference between imagining a thing and believing in its existence, between supposing a proposition and acquiescing in its truth. In the case of acquiescence or belief, the object is not only apprehended by the mind, but is held to have reality. Belief is thus the mental state or function of cognizing reality. As used in the following pages, "Belief" will mean every degree of assurance, including the highest possible certainty and conviction.

There are, as we know, two ways of studying every psychic state. First, the way of analysis: What does it consist in? What is its inner nature? Of what sort of mind stuff is it composed? Second, the way of history: What are its conditions of production, and its connection with other facts?

Into the first way we cannot go very far. *In its inner nature, belief, or the sense of reality, is a sort of feeling more allied to the emotions than to anything else.* Mr. Bagehot distinctly calls it the "emotion" of conviction. I just now spoke of it as acquiescence. It resembles more than anything what in the psychology of volition we know as consent. Consent is recognized by all to be a manifestation of our active nature. It would naturally be described by such terms as "willingness" or the "turning of our disposition." What characterizes both consent and belief is the cessation of theoretic agitation, through the advent of an idea which is inwardly stable, and fills the mind solidly to the exclusion of contradictory ideas. When this is the case, motor effects are apt to follow. Hence the states of consent and belief, characterized by repose on the purely intellectual side, are both intimately connected with subsequent practical activity. This inward stability of the mind's content is as characteristic of disbelief as of belief. But we shall presently see that we never disbelieve anything except for the reason that we believe something else which contradicts the first thing.* Disbelief is thus an incidental complication to belief, and need not be considered by itself.

The true opposites of belief, psychologically considered, *are doubt and inquiry, not disbelief.* In both these states the content of our mind is in unrest, and the emotion engendered thereby is, like the emotion of belief itself, per-

---

* Compare this psychological fact with the corresponding logical truth that all negation rests on covert assertion of something else than the thing denied. (See Bradley's *Principles of Logic,* bk. I. ch. 3.)

fectly distinct, but perfectly indescribable in words. Both sorts of emotion may be pathologically exalted. One of the charms of drunkenness unquestionably lies in the deepening of the sense of reality and truth which is gained therein. In whatever light things may then appear to us, they seem more utterly what they are, more "utterly utter" than when we are sober. This goes to a fully unutterable extreme in the nitrous oxide intoxication, in which a man's very soul will sweat with conviction, and he be all the while unable to tell what he is convinced of at all.* The pathological state opposed to this solidity and deepening has been called the questioning mania (*Grübelsucht* by the Germans). It is sometimes found as a substantive affection, paroxysmal or chronic, and consists in the inability to rest in any conception, and the need of having it confirmed and explained. "Why do I stand here where I stand?" "Why is a glass a glass, a chair a chair?" "How is it that men are only of the size they are? Why not as big as houses," etc., etc.† There is, it is true, another pathological state which is as far removed from doubt as from belief, and which some may prefer to consider the proper contrary of the latter state of mind. I refer to the feeling

---

* See that very remarkable little work, *The Anesthetic Revelation and the Gist of Philosophy,* by Benjamin P. Blood (Amsterdam, N.Y., 1874). Compare also Mind, VII, p. 206.

† "To one whose mind is healthy thoughts come and go unnoticed; with me they have to be faced, thought about in a peculiar fashion, and then disposed of as finished, and this often when I am utterly wearied and would be at peace; but the call is imperative. This goes on to the hindrance of all natural action. If I were told that the staircase was on fire and I had only a minute to escape, and the thought arose—"Have they sent for fire engines. Is it probable that the man who has the key is on hand? Is the man a careful sort of person? Will the key be hanging on a peg? Am I thinking rightly? Perhaps they don't lock the depot"—my foot would be lifted to go down; I should be conscious to excitement that I was losing my chance; but I should be unable to stir until all these absurdities were entertained and disposed of. In the most critical moments of my life, when I ought to have been so *engrossed as to leave no room for any secondary thoughts,* I have been oppressed by the inability to be at peace. And in the most ordinary circumstances it is all the same. Let me instance the other morning I went to walk. The day was biting cold, but I was unable to proceed except by jerks. Once I got arrested, my feet in a muddy pool. One foot was lifted to go, knowing that it was not good to be standing in water, but there I was fast, the cause of detention being the discussing with myself the reasons why I should not stand in that pool." (T. S. Clouston, *Clinical Lectures on Mental Diseases,* 1883, p. 43. See also Berger, in *Archiv f. Psychiatrie,* VI, p. 217.)

that everything is hollow, unreal, dead. I shall speak of this state again upon a later page. The point I wish to notice here is simply that belief and disbelief are but two aspects of one psychic state.

John Mill, reviewing various opinions about belief, comes to the conclusion that no account of it can be given:

> "What," he says, "is the difference *to our minds* between thinking of a reality and representing to ourselves an imaginary picture? I confess I can see no escape from the opinion that the distinction is ultimate and primordial. There is no more difficulty in holding it to be so than in holding the difference between a sensation and an idea to be primordial. It seems almost another aspect of the same difference. . . . I cannot help thinking, therefore, that there is in the remembrance of a real fact, as distinguished from that of a thought, an element which does not consist . . . in a difference between the mere ideas which are present to the mind in the two cases. This element, howsoever we define it, constitutes belief, and is the difference between Memory and Imagination. From whatever direction we approach, this difference seems to close our path. When we arrive at it, we seem to have reached, as it were, the central point of our intellectual nature, presupposed and built upon in every attempt we make to explain the more recondite phenomena of our mental being." *

If the words of Mill be taken to apply to the mere subjective analysis of belief—to the question, What does it feel like when we have it?—they must be held, on the whole, to be correct. Belief, the sense of reality, feels like itself—that is about as much as we can say.

Prof. Brentano, in an admirable chapter of his *Psychologie*, expresses this by saying that conception and belief (which he names *judgment*) are two different fundamental psychic phenomena. What I myself have called . . . the "object" of thought may be comparatively simple, like "Ha!-what-a-pain," or "It-thunders"; or it may be complex, like "Columbus-discovered-America-in-1492," or "There-exists-an-all-wise-Creator-of-the-world." In either case, however, the mere thought of the object may exist as

* Note to James Mill's *Analysis*, I, pp. 412–423.

something quite distinct from the belief in its reality. The belief, as Brentano says, presupposes the mere thought:

> Every object comes into consciousness in a twofold way, as simply thought of [*vorgestellt*] and as admitted [*anerkannt*] or denied. The relation is analogous to that which is assumed by most philosophers (by Kant no less than by Aristotle) to obtain between mere thought and desire. Nothing is ever desired without being thought of; but the desiring is nevertheless a second quite new and peculiar form of relation to the object, a second quite new way of receiving it into consciousness. No more is anything judged [i.e., believed or disbelieved] which is not thought of too. But we must insist that, so soon as the object of a thought becomes the object of an assenting or rejecting judgment, our consciousness steps into an entirely new relation towards it. It is then twice present in consciousness, as thought of, and as held for real or denied; just as when desire awakens for it, it is both thought and simultaneously desired (p. 266).

The commonplace doctrine of "judgment" is that it consists in the combination of "ideas" by a "copula" into a "proposition," which may be of various sorts, as affirmative, negative, hypothetical, etc. But who does not see that in a disbelieved or doubted or interrogative or conditional proposition, the ideas are combined in the same identical way in which they are in a proposition which is solidly believed? *The way in which the ideas are combined is a part of the inner constitution of the thought's object or content.* That object is sometimes an articulated whole with relations between its parts, amongst which relations, that of predicate to subject may be one. But when we have got our object with its inner constitution thus defined in a proposition, then the question comes up regarding the object as a whole: "Is it a real object? is this proposition a true proposition or not?" And in the answer *Yes* to *this* question lies that new psychic act which Brentano calls "judgment," but which I prefer to call "belief."

In every proposition, then, so far as it is believed, questioned, or disbelieved, four elements are to be distinguished, the subject, the predicate, and their relation (of whatever sort it be)—these form the *object* of belief—and finally the psychic attitude in which our mind stands towards the proposition taken as a whole—and this is the belief itself.*

Admitting, then, that this attitude is a state of consciousness *sui generis,* about which nothing more can be said in the way of internal analysis, let us proceed to the second way of studying the subject of belief: *Under what circumstances do we think things real?* We shall soon see how much matter this gives us to discuss.

THE VARIOUS ORDERS OF REALITY

Suppose a newborn mind, entirely blank and waiting for experience to begin. Suppose that it begins in the form of a visual impression (whether faint or vivid is immaterial) of a lighted candle against a dark background, and nothing else, so that whilst this image lasts it constitutes the entire universe known to the mind in question. Suppose, moreover (to simplify the hypothesis), that the candle is only imaginary, and that no "original" of it is recognized by us psychologists outside. Will this hallucinatory candle be believed in, will it have a real existence for the mind?

What possible sense (for that mind) would a suspicion have that the candle was not real? What would doubt or disbelief of it imply? When *we,* the onlooking psychologists, say the candle is unreal, we mean something quite definite, viz., that there is a world known to *us* which *is* real, and to which we perceive that the candle does not belong; it belongs exclusively to that individual mind, has no *status* anywhere else, etc. It exists, to be sure, in a fashion, for it forms the content of that mind's hallucination; but the hallucination itself, though unquestionably it is a sort of existing fact, has no knowledge of *other* facts; and since those *other* facts are the realities *par excellence* for us, and the only things we believe in, the candle is simply outside of our reality and belief altogether.

By the hypothesis, however, the *mind which sees the candle* can spin no such considerations as these about it, for of other facts, actual or possible, it has no inkling whatever. That candle is its all, its absolute. Its entire faculty of attention is absorbed by it. It *is,* it is *that;* it is

---

* For an excellent account of the history of opinion on this subject see A. Marty, in *Vierteljahrsch. f. wiss. Phil.,* VII, (1884), 161 ff.

there; no other possible candle, or quality of this candle, no other possible place, or possible object in the place, no alternative, in short, suggests itself as even conceivable; so how can the mind help believing the candle real? The supposition that it might possibly not do so is, under the supposed conditions, unintelligible.*

This is what Spinoza long ago announced:

> "Let us conceive a boy," he said, "imagining to himself a horse, and taking note of nothing else. As this imagination involves the existence of the horse, *and the boy has no perception which annuls its existence,* he will necessarily contemplate the horse as present, nor will he be able to doubt of its existence, however little certain of it he may be. I deny that a man in so far as he imagines [*percipit*] affirms nothing. For what is it to imagine a winged horse but to affirm that the horse [that horse, namely] has wings? For if the mind had nothing before it but the winged horse it would contemplate the same as present, would have no cause to doubt of its existence, nor any power of dissenting from its existence, unless the imagination of the winged horse were joined to an idea which contradicted [*tollit*] its existence." (Ethics, II. 49, Scholium.)

The sense that anything we think of is unreal can only come, then, when that thing is contradicted by some other thing of which we think. *Any object which remains uncontradicted is ipso facto believed and posited as absolute reality.*

Now, how comes it that one thing thought of can be contradicted by another? It cannot unless it begins the quarrel by saying something inadmissible about that other. Take the mind with the candle, or the boy with the horse. If either of them say, "That candle or that horse, even when I don't see it, exists in *the outer world,*" he pushes into "the outer world" an object which may be incompatible with everything which he otherwise knows of that world. If so, he must take his choice of which to hold by, the present perceptions or the other knowledge of the world. If he holds to the other knowledge, the present per-

---

* We saw near the end of Chapter XIX that a candle image taking exclusive possession of the mind in this way would probably acquire the sensational vividness. But this physiological accident is logically immaterial to the argument in the text, which ought to apply as well to the dimmest sort of mental image as to the brightest sensation.

ceptions are contradicted, *so far as their relation to that world goes.* Candle and horse, whatever they may be, are not existents in outward space. They are existents, of course; they are mental objects; mental objects have existence as mental objects. But they are situated in their own spaces, the space in which they severally appear, and neither of those spaces is the space in which the realities called "the outer world" exist.

Take again the horse with wings. If I merely dream of a horse with wings, my horse interferes with nothing else and has not to be contradicted. That horse, its wings, and its place are all equally real. That horse exists no otherwise than as winged, and is moreover really there, for that place exists no otherwise than as the place of that horse, and claims as yet no connection with the other places of the world. But if with this horse I make an inroad into the *world otherwise known,* and say, for example, "That is my old mare Maggie, having grown a pair of wings where she stands in her stall," the whole case is altered; for now the horse and place are identified with a horse and place otherwise known, and *what* is known of the latter objects is incompatible with what is perceived with the former. "Maggie in her stall with wings! Never!" The wings are unreal, then, visionary. I have dreamed a lie about Maggie in her stall.

The reader will recognize in these two cases the two sorts of judgment called in the logic books existential and attributive respectively. "The candle exists as an outer reality" is an existential, "My Maggie has got a pair of wings" is an attributive, proposition; * and it follows from what was first said that *all propositions, whether attributive or existential, are believed through the very fact of*

---

* In both existential and attributive judgments a synthesis is represented. The syllable *ex* in the word Existence, *da* in the word *Dasein,* express it. "The candle exists" is equivalent to "The candle is *over there.*" And the "over there" means real space, space related to other reals. The proposition amounts to saying: "The candle is in the same space with other reals." It affirms of the candle a very concrete predicate—namely, this relation to other particular concrete things. *Their* real existence, as we shall later see, resolves itself into their peculiar relation to *ourselves.* Existence is thus no substantive quality when we predicate it of any object; it is a relation, ultimately terminating in ourselves, and at the moment when it terminates, becoming a *practical* relation. But of this more anon. I only wish now to indicate the superficial nature of the distinction between the existential and the attributive proposition.

being conceived, unless they clash with other propositions believed at the same time, by affirming that their terms are the same with the terms of these other propositions. A dream candle has existence, true enough; but not the same existence (existence for itself, namely, or *extra mentem meam*) which the candles of waking perception have. A dream horse has wings; but then neither horse nor wings are the same with any horses or wings known to memory. That we can at any moment think of the same thing which at any former moment we thought of is the ultimate law of our intellectual constitution. But when we now think of it incompatibly with our other ways of thinking it, then we must choose which way to stand by, for we cannot continue to think in two contradictory ways at once. *The whole distinction of real and unreal, the whole psychology of belief, disbelief, and doubt, is thus grounded on two mental facts—first, that we are liable to think differently of the same; and second, that when we have done so, we can choose which way of thinking to adhere to and which to disregard.*

The subjects adhered to become real subjects, the attributes adhered to real attributes, the existence adhered to real existence; whilst the subjects disregarded become imaginary subjects, the attributes disregarded erroneous attributes, and the existence disregarded an existence in no man's land, in the limbo "where footless fancies dwell." The real things are, in M. Taine's terminology, the *reductives* of the things judged unreal.

THE MANY WORLDS

Habitually and practically we do not *count* these disregarded things as existents at all. For them *Væ victis* is the law in the popular philosophy; they are not even treated as appearances; they are treated as if they were mere waste, equivalent to nothing at all. To the genuinely philosophic mind, however, they still have existence, though not the same existence, as the real things. *As* objects of fancy, *as* errors, *as* occupants of dreamland, etc., they are in their way as indefeasible parts of life, as undeniable features of the Universe, as the realities are in their way. The total world of which the philosophers must take account is thus composed of the realities *plus* the fancies and illusions.

Two subuniverses, at least, connected by relations which philosophy tries to ascertain! Really there are more than two subuniverses of which we take account, some of us of this one, and others of that. For there are various categories both of illusion and of reality, and alongside of the world of absolute error (i.e., error confined to single individuals) but still within the world of absolute reality (i.e., reality believed by the complete philosopher) there is the world of collective error, there are the worlds of abstract reality, of relative or practical reality, of ideal relations, and there is the supernatural world. The popular mind conceives of all these subworlds more or less disconnectedly; and when dealing with one of them, forgets for the time being its relations to the rest. The complete philosopher is he who seeks not only to assign to every given object of his thought its right place in one or other of these subworlds, but he also seeks to determine the relation of each subworld to the others in the total world which *is*.

The most important subuniverses commonly discriminated from each other and recognized by most of us as existing, each with its own special and separate style of existence, are the following:

1. The world of sense, or of physical "things" as we instinctively apprehend them, with such qualities as heat, color, and sound, and such "forces" as life, chemical affinity, gravity, electricity, all existing as such within or on the surface of the things.

2. The world of science, or of physical things as the learned conceive them, with secondary qualities and "forces" (in the popular sense) excluded, and nothing real but solids and fluids and their "laws" (i.e., customs) of motion.*

3. The world of ideal relations, or abstract truths believed or believable by all, and expressed in logical, mathematical, metaphysical, ethical, or æsthetic propositions.

4. The world of "idols of the tribe," illusions or prejudices common to the race. All educated people recognize these as forming one subuniverse. The motion of the sky round the earth, for example, belongs to this world. That motion is not a recognized item of any of the other

---

* I define the scientific universe here in the radical mechanical way. Practically, it is oftener thought of in a mongrel way and resembles in more points the popular physical world.

worlds; but as an "idol of the tribe" it really exists. For certain philosophers "matter" exists only as an idol of the tribe. For science, the "secondary qualities" of matter are but "idols of the tribe."

5. The various supernatural worlds, the Christian heaven and hell, the world of the Hindu mythology, the world of Swedenborg's *visa et audita,* etc. Each of these is a consistent system, with definite relations among its own parts. Neptune's trident, e.g., has no status of reality whatever in the Christian heaven; but within the classic Olympus certain definite things are true of it, whether one believe in the reality of the classic mythology as a whole or not. The various worlds of deliberate fable may be ranked with these worlds of faith—the world of the *Iliad,* that of *King Lear,* of the *Pickwick Papers,* etc.*

6. The various worlds of individual opinion, as numerous as men are.

7. The worlds of sheer madness and vagary, also indefinitely numerous.

Every object we think of gets at last referred to one world or another of this or of some similar list. It settles into our belief as a commonsense object, a scientific object, an abstract object, a mythological object, an object of some one's mistaken conception, or a madman's object; and it reaches this state sometimes immediately, but often only after being hustled and bandied about amongst other objects until it finds some which will tolerate its presence and stand in relations to it which nothing contradicts. The molecules and ether waves of the scientific world, for example, simply kick the object's warmth and color out, they refuse to have any relations with them. But the world of "idols of the tribe" stands ready to take them in. Just so the world of classic myth takes up the winged horse; the world of individual hallucination, the vision of the candle;

---

* It thus comes about that we can say such things as that Ivanhoe did not *really* marry Rebecca, as Thackeray *falsely* makes him do. The real Ivanhoe world is the one which Scott wrote down for us. *In that world* Ivanhoe does *not* marry Rebecca. The objects within that world are knit together by perfectly definite relations, which can be affirmed or denied. Whilst absorbed in the novel, we turn our backs on all other worlds, and, for the time, the Ivanhoe world remains our absolute reality. When we wake from the spell, however, we find a still more real world, which reduces Ivanhoe, and all things connected with him, to the fictive status, and relegates them to one of the subuniverses grouped under Number 5.

the world of abstract truth, the proposition that justice is kingly, though no actual king be just. The various worlds themselves, however, appear (as aforesaid) to most men's minds in no very definitely conceived relation to each other, and our attention, when it turns to one, is apt to drop the others for the time being out of its account. Propositions concerning the different worlds are made from "different points of view"; and in this more or less chaotic state the consciousness of most thinkers remains to the end. Each world *whilst it is attended to* is real after its own fashion; only the reality lapses with the attention.

THE WORLD OF "PRACTICAL REALITIES"

Each thinker, however, has dominant habits of attention; and these *practically elect from among the various worlds some one to be for him the world of ultimate realities*. From this world's objects he does not appeal. Whatever positively contradicts them must get into another world or die. The horse, e.g., may have wings to its heart's content, so long as it does not pretend to be the real world's horse—*that* horse is absolutely wingless. For most men, as we shall immediately see, the "things of sense" hold this prerogative position, and are the absolutely real world's nucleus. Other things, to be sure, may be real for this man or for that—things of science, abstract moral relations, things of the Christian theology, or what not. But even for the special man, these things are usually real with a less real reality than that of the things of sense. They are taken less seriously; and the very utmost that can be said for anyone's belief in them is that it is as strong as his "belief in his own senses." *

* The world of dreams is our real world whilst we are sleeping, because our attention then lapses from the sensible world. Conversely, when we wake the attention usually lapses from the dream world and that becomes unreal. But if a dream haunts us and compels our attention during the day it is very apt to remain figuring in our consciousness as a sort of subuniverse alongside of the waking world. Most people have probably had dreams which it is hard to imagine not to have been glimpses into an actually existing region of being, perhaps a corner of the "spiritual world." And dreams have accordingly in all ages been regarded as revelations, and have played a large part in furnishing forth mythologies and creating themes for faith to lay hold upon. The "larger universe," here, which helps us to believe both in the dream and in the waking real-

In all this the everlasting partiality of our nature shows itself, our inveterate propensity to choice. For, in the strict and ultimate sense of the word existence, everything which can be thought of at all exists as *some* sort of object, whether mythical object, individual thinker's object, or object in outer space and for intelligence at large. Errors, fictions, tribal beliefs are parts of the whole great Universe which God has made, and He must have meant all these things to be in it, each in its respective place. But for us finite creatures, " 'tis to consider too curiously to consider so." The mere fact of appearing as an object at all is not enough to constitute reality. That may be metaphysical reality, reality for God; but what we need is practical reality, reality for ourselves; and, to have that, an object must not only appear, but it must appear both *interesting* and *important*. The worlds whose objects are neither interesting nor important we treat simply negatively, we brand them as *un*real.

In the relative sense, then, the sense in which we contrast reality with simple *un*reality, and in which one thing is said to have *more* reality than another, and to be more believed, *reality means simply relation to our emotional and active life.* This is the only sense which the word ever has in the mouths of practical men. *In this sense, whatever excites and stimulates our interest is real;* whenever an object so appeals to us that we turn to it, accept it, fill our mind with it, or practically take account of it, so far it is real for us, and we believe it. Whenever, on the contrary, we ignore it, fail to consider it or act upon it despise it, reject it, forget it, so far it is unreal for us and disbelieved. Hume's account of the matter was then essentially correct, when he said that belief in anything was simply the having the idea of it in a lively and active manner:

> I say, then, that belief is nothing but a more vivid, lively, forcible, firm, steady conception of an object than the imagination alone is ever able to attain. . . . It con-

---

ity which is its immediate reductive, is the *total* universe, of Nature *plus* the Supernatural. The dream holds true, namely, in one half of that universe; the waking perceptions in the other half. Even today dream objects figure among the realities in which some "psychic researchers" are seeking to rouse our belief. All our theories, not only those about the supernatural, but our philosophic and scientific theories as well, are like our dreams in rousing such different degrees of belief in different minds.

sists not in the peculiar nature or order of the ideas, but in the *manner* of their conception and in their *feeling* to the mind. I confess that it is impossible perfectly to explain this feeling or manner of conception. . . . Its true and proper name . . . is *belief,* which is a term that everyone sufficiently understands in common life. And in philosophy we can go no farther than assert that belief is something felt by the mind, which distinguishes the idea of the judgment from the fictions of the imagination.* It gives them more weight and influence; makes them appear of greater importance; enforces them in the mind; gives them a superior influence on the passions, and renders them the governing principle in our actions.†

Or as Professor Bain puts it: "In its essential character, belief is a phase of our active nature—otherwise called the Will." ‡

The object of belief, then, reality or real existence, is something quite different from all the other predicates which a subject may possess. Those are properties intellectually or sensibly intuited. When we add any one of them to the subject, we increase the intrinsic content of the latter, we enrich its picture in our mind. But adding reality does not enrich the picture in any such inward way; it leaves it inwardly as it finds it, and only fixes it and stamps it into *us*.

> "The real," as Kant says, "contains no more than the possible. A hundred real dollars do not contain a penny more than a hundred possible dollars. . . . By whatever, and by however many, predicates I may think a thing, nothing is added to it if I add that the thing exists. . . . Whatever, therefore, our concept of an object may contain, we must always step outside of it in order to attribute to it existence." §

---

* Distinguishes realities from unrealities, the essential from the rubbishy and neglectable.

† *Inquiry Concerning Human Understanding,* sec. v. pt. 2 (slightly transposed in my quotation).

‡ Note to James Mill's *Analysis,* I., p. 394.

§ *Critique of Pure Reason,* trans. Müller, II. 515–517. Hume also:

> When, after the simple conception of anything, we would conceive it as existent, we in reality make no addition to, or alteration of, our first idea. Thus, when we affirm that God is existent, we simply form the idea of such a being as He is represented to us; nor is the existence which we attribute to Him conceived by a particular idea, which we join to His other qualities, and can again separate and distinguish from

The "stepping outside" of it is the establishment either of immediate practical relations between it and ourselves, or of relations between it and other objects with which we have immediate practical relations. Relations of this sort, which are as yet not transcended or superseded by others, are *ipso facto* real relations, and confer reality upon their objective term. *The fons et origo of all reality, whether from the absolute or the practical point of view, is thus subjective, is ourselves.* As bare logical thinkers, without emotional reaction, we give reality to whatever objects we think of, for they are really phenomena, or objects of our passing thought, if nothing more. But, *as thinkers with emotional reaction, we give what seems to us a still higher degree of reality to whatever things we select and emphasize and turn to* WITH A WILL. These are our *living* realities; and not only these, but all the other things which are intimately connected with these. Reality, starting from our Ego, thus sheds itself from point to point—first, upon all objects which have an immediate sting of interest for our Ego in them, and next, upon the objects most continuously related with these. It only fails when the connecting thread is lost. A whole system may be real, if it only hang to our Ego by one immediately *stinging* term. But what contradicts any such stinging term, even though it be another stinging term itself, is either not believed, or only believed after settlement of the dispute.

We reach thus the important conclusion that *our own reality, that sense of our own life which we at every moment possess, is the ultimate of ultimates for our belief.* "As sure as I exist!"—this is our uttermost warrant for the being of all other things. As Descartes made the indubitable reality of the *cogito* go bail for the reality of all that the *cogito* involved, so we all of us, feeling our own present reality with absolutely coercive force, ascribe an all

---

them. . . . The belief of the existence joins no new idea to those which compose the ideas of the object. When I think of God, when I think of Him as existent, and when I believe Him to be existent, my idea of Him neither increases nor diminishes. But as 'tis certain there is a great difference betwixt the simple conception of the existence of an object and the belief of it, and as this difference lies not in the facts or compositions of the idea which we conceive, it follows that it must lie in the manner in which we conceive it. (*Treatise of Human Nature,* pt. III. sec. 7.)

but equal degree of reality, first to whatever things we lay hold on with a sense of personal need, and second, to whatever farther things continuously belong with these. *"Mein Jetzt und Hier,"* as Professor Lipps says, *"ist der letzte Angelpunkt für alle Wirklichkeit, also alle Erkenntniss."*

The world of living realities as contrasted with unrealities is thus anchored in the Ego, considered as an active and emotional term.* That is the hook from which the rest dangles, the absolute support. And as from a painted hook it has been said that one can only hang a painted chain, so conversely, from a real hook only a real chain can properly be hung. *Whatever things have intimate and continuous connection with my life are things of whose reality I cannot doubt.* Whatever things fail to establish this connection are things which are practically no better for me than if they existed not at all.

In certain forms of melancholic perversion of the sensibilities and reactive powers, nothing touches us intimately, rouses us, or wakens natural feeling. The consequence is the complaint so often heard from melancholic patients, that nothing is believed in by them as it used to be, and that all sense of reality is fled from life. They are sheathed in india-rubber; nothing penetrates to the quick or draws blood, as it were. . . .

THE INFLUENCE OF EMOTION AND ACTIVE IMPULSE ON BELIEF

The quality of arousing emotion, of shaking, moving us or inciting us to action, has as much to do with our belief in an object's reality as the quality of giving pleasure or pain. In Chapter XXIV I shall seek to show that our emotions probably owe their pungent quality to the bodily sensations which they involve. Our tendency to believe in emotionally exciting objects (objects of fear, desire, etc.) is thus explained without resorting to any fundamentally new principle of choice. Speaking generally, the more a conceived object *excites* us, the more reality it has. The

---

* I use the notion of the Ego here, as common sense uses it. Nothing is prejudged as to the results (or absence of results) of ulterior attempts to analyze the notion.

object excites us differently at different times. Moral and religious truths come "home" to us far more on some occasions than on others. As Emerson says, "There is a difference between one and another hour of life in their authority and subsequent effect. Our faith comes in moments, . . . yet there is a depth in those brief moments which constrains us to ascribe more reality to them than to all other experiences." The "depth" is partly, no doubt, the insight into wider systems of unified relation, but far more often than that it is the emotional thrill. Thus, to descend to more trivial examples, a man who has no belief in ghosts by daylight will temporarily believe in them when, alone at midnight, he feels his blood curdle at a mysterious sound or vision, his heart thumping, and his legs impelled to flee. The thought of falling when we walk along a curbstone awakens no emotion of dread; so no sense of reality attaches to it, and we are sure we shall not fall. On a precipice's edge, however, the sickening emotion which the notion of a possible fall engenders makes us believe in the latter's imminent reality, and quite unfits us to proceed.

The greatest proof that a man is *sui compos* is his ability to suspend belief in presence of an emotionally exciting idea. To give this power is the highest result of education. In untutored minds the power does not exist. *Every exciting thought in the natural man carries credence with it. To conceive with passion is* eo ipso *to affirm. . . .*

The reason of the belief is undoubtedly the bodily commotion which the exciting idea sets up. "Nothing which I can feel like *that* can be false." All our religious and supernatural beliefs are of this order. The surest warrant for immortality is the yearning of our bowels for our dear ones; for God, the sinking sense it gives us to imagine no such Providence or help. So of our political or pecuniary hopes and fears, and things and persons dreaded and desired . . .

BELIEF IN OBJECTS OF THEORY

Now the merely conceived or imagined objects which our mind represents as hanging to the sensations (causing them, etc.), filling the gaps between them, and weaving their interrupted chaos into order are innumerable. Whole systems of them conflict with other systems, and our choice of which system shall carry our belief is governed by principles which are simple enough, however subtle and difficult may be their application to details. *The conceived system, to pass for true, must at least include the reality of the sensible objects in it, by explaining them as effects on us, if nothing more. The system which includes the most of them, and definitely explains or pretends to explain the most of them, will, ceteris paribus, prevail.* It is needless to say how far mankind still is from having excogitated such a system. But the various materialisms, idealisms, and hylozoisms show with what industry the attempt is forever made. It is conceivable that several rival theories should equally well include the actual order of our sensations in their scheme, much as the one-fluid and two-fluid theories of electricity formulated all the common electrical phenomena equally well. The sciences are full of these alternatives. Which theory is then to be believed? *That theory will be most generally believed which, besides offering us objects able to account satisfactorily for our sensible experience, also offers those which are most interesting, those which appeal most urgently to our esthetic, emotional, and active needs.* So here, in the higher intellectual life, the same selection among general conceptions goes on which went on among the sensations themselves . . .

(viii) EMOTION

EMOTION FOLLOWS UPON THE BODILY EXPRESSION IN THE COARSER EMOTIONS AT LEAST

Our natural way of thinking about these coarser emotions is that the mental perception of some fact excites the mental affection called the emotion, and that this latter state of mind gives rise to the bodily expression. My theory, on the contrary, is that *the bodily changes follow directly the perception of the exciting fact, and that our feeling of the same changes as they occur* IS *the emotion.* Common sense says, we lose our fortune, are sorry, and weep; we meet a bear, are frightened, and run; we are insulted by a rival, are angry, and strike. The hypothesis here to be defended says that this order of sequence is incorrect, that the one mental state is not immediately induced by the other, that the bodily manifestations must first be interposed between, and that the more rational statement is that we feel sorry because we cry, angry because we strike, afraid because we tremble, and not that we cry, strike, or tremble because we are sorry, angry, or fearful, as the case may be. Without the bodily states following on the perception, the latter would be purely cognitive in form, pale, colorless, destitute of emotional warmth. We might then see the bear, and judge it best to run, receive the insult and deem it right to strike, but we should not actually *feel* afraid or angry.

Stated in this crude way, the hypothesis is pretty sure to meet with immediate disbelief. And yet neither many nor farfetched considerations are required to mitigate its paradoxical character, and possibly to produce conviction of its truth.

To begin with, no reader of the last two chapters will be inclined to doubt the fact that *objects do excite bodily changes* by a preorganized mechanism, or the farther fact that *the changes are so indefinitely numerous and subtle that the entire organism may be called a sounding board,* which every change of consciousness, however slight, may make reverberate. The various permutations and combinations of which these organic activities are susceptible make it abstractly possible that no shade of emotion, however slight, should be without a bodily reverberation as unique, when taken in its totality, as is the mental mood itself. The immense number of parts modified in each emotion is what makes it so difficult for us to reproduce in cold blood the total and integral expression of any one of them. We may catch the trick with the voluntary muscles, but fail with the skin, glands, heart, and other viscera. Just as an artificially imitated sneeze lacks something of the reality, so the attempt to imitate an emotion in the absence of its normal instigating cause is apt to be rather "hollow."

The next thing to be noticed is this, that *every one of the bodily changes, whatsoever it be, if* FELT, *acutely or obscurely, the moment it occurs.* If the reader has never paid attention to this matter, he will be both interested and astonished to learn how many different local bodily feelings he can detect in himself as characteristic of his various emotional moods. It would be perhaps too much to expect him to arrest the tide of any strong gust of passion for the sake of any such curious analysis as this; but he can observe more tranquil states, and that may be assumed here to be true of the greater which is shown to be true of the less. Our whole cubic capacity is sensibly alive; and each morsel of it contributes its pulsations of feeling, dim or sharp, pleasant, painful, or dubious, to that sense of personality that every one of us unfailingly carries with him. It is surprising what little items give accent to these complexes of sensibility. When worried by any slight trouble, one may find that the focus of one's bodily consciousness is the contraction, often quite inconsiderable, of the eyes and brows. When momentarily embarrassed, it is something in the pharynx that compels either a swallow, a clearing of the throat, or a slight cough; and so on for as many more instances as might be named. Our concern here being with the general view rather than with the details, I will not linger to discuss these, but, assuming the point admitted that every change that occurs must be felt, I will pass on.

I now proceed to urge the vital point of my whole theory, which is this: *If we fancy some strong emotion, and then try to abstract from our consciousness of it all the feelings of its bodily symptoms, we find we have nothing left behind,* no "mind-stuff" out of which the emotion can be constituted, and that a cold and neutral state of intellectual perception is all that remains. It is true that, although most people when asked say that their introspection verifies this statement, some persist in saying theirs does not. Many cannot be made to understand the question. When you beg them to imagine away every feeling of laughter and of tendency to laugh from their consciousness of the ludicrousness of an object, and then to tell you what the feeling of its ludicrousness would be like, whether it be anything more than the perception that the object belongs to the class "funny," they persist in replying that the thing proposed is a physical impossibility, and that they always *must* laugh if they see a funny object. Of course the task proposed is not the practical one of seeing a ludicrous object and annihilating one's tendency to laugh. It is the purely speculative one of subtracting certain elements of feeling from an emotional state supposed to exist in its fulness, and saying what the residual elements are. I cannot help thinking that all who rightly apprehend this problem will agree with the proposition above laid down. What kind of an emotion of fear would be left if the feeling neither of quickened heartbeats nor of shallow breathing, neither of trembling lips nor of weakened limbs, neither of gooseflesh nor of visceral stirrings, were present, it is quite impossible for me to think. Can one fancy the state of rage and picture no ebullition in the chest, no flushing of the face, no dilatation of the nostrils, no clenching of the teeth, no impulse to vigorous action, but in their stead limp muscles, calm breathing, and a placid face? The present writer, for one, certainly cannot. The rage is as completely evaporated as the sensation of its so-called manifestations, and the only thing that can possibly be supposed to take its place is some cold-blooded and dispassionate judicial sentence, confined entirely to the intellectual realm, to the effect that a certain person or persons merit chastisement for their sins. In like manner of grief: what would it be without its tears, its sobs, its suffocation of the heart, its pang in the breastbone? A feelingless cognition that certain circumstances are deplorable, and nothing more. Every passion in turn tells the same story. A purely disembodied human emotion is a nonentity. I do not say that it is a contradiction in the nature of things, or that pure spirits are necessarily condemned to cold intellectual lives; but I say that for *us*, emotion dissociated from all bodily feeling is inconceivable. The more closely I scrutinize my states, the more persuaded I become that whatever moods, affections, and passions I have are in very truth constituted by, and made up of, those bodily changes which we ordinarily call their expression or consequence . . .

Some movements of expression can be accounted for as *weakened repetitions of movements which formerly* (when they were stronger) *were of utility to the subject.* Others are similarly weakened repetitions of movements which under other conditions were *physiologically necessary effects.* Of the latter reactions the respiratory disturbances in anger and fear might be taken as examples—organic reminiscences, as it were, reverberations in imagination of the blowings of the man making a series of combative efforts, of the pantings of one in precipitate flight. Such at least is a suggestion made by Mr. Spencer which has found approval. And he also was the first, so far as I know, to suggest that other movements in anger and fear could be explained by the nascent excitation of formerly useful acts.

"To have in a slight degree," he says, "such psychical states as accompany the reception of wounds, and are experienced during flight, is to be in a state of what we call fear. And to have in a slight degree such psychical states as the processes of catching, killing, and eating imply, is to have the desires to catch, kill, and eat. That the propensities to the acts are nothing else than nascent excitations of the psychical state involved in the acts, is proved by the natural language of the propensities. Fear, when strong, expresses itself in cries, in efforts to escape, in palpitations, in tremblings; and these are just the manifestations that go along with an actual suffering of the evil feared. The destructive passion is shown in a general tension of the muscular system, in gnashing of teeth and protrusion of the claws, in dilated eyes and nostrils, in growls; and these are weaker forms of the actions that accompany the killing of prey. To such objective evidences every one can add subjective evidences. Every one can testify that the psychical state called fear consists of mental representations of certain painful results; and that the one called anger consists of mental representations of the actions and impressions which would occur while inflicting some kind of pain." *

About fear I shall have more to say presently. Meanwhile the principle of *revival in weakened form of reactions useful in more violent dealings with the object inspiring the emotion,* has found many applications. So slight a symptom as the snarl or sneer, the one-sided uncovering of the upper teeth, is accounted for by Darwin as a survival from the time when our ancestors had large canines, and unfleshed them (as dogs now do) for attack. Similarly the raising of the eyebrows in outward attention, the opening of the mouth in astonishment, come, according to the same author, from the utility of these movements in extreme cases. The raising of the eyebrows goes with the opening of the eye for better vision; the opening of the mouth with the intensest listening, and with the rapid catching of the breath which precedes muscular effort. The distention of the nostrils in anger is interpreted by Spencer as an echo of the way in which our ancestors had

* *Psychol.,* § 213.

to breathe when, during combat, their "mouth was filled up by a part of an antagonist's body that had been seized(!)." The trembling of fear is supposed by Mantegazza to be for the sake of warming the blood(!). The reddening of the face and neck is called by Wundt a compensatory arrangement for relieving the brain of the blood pressure which the simultaneous excitement of the heart brings with it. The effusion of tears is explained both by this author and by Darwin to be a blood-withdrawing agency of a similar sort. . . .

(ix) ACTION AND WILL

ACTION AFTER DELIBERATION

We are now in a position to describe *what happens in deliberate action*, or when the mind is the seat of many ideas related to each other in antagonistic or in favorable ways.* One of the ideas is that of an act. By itself this idea would prompt a movement; some of the additional considerations, however, which are present to consciousness block the motor discharge, whilst others, on the contrary, solicit it to take place. The result is that peculiar feeling of inward unrest known as *indecision*. Fortunately it is too familiar to need description, for to describe it would be impossible. As long as it lasts, with the various objects before the attention, we are said to *deliberate;* and when finally the original suggestion either prevails and makes the movement take place, or gets definitively quenched by its antagonists, we are said to *decide,* or to *utter our voluntary fiat* in favor of one or the other course. The reinforc-

* I use the common phraseology here for mere convenience' sake. The reader who has made himself acquainted with Chapter IX will always understand, when he hears of many ideas simultaneously present to the mind and acting upon each other, that what is really meant is a mind with one idea before it, of many objects, purposes, reasons, motives related to each other, some in a harmonious and some in an antagonistic way. With this caution I shall not hesitate from time to time to fall into the popular Lockian speech, erroneous though I believe it to be.

ing and inhibiting ideas meanwhile are termed the *reasons* or *motives* by which the decision is brought about.

The process of deliberation contains endless degrees of complication. At every moment of it our consciousness is of an extremely complex object, namely the existence of the whole set of motives and their conflict . . . Of this object, the totality of which is realized more or less dimly all the while, certain parts stand out more or less sharply at one moment in the foreground, and at another moment other parts, in consequence of the oscillations of our attention, and of the "associative" flow of our ideas. But no matter how sharp the foreground reasons may be, or how imminently close to bursting through the dam and carrying the motor consequences their own way, the background, however dimly felt, is always there; and its presence (so long as the indecision actually lasts) serves as an effective check upon the irrevocable discharge. The deliberation may last for weeks or months, occupying at intervals the mind. The motives which yesterday seemed full of urgency and blood and life today feel strangely weak and pale and dead. But as little today as tomorrow is the question finally resolved. Something tells us that all this is provisional; that the weakened reasons will wax strong again, and the stronger weaken; that equilibrium is unreached; that testing our reasons, not obeying them, is still the order of the day, and that we must wait awhile, patient or impatiently, until our mind is made up "for good and all." This inclining first to one then to another future, both of which we represent as possible, resembles the oscillations to and fro of a material body within the limits of its elasticity. There is inward strain, but no outward rapture. And this condition, plainly enough, is susceptible of indefinite continuance, as well in the physical mass as in the mind. If the elasticity give way, however, if the dam ever do break, and the currents burst the crust, vacillation is over and decision is irrevocably there.

The decision may come in either of many modes. I will try briefly to sketch the most characteristic types of it, merely warning the reader that this is only an introspective account of symptoms and phenomena, and that all questions of causal agency, whether neural or spiritual, are relegated to a later page.

The particular reasons for or against action are of

course infinitely various in concrete cases. But certain motives are more or less constantly in play. One of these is *impatience of the deliberative state;* or to express it otherwise, proneness to act or to decide merely because action and decision are, as such, agreeable, and relieve the tension of doubt and hesitancy. Thus it comes that we will often take any course whatever which happens to be most vividly before our minds, at the moment when this impulse to decisive action becomes extreme.

Against this impulse we have the *dread of the irrevocable,* which often engenders a type of character incapable of prompt and vigorous resolve, except perhaps when surprised into sudden activity. These two opposing motives twine round whatever other motives may be present at the moment when decision is imminent, and tend to precipitate or retard it. The conflict of these motives so far as they alone affect the matter of decision is a conflict as to *when* it shall occur. One says "now," the other says "not yet."

Another constant component of the web of motivation is the impulse to persist in a decision once made. There is no more remarkable difference in human character than that between resolute and irresolute natures. Neither physiological nor the psychical grounds of this difference have yet been analyzed. Its symptom is that whereas in the irresolute all decisions are provisional and liable to be reversed, in the resolute they are settled once for all and not disturbed again. Now into every one's deliberations the representation of one alternative will often enter with such sudden force as to carry the imagination with itself exclusively, and to produce an apparently settled decision in its own favor. These premature and spurious decisions are of course known to everyone. They often seem ridiculous in the light of the considerations that succeed them. But it cannot be denied that in the resolute type of character the accident that one of them has once been made does afterwards enter as a motive additional to the more genuine reasons why it should not be revoked, or if provisionally revoked, why it should be made again. How many of us persist in a precipitate course which, but for a moment of heedlessness, we might never have entered upon, simply because we hate to "change our mind."

FIVE TYPES OF DECISION

Turning now to the form of the decision itself, we may distinguish four chief types. The first may be called *the reasonable type*. It is that of those cases in which the arguments for and against a given course seem gradually and almost insensibly to settle themselves in the mind and to end by leaving a clear balance in favor of one alternative, which alternative we then adopt without effort or constraint. Until this rational balancing of the books is consummated we have a calm feeling that the evidence is not yet all in, and this keeps action in suspense. But some day we wake with the sense that we see the thing rightly, that no new light will be thrown on the subject by farther delay, and that the matter had better be settled *now*. In this easy transition from doubt to assurance we seem to ourselves almost passive; the "reasons" which decide us appearing to flow in from the nature of things, and to owe nothing to our will. We have, however, a perfect sense of being *free*, in that we are devoid of any feeling of coercion. The conclusive reason for the decision in these cases usually is the discovery that we can refer the case to a *class* upon which we are accustomed to act unhesitatingly in a certain stereotyped way. It may be said in general that a great part of every deliberation consists in the turning over of all the possible modes of *conceiving* the doing or not doing of the act in point. The moment we hit upon a conception which lets us apply some principle of action which is a fixed and stable part of our Ego, our state of doubt is at an end. Persons of authority, who have to make many decisions in the day, carry with them a set of heads of classification, each bearing its motor consequence, and under these they seek as far as possible to range each new emergency as it occurs. It is where the emergency belongs to a species without precedent, to which consequently no cut-and-dried maxim will apply, that we feel most at a loss, and are distressed at the indeterminateness of our task. As soon, however, as we see our way to a familiar classification, we are at ease again. *In action as in reasoning, then, the great thing is the quest of the right conception.* The concrete dilemmas do not come to us with labels gummed upon their backs. We may name them by many names. The wise man is he who succeeds in finding the name which suits the needs of the particular occasion best. A "reasonable" character is one who has a store of stable and worthy ends, and who does not decide about an action till he has calmly ascertained whether it be ministerial or detrimental to any one of these.

In the next two types of decision, the final fiat occurs before the evidence is all "in." It often happens that no paramount and authoritative reason for either course will come. Either seems a case of a Good, and there is no umpire as to which good should yield its place to the other. We grow tired of long hesitation and inconclusiveness, and the hour may come when we feel that even a bad decision is better than no decision at all. Under these conditions it will often happen that some accidental circumstance, supervening at a particular movement upon our mental weariness, will upset the balance in the direction of one of the alternatives, to which then we feel ourselves committed, although an opposite accident at the same time might have produced the opposite result.

In the *second type* of case our feeling is to a certain extent that of letting ourselves drift with a certain indifferent acquiescence in a direction accidentally determined *from without,* with the conviction that, after all, we might as well stand by this course as by the other, and that things are in any event sure to turn out sufficiently right.

In the *third type* the determination seems equally accidental, but it comes from within, and not from without. It often happens, when the absence of imperative principle is perplexing and suspense distracting, that we find ourselves acting, as it were, automatically, and as if by a spontaneous discharge of our nerves, in the direction of one of the horns of the dilemma. But so exciting is this sense of motion after our intolerable pent-up state, that we eagerly throw ourselves into it. "Forward now!" we inwardly cry, "though the heavens fall." This reckless and exultant espousal of an energy so little premeditated by us that we feel rather like passive spectators cheering on the display of some extraneous force than like voluntary agents, is a type of decision too abrupt and tumultuous to occur often in humdrum and cool-blooded natures. But it is probably frequent in persons of strong emotional endowment and unstable or vacillating character. And in men of the world-shaking type, the Napoleons, Luthers, etc., in whom tenacious passion combines with ebullient activity, when by any chance the passion's outlet has been dammed by scruples or apprehensions, the resolution is probably often of this catastrophic kind. The flood breaks quite unexpectedly through the dam. That it should so often do so is quite sufficient to account for the tendency of these characters to a fatalistic mood of mind. And the fatalistic mood itself is sure to reinforce the strength of the energy just started on its exciting path of discharge.

There is a *fourth form* of decision, which often ends deliberation as suddenly as the third form does. It comes when, in consequence of some outer experience or some inexplicable inward change, *we suddenly pass from the easy and careless to the sober and strenuous mood,* or possibly the other way. The whole scale of values of our motives and impulses then undergoes a change like that which a change of the observer's level produces on a view. The most sobering possible agents are objects of grief and fear. When one of these affects us, all "light fantastic" notions lose their motive power, all solemn ones find theirs multiplied manyfold. The consequence is an instant abandonment of the more trivial projects with which we had been dallying, and an instant practical acceptance of the more grim and earnest alternative which till then could not extort our mind's consent. All those "changes of heart," "awakenings of conscience," etc., which make new men of so many of us, may be classed under this head. The character abruptly rises to another "level," and deliberation comes to an immediate end.*

In the *fifth and final type* of decision, the feeling that the evidence is all in, and that reason has balanced the books, may be either present or absent. But in either case we feel, in deciding, as if we ourselves by our own wilful act inclined the beam; in the former case by adding our living effort to the weight of the logical reason which, taken alone, seems powerless to make the act discharge; in the latter by a kind of creative contribution of something instead of a reason which does a reason's work. The slow dead heave of the will that is felt in these instances makes of them a class altogether different subjectively from all

---

* My attention was first emphatically called to this class of decisions by my colleague, Professor C. C. Everett.

the three preceding classes. What the heave of the will betokens metaphysically, what the effort might lead us to infer about a will power distinct from motives, are not matters that concern us yet. Subjectively and phenomenally, the *feeling of effort*, absent from the former decisions, accompanies these. Whether it be the dreary resignation for the sake of austere and naked duty of all sorts of rich mundane delights, or whether it be the heavy resolve that of two mutually exclusive trains of future fact, both sweet and good, and with no strictly objective or imperative principle of choice between them, one shall forevermore become impossible, while the other shall become reality, it is a desolate and acrid sort of act, an excursion into a lonesome moral wilderness. If examined closely, its chief difference from the three former cases appears to be that in those cases the mind at the moment of deciding on the triumphant alternative dropped the other one wholly or nearly out of sight, whereas here both alternatives are steadily held in view, and in the very act of murdering the vanquished possibility the chooser realizes how much in that instant he is making himself lose. It is deliberately driving a thorn into one's flesh; and the sense of *inward effort* with which the act is accompanied is an element which sets the fourth type of decisions in strong contrast with the previous three varieties, and makes of it an altogether peculiar sort of mental phenomenon. The immense majority of human decisions are decisions without effort. In comparatively few of them, in most people, does effort accompany the final act. We are, I think, misled into supposing that effort is more frequent than it is, by the fact that *during deliberation* we so often have a feeling of how great an effort it would take to make a decision *now*. Later, after the decision has made itself with ease, we recollect this and erroneously suppose the effort also to have been made then.

The existence of the effort as a phenomenal fact in our consciousness cannot of course be doubted or denied. Its significance, on the other hand, is a matter about which the gravest difference of opinion prevails. Questions as momentous as that of the very existence of spiritual causality, as vast as that of universal predestination or free will, depend on its interpretation. It therefore becomes essential that we study with some care the conditions under which the feeling of volitional effort is found. . . .

VIII. The Will to Believe*

In the recently published Life by Leslie Stephen of his brother, Fitz-James, there is an account of a school to which the latter went when he was a boy. The teacher, a certain Mr. Guest, used to converse with his pupils in this wise: "Gurney, what is the difference between justification and sanctification?—Stephen, prove the omnipotence of God!" etc. In the midst of our Harvard freethinking and indifference we are prone to imagine that here at your good old orthodox College conversation continues to be somewhat upon this order; and to show you that we at Harvard have not lost all interest in these vital subjects, I have brought with me tonight something like a sermon on justification by faith to read to you—I mean an essay in justification *of* faith, a defense of our right to adopt a believing attitude in religious matters, in spite of the fact that our merely logical intellect may not have been coerced. "The Will to Believe," accordingly, is the title of my paper.

I have long defended to my own students the lawfulness of voluntarily adopted faith; but as soon as they have got well imbued with the logical spirit, they have as a rule refused to admit my contention to be lawful philosophically, even though in point of fact they were personally all the time chock full of some faith or other themselves. I am all the while, however, so profoundly convinced that my own position is correct, that your invitation has seemed to me a good occasion to make my statements more clear. Perhaps

* An Address to the Philosophical Clubs of Yale and Brown Universities. Published in the *New World*, (June, 1896), pp. 327–347.

your minds will be more open than those with which I have hitherto had to deal. I will be as little technical as I can, though I must begin by setting up some technical distinctions that will help us in the end.

i

Let us give the name of *hypothesis* to anything that may be proposed to our belief; and just as the electricians speak of live and dead wires, let us speak of any hypothesis as either *live* or *dead*. A live hypothesis is one which appeals as a real possibility to him to whom it is proposed. If I ask you to believe in the Mahdi, the notion makes no electric connection with your nature—it refuses to scintillate with any credibility at all. As an hypothesis it is completely dead. To an Arab, however (even if he be not one of the Mahdi's followers), the hypothesis is among the mind's possibilities: it is alive. This shows that deadness and liveness in an hypothesis are not intrinsic properties, but relations to the individual thinker. They are measured by his willingness to act. The maximum of liveness in an hypothesis means willingness to act irrevocably. Practically, that means belief; but there is some believing tendency wherever there is willingness to act at all.

Next, let us call the decision between two hypotheses an *option*. Options may be of several kinds. They may be—1, *living* or *dead;* 2, *forced* or *avoidable;* 3, *momentous* or *trivial;* and for our purposes we may call an option a *genuine* option when it is of the forced, living, and momentous kind.

1. A living option is one in which both hypotheses are live ones. If I say to you: "Be a theosophist or be a Mohammedan," it is probably a dead option, because for you neither hypothesis is likely to be alive. But if I say: "Be an agnostic or be a Christian," it is otherwise: trained as you are, each hypothesis makes some appeal, however small, to your belief.

2. Next, if I say to you: "Choose between going out with your umbrella or without it," I do not offer you a genuine option, for it is not forced. You can easily avoid it by not going out at all. Similarly, if I say, "Either love me

or hate me," "Either call my theory true or call it false," your option is avoidable. You may remain indifferent to me, neither loving nor hating and you may decline to offer any judgment as to my theory. But if I say, "Either accept this truth or go without it," I put on you a forced option, for there is no standing place outside of the alternative. Every dilemma based on a complete logical disjunction, with no possibility of not choosing, is an option of this forced kind.

3. Finally, if I were Dr. Nansen and proposed to you to join my North Pole expedition, your option would be momentous; for this would probably be your only similar opportunity, and your choice now would either exclude you from the North Pole sort of immortality altogether or put at least the chance of it into your hands. He who refuses to embrace a unique opportunity loses the prize as surely as if he tried and failed. *Per contra,* the option is trivial when the opportunity is not unique, when the stake is insignificant, or when the decision is reversible if it later prove unwise. Such trivial options abound in the scientific life. A chemist finds an hypothesis live enough to spend a year in its verification: he believes in it to that extent. But if his experiments prove inconclusive either way, he is quit for his loss of time, no vital harm being done.

It will facilitate our discussion if we keep all these distinctions well in mind.

ii

The next matter to consider is the actual psychology of human opinion. When we look at certain facts, it seems as if our passional and volitional nature lay at the root of all our convictions. When we look at others, it seems as if they could do nothing when the intellect had once said its say. Let us take the latter facts up first.

Does it not seem preposterous on the very face of it to talk of our opinions being modifiable at will? Can our will either help or hinder our intellect in its perceptions of truth? Can we, by just willing it, believe that Abraham Lincoln's existence is a myth, and that the portraits of him in *McClure's Magazine* are all of some one else? Can we, by any effort of our will, or by any strength of wish that it were true, believe ourselves well and about when we are roaring with rheumatism in bed, or feel certain that the sum of the two one-dollar bills in our pocket must be a hundred dollars? We can *say* any of these things, but we are absolutely impotent to believe them; and of just such things is the whole fabric of the truths that we do believe in made up—matters of fact, immediate or remote, as Hume said, and relations between ideas, which are either there or not there for us if we see them so, and which if not there cannot be put there by any action of our own.

In Pascal's Thoughts there is a celebrated passage known in literature as Pascal's wager. In it he tries to force us into Christianity by reasoning as if our concern with truth resembled our concern with the stakes in a game of chance. Translated freely his words are these: You must either believe or not believe that God is—which will you do? Your human reason cannot say. A game is going on between you and the nature of things which at the day of judgment will bring out either heads or tails. Weigh what your gains and your losses would be if you should stake all you have on heads, or God's existence: if you win in such case, you gain eternal beatitude; if you lose, you lose nothing at all. If there were an infinity of chances, and only one for God in this wager, still you ought to stake your all on God; for though you surely risk a finite loss by this procedure, any finite loss is reasonable, even a certain one is reasonable, if there is but the possibility of infinite gain. Go, then, and take holy water, and have masses said; belief will come and stupefy your scruples—*Cela vous fera croire et vous abêtira.* Why should you not? At bottom, what have you to lose?

You probably feel that when religious faith expresses itself thus, in the language of the gaming table, it is put to its last trumps. Surely Pascal's own personal belief in masses and holy water had far other springs; and this celebrated page of his is but an argument for others, a last desperate snatch at a weapon against the hardness of the unbelieving heart. We feel that a faith in masses and holy water adopted wilfully after such a mechanical calculation would lack the inner soul of faith's reality; and if we were ourselves in the place of the Deity, we should probably take particular pleasure in cutting off believers of this pattern from their infinite reward. It is evident that unless there be some preexisting tendency to believe in masses and holy water, the option offered to the will by Pascal is not a living option. Certainly no Turk ever took to masses and holy water on its account; and even to us Protestants these means of salvation seem such foregone impossibilities that Pascal's logic, invoked for them specifically, leaves us unmoved. As well might the Mahdi write to us, saying, "I am the Expected One whom God has created in his effulgence. You shall be infinitely happy if you confess me; otherwise you shall be cut off from the light of the sun. Weigh, then, your infinite gain if I am genuine against your finite sacrifice if I am not!" His logic would be that of Pascal; but he would vainly use it on us, for the hypothesis he offers us is dead. No tendency to act on it exists in us to any degree.

The talk of believing by our volition seems, then, from one point of view, simply silly. From another point of view it is worse than silly, it is vile. When one turns to the magnificent edifice of the physical sciences, and sees how it was reared; what thousands of disinterested moral lives of men lie buried in its mere foundations; what patience and postponement, what choking down of preference, what submission to the icy laws of outer fact are wrought into its very stones and mortar; how absolutely impersonal it stands in its vast augustness—then how besotted and contemptible seems every little sentimentalist who comes blowing his voluntary smoke wreaths, and pretending to decide things from out of his private dream! Can we wonder if those bred in the rugged and manly school of science should feel like spewing such subjectivism out of their mouths? The whole system of loyalties which grow up in the schools of science go dead against its toleration; so that it is only natural that those who have caught the scientific fever should pass over to the opposite extreme, and write sometimes as if the incorruptibly truthful intellect ought positively to prefer bitterness and unacceptableness to the heart of its cup.

> It fortifies my soul to know
> That, though I perish, Truth is so—

sings Clough, while Huxley exclaims: "My only consolation lies in the reflection that, however bad our posterity may become, so far as they hold by the plain rule of not pretending to believe what they have no reason to believe, because it may be to their advantage so to pretend [the word "pretend" is surely here redundant], they will not have reached the lowest depth of immorality." And that delicious *enfant terrible* Clifford writes: "Belief is desecrated when given to unproved and unquestioned statements of the solace and private pleasure of the believer. . . . Whoso would deserve well of his fellows in this matter will guard the purity of his belief with a very fanaticism of jealous care, lest at any time it should rest on an unworthy object, and catch a stain which can never be wiped away. . . . If [a] belief has been accepted on insufficient evidence [even though the belief be true, as Clifford on the same page explains] the pleasure is a stolen one. . . . It is sinful because it is stolen in defiance of our duty to mankind. That duty is to guard ourselves from such beliefs as from a pestilence which may shortly master our own body and then spread to the rest of the town. . . . It is wrong always, everywhere, and for every one, to believe anything upon insufficient evidence."

iii

All this strikes one as healthy, even when expressed, as by Clifford, with somewhat too much of robustious pathos in the voice. Free will and simple wishing do seem, in the matter of our credences, to be only fifth wheels to the coach. Yet if any one should thereupon assume that intellectual insight is what remains after wish and will and sentimental preference have taken wing, or that pure reason is what then settles our opinions, he would fly quite as directly in the teeth of the facts.

It is only our already dead hypotheses that our willing nature is unable to bring to life again. But what has made them dead for us is for the most part a previous action of our willing nature of an antagonistic kind. When I say "willing nature," I do not mean only such deliberate volitions as may have set up habits of belief that we cannot now escape from—I mean all such factors of belief as fear and hope, prejudice and passion, imitation and partisanship, the circumpressure of our caste and set. As a matter of fact we find ourselves believing, we hardly know how or why. Mr. Balfour gives the name of "authority" to all those influences, born of the intellectual climate, that make hypotheses possible or impossible for us, alive or dead. Here in this room, we all of us believe in molecules and the conservation of energy, in democracy and necessary progress, in Protestant Christianity and the duty of fighting for "the doctrine of the immortal Monroe," all for no reasons worthy of the name. We see into these matters with no more inner clearness, and probably with much less, than any disbeliever in them might possess. His unconventionality would probably have some grounds to show for its conclusions; but for us, not insight, but the *prestige* of the opinions, is what makes the spark shoot from them and light up our sleeping magazines of faith. Our reason is quite satisfied, in nine hundred and ninety-nine cases out of every thousand of us, if it can find a few arguments that will do to recite in case our credulity is criticized by some one else. Our faith is faith in some one else's faith, and in the greatest matters this is most the case. Our belief in truth itself, for instance, that there is a truth, and that our minds and it are made for each other —what is it but a passionate affirmation of desire, in which our social system backs us up? We want to have a truth; we want to believe that our experiments and studies and discussions must put us in a continually better and better position towards it; and on this line we agree to fight out our thinking lives. But if a pyrrhonistic sceptic asks us *how we know* all this, can our logic find a reply? No! certainly it cannot. It is just one volition against another—we willing to go in for life upon a trust or assumption which he, for his part, does not care to make.*

As a rule we disbelieve all facts and theories for which we have no use. Clifford's cosmic emotions find no use for Christian feelings. Huxley belabors the bishops because there is no use for sacerdotalism in his scheme of life. Newman, on the contrary, goes over to Romanism, and finds all sorts of reasons good for staying there, because a priestly system is for him an organic need and delight. Why do so few "scientists" even look at the evidence for telepathy, so called? Because they think, as a leading biologist, now dead, once said to me, that even if such a thing

---

* Compare the admirable page 310 in S. H. Hodgson's *Time and Space*, (London, 1865).

were true, scientists ought to band together to keep it suppressed and concealed. It would undo the uniformity of Nature and all sorts of other things without which scientists cannot carry on their pursuits. But if this very man had been shown something which as a scientist he might *do* with telepathy, he might not only have examined the evidence, but even have found it good enough. This very law which the logicians would impose upon us—if I may give the name of logicians to those who would rule out our willing nature here—is based on nothing but their own natural wish to exclude all elements for which they, in their professional quality of logicians, can find no use.

Evidently, then, our nonintellectual nature does influence our convictions. There are passional tendencies and volitions which run before and others which come after belief, and it is only the latter that are too late for the fair; and they are not too late when the previous passional work has been already in their own direction. Pascal's argument, instead of being powerless, then seems a regular clincher, and is the last stroke needed to make our faith in masses and holy water complete. The state of things is evidently far from simple; and pure insight and logic, whatever they might do ideally, are not the only things that really do produce our creeds.

iv

Our next duty, having recognized this mixed-up state of affairs, is to ask whether it be simply reprehensible and pathological, or whether, on the contrary, we must treat it as a normal element in making up our minds. The thesis I defend is, briefly stated, this: *Our passional nature not only lawfully may, but must, decide an option between propositions, whenever it is a genuine option that cannot by its nature be decided on intellectual grounds; for to say, under such circumstances, "Do not decide, but leave the question open," is itself a passional decision—just like deciding yes or no—and is attended with the same risk of losing the truth.* The thesis thus abstractly expressed will, I trust, soon become quite clear. But I must first indulge in a bit more of preliminary work.

v

It will be observed that for the purposes of this discussion we are on "dogmatic" ground—ground, I mean, which leaves systematic philosophical scepticism altogether out of account. The postulate that there is truth, and that it is the destiny of our minds to attain it, we are deliberately resolving to make, though the sceptic will not make it. We part company with him, therefore, absolutely, at this point. But the faith that truth exists, and that our minds can find it, may be held in two ways. We may talk of the *empiricist* way and of the *absolutist* way of believing in truth. The absolutists in this matter say that we not only can attain to knowing truth, but we can *know when* we have attained to knowing it; while the empiricists think that although we may attain it, we cannot infallibly know when. To *know* is one thing, and to know for certain *that* we know is another. One may hold to the first being possible without the second; hence the empiricists and the absolutists, although neither of them is a sceptic in the usual philosophic sense of the term, show very different degrees of dogmatism in their lives.

If we look at the history of opinions, we see that the empiricist tendency has largely prevailed in science, while in philosophy the absolutist tendency has had everything its own way. The characteristic sort of happiness, indeed, which philosophies yield has mainly consisted in the conviction felt by each successive school or system that by it bottom certitude had been attained. "Other philosophies are collections of opinions, mostly false; *my* philosophy gives standing ground forever"—who does not recognize in this the keynote of every system worthy of the name? A system, to be a system at all, must come as a *closed* system, reversible in this or that detail, perchance, but in its essential features never!

Scholastic orthodoxy, to which one must always go when one wishes to find perfectly clear statement, has beautifully elaborated this absolutist conviction in a doctrine which it calls that of "objective evidence." If, for example, I am unable to doubt that I now exist before you, that two is less than three, or that if all men are mortal then I am mortal too, it is because these things illumine my intellect irresistibly. The final ground of this objective evidence possessed by certain propositions is the *adæquatio intellectûs nostri cum rê.* The certitude it brings involves an *aptitudinem ad extorquendum certum assensum* on the part of the truth envisaged, and on the side of the subject a *quietem in cognitione,* when once the object is mentally received, that leaves no possibility of doubt behind; and in the whole transaction nothing operates but the *entitas ipsa* of the object and the *entitas ipsa* of the mind. We slouchy modern thinkers dislike to talk in Latin—indeed, we dislike to talk in set terms at all; but at bottom our own state of mind is very much like this whenever we uncritically abandon ourselves: You believe in objective evidence, and I do. Of some things we feel that we are certain: we know, and we know that we do know. There is something that gives a click inside of us, a bell that strikes twelve, when the hands of our mental clock have swept the dial and meet over the meridian hour. The greatest empiricists among us are only empiricists on reflection: when left to their instincts, they dogmatize like infallible popes. When the Cliffords tell us how sinful it is to be Christians on such "insufficient evidence," insufficiency is really the last thing they have in mind. For them the evidence is absolutely sufficient, only it makes the other way. They believe so completely in an anti-Christian order of the universe that there is no living option: Christianity is a dead hypothesis from the start.

vi

But now, since we are all such absolutists by instinct, what in our quality of students of philosophy ought we to do about the fact? Shall we espouse and indorse it? Or shall we treat it as a weakness of our nature from which we must free ourselves, if we can?

I sincerely believe that the latter course is the only one we can follow as reflective men. Objective evidence and certitude are doubtless very fine ideals to play with, but where on this moonlit and dream-visited planet are they found? I am, therefore, myself a complete empiricist so far as my theory of human knowledge goes. I live, to be sure, by the practical faith that we must go on experiencing and thinking over our experience, for only thus can our opinions grow more true; but to hold any one of them—I absolutely do not care which—as if it never could be reinterpretable or corrigible, I believe to be a tremendously mistaken attitude, and I think that the whole history of philosophy will bear me out. There is but one indefectibly certain truth, and that is the truth that pyrrhonistic scepticism itself leaves standing—the truth that the present phenomenon of consciousness exists. That, however, is the bare starting point of knowledge, the mere admission of a stuff to be philosophized about. The various philosophies are but so many attempts at expressing what this stuff really is. And if we repair to our libraries what disagreement do we discover! Where is a certainly true answer found? Apart from abstract propositions of comparison (such as two and two are the same as four), propositions which tell us nothing by themselves about concrete reality, we find no proposition ever regarded by any one as evidently certain that has not either been called a falsehood, or at least had its truth sincerely questioned by some one else. The transcending of the axioms of geometry, not in play but in earnest, by certain of our contemporaries (as Zöllner and Charles H. Hinton), and the rejection of the whole Aristotelian logic by the Hegelians, are striking instances in point.

No concrete test of what is really true has ever been agreed upon. Some make the criterion external to the moment of perception, putting it either in revelation, the *consensus gentium*, the instincts of the heart, or the systematized experience of the race. Others make the perceptive moment its own test—Descartes, for instance, with his clear and distinct ideas guaranteed by the veracity of God; Reid with his "common sense"; and Kant with his forms of synthetic judgment *a priori*. The inconceivability of the opposite; the capacity to be verified by sense; the possession of complete organic unity or self-relation, realized when a thing is its own other—are standards which, in turn, have been used. The much lauded objective evidence is never triumphantly there; it is a mere aspiration or *Grenzbegriff*, marking the infinitely remote ideal of our thinking life. To claim that certain truths now possess it, is simply to say that when you think them true and they *are* true, then their evidence is objective, otherwise it is not. But practically one's conviction that the evidence one goes by is of the real objective brand, is only one more subjective opinion added to the lot. For what a contradictory array of opinions have objective evidence and absolute certitude been claimed! The world is rational through and through—its existence is an ultimate brute fact; there is a personal God—a personal God is inconceivable; there is an extramental physical world immediately known—the mind can only know its own ideas; a moral imperative exists—obligation is only the resultant of desires; a permanent spiritual principle is in every one—there are only shifting states of mind; there is an endless chain of causes—there is an absolute first cause; an eternal necessity—a freedom; a purpose—no purpose; a primal One—a primal Many; a universal continuity—an essential discontinuity in things; an infinity—no infinity. There is this—there is that; there is indeed nothing which some one has not thought absolutely true, while his neighbor deemed it absolutely false; and not an absolutist among them seems ever to have considered that the trouble may all the time be essential and that the intellect, even with truth directly in its grasp, may have no infallible signal for knowing whether it be truth or no. When, indeed, one remembers that the most striking practical application to life of the doctrine of objective certitude has been the conscientious labors of the Holy Office of the Inquisition, one feels less tempted than ever to lend the doctrine a respectful ear.

But please observe, now, that when as empiricists we give up the doctrine of objective certitude, we do not thereby give up the quest or hope of truth itself. We still pin our faith on its existence, and still believe that we gain an ever better position toward it by systematically continuing to roll up experiences and think. Our great difference from the scholastic lies in the way we face. The strength of his system lies in the principles, the origin, the *terminus a quo* of his thought; for us the strength is in the outcome, the upshot, the *terminus ad quem*. Not where it comes from but what it leads to is to decide. It matters not to an empiricist from what quarter an hypothesis may come to him: he may have acquired it by fair means or by foul;

passion may have whispered or accident suggested it; but if the total drift of thinking continues to confirm it, that is what he means by its being true.

vii

One more point, small but important, and our preliminaries are done. There are two ways of looking at our duty in the matter of opinion—ways entirely different, and yet ways about whose difference the theory of knowledge seems hitherto to have shown very little concern. *We must know the truth;* and *we must avoid error*—these are our first and great commandments as would-be knowers; but they are not two ways of stating an identical commandment, they are two separable laws. Although it may indeed happen that when we believe the truth A, we escape as an incidental consequence from believing the falsehood B, it hardly ever happens that by merely disbelieving B we necessarily believe A. We may in escaping B fall into believing other falsehoods, C or D, just as bad as B; or we may escape B by not believing anything at all, not even A.

Believe truth! Shun error!—these, we see, are two materially different laws; and by choosing between them we may end by coloring differently our whole intellectual life. We may regard the chase for truth as paramount and the avoidance of error as secondary; or we may, on the other hand, treat the avoidance of error as more imperative, and let truth take its chance. Clifford, in the instructive passage which I have quoted, exhorts us to the latter course. Believe nothing, he tells us, keep your mind in suspense forever, rather than by closing it on insufficient evidence incur the awful risk of believing lies. You, on the other hand, may think that the risk of being in error is a very small matter when compared with the blessings of real knowledge, and be ready to be duped many times in your investigation rather than postpone indefinitely the chance of guessing true. I myself find it impossible to go with Clifford. We must remember that these feelings of our duty about either truth or error are in any case only expressions of our passional life. Biologically considered, our minds are as ready to grind out falsehood as veracity, and he who says, "Better go without belief forever than believe a lie!" merely shows his own preponderant private horror of becoming a dupe. He may be critical of many of his desires and fears, but this fear he slavishly obeys. He cannot imagine any one questioning its binding force. For my own part, I have also a horror of being duped; but I can believe that worse things than being duped may happen to a man in this world: so Clifford's exhortation has to my ears a thoroughly fantastic sound. It is like a general informing his soldiers that it is better to keep out of battle forever than to risk a single wound. Not so are victories either over enemies or over nature gained. Our errors are surely not such awfully solemn things. In a world where we are so certain to incur them in spite of all our caution, a certain lightness of heart seems healthier than this excessive nervousness on their behalf. At any rate, it seems the fittest thing for the empiricist philosopher.

viii

And now, after all this introduction, let us go straight at our question. I have said, and now repeat it, that not only as a matter of fact do we find our passional nature influencing us in our opinions, but that there are some options between opinions in which this influence must be regarded both as an inevitable and as a lawful determinant of our choice.

I fear here that some of you my hearers will begin to scent danger, and lend an inhospitable ear. Two first steps of passion you have indeed had to admit as necessary—we must think so as to avoid dupery, and we must think so as to gain truth; but the surest path to those ideal consummations, you will probably consider, is from now onwards to take no further passional step.

Well, of course, I agree as far as the facts will allow. Wherever the option between losing truth and gaining it is not momentous, we can throw the change of *gaining truth* away, and at any rate save ourselves from any chance of *believing falsehood,* by not making up our minds at all till objective evidence has come. In scientific questions, this is almost always the case; and even in human affairs in general, the need of acting is seldom so urgent that a false belief to act on is better than no belief at all. Law courts, indeed, have to decide on the best evidence attainable for the moment, because a judge's duty is to make law as well as to ascertain it, and (as a learned judge once said to me) few cases are worth spending much time over: the great thing is to have them decided on *any* acceptable principle, and got out of the way. But in our dealings with objective nature we obviously are recorders, not makers, of the truth; and decisions for the mere 'sake of deciding promptly and getting on to the next business would be wholly out of place. Throughout the breadth of physical nature facts are what they are quite independently of us, and seldom is there any such hurry about them that the risks of being duped by believing a premature theory need be faced. The questions here are always trivial options, the hypotheses are hardly living (at any rate not living for us spectators), the choice between believing truth or falsehood is seldom forced. The attitude of sceptical balance is therefore the absolutely wise one if we would escape mistakes. What difference, indeed, does it make to most of us whether we have or have not a theory of the roentgen rays, whether we believe or not in mind stuff, or have a conviction about the causality of conscious states? It makes no difference. Such options are not forced on us. On every account it is better not to make them, but still keep weighing reasons *pro et contra* with an indifferent hand.

I speak, of course, here of the purely judging mind. For purposes of discovery such indifference is to be less highly recommended, and science would be far less advanced than she is if the passionate desire of individuals to get their own faiths confirmed had been kept out of the game. See for example the sagacity which Spencer and Weismann now display. On the other hand, if you want an absolute duffer in an investigation, you must, after all, take the man who has no interest whatever in its results: he is the warranted incapable, the positive fool. The most useful investigator, because the most sensitive observer, is always he whose eager interest in one side of the question is balanced by an equally keen nervousness lest he become deceived.* Science has organized this nervousness into a regular *technique,* her so-called method of verification; and she has fallen so deeply in love with the method that one may even say she has ceased to care for truth by itself at all. It is only truth as technically verified that interests her. The truth of truths might come in merely affirmative form, and she would decline to touch it. Such truth as that, she might repeat with Clifford, would be stolen in defiance of her duty to mankind. Human passions, however, are stronger than technical rules. "Le cœur a ses raisons," as Pascal says, "que la raison ne connaît pas"; and however indifferent to all but the bare rules of the game the umpire, the abstract intellect, may be, the concrete players who furnish him the materials to judge of are usually, each one of them, in love with some pet "live hypothesis" of his own. Let us agree, however, that wherever there is no forced option, the dispassionately judicial intellect with no pet hypothesis, saving us, as it does, from dupery at any rate, ought to be our ideal.

The question next arises: Are there not somewhere forced options in our speculative questions, and can we (as men who may be interested at least as much in positively gaining truth as in merely escaping dupery) always wait with impunity till the coercive evidence shall have arrived? It seems *a priori* improbable that the truth should be so nicely adjusted to our needs and powers as that. In the great boarding house of nature, the cakes and the butter and the syrup seldom come out so even and leave the plates so clean. Indeed, we should view them with scientific suspicion if they did.

ix

Moral questions immediately present themselves as questions whose solution cannot wait for sensible proof. A moral question is a question not of what sensibly exists, but of what is good, or would be good if it did exist. Science can tell us what exists; but to compare the *worths,* both of what exists and of what does not exist, we must

---

* Compare Wilfrid Ward's Essay, "The Wish to Believe," in his *Witnesses to the Unseen* (Macmillan & Co., 1893).

consult not science, but what Pascal calls our heart. Science herself consults her heart when she lays it down that the infinite ascertainment of fact and correction of false belief are the supreme goods for man. Challenge the statement, and science can only repeat it oracularly, or else prove it by showing that such ascertainment and correction bring man all sorts of other goods which man's heart in turn declares. The question of having moral beliefs at all or not having them is decided by our will. Are our moral preferences true or false, or are they only odd biological phenomena, making things good or bad for *us*, but in themselves indifferent? How can your pure intellect decide? If your heart does not *want* a world of moral reality, your head will assuredly never make you believe in one. Mephistophelian scepticism, indeed, will satisfy the head's play instincts much better than any rigorous idealism can. Some men (even at the student age) are so naturally cool-hearted that the moralistic hypothesis never has for them any pungent life, and in their supercilious presence the hot young moralist always feels strangely ill at ease. The appearance of knowingness is on their side, of naïveté and gullibility on his. Yet, in the inarticulate heart of him, he clings to it that he is not a dupe, and that there is a realm in which (as Emerson says) all their wit and intellectual superiority is no better than the cunning of a fox. Moral scepticism can no more be refuted or proved by logic than intellectual scepticism can. When we stick to it that there *is* truth (be it of either kind), we do so with our whole nature, and resolve to stand or fall by the results. The sceptic with his whole nature adopts the doubting attitude; but which of us is the wiser, Omniscience only knows.

Turn now from these wide questions of good to a certain class of questions of fact, questions concerning personal relations, states of mind between one man and another. *Do you like me or not?*—for example. Whether you do or not depends, in countless instances, on whether I meet you halfway, am willing to assume that you must like me, and show you trust and expectation. The previous faith on my part in your liking's existence is in such cases what makes your liking come. But if I stand aloof, and refuse to budge an inch until I have objective evidence, until you shall have done something apt, as the absolutists say, *ad extorquendum assensum meum,* ten to one your liking never comes. How many women's hearts are vanquished by the mere sanguine insistence of some man that they *must* love him! he will not consent to the hypothesis that they cannot. The desire for a certain kind of truth here brings about that special truth's existence; and so it is in innumerable cases of other sorts. Who gains promotions, boons, appointments, but the man in whose life they are seen to play the part of life hypotheses, who discounts them, sacrifices other things for their sake before they have come, and takes risks for them in advance? His faith acts on the powers above him as a claim, and creates its own verification.

A social organism of any sort whatever, large or small, is what it is because each member proceeds to his own duty with a trust that the other members will simultaneously do theirs. Wherever a desired result is achieved by the cooperation of many independent persons, its existence as a fact is a pure consequence of the percursive faith in one another of those immediately concerned. A government, an army, a commercial system, a ship, a college, an athletic team, all exist on this condition, without which not only is nothing achieved, but nothing is even attempted. A whole train of passengers (individually brave enough) will be looted by a few highwaymen, simply because the latter can count on one another, while each passenger fears that if he makes a movement of resistance, he will be shot before any one else backs him up. If we believed that the whole car-full would rise at once with us, we should each severally rise, and train robbing would never even be attempted. There are, then, cases where a fact cannot come at all unless a preliminary faith exists in its coming. *And where faith in a fact can help create the fact,* that would be an insane logic which should say that faith running ahead of scientific evidence is the "lowest kind of immorality" into which a thinking being can fall. Yet such is the logic by which our scientific absolutists pretend to regulate our lives!

x

In truths dependent on our personal action, then, faith based on desire is certainly a lawful and possibly an indispensable thing.

But now, it will be said, these are all childish human cases, and have nothing to do with great cosmical matters, like the question of religious faith. Let us then pass on to that. Religions differ so much in their accidents that in discussing the religious question we must make it very generic and broad. What then do we now mean by the religious hypothesis? Science says things are; morality says some things are better than other things; and religion says essentially two things.

First, she says that the best things are the more eternal things, the overlapping things, the things in the universe that throw the last stone, so to speak, and say the final word. "Perfection is eternal"—this phrase of Charles Secrétan seems a good way of putting this first affirmation of religion, an affirmation which obviously cannot yet be verified scientifically at all.

The second affirmation of religion is that we are better off even now if we believe her first affirmation to be true.

Now, let us consider what the logical elements of this situation are *in case the religious hypothesis in both its branches be really true.* (Of course, we must admit that possibility at the outset. If we are to discuss the question at all, it must involve a living option. If for any of you religion be a hypothesis that cannot, by any living possibility be true, then you need go no farther. I speak to the "saving remnant" alone.) So proceeding, we see, first, that religion offers itself as a *momentous* option. We are supposed to gain even now, by our belief, and to lose by our nonbelief, a certain vital good. Secondly, religion is a *forced* option, so far as that good goes. We cannot escape the issue by remaining sceptical and waiting for more light, because, although we do avoid error in that way *if religion be untrue,* we lose the good, *if it be true,* just as certainly as if we positively chose to disbelieve. It is as if a man should hesitate indefinitely to ask a certain woman to marry him because he was not perfectly sure that she would prove an angel after he brought her home. Would he not cut himself off from that particular angel possibility as decisively as if he went and married someone else? Scepticism, then, is not avoidance of option; it is option of a certain particular kind of risk. *Better risk loss of truth than chance of error*—that is your faith vetoer's exact position. He is actively playing his stake as much as the believer is; he is backing the field against the religious hypothesis, just as the believer is backing the religious hypothesis against the field. To preach scepticism to us as a duty until "sufficient evidence" for religion be found, is tantamount therefore to telling us, when in presence of the religious hypothesis, that to yield to our fear of its being error is wiser and better than to yield to our hope that it may be true. It is not intellect against all passions, then; it is only intellect with one passion laying down its law. And by what, forsooth, is the supreme wisdom of this passion warranted? Dupery for dupery, what proof is there that dupery through hope is so much worse than dupery through fear? I, for one, can see no proof; and I simply refuse obedience to the scientist's command to imitate his kind of option, in a case where my own stake is important enough to give the right to choose my own form of risk. If religion be true and the evidence for it be still insufficient, I do not wish, by putting your extinguisher upon my nature (which feels to me as if it had after all some business in this matter), to forfeit my sole chance in life of getting upon the winning side—that chance depending, of course, on my willingness to run the risk of acting as if my passional need of taking the world religiously might be prophetic and right.

All this is on the supposition that it really may be prophetic and right, and that, even to us who are discussing the matter, religion is a live hypothesis which may be true. Now, to most of us religion comes in a still further way that makes a veto on our active faith even more illogical. The more perfect and more eternal aspect of the universe is represented in our religions as having personal form. The universe is no longer a mere *It* to us, but a *Thou*, if we are religious; and any relation that may be possible from person to person might be possible here. For instance, although in one sense we are passive portions of the universe, in another we show a curious autonomy, as if we were small active centers on our own account. We feel, too, as if the appeal of religion to us were made to our own active good will, as if evidence might be forever withheld from us unless we met the hypothesis halfway. To take a trivial illustration: just as a man who in a company of gentlemen made no advances, asked a warrant for every concession, and believed no one's word without proof, would cut himself off by such churlishness from all the social rewards that a more trusting spirit would earn —so here, one who should shut himself up in snarling logicality and try to make the gods extort his recognition willy-nilly, or not get it at all, might cut himself off forever from his only opportunity of making the gods' acquaintance. This feeling, forced on us we know not whence, that by obstinately believing that there are gods (although not to do so would be so easy both for our logic and our life) we are doing the universe the deepest service we can, seems part of the living essence of the religious hypothesis. If the hypothesis *were* true in all its parts, including this one, then pure intellectualism, with its veto on our making willing advances, would be an absurdity; and some participation of our sympathetic nature would be logically required. I, therefore, for one, cannot see my way to accepting the agnostic rules for truth seeking, or wilfully agree to keep my willing nature out of the game. I cannot do so for this plain reason, that *a rule of thinking which would absolutely prevent me from acknowledging certain kinds of truth if those kinds of truth were really there would be an irrational rule.* That for me is the long and short of the formal logic of the situation, no matter what the kinds of truth might materially be.

I confess I do not see how this logic can be escaped. But sad experience makes me fear that some of you may still shrink from radically saying with me, *in abstracto,* that we have the right to believe at our own risk any hypothesis that is live enough to tempt our will. I suspect, however, that if this is so, it is because you have got away from the abstract logical point of view altogether, and are thinking (perhaps without realizing it) of some particular religious hypothesis which for you is dead. The freedom to "believe what we will" you apply to the case of some patent superstition; and the faith you think of is the faith defined by the schoolboy when he said, "Faith is when you

believe something that you know ain't true." I can only repeat that this is misapprehension. *In concreto,* the freedom
to believe can only cover living options which the intellect
of the individual cannot by itself resolve; and living options never seem absurdities to him who has them to consider. When I look at the religious question as it really
puts itself to concrete men, and when I think of all the
possibilities which both practically and theoretically it involves, then this command that we shall put a stopper on
our heart, instincts, and courage, and *wait*—acting of
course meanwhile more or less as if religion were *not*
true*—till doomsday, or till such time as our intellect and
senses working together may have raked in evidence
enough—this command, I say, seems to me the queerest
idol ever manufactured in the philosophic cave. Were we
scholastic absolutists, there might be more excuse. If we
had an infallible intellect with its objective certitudes, we
might feel ourselves disloyal to such a perfect organ of
knowledge in not trusting to it exclusively, in not waiting
for its releasing word. But if we are empiricists, if we believe that no bell in us tolls to let us know for certain
when truth is in our grasp, then it seems a piece of idle
fantasticality to preach so solemnly our duty of waiting
for the bell. Indeed we *may* wait if we will—I hope you
do not think that I am denying that—but if we do so, we
do so at our peril as much as if we believed. In either case
we *act,* taking our life in our hands. No one of us ought to
issue vetoes to the other, nor should we bandy words of
abuse. We ought, on the contrary, delicately and profoundly to respect one another's mental freedom: then
only shall we bring about the intellectual republic; then
only shall we have that spirit of inner tolerance without
which all our outer tolerance is soulless, and which is em-

---

* Since belief is measured by action, he who forbids us to believe
religion to be true, necessarily also forbids us to act as we should if
we did believe it to be true. The whole defense of religious faith
hinges upon action. If the action required or inspired by the religious hypothesis is in no way different from that dictated by the
naturalistic hypothesis, then religious faith is a pure superfluity, better pruned away, and controversy about its legitimacy is a piece of
idle trifling, unworthy of serious minds. I myself believe, of course,
that the religious hypothesis gives to the world an expression which
specifically determines our reactions, and makes them in a large
part unlike what they might be on a purely naturalistic scheme of
belief.

piricism's glory; then only shall we live and let live, in speculative as well as in practical things.

I began by a reference to Fitz-James Stephen; let me end by a quotation from him.

> What do you think of yourself? What do you think of the world? . . . These are questions with which all must deal as it seems good to them. They are riddles of the Sphinx, and in some way or other we must deal with them. . . . In all important transactions of life we have to take a leap in the dark. . . . If we decide to leave the riddles unanswered, that is a choice; if we waver in our answer, that, too, is a choice: but whatever choice we make, we make it at our peril. If a man chooses to turn his back altogether on God and the future, no one can prevent him; no one can show beyond reasonable doubt that he is mistaken. If a man thinks otherwise and acts as he thinks, I do not see that any one can prove that *he* is mistaken. Each must act as he thinks best; and if he is wrong, so much the worse for him. We stand on a mountain pass in the midst of whirling snow and blinding mist, through which we get glimpses now and then of paths which may be deceptive. If we stand still we shall be frozen to death. If we take the wrong road we shall be dashed to pieces. We do not certainly know whether there is any right one. What must we do? "Be strong and of a good courage." Act for the best, hope for the best, and take what comes. . . . If death ends all, we cannot meet death better.*

* *Liberty, Equality, Fraternity*, 2nd ed. (London, 1874), p. 353.

IX. What Pragmatism Means*

Some years ago, being with a camping party in the mountains, I returned from a solitary ramble to find every one engaged in a ferocious metaphysical dispute. The *corpus* of the dispute was a squirrel—a live squirrel supposed to be clinging to one side of a tree trunk; while over against the tree's opposite side a human being was imagined to stand. This human witness tries to get sight of the squirrel by moving rapidly round the tree, but no matter how fast he goes, the squirrel moves as fast in the opposite direction, and always keeps the tree between himself and the man, so that never a glimpse of him is caught. The resultant metaphysical problem now is this: *Does the man go round the squirrel or not?* He goes round the tree, sure enough, and the squirrel is on the tree; but does he go round the squirrel? In the unlimited leisure of the wilderness, discussion had been worn threadbare. Every one had taken sides, and was obstinate; and the numbers on both sides were even. Each side, when I appeared therefore appealed to me to make it a majority. Mindful of the scholastic adage that whenever you meet a contradiction you must make a distinction, I immediately sought and found one, as follows: "Which party is right," I said, "depends on what you *practically mean* by 'going round' the squirrel. If you mean passing from the north of him to the east, then to the south, then to the west, and then to the north of him again, obviously the man does go round him, for he occupies these successive positions. But if on the contrary you mean being first in front of him, then on the right of him, then behind him, then on his left, and finally in front again, it is quite as obvious that the man fails to go round him, for by the compensating movements the squirrel makes, he keeps his belly turned towards the man

* Chapter II of *Pragmatism* (New York: 1907).

all the time, and his back turned away. Make the distinction, and there is no occasion for any farther dispute. You are both right and both wrong according as you conceive the verb 'to go round' in one practical fashion or the other."

Although one or two of the hotter disputants called my speech a shuffling evasion, saying they wanted no quibbling or scholastic hairsplitting, but meant just plain honest English "round," the majority seemed to think that the distinction had assuaged the dispute.

I tell this trivial anecdote because it is a peculiarly simple example of what I wish now to speak of as *the pragmatic method.* The pragmatic method is primarily a method of settling metaphysical disputes that otherwise might be interminable. Is the world one or many?—fated or free?—material or spiritual?—here are notions either of which may or may not hold good of the world; and disputes over such notions are unending. The pragmatic method in such cases is to try to interpret each notion by tracing its respective practical consequences. What difference would it practically make to any one if this notion rather than that notion were true? If no practical difference whatever can be traced, then the alternatives mean practically the same thing, and all dispute is idle. Whenever a dispute is serious, we ought to be able to show some practical difference that must follow from one side or the other's being right.

A glance at the history of the idea will show you still better what pragmatism means. The term is derived from the same Greek word πράγμα, meaning action, from which our words "practice" and "practical" come. It was first introduced into philosophy by Mr. Charles Peirce in 1878. In an article entitled "How to Make Our Ideas Clear," in the *Popular Science Monthly* for January of that year * Mr. Peirce, after pointing out that our beliefs are really rules for action, said that, to develop a thought's meaning, we need only determine what conduct it is fitted to produce: that conduct is for us its sole significance. And the tangible fact at the root of all our thought distinctions, however subtle, is that there is no one of them so fine as to consist in anything but a possible difference of

---

* Translated in the *Revue Philosophique* for January, 1879 (vol. vii). [See Section IV, p. 78, above.]

practice. To attain perfect clearness in our thoughts of an object, then, we need only consider what conceivable effects of a practical kind the object may involve—what sensations we are to expect from it, and what reactions we must prepare. Our conception of these effects, whether immediate or remote, is then for us the whole of our conception of the object, so far as that conception has positive significance at all.

This is the principle of Peirce, the principle of pragmatism. It lay entirely unnoticed by any one for twenty years, until I, in an address before Professor Howison's philosophical union at the university of California, brought it forward again and made a special application of it to religion. By that date (1898) the times seemed ripe for its reception. The word "pragmatism" spread, and at present it fairly spots the pages of the philosophic journals. On all hands we find the "pragmatic movement" spoken of, sometimes with respect, sometimes with contumely, seldom with clear understanding. It is evident that the term applies itself conveniently to a number of tendencies that hitherto have lacked a collective name, and that it has "come to stay."

To take in the importance of Peirce's principle, one must get accustomed to applying it to concrete cases. I found a few years ago that Ostwald, the illustrious Leipzig chemist, had been making perfectly distinct use of the principle of pragmatism in his lectures on the philosophy of science, though he had not called it by that name.

"All realities influence our practice," he wrote me, "and that influence is their meaning for us. I am accustomed to put questions to my classes in this way: In what respects would the world be different if this alternative or that were true? If I can find nothing that would become different, then the alternative has no sense."

That is, the rival views mean practically the same thing, and meaning, other than practical, there is for us none. Ostwald in a published lecture gives this example of what he means. Chemists have long wrangled over the inner constitution of certain bodies called "tautomerous." Their properties seemed equally consistent with the notion that an instable hydrogen atom oscillates inside of them, or that they are instable mixtures of two bodies. Controversy raged, but never was decided. "It would never have begun," says Ostwald, "if the combatants had asked themselves what particular experimental fact could have been made different by one or the other view being correct. For it would then have appeared that no difference of fact could possibly ensue; and the quarrel was as unreal as if, theorizing in primitive times about the raising of dough by yeast, one party should have invoked a 'brownie,' while another insisted on an 'elf' as the true cause of the phenomenon." *

It is astonishing to see how many philosophical disputes collapse into insignificance the moment you subject them to this simple test of tracing a concrete consequence. There can *be* no difference anywhere that doesn't *make* a difference elsewhere—no difference in abstract truth that doesn't express itself in a difference in concrete fact and in conduct consequent upon that fact, imposed on somebody, somehow, somewhere, and somewhen. The whole function of philosophy ought to be to find out what definite difference it will make to you and me, at definite instants of our life, if this world formula or that world formula be the true one.

There is absolutely nothing new in the pragmatic method. Socrates was an adept at it. Aristotle used it methodically. Locke, Berkeley, and Hume made momentous contributions to truth by its means. Shadworth Hodgson keeps insisting that realities are only what they are "known as." But these forerunners of pragmatism used it in fragments: they were preluders only. Not until in our time has it generalized itself, become conscious of a universal mission, pretended to a conquering destiny. I believe in that destiny, and I hope I may end by inspiring you with my belief.

Pragmatism represents a perfectly familiar attitude in philosophy, the empiricist attitude, but it represents it, as it seems to me, both in a more radical and in a less objectionable form than it has ever yet assumed. A pragmatist turns his back resolutely and once for all upon a lot of

---

* "Theorie und Praxis," *Zeitsch. des Oesterreichischen Ingenieur u. Architecten-Vereines* (1905), Nr. 4 u. 6. I find a still more radical pragmatism than Ostwald's in an address by Professor W. S. Franklin: "I think that the sickliest notion of physics, even if a student gets it, is that it is 'the science of masses, molecules, and the ether.' And I think that the healthiest notion, even if a student does not wholly get it, is that physics is the science of the ways of taking hold of bodies and pushing them!" from *Science* vol. (January 2, 1903).

inveterate habits dear to professional philosophers. He turns away from abstraction and insufficiency, from verbal solutions, from bad *a priori* reasons, from fixed principles, closed systems, and pretended absolutes and origins. He turns towards concreteness and adequacy, towards facts, towards action and towards power. That means the empiricist temper regnant and the rationalist temper sincerely given up. It means the open air and possibilities of nature, as against dogma, artificiality, and the pretense of finality in truth.

At the same time it does not stand for any special results. It is a method only. But the general triumph of that method would mean an enormous change in what I called in my last lecture the "temperament" of philosophy. Teachers of the ultrarationalistic type would be frozen out, much as the courtier type is frozen out in republics, as the ultramontane type of priest is frozen out in protestant lands. Science and metaphysics would come much nearer together, would in fact work absolutely hand in hand.

Metaphysics has usually followed a very primitive kind of quest. You know how men have always hankered after unlawful magic, and you know what a great part in magic *words* have always played. If you have his name, or the formula of incantation that binds him, you can control the spirit, genie, afrite, or whatever the power may be. Solomon knew the names of all the spirits, and having their names, he held them subject to his will. So the universe has always appeared to the natural mind as a kind of enigma, of which the key must be sought in the shape of some illuminating or power-bringing word or name. That word names the universe's *principle,* and to possess it is after a fashion to possess the universe itself. "God," "Matter," "Reason," "the Absolute," "Energy," are so many solving names. You can rest when you have them. You are at the end of your metaphysical quest.

But if you follow the pragmatic method, you cannot look on any such word as closing your quest. You must bring out of each word its practical cash value, set it at work within the stream of your experience. It appears less as a solution, then, than as a program for more work, and more particularly as an indication of the ways in which existing realities may be *changed.*

Theories thus become instruments, not answers to enigmas, in which we can rest. We don't lie back upon them, we move forward, and, on occasion, make nature over again by their aid. Pragmatism unstiffens all our theories, limbers them up and sets each one at work. Being nothing essentially new, it harmonizes with many ancient philosophic tendencies. It agrees with nominalism for instance, in always appealing to particulars; with utilitarianism in emphasizing practical aspects; with positivism in its disdain for verbal solutions, useless questions and metaphysical abstractions.

All these, you see, are *anti-intellectualist* tendencies. Against rationalism as a pretension and a method pragmatism is fully armed and militant. But, at the outset, at least, it stands for no particular results. It has no dogmas, and no doctrines save its method. As the young Italian pragmatist Papini has well said, it lies in the midst of our theories, like a corridor in a hotel. Innumerable chambers open out of it. In one you may find a man writing an atheistic volume; in the next some one on his knees praying for faith and strength; in a third a chemist investigating a body's properties. In a fourth a system of idealistic metaphysics is being excogitated; in a fifth the impossibility of metaphysics is being shown. But they all own the corridor, and all must pass through it if they want a practicable way of getting into or out of their respective rooms.

No particular results then, so far, but only an attitude of orientation, is what the pragmatic method means. *The attitude of looking away from first things, principles, "categories," supposed necessities; and of looking towards last things, fruits, consequences, facts.*

So much for the pragmatic method! You may say that I have been praising it rather than explaining it to you, but I shall presently explain it abundantly enough by showing how it works on some familiar problems. Meanwhile the word pragmatism has come to be used in a still wider sense, as meaning also a certain *theory of truth*. I mean to give a whole lecture to the statement of that theory, after first paving the way, so I can be very brief now. But brevity is hard to follow, so I ask for your redoubled attention for a quarter of an hour. If much remains obscure, I hope to make it clearer in the later lectures.

One of the most successfully cultivated branches of philosophy in our time is what is called inductive logic, the study of the conditions under which our sciences have evolved. Writers on this subject have begun to show a singular unanimity as to what the laws of nature and elements of fact mean, when formulated by mathematicians, physicists and chemists. When the first mathematical, logical, and natural uniformities, the first laws, were discovered, men were so carried away by the clearness, beauty and simplification that resulted, that they believed themselves to have deciphered authentically the eternal thoughts of the Almighty. His mind also thundered and reverberated in syllogisms. He also thought in conic sections, squares and roots and ratios, and geometrized like Euclid. He made Kepler's laws for the planets to follow; he made velocity increase proportionally to the time in falling bodies; he made the law of the sines for light to obey when refracted; he established the classes, orders, families and genera of plants and animals, and fixed the distances between them. He thought the archetypes of all things, and devised their variations; and when we rediscover any one of these his wondrous institutions, we seize his mind in its very literal intention.

But as the sciences have developed farther, the notion has gained ground that most, perhaps all, of our laws are only approximations. The laws themselves, moreover, have grown so numerous that there is no counting them; and so many rival formulations are proposed in all the branches of science that investigators have become accustomed to the notion that no theory is absolutely a transcript of reality, but that any one of them may from some point of view be useful. Their great use is to summarize old facts and to lead to new ones. They are only a man-made language, a conceptual shorthand, as some one calls them, in which we write our reports of nature; and languages, as is well known, tolerate much choice of expression and many dialects.

Thus human arbitrariness has driven divine necessity from scientific logic. If I mention the names of Sigwart, Mach, Ostwald, Pearson, Milhaud, Poincaré, Duhem, Ruyssen, those of you who are students will easily identify the tendency I speak of, and will think of additional names.

Riding now on the front of this wave of scientific logic Messrs. Schiller and Dewey appear with their pragmatistic account of what truth everywhere signifies. Everywhere, these teachers say, "truth" in our ideas and beliefs means the same thing that it means in science. It means, they say, nothing but this, *that ideas (which themselves are but parts of our experience) become true just in so far as they help us to get into satisfactory relation with other parts of our experience,* to summarize them and get about among them by conceptual shortcuts instead of following the interminable succession of particular phenomena. Any idea upon which we can ride, so to speak; any idea that will carry us prosperously from any one part of our experience to any other part, linking things satisfactorily, working securely, simplifying, saving labor; is true for just so much, true in so far forth, true *instrumentally.* This is the "instrumental" view of truth taught so successfully at Chicago, the view that truth in our ideas means their power to "work," promulgated so brilliantly at Oxford.

Messrs. Dewey, Schiller and their allies, in reaching this general conception of all truth, have only followed the example of geologists, biologists and philologists. In the establishment of these other sciences, the successful stroke was always to take some simple process actually observable in operation—as denudation by weather, say, or variation from parental type, or change of dialect by incorporation of new words and pronunciations—and then to generalize it, making it apply at all times, and produce great results by summating its effects through the ages.

The observable process which Schiller and Dewey particularly singled out for generalization is the familiar one by which any individual settles into *new opinions.* The process here is always the same. The individual has a stock of old opinions already, but he meets a new experience that puts them to a strain. Somebody contradicts them; or in a reflective moment he discovers that they contradict each other; or he hears of facts with which they are incompatible; or desires arise in him which they cease to satisfy. The result is an inward trouble to which his mind till then had been a stranger, and from which he seeks to escape by modifying his previous mass of opinions. He saves as much of it as he can, for in this matter of belief we are all extreme conservatives. So he tries to change first this opinion, and then that (for they resist change very variously), until at last some new idea comes up which he can graft upon the ancient stock with a minimum of disturbance of the latter, some idea that mediates between the stock and the new experience and runs them into one another most felicitously and expediently.

This new idea is then adopted as the true one. It preserves the older stock of truths with a minimum of modification, stretching them just enough to make them admit the novelty, but conceiving that in ways as familiar as the case leaves possible. An *outrée* explanation, violating all our preconceptions, would never pass for a true account of a novelty. We should scratch round industriously till we found something less excentric. The most violent revolutions in an individual's beliefs leave most of his old order standing. Time and space, cause and effect, nature and history, and one's own biography remain untouched. New truth is always a go-between, a smoother-over of transitions. It marries old opinion to new fact so as ever to show a minimum of jolt, a maximum of continuity. We hold a theory true just in proportion to its success in solving this "problem of maxima and minima." But success in solving this problem is eminently a matter of approximation. We say this theory solves it on the whole more satisfactorily than that theory; but that means more satisfactorily to ourselves, and individuals will emphasize their points of satisfaction differently. To a certain degree, therefore, everything here is plastic.

The point I now urge you to observe particularly is the part played by the older truths. Failure to take account of it is the source of much of the unjust criticism leveled against pragmatism. Their influence is absolutely controlling. Loyalty to them is the first principle—in most cases it is the only principle; for by far the most usual way of handling phenomena so novel that they would make for a serious rearrangement of our preconception is to ignore them altogether, or to abuse those who bear witness for them.

You doubtless wish examples of this process of truth's growth, and the only trouble is their superabundance. The simplest case of new truth is of course the mere numerical addition of new kinds of facts, or of new single facts of old kinds, to our experience—an addition that involves no alteration in the old beliefs. Day follows day, and its contents are simply added. The new contents themselves are not true, they simply *come* and *are*. Truth is *what we say about* them, and when we say that they have come, truth is satisfied by the plain additive formula.

But often the day's contents oblige a rearrangement. If I should now utter piercing shrieks and act like a maniac on this platform, it would make many of you revise your ideas as to the probable worth of my philosophy. "Radium" came the other day as part of the day's content, and seemed for a moment to contradict our ideas of the whole order of nature, that order having come to be identified with what is called the conservation of energy. The mere sight of radium paying heat away indefinitely out of its own pocket seemed to violate that conservation. What to think? If the radiations from it were nothing but an escape of unsuspected "potential" energy, preexistent inside of the atoms, the principle of conservation would be saved. The discovery of "helium" as the radiation's outcome, opened a way to this belief. So Ramsay's view is generally held to be true, because, although it extends our old ideas of energy, it causes a minimum of alteration in their nature.

I need not multiply instances. A new opinion counts as "true" just in proportion as it gratifies the individual's desire to assimilate the novel in his experience to his beliefs in stock. It must both lean on old truth and grasp new fact; and its success (as I said a moment ago) in doing this, is a matter for the individual's appreciation. When old truth grows, then, by new truth's addition, it is for subjective reasons. We are in the process and obey the reasons. That new idea is truest which performs most felicitously its function of satisfying our double urgency. It makes itself true, gets itself classed as true, by the way it works; grafting itself then upon the ancient body of truth, which thus grows much as a tree grows by the activity of a new layer of cambium.

Now Dewey and Schiller proceed to generalize this observation and to apply it to the most ancient parts of truth. They also once were plastic. They also were called true for human reasons. They also mediated between still earlier truths and what in those days were novel observations. Purely objective truth, truth in whose establishment the function of giving human satisfaction in marrying previous parts of experience with newer parts played no role whatever, is nowhere to be found. The reason why we call things true is the reason why they *are* true, for "to be true" *means* only to perform this marriage function.

The trail of the human serpent is thus over everything. Truth independent; truth that we *find* merely; truth no longer malleable to human need; truth incorrigible, in a word; such truth exists indeed superabundantly—or is supposed to exist by rationalistically minded thinkers; but then it means only the dead heart of the living tree, and its being there means only that truth also has its paleontology, and its "prescription," and may grow stiff with years of veteran service and petrified in men's regard by sheer antiquity. But how plastic even the oldest truths nevertheless really are has been vividly shown in our day by the transformation of logical and mathematical ideas, a transformation which seems even to be invading physics. The ancient formulas are reinterpreted as special expressions of much wider principles, principles that our ancestors never got a glimpse of in their present shape and formulation.

Mr. Schiller still gives to all this view of truth the name of "Humanism," but, for this doctrine too, the name of pragmatism seems fairly to be in the ascendant, so I will treat it under the name of pragmatism in these lectures.

Such then would be the scope of pragmatism—first, a method; and second, a genetic theory of what is meant by truth. And these two things must be our future topics.

What I have said of the theory of truth will, I am sure, have appeared obscure and unsatisfactory to most of you by reason of its brevity. I shall make amends for that hereafter. In a lecture on "common sense" I shall try to show what I mean by truths grown petrified by antiquity. In another lecture I shall expatiate on the idea that our thoughts become true in proportion as they successfully exert their go-between function. In a third I shall show how hard it is to discriminate subjective from objective factors in Truth's development. You may not follow me wholly in these lectures; and if you do, you may not wholly agree with me. But you will, I know, regard me at least as serious, and treat my effort with respectful consideration.

You will probably be surprised to learn, then, that Messrs. Schiller's and Dewey's theories have suffered a hailstorm of contempt and ridicule. All rationalism has risen against them. In influential quarters Mr. Schiller, in particular, has been treated like an impudent schoolboy who deserves a spanking. I should not mention this, but for the fact that it throws so much sidelight upon that rationalistic temper to which I have opposed the temper of pragmatism. Pragmatism is uncomfortable away from facts. Rationalism is comfortable only in the presence of abstractions. This pragmatist talk about truths in the plural, about their utility and satisfactoriness, about the success with which they "work," etc., suggests to the typical intellectualist mind a sort of coarse lame second-rate makeshift article of truth. Such truths are not real truth. Such tests are merely subjective. As against this, objective truth must be something nonutilitarian, haughty, refined, remote, august, exalted. It must be an absolute correspondence of our thoughts with an equally absolute reality. It must be what we *ought* to think unconditionally. The conditioned ways in which we *do* think are so much irrelevance and matter for psychology. Down with psychology, up with logic, in all this question!

See the exquisite contrast of the types of mind! The pragmatist clings to facts and concreteness, observes truth at its work in particular cases, and generalizes. Truth, for him, becomes a class name for all sorts of definite working values in experience. For the rationalist it remains a pure abstraction, to the bare name of which we must defer. When the pragmatist undertakes to show in detail just *why* we must defer, the rationalist is unable to recognize the concretes from which his own abstraction is taken. He accuses us of *denying* truth; whereas we have only sought to trace exactly why people follow it and always ought to follow it. Your typical ultra-abstractionist fairly shudders at concreteness: other things equal, he positively prefers the pale and spectral. If the two universes were offered, he would always choose the skinny outline rather than the rich thicket of reality. It is so much purer, clearer, nobler.

I hope that as these lectures go on, the concreteness and closeness to facts of the pragmatism which they advocate may be what approves itself to you as its most satisfactory peculiarity. It only follows here the example of the sister sciences, interpreting the unobserved by the observed. It brings old and new harmoniously together. It converts the absolutely empty notion of a static relation of "correspondence" (what that may mean we must ask later) between our minds and reality, into that of a rich and active commerce (that any one may follow in detail and understand) between particular thoughts of ours, and the great universe of other experiences in which they play their parts and have their uses.

But enough of this at present? The justification of what I say must be postponed. I wish now to add a word in further explanation of the claim I made at our last meeting, that pragmatism may be a happy harmonizer of empiricist ways of thinking with the more religious demands of human beings.

Men who are strongly of the fact-loving temperament, you may remember me to have said, are liable to be kept at a distance by the small sympathy with facts which that philosophy from the present-day fashion of idealism offers them. It is far too intellectualistic. Old-fashioned theism was bad enough, with its notion of God as an exalted monarch, made up of a lot of unintelligible or preposterous "attributes"; but, so long as it held strongly by the argument from design, it kept some touch with concrete realities. Since, however, darwinism has once for all displaced design from the minds of the "scientific," theism has lost that foothold; and some kind of an immanent or pantheistic deity working *in* things rather than above them is, if any, the kind recommended to our contemporary imagination. Aspirants to a philosophic religion turn, as a rule, more hopefully nowadays toward idealistic pantheism than toward the older dualistic theism, in spite of the fact that the latter still counts able defenders.

But, as I said in my first lecture, the brand of pantheism offered is hard for them to assimilate if they are lovers of fact, or empirically minded. It is the absolutistic brand, spurning the dust and reared upon pure logic. It keeps no connection whatever with concreteness. Affirming the Absolute Mind, which is its substitute for God, to be the rational presupposition of all particulars of fact, whatever they may be, it remains supremely indifferent to what the particular facts in our world actually are. Be they what they may, the Absolute will father them. Like the sick lion in Aesop's fable, all footprints lead into his den, but *nulla vestigia retrorsum*. You cannot redescend into the world of particulars by the Absolute's aid, or deduce any necessary consequences of detail important for your life from your idea of his nature. He gives you indeed the assurance that all is well with *Him*, and for his eternal way of thinking; but thereupon he leaves you to be finitely saved by your own temporal devices.

Far be it from me to deny the majesty of this conception, or its capacity to yield religious comfort to a most respectable class of minds. But from the human point of view, no one can pretend that it doesn't suffer from the faults of remoteness and abstractness. It is eminently a product of what I have ventured to call the rationalistic temper. It disdains empiricism's needs. It substitutes a pallid outline for the real world's richness. It is dapper, it is noble in the bad sense, in the sense in which to be noble is to be inapt for humble service. In this real world of sweat and dirt, it seems to me that when a view of things is "noble," that ought to count as a presumption against its truth, and as a philosophic disqualification. The prince of darkness may be a gentleman, as we are told he is, but whatever the God of earth and heaven is, he can surely be no gentleman. His menial services are needed in the dust of our human trials, even more than his dignity is needed in the empyrean.

Now pragmatism, devoted though she be to facts, has no such materialistic bias as ordinary empiricism labors under. Moreover, she has no objection whatever to the realizing of abstractions, so long as you get about among particulars with their aid and they actually carry you somewhere. Interested in no conclusions but those which our minds and our experiences work out together, she has no *a priori* prejudices against theology. *If theological ideas prove to have a value for concrete life, they will be true, for pragmatism, in the sense of being good for so much. For how much more they are true, will depend entirely on their relations to the other truths that also have to be acknowledged.*

What I said just now about the Absolute, of transcendental idealism, is a case in point. First, I called it majestic and said it yielded religious comfort to a class of minds, and then I accused it of remoteness and sterility. But so far as it affords such comfort, it surely is not sterile; it has that amount of value; it performs a concrete function. As a good pragmatist, I myself ought to call the Absolute true "in so far forth," then; and I unhesitatingly now do so.

But what does *true in so far forth* mean in this case? To answer, we need only apply the pragmatic method. What do believers in the Absolute mean by saying that their belief affords them comfort? They mean that since, in the Absolute finite evil is "overruled" already, we may, therefore, whenever we wish, treat the temporal as if it were potentially the eternal, be sure that we can trust its outcome, and, without sin, dismiss our fear and drop the worry of our finite responsibility. In short, they mean that we have a right ever and anon to take a moral holiday, to let the world wag in its own way, feeling that its issues are in better hands than ours and are none of our business.

The universe is a system of which the individual members may relax in their anxieties occasionally, in which the don't-care mood is also right for men, and moral holidays in order—that, if I mistake not, is part, at least, of what the Absolute is "known-as," that is the great difference in our particular experiences which his being true makes, for us, that is his cash-value when he is pragmatically interpreted. Farther than that the ordinary lay reader in philosophy who thinks favorably of absolute idealism does not venture to sharpen his conceptions. He can use the Absolute for so much, and so much is very previous. He is pained at hearing you speak incredulously of the Absolute, therefore, and disregards your criticisms because they deal with aspects of the conception that he fails to follow.

If the Absolute means this, and means no more than this, who can possibly deny the truth of it? To deny it would be to insist that men should never relax, and that holidays are never in order.

I am well aware how odd it must seem to some of you to hear me say that an idea is "true" so long as to believe it is profitable to our lives. That it is *good*, for as much as it profits, you will gladly admit. If what we do by its aid is good, you will allow the idea itself to be good in so far forth, for we are the better for possessing it. But is it not a strange misuse of the word "truth," you will say, to call ideas also "true" for this reason?

To answer this difficulty fully is impossible at this stage of my account. You touch here upon the very central point of Messrs. Schiller's, Dewey's and my own doctrine of truth, which I can not discuss with detail until my sixth lecture. Let me now say only this, that truth is *one species of good*, and not, as is usually supposed, a category distinct from good, and coordinate with it. *The true is the name of whatever proves itself to be good in the way of belief, and good, too, for definite, assignable reasons.* Surely you must admit this, that if there were *no* good for life in true ideas, or if the knowledge of them were positively disadvantageous and false ideas the only useful ones, then the current notion that truth is divine and precious, and its pursuit a duty, could never have grown up or become a dogma. In a world like that, our duty would be to *shun* truth, rather. But in this world, just as certain foods are not only agreeable to our taste, but good for our teeth, our stomach, and our tissues; so certain ideas are not only agreeable to think about, or agreeable as supporting other ideas that we are fond of, but they are also helpful in life's practical struggles. If there be any life that it is really better we should lead, and if there be any idea which, if believed in, would help us to lead that life, then it should be really *better for us* to believe in that idea, *unless, indeed, belief in it incidentally clashed with other greater vital benefits.*

"What would be better for us to believe!" This sounds very like a definition of truth. It comes very near to saying "what we *ought* to believe": and in *that* definition none of you would find any oddity. Ought we ever not to believe what it is *better for us* to believe? And can we then keep the notion of what is better for us, and what is true for us, permanently apart?

Pragmatism says no, and I fully agree with her. Probably you also agree, so far as the abstract statement goes, but with a suspicion that if we practically did believe everything that made for good in our own personal lives, we should be found indulging all kinds of fancies about this world's affairs, and all kinds of sentimental superstitions about a world hereafter. Your suspicion here is undoubtedly well founded, and it is evident that something happens when you pass from the abstract to the concrete that complicates the situation.

I said just now that what is better for us to believe is true *unless the belief incidentally clashes with some other vital benefit.* Now in real life what vital benefits is any particular belief of ours most liable to clash with? What indeed except the vital benefits yielded by *other beliefs* when these prove incompatible with the first ones? In other words, the greatest enemy of any one of our truths may be the rest of our truths. Truths have once for all this desperate instinct of self-preservation and of desire to extinguish whatever contradicts them. My belief in the Absolute, based on the good it does me, must run the gauntlet of all my other beliefs. Grant that it may be true in giving me a moral holiday. Nevertheless, as I conceive it—and let me speak now confidentially, as it were, and merely in my own private person,—it clashes with other truths of mine whose benefits I hate to give up on its account. It happens to be associated with a kind of logic of which I am the enemy, I find that it entangles me in metaphysical paradoxes that are inacceptable, etc., etc. But as I have enough trouble in life already without adding the trouble of carrying these intellectual inconsistencies, I personally just give up the Absolute. I just *take* my moral holidays; or else as a professional philosopher, I try to justify them by some other principle.

If I could restrict my notion of the Absolute to its bare holiday-giving value, it wouldn't clash with my other truths. But we can not easily thus restrict our hypotheses. They carry supernumerary features, and these it is that clash so. My disbelief in the Absolute means then disbelief in those other supernumerary features, for I fully believe in the legitimacy of taking moral holidays.

You see by this what I meant when I called pragmatism a mediator and reconciler and said, borrowing the word from Papini, that she "unstiffens" our theories. She has in fact no prejudices whatever, no obstructive dogmas, no rigid canons of what shall count as proof. She is completely genial. She will entertain any hypothesis, she will consider any evidence. It follows that in the religious field she is at a great advantage both over positivistic empiricism, with its antitheological bias, and over religious rationalism, with its exclusive interest in the remote, the noble, the simple, and the abstract, in the way of conception.

In short, she widens the field of search for God. Rationalism sticks to logic and the empyrean. Empiricism sticks to the external senses. Pragmatism is willing to take anything, to follow either logic or the senses and to count the humblest and most personal experiences. She will count mystical experiences if they have practical consequences. She will take a God who lives in the very dirt of private fact—if that should seem a likely place to find him.

Her only test of probable truth is what works best in the way of leading us, what fits every part of life best and combines with the collectivity of experience's demands, nothing being omitted. If theological ideas should do this, if the notion of God, in particular, should prove to do it, how could pragmatism possibly deny God's existence? She could see no meaning in treating as "not true" a notion that was pragmatically so successful. What other kind of truth could there be, for her, than all this agreement with concrete reality?

In my last lecture I shall return again to the relations of pragmatism with religion. But you see already how democratic she is. Her manners are as various and flexible, her resources as rich and endless, and her conclusions as friendly as those of mother nature.

X. Pragmatism's Conception of Truth*

When Clerk-Maxwell was a child it is written that he had a mania for having everything explained to him, and that when people put him off with vague verbal accounts of any phenomenon he would interrupt them impatiently by saying, "Yes; but I want you to tell me the *particular go* of it!" Had his question been about truth, only a pragmatist could have told him the particular go of it. I believe that our contemporary pragmatists, especially Messrs. Schiller and Dewey, have given the only tenable account of this subject. It is a very ticklish subject, sending subtle rootlets into all kinds of crannies, and hard to treat in the sketchy way that alone befits a public lecture. But the Schiller–Dewey view of truth has been so ferociously attacked by rationalistic philosophers, and so abominably misunderstood, that here, if anywhere, is the point where a clear and simple statement should be made.

I fully expect to see the pragmatist view of truth run through the classic stages of a theory's career. First, you know, a new theory is attacked as absurd; then it is admitted to be true, but obvious and insignificant; finally it is seen to be so important that its adversaries claim that they themselves discovered it. Our doctrine of truth is at present in the first of these three stages, with symptoms of the second stage having begun in certain quarters. I wish that this lecture might help it beyond the first stage in the eyes of many of you.

Truth, as any dictionary will tell you, is a property of certain of our ideas. It means their "agreement," as falsity means their disagreement, with "reality." Pragmatists and intellectualists both accept this definition as a matter of

* Chapter VI of *Pragmatism* (New York: 1907).

course. They begin to quarrel only after the question is raised as to what may precisely be meant by the term "agreement," and what by the term "reality," when reality is taken as something for our ideas to agree with.

In answering these questions the pragmatists are more analytic and painstaking, the intellectualists more offhand and irreflective. The popular notion is that a true idea must copy its reality. Like other popular views, this one follows the analogy of the most usual experience. Our true ideas of sensible things do indeed copy them. Shut your eyes and think of yonder clock on the wall, and you get just such a true picture or copy of its dial. But your idea of its "works" (unless you are a clockmaker) is much less of a copy, yet it passes muster, for it in no way clashes with the reality. Even though it should shrink to the mere word "works," that word still serves you truly; and when you speak of the "timekeeping function" of the clock, or of its spring's "elasticity," it is hard to see exactly what your ideas can copy.

You perceive that there is a problem here. Where our ideas cannot copy definitely their object, what does agreement with that object mean? Some idealists seem to say that they are true whenever they are what God means that we ought to think about that object. Others hold the copy view all through, and speak as if our ideas possessed truth just in proportion as they approach to being copies of the Absolute's eternal way of thinking.

These views, you see, invite pragmatistic discussion. But the great assumption of the intellectualists is that truth means essentially an inert static relation. When you've got your rule idea of anything, there's an end of the matter. You're in possession; you *know;* you have fulfilled your thinking destiny. You are where you ought to be mentally; you have obeyed your categorical imperative; and nothing more need follow on that climax of your rational destiny. Epistemologically you are in stable equilibrium.

Pragmatism, on the other hand, asks its usual question. "Grant an idea or belief to be true," it says, "what concrete difference will its being true make in any one's actual life? How will the truth be realized? What experiences will be different from those which would obtain if the belief were false? What, in short, is the truth's cash value in experiential terms?"

The moment pragmatism asks this question, it sees the

answer: *True ideas are those that we can assimilate, validate, corroborate and verify. False ideas are those that we can not.* That is the practical difference it makes to us to have true ideas; that, therefore, is the meaning of truth, for it is all that truth is known-as.

This thesis is what I have to defend. The truth of an idea is not a stagnant property inherent in it. Truth *happens* to an idea. It *becomes* true, is *made* true by events. Its verity *is* in fact an event, a process: the process namely of its verifying itself, its veri-*fication*. Its validity is the process of its valid-*ation*.

But what do the words verification and validation themselves pragmatically mean? They again signify certain practical consequences of the verified and validated idea. It is hard to find any one phrase that characterizes these consequences better than the ordinary agreement formula —just such consequences being what we have in mind whenever we say that our ideas "agree" with reality. They lead us, namely, through the acts and other ideas which they instigate, into or up to, or toward, other parts of experience with which we feel all the while—such feeling being among our potentialities—that the original ideas remain in agreement. The connections and transitions come to us from point to point as being progressive, harmonious, satisfactory. This function of agreeable leading is what we mean by an idea's verification. Such an account is vague and it sounds at first quite trivial, but it has results which it will take the rest of my hour to explain.

Let me begin by reminding you of the fact that the possession of true thoughts means everywhere the possession of invaluable instruments of action; and that our duty to gain truth, so far from being a blank command from out of the blue, or a "stunt" self-imposed by our intellect, can account for itself by excellent practical reasons.

The importance to human life of having true beliefs about matters of fact is a thing too notorious. We live in a world of realities that can be infinitely useful or infinitely harmful. Ideas that tell us which of them to expect count as the true ideas in all this primary sphere of verification, and the pursuit of such ideas is a primary human duty. The possession of truth, so far from being here an end in itself, is only a preliminary means towards other vital satisfactions. If I am lost in the woods and starved, and find what looks like a cow path, it is of the utmost importance that I should think of a human habitation at the end of it, for if I do so and follow it, I save myself. The true thought is useful here because the house which is its object is useful. The practical value of true ideas is thus primarily derived from the practical importance of their objects to us. Their objects are, indeed, not important at all times. I may on another occasion have no use for the house; and then my idea of it, however verifiable, will be practically irrelevant and had better remain latent. Yet since almost any object may some day become temporarily important, the advantage of having a general stock of *extra* truths, of ideas that shall be true of merely possible situations, is obvious. We store such extra truths away in our memories, and with the overflow we fill our books of reference. Whenever such an extra truth becomes practically relevant to one of our emergencies, it passes from cold storage to do work in the world and our belief in it grows active. You can say of it then either that "it is useful because it is true" or that "it is true because it is useful." Both these phrases mean exactly the same thing, namely that here is an idea that gets fulfilled and can be verified. True is the name for whatever idea starts the verification process, useful is the name for its completed function in experience. True ideas would never have been singled out as such, would never have acquired a class name, least of all a name suggesting value, unless they had been useful from the outset in this way.

From this simple cue pragmatism gets her general notion of truth as something essentially bound up with the way in which one moment in our experience may lead us towards other moments which it will be worth while to have been led to. Primarily, and on the commonsense level, the truth of a state of mind means this function of *a leading that is worth while*. When a moment in our experience, of any kind whatever, inspires us with a thought that is true, that means that sooner or later we dip by that thought's guidance into the particulars of experience again and make advantageous connection with them. This is a vague enough statement, but I beg you to retain it, for it is essential.

Our experience meanwhile is all shot through with regularities. One bit of it can warn us to get ready for another bit, can "intend" or be "significant of" that remoter object.

The object's advent is the significance's verification. Truth, in these cases, meaning nothing but eventual verification, is manifestly incompatible with waywardness on our part. Woe to him whose beliefs play fast and loose with the order which realities follow in his experience; they will lead him nowhere or else make false connections.

By "realities" or "objects" here, we mean either things of common sense, sensibly present, or else commonsense relations, such as dates, places, distances, kinds, activities. Following our mental image of a house along the cow path, we actually come to see the house; we get the image's full verification. *Such simply and fully verified leadings are certainly the originals and prototypes of the truth process.* Experience offers indeed other forms of truth process, but they are all conceivable as being primary verifications arrested, multiplied or substituted one for another.

Take, for instance, yonder object on the wall. You and I consider it to be a "clock," although no one of us has seen the hidden works that make it one. We let our notion pass for true without attempting to verify. If truths mean verification process essentially, ought we then to call such unverified truths as this abortive? No, for they form the overwhelmingly large number of the truths we live by. Indirect as well as direct verifications pass muster. Where circumstantial evidence is sufficient, we can go without eye-witnessing. Just as we here assume Japan to exist without ever having been there, because it *works* to do so, everything we know conspiring with the belief, and nothing interfering, so we assume that thing to be a clock. We *use* it as a clock, regulating the length of our lecture by it. The verification of the assumption here means its leading to no frustration or contradiction. Verifi*ability* of wheels and weights and pendulum is as good as verification. For one truth process completed there are a million in our lives that function in this state of nascency. They turn us *toward* direct verification; lead us into the *surroundings* of the objects they envisage; and then, if everything runs on harmoniously, we are so sure that verification is possible that we omit it, and are usually justified by all that happens.

Truth lives, in fact, for the most part on a credit system. Our thoughts and beliefs "pass," so long as nothing challenges them, just as bank notes pass so long as nobody refuses them. But this all points to direct face-to-face verifications somewhere, without which the fabric of truth collapses like a financial system with no cash basis whatever. You accept my verification of one thing, I yours of another. We trade on each other's truth. But beliefs verified concretely by *somebody* are the posts of the whole superstructure.

Another great reason—beside economy of time—for waiving complete verification in the usual business of life is that all things exist in kinds and not singly. Our world is found once for all to have that peculiarity. So that when we have once directly verified our ideas about one specimen of a kind, we consider ourselves free to apply them to other specimens without verification. A mind that habitually discerns the kind of thing before it, and acts by the law of the kind immediately, without pausing to verify, will be a "true" mind in ninety-nine out of a hundred emergencies, proved so by its conduct fitting everything it meets, and getting no refutation.

Indirectly or only potentially verifying processes may thus be true as well as full verification processes. They work as true processes would work, give us the same advantages, and claim our recognition for the same reasons. All this on the commonsense level of matters of fact, which we are alone considering.

But matters of fact are not our only stock in trade. *Relations among purely mental ideas* form another sphere where true and false beliefs obtain, and here the beliefs are absolute, or unconditional. When they are true they bear the name either of definitions or of principles. It is either a principle or a definition that 1 and 1 make 2, that 2 and 1 make 3, and so on; that white differs less from gray than it does from black; that when the cause begins to act the effect also commences. Such propositions hold of all possible "ones," of all conceivable "whites" and "grays" and "causes." The objects here are mental objects. Their relations are perceptually obvious at a glance, and no sense verification is necessary. Moreover, once true, always true, of those same mental objects. Truth here has an "eternal" character. If you can find a concrete thing anywhere that is "one" or "white" or "gray" or an "effect," then your principles will everlastingly apply to it. It is but a case of ascertaining the kind, and then applying the law of its kind to the particular object. You are sure to get truth if you can but name the kind rightly, for your mental relations hold good of everything of that kind without exception. If you then, nevertheless, failed to get truth concretely, you would say that you had classed your real objects wrongly.

In this realm of mental relations, truth again is an affair of leading. We relate one abstract idea with another, framing in the end great systems of logical and mathematical truth, under the respective terms of which the sensible facts of experience eventually arrange themselves, so that our eternal truths hold good of realities also. This marriage of fact and theory is endlessly fertile. What we say is here already true in advance of special verification, *if we have subsumed our objects rightly.* Our ready-made ideal framework for all sorts of possible objects follows from the very structure of our thinking. We can no more play fast and loose with these abstract relations than we can do so with our sense experiences. They coerce us; we must treat them consistently, whether or not we like the results. The rules of addition apply to our debts as rigorously as to our assets. The hundredth decimal of π, the ratio of the circumference to its diameter, is predetermined ideally now, though no one may have computed it. If we should ever need the figure in our dealings with an actual circle we should need to have it given rightly, calculated by the usual rules; for it is the same kind of truth that those rules elsewhere calculate.

Between the coercions of the sensible order and those of the ideal order, our mind is thus wedged tightly. Our ideas must agree with realities, be such realities concrete or abstract, be they facts or be they principles, under penalty of endless inconsistency and frustration.

So far, intellectualists can raise no protest. They can only say that we have barely touched the skin of the matter.

Realities mean, then, either concrete facts, or abstract kinds of thing and relations perceived intuitively between them. They furthermore and thirdly mean, as things that new ideas of ours must no less take account of, the whole body of other truths already in our possession. But what now does "agreement" with such threefold realities mean? —to use again the definition that is current,

Here it is that pragmatism and intellectualism begin to

part company. Primarily, no doubt, to agree means to copy, but we saw that the mere word "clock" would do instead of a mental picture of its works, and that of many realities our ideas can only be symbols and not copies. "Past time," "power," "spontaneity"—how can our mind copy such realities?

To "agree" in the widest sense with a reality *can only mean to be guided either straight up to it or into its surroundings, or to be put into such working touch with it as to handle either it or something connected with it better than if we disagreed.* Better either intellectually or practically! And often agreement will only mean the negative fact that nothing contradictory from the quarter of that reality comes to interfere with the way in which our ideas guide us elsewhere. To copy a reality is, indeed, one very important way of agreeing with it, but it is far from being essential. The essential thing is the process of being guided. Any idea that helps us to *deal*, whether practically or intellectually, with either the reality or its belongings, that doesn't entangle our progress in frustrations, that *fits*, in fact, and adapts our life to the reality's whole setting, will agree sufficiently to meet the requirement. It will hold true of that reality.

Thus, *names* are just as "true" or "false" as definite mental pictures are. They set up similar verification processes, and lead to fully equivalent practical results.

All human thinking gets discursified; we exchange ideas; we lend and borrow verifications, get them from one another by means of social intercourse. All truth thus gets verbally built out, stored up, and made available for every one. Hence, we must *talk* consistently just as we must *think* consistently: for both in talk and thought we deal with kinds. Names are arbitrary, but once understood they must be kept to. We mustn't now call Abel "Cain" or Cain "Abel." If we do, we ungear ourselves from the whole book of Genesis, and from all its connections with the universe of speech and fact down to the present time. We throw ourselves out of whatever truth that entire system of speech and fact may embody.

The overwhelming majority of our true ideas admit of no direct or face-to-face verification—those of past history, for example, as of Cain and Abel. The stream of time can be remounted only verbally, or verified indirectly by the present prolongations or effects of what the past harbored. Yet if they agree with these verbalities and effects, we can know that our ideas of the past are true. *As true as past time itself was,* so true was Julius Cæsar, so true were antediluvian monsters, all in their proper dates and settings. That past time itself was, is guaranteed by its coherence with everything that's present. True as the present *is,* the past *was* also.

Agreement thus turns out to be essentially an affair of leading—leading that is useful because it is into quarters that contain objects that are important. True ideas lead us into useful verbal and conceptual quarters as well as directly up to useful sensible termini. They lead to consistency, stability and flowing human intercourse. They lead away from excentricity and isolation, from foiled and barren thinking. The untrammeled flowing of the leading process, its general freedom from clash and contradiction, passes for its indirect verification; but all roads lead to Rome, and in the end and eventually, all true processes must lead to the face of directly verifying sensible experiences *somewhere,* which somebody's ideas have copied.

Such is the large loose way in which the pragmatist interprets the word agreement. He treats it altogether practically. He lets it cover any process of conduction from a present idea to a future terminus, provided only it run prosperously. It is only thus that "scientific" ideas, flying as they do beyond common sense, can be said to agree with their realities. It is, as I have already said, *as if* reality were made of ether, atoms or electrons, but we mustn't think so literally. The term "energy" doesn't even pretend to stand for anything "objective." It is only a way of measuring the surface of phenomena so as to string their changes on a simple formula.

Yet in the choice of these man-made formulas we can not be capricious with impunity any more than we can be capricious on the commonsense practical level. We must find a theory that will *work;* and that means something extremely difficult; for our theory must mediate between all previous truths and certain new experiences. It must derange common sense and previous belief as little as possible, and it must lead to some sensible terminus or other that can be verified exactly. To "work" means both these things; and the squeeze is so tight that there is little loose play for any hypothesis. Our theories are wedged and controlled as nothing else is. Yet sometimes alternative theoretic formulas are equally compatible with all the truths we know, and then we choose between them for subjective reasons. We choose the kind of theory to which we are already partial; we follow "elegance" or "economy." Clerk-Maxwell somewhere says it would be "poor scientific taste" to choose the more complicated of two equally well-evidenced conceptions; and you will all agree with him. Truth in science is what gives us the maximum possible sum of satisfactions, taste included, but consistency both with previous truth and with novel fact is always the most imperious claimant.

I have led you through a very sandy desert. But now, if I may be allowed so vulgar an expression, we begin to taste the milk in the cocoanut. Our rationalist critics here discharge their batteries upon us, and to reply to them will take us out from all this dryness into full sight of a momentous philosophical alternative.

Our account of truth is an account of truths in the plural, of processes of leading, realized *in rebus,* and having only this quality in common, that they *pay.* They pay by guiding us into or towards some part of a system that dips at numerous points into sense percepts, which we may copy mentally or not, but with which at any rate we are now in the kind of commerce vaguely designated as verification. Truth for us is simply a collective name for verification processes, just as health, wealth, strength, etc., are names for other processes connected with life, and also pursued because it pays to pursue them. Truth is *made,* just as health, wealth, and strength are made, in the course of experience.

Here rationalism is instantaneously up in arms against us. I can imagine a rationalist to talk as follows:

"Truth is not made," he will say, "it absolutely obtains, being a unique relation that does not wait upon any process, but shoots straight over the head of experience and hits its reality every time. Our belief that yon thing on the wall is a clock is true already, although no one in the whole history of the world should verify it. The bare quality of standing in that transcendent relation is what makes any thought true that possesses it, whether or not there be verification. You pragmatists put the cart before the horse in making truth's being reside in verification processes. These are merely signs of its being, merely our lame ways of ascertaining after the fact which of our ideas already has possessed the wondrous quality. The quality itself is timeless, like all essences and natures. Thoughts partake of it directly, as they partake of falsity or of irrelevancy. It can't be analyzed away into pragmatic consequences."

The whole plausibility of this rationalist tirade is due to the fact to which we have already paid so much attention. In our world, namely, abounding as it does in things of similar kinds and similarly associated, one verification serves for others of its kind, and one great use of knowing things is to be led not so much to them as to their associates, especially to human talk about them. The quality of truth, obtaining *ante rem,* pragmatically means, then, the fact that in such a world innumerable ideas work better by their indirect or possible than by their direct and actual verification. Truth *ante rem* means only verifiability, then; or else it is a case of the stock rationalist trick of treating the *name* of a concrete phenomenal reality as an independent prior entity, and placing it behind the reality as its explanation. Professor Mach quotes somewhere an epigram of Lessing's:

> Sagt Hänschen Schlau zu Vetter Fritz,
> "Wie kommt es, Vetter Fritzen,
> Dass grad' die Reichsten in der Welt,
> Das meiste Geld besitzen?"

Hänschen Schlau here treats the principle "wealth" as something distinct from the facts denoted by the man's being rich. It antedates them; the facts become only a sort of secondary coincidence with the rich man's essential nature.

In the case of "wealth" we all see the fallacy. We know that wealth is but a name for concrete processes that certain men's lives play a part in, and not a natural excellence found in Messrs. Rockefeller and Carnegie, but not in the rest of us.

Like wealth, health also lives *in rebus.* It is a name for processes, as digestion, circulation, sleep, etc., that go on happily, though in this instance we are more inclined to think of it as a principle and to say the man digests and sleeps so well *because* he is so healthy.

With "strength" we are, I think, more rationalistic still, and decidedly inclined to treat it as an excellence preexisting in the man and explanatory of the herculean performances of his muscles.

With "truth" most people go over the border entirely, and treat the rationalistic account as self-evident. But really all these words in *th* are exactly similar. Truth exists *ante rem* just as much and as little as the other things do.

The scholastics, following Aristotle, made much of the distinction between habit and act. Health *in actu* means, among other things, good sleeping and digesting. But a healthy man need not always be sleeping, or always digesting, any more than a wealthy man need be always handling money, or a strong man always lifting weights. All such qualities sink to the status of "habits" between their times of exercise; and similarly truth becomes a habit of certain of our ideas and beliefs in their intervals of rest from their verifying activities. But those activities are the root of the whole matter, and the condition of there being any habit to exist in the intervals.

"The true," to put it very briefly, *is only the expedient in the way of our thinking, just as "the right" is only the expedient in the way of our behaving.* Expedient in almost any fashion; and expedient in the long run and on the whole of course; for what meets expediently all the experience in sight won't necessarily meet all farther experiences equally satisfactorily. Experience, as we know, has ways of *boiling over,* and making us correct our present formulas.

The "absolutely" true, meaning what no further experience will ever alter, is that ideal vanishing point towards which we imagine that all our temporary truths will some day converge. It runs on all fours with the perfectly wise man, and with the absolutely complete experience; and, if these ideals are ever realized, they will all be realized together. Meanwhile we have to live today by what truth we can get today, and be ready tomorrow to call it falsehood. Ptolemaic astronomy, euclidean space, aristotelian logic, scholastic metaphysics, were expedient for centuries, but human experience has boiled over those limits, and we now call these things only relatively true, or true within those borders of experience. "Absolutely" they are false; for we know that those limits were casual, and might have been transcended by past theorists just as they are by present thinkers.

When new experiences lead to retrospective judgments, using the past tense, what these judgments utter *was* true, even though no past thinker had been led there. We live forward, a Danish thinker has said, but we understand backward. The present sheds a backward light on the world's previous processes. They may have been truth processes for the actors in them. They are not so for one who knows the later revelations of the story.

This regulative notion of a potential better truth to be established later, possibly to be established some day absolutely, and having powers of retroactive legislation, turns its face, like all pragmatist notions, towards concreteness of fact, and towards the future. Like the half truths, the absolute truth will have to be *made,* made as a relation incidental to the growth of a mass of verification experience, to which the half true ideas are all along contributing their quota.

I have already insisted on the fact that truth is made largely out of previous truths. Men's beliefs at any time are so much experience *funded.* But the beliefs are themselves parts of the sum total of the world's experience, and become matter, therefore, for the next day's funding operations. So far as reality means experienceable reality, both it and the truths men gain about it are everlastingly in process of mutation—mutation toward a definite goal, it may be—but still mutation.

Mathematicians can solve problems with two variables. On the Newtonian theory, for instance, acceleration varies with distance, but distance also varies with acceleration. In the realm of truth processes facts come independently and determine our beliefs provisionally. But these beliefs make us act, and as fast as they do so, they bring into sight or into existence new facts which redetermine the beliefs accordingly. So the whole coil and ball of truth, as it rolls up, is the product of a double influence. Truths emerge from facts; but they dip forward into facts again and add to them; which facts again create or reveal new truth (the word is indifferent) and so on indefinitely. The "facts" themselves meanwhile are not *true.* They simply *are.* Truth is the function of the beliefs that start and terminate among them.

The case is like a snowball's growth, due as it is to the distribution of the snow on the one hand, and to the successive pushes of the boys on the other, with these factors codetermining each other incessantly.

The most fateful point of difference between being a rationalist and being a pragmatist is now fully in sight. Experience is in mutation, and our psychological ascertainments of truth are in mutation—so much rationalism will allow; but never that either reality itself or truth itself is mutable. Reality stands complete and ready-made from all eternity, rationalism insists, and the agreement of our ideas with it is that unique unanalyzable virtue in them of which she has already told us. As that intrinsic excellence, their truth has nothing to do with our experiences. It adds nothing to the content of experience. It makes no difference to reality itself; it is supervenient, inert, static, a reflection merely. It doesn't *exist*, it *holds* or *obtains*, it belongs to another dimension from that of either facts or fact relations, belongs, in short, to the epistemological dimension—and with that big word rationalism closes the discussion.

Thus, just as pragmatism faces forward to the future, so does rationalism here again face backward to a past eternity. True to her inveterate habit, rationalism reverts to "principles," and thinks that when an abstraction once is named, we own an oracular solution.

The tremendous pregnancy in the way of consequences for life of this radical difference of outlook will only become apparent in my later lectures. I wish meanwhile to close this lecture by showing that rationalism's sublimity does not save it from inanity.

When, namely, you ask rationalists, instead of accusing pragmatism of desecrating the notion of truth, to define it themselves by saying exactly what *they* understand by it, the only positive attempts I can think of are these two:
1. "Truth is the system of propositions which have an unconditional claim to be recognized as valid." *
2. Truth is a name for all those judgments which we find ourselves under obligation to make by a kind of imperative duty.†

The first thing that strikes one in such definitions is their unutterable triviality. They are absolutely true, of course, but absolutely insignificant until you handle them pragmatically. What do you mean by "claim" here, and what do you mean by "duty"? As summary names for the

---

* A. E. Taylor, *Philosophical Review*, vol. XIV, p. 288.

† H. Rickert, *Der Gegenstand der Erkenntniss*, ch. on "Die Urtheilsnothwendigkeit."

concrete reasons why thinking in true ways is overwhelmingly expedient and good for mortal men, it is all right to talk of claims on reality's part to be agreed with, and of obligations on our part to agree. We feel both the claims and the obligations, and we feel them for just those reasons.

But the rationalists who talk of claim and obligation *expressly say that they have nothing to do with our practical interests or personal reasons.* Our reasons for agreeing are psychological facts, they say, relative to each thinker, and to the accidents of his life. They are his evidence merely, they are no part of the life of truth itself. That life transacts itself in a purely logical or epistemological, as distinguished from a psychological, dimension, and its claims antedate and exceed all personal motivations whatsoever. Though neither man nor God should ever ascertain truth. the word would still have to be defined as that which *ought* to be ascertained and recognized.

There never was a more exquisite example of an idea abstracted from the concretes of experience and then used to oppose and negate what it was abstracted from.

Philosophy and common life abound in similar instances. The "sentimentalist fallacy" is to shed tears over abstract justice and generosity, beauty, etc., and never to know these qualities when you meet them in the street, because the circumstances make them vulgar. Thus I read in the privately printed biography of an eminently rationalistic mind: "It was strange that with such admiration for beauty in the abstract, my brother had no enthusiasm for fine architecture, for beautiful painting, or for flowers." And in almost the last philosophic work I have read, I find such passages as the following: "Justice is ideal, solely ideal. Reason conceives that it ought to exist, but experience shows that it cannot. . . . Truth, which ought to be, cannot be. . . . Reason is deformed by experience. As soon as reason enters experience it becomes contrary to reason."

The rationalist's fallacy here is exactly like the sentimentalist's. Both extract a quality from the muddy particulars of experience, and find it so pure when extracted that they contrast it with each and all its muddy instances as an opposite and higher nature. All the while it is *their* nature. It is the nature of truths to be validated, verified. It pays for our ideas to be validated. Our obligation to seek truth is part of our general obligation to do what pays. The payments true ideas bring are the sole why of our duty to follow them. Identical whys exist in the case of wealth and health.

Truth makes no other kind of claim and imposes no other kind of ought than health and wealth do. All these claims are conditional; the concrete benefits we gain are what we mean by calling the pursuit a duty. In the case of truth, untrue beliefs work as perniciously in the long run as true beliefs work beneficially. Talking abstractly, the quality "true" may thus be said to grow absolutely precious and the quality "untrue" absolutely damnable: the one may be called good, the other bad, unconditionally. We ought to think the true, we ought to shun the false, imperatively.

But if we treat all this abstraction literally and oppose it to its mother soil in experience, see what a preposterous position we work ourselves into.

We cannot then take a step forward in our actual thinking. When shall I acknowledge this truth and when that? Shall the acknowledgment be loud?—or silent? If sometimes loud, sometimes silent, which *now?* When may a truth go into cold storage in the encyclopedia? and when shall it come out for battle? Must I constantly be repeating the truth "twice two are four" because of its eternal claim on recognition? or is it sometimes irrelevant? Must my thoughts dwell night and day on my personal sins and blemishes, because I truly have them?—or may I sink and ignore them in order to be a decent social unit, and not a mass of morbid melancholy and apology?

It is quite evident that our obligation to acknowledge truth, so far from being unconditional, is tremendously conditioned. Truth with a big T, and in the singular, claims abstractly to be recognized, of course; but concrete truths in the plural need be recognized only when their recognition is expedient. A truth must always be preferred to a falsehood when both relate to the situation; but when neither does, truth is as little of a duty as falsehood. If you ask me what o'clock it is and I tell you that I live at 95 Irving Street, my answer may indeed be true, but you don't see why it is my duty to give it. A false address would be as much to the purpose.

With this admission that there are conditions that limit the application of the abstract imperative, *the pragmatistic treatment of truth sweeps back upon us in its fulness.* Our duty to agree with reality is seen to be grounded in a perfect jungle of concrete expediencies.

When Berkeley had explained what people meant by matter, people thought that he denied matter's existence. When Messrs. Schiller and Dewey now explain what people mean by truth, they are accused of denying *its* existence. These pragmatists destroy all objective standards, critics say, and put foolishness and wisdom on one level. A favorite formula for describing Mr. Schiller's doctrines and mine is that we are persons who think that by saying whatever you find it pleasant to say and calling it truth you fulfil every pragmatistic requirement.

I leave it to you to judge whether this be not an impudent slander. Pent in, as the pragmatist more than any one else sees himself to be, between the whole body of funded truths squeezed from the past and the coercions of the world of sense about him, who so well as he feels the immense pressure of objective control under which our minds perform their operations? If any one imagines that this law is lax, let him keep its commandment one day, says Emerson. We have heard much of late of the uses of the imagination in science. It is high time to urge the use of a little imagination in philosophy. The unwillingness of some of our critics to read any but the silliest of possible meanings into our statements is as discreditable to their imaginations as anything I know in recent philosophic history. Schiller says the true is that which "works." Thereupon he is treated as one who limits verification to the lowest material utilities. Dewey says truth is what gives "satisfaction." He is treated as one who believes in calling everything true which, if it were true, would be pleasant.

Our critics certainly need more imagination of realities. I have honestly tried to stretch my own imagination and to read the best possible meaning into the rationalist conception, but I have to confess that it still completely baffles me. The notion of a reality calling on us to "agree" with it, and that for no reasons, but simply because its claim is "unconditional" or "transcendent," is one that I can make neither head nor tail of. I try to imagine myself as the sole reality in the world, and then to imagine what more I would "claim" if I were allowed to. If you suggest the possibility of my claiming that a mind should come into being from out of the void inane and stand and *copy* me, I can indeed imagine what the copying might mean, but I can conjure up no motive. What good it would do me to be copied, or what good it would do that mind to copy me, if further consequences are expressly and in principle ruled out as motives for the claim (as they are by our rationalist authorities) I can not fathom. When the Irishman's admirers ran him along to the place of banquet in a sedan chair with no bottom, he said, "Faith, if it wasn't for the honor of the thing, I might as well have come on foot." So here: but for the honor of the thing, I might as well have remained uncopied. Copying is one genuine mode of knowing (which for some strange reason our contemporary transcendentalists seem to be tumbling over each other to repudiate); but when we get beyond copying, and fall back on unnamed forms of agreeing that are expressly denied to be either copyings or leadings or fittings, or any other processes pragmatically definable, the *what* of the "agreement" claimed becomes as unintelligible as the why of it. Neither content nor motive can be imagined for it. It is an absolutely meaningless abstraction.*

Surely in this field of truth it is the pragmatists and not the rationalists who are the more genuine defenders of the universe's rationality.

---

* I am not forgetting that Professor Rickert long ago gave up the whole notion of truth being founded on agreement with reality. Reality according to him, is whatever agrees with truth, and truth is founded solely on our primal duty. This fantastic flight, together with Mr. Joachim's candid confession of failure in his book *The Nature of Truth*, seems to me to mark the bankruptcy of rationalism when dealing with this subject. Rickert deals with part of the pragmatistic position under the head of what he calls "Relativismus." I can not discuss his text here. Suffice it to say that his argumentation in that chapter is so feeble as to seem almost incredible in so generally able a writer.

XI. The Tigers in India *

There are two ways of knowing things, knowing them immediately or intuitively, and knowing them conceptually or representatively. Although such things as the white paper before our eyes can be known intuitively, most of the things we know, the tigers now in India, for example, or the scholastic system of philosophy, are known only representatively or symbolically.

Suppose, to fix our ideas, that we take first a case of conceptual knowledge; and let it be our knowledge of the tigers in India, as we sit here. Exactly what do we *mean* by saying that we here know the tigers? What is the precise fact that the cognition so confidently claimed is *known-as*, to use Shadworth Hodgson's inelegant but valuable form of words?

Most men would answer that what we mean by knowing the tigers is having them, however absent in body, become in some way present to our thought; or that our knowledge of them is known as presence of our thought to them. A great mystery is usually made of this peculiar presence in absence; and the scholastic philosophy, which is only common sense grown pedantic, would explain it as a peculiar kind of existence, called *intentional inexistence,* of the tigers in our mind. At the very least, people would say that what we mean by knowing the tigers is mentally *pointing* towards them as we sit here.

But now what do we mean by *pointing,* in such a case as this? What is the pointing known-as, here?

To this question I shall have to give a very prosaic

* Extracts from a presidential address before the American Psychological Association, published in the *Psychological Review,* vol. II (1895), p. 105.

answer—one that traverses the prepossessions not only of common sense and scholasticism, but also those of nearly all the epistemological writers whom I have ever read. The answer, made brief, is this: The pointing of our thought to the tigers is known simply and solely as a procession of mental associates and motor consequences that follow on the thought, and that would lead harmoniously, if followed out, into some ideal or real context, or even into the immediate presence, of the tigers. It is known as our rejection of a jaguar, if that beast were shown us as a tiger; as our assent to a genuine tiger if so shown. It is known as our ability to utter all sorts of propositions which don't contradict other propositions that are true of the real tigers. It is even known, if we take the tigers very seriously, as actions of ours which may terminate in directly intuited tigers, as they would if we took a voyage to India for the purpose of tiger hunting and brought back a lot of skins of the striped rascals which we had laid low. In all this there is no self-transcendency in our mental images *taken by themselves*. They are one phenomenal fact; the tigers are another; and their pointing to the tigers is a perfectly commonplace intraexperiential relation, *if you once grant a connecting world to be there*. In short, the ideas and the tigers are in themselves as loose and separate, to use Hume's language, as any two things can be; and pointing means here an operation as external and adventitious as any that nature yields.*

I hope you may agree with me now that in representative knowledge there is no special inner mystery, but only an outer chain of physical or mental intermediaries connecting thought and thing. *To know an object is here to lead to it through a context which the world supplies. . . .*

Let us next pass on to the case of immediate or intuitive acquaintance with an object, and let the object be the white paper before our eyes. The thought stuff and the thing stuff are here indistinguishably the same in nature, as we saw a moment since, and there is no context of intermediaries or associates to stand between and separate the

---

* A stone in one field may "fit," we say, a hole in another field. But the relation of "fitting," so long as no one carries the stone to the hole and drops it in, is only one name for the fact that such an act *may* happen. Similarly with the knowing of the tigers here and now. It is only an anticipatory name for a further associative and terminative process that *may* occur.

thought and thing. There is no "presence in absence" here, and no "pointing," but rather an all-round embracing of the paper by the thought; and it is clear that the knowing cannot now be explained exactly as it was when the tigers were its object. Dotted all through our experience are states of immediate acquaintance just like this. Somewhere our belief always does rest on ultimate data like the whiteness, smoothness, or squareness of this paper. Whether such qualities be truly ultimate aspects of being, or only provisional suppositions of ours, held to till we get better informed, is quite immaterial for our present inquiry. So long as it is believed in, we see our object face to face. What now do we mean by "knowing" such a sort of object as this? For is this also the way in which we should know the tiger if our conceptual idea of him were to terminate by having led us to his lair?

This address must not become too long, so I must give my answer in the fewest words. And let me first say this: So far as the white paper or other ultimate datum of our experience is considered to enter also into some one else's experience, and we, in knowing it, are held to know it there as well as here; so far, again, as it is considered to be a mere mask for hidden molecules that other now impossible experiences of our own might some day lay bare to view; so far it is a case of tigers in India again—the things known being absent experiences, the knowing can only consist in passing smoothly towards them through the intermediary context that the world supplies. But if our own private vision of the paper be considered in abstraction from every other event, as if it constituted by itself the universe (and it might perfectly well do so, for aught we can understand to the contrary), then the paper seen and the seeing of it are only two names for one indivisible fact which, properly named, is *the datum, the phenomenon, or the experience.* The paper is in the mind and the mind is around the paper, because paper and mind are only two names that are given later to the one experience, when, taken in a larger world of which it forms a part, its connections are traced in different directions.* *To know*

---

* What is meant by this is that "the experience" can be referred to either of two great associative systems, that of the experiencer's mental history, or that of the experienced facts of the world. Of both of these systems it forms part, and may be regarded, indeed, as one of their points of intersection. One might let a vertical line

immediately, then, or intuitively, is for mental content and object to be identical. This is a very different definition from that which we gave of representative knowledge; but neither definition involves those mysterious notions of self-transcendency and presence in absence which are such essential parts of the ideas of knowledge, both of philosophers and of common men.*

---

stand for the mental history; but the same object, O, appears also in the mental history of different persons, represented by the other vertical lines. It thus ceases to be the private property of one experience, and becomes, so to speak, a shared or public thing. We

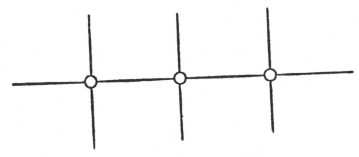

can track its outer history in this way, and represent it by the horizontal line. [It is also known representatively at other points of the vertical lines, or intuitively there again, so that the line of its outer history would have to be looped and wandering, but I make it straight for simplicity's sake.] In any case, however, it is the same *stuff* that figures in all the sets of lines.

* The reader will observe that the text is written from the point of view of *naïf* realism or common sense, and avoids raising the idealistic controversy.

XII. The Meaning of the Word "Truth"*

My account of truth is realistic, and follows the epistemological dualism of common sense. Suppose I say to you "The thing exists"—is that true or not? How can you tell? Not till my statement has developed its meaning farther is it determined as being true, false, or irrelevant to reality altogether. But if now you ask "what thing?" and I reply "a desk"; if you ask "where?" and I point to a place; if you ask "does it exist materially, or only in imagination?" and I say "materially"; if moreover I say "I mean that desk," and then grasp and shake a desk which you see just as I have described it, you are willing to call my statement true. But you and I are commutable here; we can exchange places; and, as you go bail for my desk, so I can go bail for yours.

This notion of a reality independent of either of us, taken from ordinary social experience, lies at the base of the pragmatist definition of truth. With some such reality any statement, in order to be counted true, must agree. Pragmatism defines "agreeing" to mean certain ways of "working," be they actual or potential. Thus, for my statement "the desk exists" to be true of a desk recognized as real by you, it must be able to lead me to shake your desk, to explain myself by words that suggest that desk to your mind, to make a drawing that is like the desk you see, etc. Only in such ways as this is there sense in saying it agrees with *that* reality, only thus does it gain for me the satisfaction of hearing you corroborate me. Reference then to

* Remarks at the meeting of the American Philosophical Association, Cornell University, December, 1907.

something determinate, and some sort of adaptation to it worthy of the name of agreement, are thus constituent elements in the definition of any statement of mine as "true." You cannot get at either the reference or the adaptation with out using the notion of the workings. *That* the thing is, *what* it is, and *which* it is (of all the possible things with that what) are points determinable only by the pragmatic method. The "which" means a possibility of pointing, or of otherwise singling out the special object; the "what" means choice on our part of an essential aspect to conceive it by (and this is always relative to what Dewey calls our own "situation"); and the "that" means our assumption of the attitude of belief, the reality-recognizing attitude. Surely for understanding what the word "true" means as applied to a statement, the mention of such workings is indispensable. Surely if we leave them out the subject and the object of the cognitive relation float—in the same universe, 'tis true—but vaguely and ignorantly and without mutual contact or mediation.

Our critics nevertheless call the workings inessential. No functional possibilities "make" our beliefs true, they say; they are true inherently, true positively, born "true" as the Count of Chambord was born "Henri-Cinq." Pragmatism insists, on the contrary, that statements and beliefs are thus inertly and statically true only by courtesy: they practically pass for true; but you *cannot define what you mean* by calling them true without referring to their functional possibilities. These give its whole *logical content* to that relation to reality on a belief's part to which the name "truth" is applied, a relation which otherwise remains one of mere coexistence or bare witness.

The foregoing statements reproduce the essential content of the lecture on Truth in my book *Pragmatism*. Schiller's doctrine of "humanism," Dewey's "Studies in logical theory," and my own "radical empiricism," all involve this general notion of truth as "working," either actual or conceivable. But they envelop it as only one detail in the midst of much wider theories that aim eventually at determining the notion of what "reality" at large is in its ultimate nature and constitution.

John Dewey

INTRODUCTION

John Dewey (1859–1952) was born in Burlington, Vermont, and educated at the University of Vermont and Johns Hopkins University. From 1884 to 1894 he taught at the University of Michigan where he established lasting friendships with James J. Tufts and George Herbert Mead and for one year at the University of Minnesota. In 1894 he left Michigan to go to the University of Chicago as Professor of Pedagogy. There he founded his "laboratory school," which became world famous and one of the sources of the later movement of "progressive education." His influential book *The School and Society* (1900) presents the theory and aim of this school. In 1904 Dewey moved to Columbia University where he worked for the rest of his career. He traveled in Europe and the Orient and in 1918 lectured in China and Japan. Always a prolific writer, Dewey wrote his best known books during his association with Columbia: *Ethics* (1908, with James Tufts), *The Influence of Darwin on Philosophy* (1910), *How We Think* (1910), *Democracy and Education* (1916), *Reconstruction in Philosophy* (1920), *Human Nature and Conduct* (1922), *Experience and Nature* (1925), *The Quest for Certainty* (1929), *Art as Experience* (1934), *Logic: the Theory of Inquiry* (1939). During these years Dewey achieved renown as the philosophic exponent of pragmatism, progressive education, and liberal causes, among them, teachers' rights.

Dewey's ninety-three years spanned three major revolutions in science. Born in the year that Darwin's *Origin of Species* appeared (1859), a witness to the impact of Einstein's theory of relativity on physics, Dewey died in 1952, seven years after the Bomb had fallen on Hiroshima when men were struggling to understand the ominous advent of the atomic age. All three of these revolutions had their origins within science, but their most violent and disturbing effects were felt in regions of social and moral experience. It is not surprising, therefore, that one fixed concern threaded the years of Dewey's philosophic activity: the relation of scientific knowledge to human values (the substance of the Introduction to the present book). The chief task of philosophy, according to Dewey, was to find a responsible and rational solution to the divisive and destructive cleavage between science and values:

> The problem of restoring integration and cooperation between man's beliefs about the world in which he lives and his beliefs about values and purposes that should direct his conduct is the deepest problem of modern life. It is the problem of any philosophy that is not isolated from life.

The central problem of philosophy is

> the relation that exists between the beliefs about the nature of things due to natural science to beliefs about value—using that word to designate whatever is taken to have rightful authority in the direction of conduct.*

Dewey's thought exhibits a gradual transition from early Hegelian and neo-kantian idealism to a philosophic naturalism. A turning point in this development, as Dewey tells us (see I, p. 35), was the appearance of James' *Principles of Psychology*. Dewey had studied under Peirce at Johns Hopkins but felt his influence considerably later. While Dewey's intellectual history had its marked changes in subject matter and methods of analysis, however, there was continuity—appropriately so, for a philosopher who made so much of continuity—in which something of the old was carried in the new. Throughout his life, Dewey was especially interested in education. This is as it should be, for in the theory and practice of education all the fundamental and vital ideas of philosophy come to trial: the nature of learning (thus, the theory of mind, the relation of mind and body, individual and society, man and nature, thought and action), knowledge and ethical judgment, the formation of moral ideals and social goals. In the 1890s Dewey was arguing that the "ultimate sci-

* *The Quest For Certainty* (New York, 1929), pp. 255–256. See p. 291, below.

ence"—thus the science basic to education—was psychology.

> Psychology is the ultimate science because it declares what experience in its totality is. It fixes the worth and meaning of its various elements by showing their development and place within this whole. It is, in short, philosophic method.*

Moreover, since the other sciences deal with things known, but psychology deals with the process of knowing,

> This science . . . is a central science, for its *subject matter,* knowledge, is involved in them all.†

In time the idealistic psychology made way for one increasingly behavioristic and social. The older concepts and more traditional categories of analysis are transformed: a dialectic of "Universal consciousness" and "finite Self" becomes replaced by the interaction of "culture" and "individual," nature and experience. There is a broadening of *psychology* into *instrumentalism* (on which see Dewey's description in I, p. 34), and the latter has its culmination in the theory of *inquiry*. That theory, for Dewey, in its scope and depth, can rightly be said to fulfill his earlier conception of psychology as the ultimate science and method of philosophy.

Over the course of these changes, however, Dewey continued to affirm his conviction of the fundamental importance of education, "the supreme art," as the condition of growth, the means of renewal and transmission of social experience. Generally, then, it was in the idea and institution of education that Dewey found the answer to his own urgently stated challenge to philosophy. The integration of the methods and products of knowledge due to natural science and ideals of conduct has its basis here: in the operations of the school, in a narrow and formal sense, and, ideally, less formally, in society; for society is not an end but a means of living and it itself is the central educational institution of civilized man. *Philosophy* Dewey once defined as "the general theory of education." His own philosophy of education, as stated in his major work on the subject, connected "the growth of democracy with the development of the experimental method in the sciences, evolu-

---

* "Psychology as Philosophic Method," *Mind*, XI (1886), p. 153.
† *Psychology* (New York, 1887), pp. 9–10.

tionary ideas in the biological sciences, and the industrial reorganization." *

The technical philosophic core of much of Dewey's writing on psychology, education, and logic was his conception of the organic and social conditions of behavior and action. "Action" has a special meaning for Dewey, as it also does in current philosophy. Dewey comments on the mind-body dualism which has established itself in so much of Western thought.

> I do not know of anything so disastrously affected by the tradition of separation and isolation as is this particular theme of body-mind. In its discussion are reflected the splitting off from each other of religion, morals and science; the divorce of philosophy from science and of both from the arts of conduct.†

Even our ordinary language perpetuates the mind-body dualism. For we have no word for the "mind-body in a unified wholeness of operation." Thus we speak of mind *and* body, or body *and* mind, as if we were referring to two conjoined substances or processes.

> In contrast to such a notion . . . when we take the standpoint of human action, of life in operation, body presents itself as the mechanism, the instrumentality of behavior, and mind as its function, its fruit and consummation.‡

Dewey points out that one feature of body as "means" and its study as one aspect of action is its physical chemical system; and in this respect it shares traits with other kinds of objects and inanimate nature. By virtue of this relation, all the sciences of physical nature become available as intellectual tools for the study and control of bodily changes. But this is not the only feature of the body, or else it would be indistinguishable from nonliving things, and the distinct aspects of bodily behavior and human action would become mysterious. The other feature is

> that chemicophysical processes go on in ways and by interactions which have reference to the needs of the organism as a whole . . . Organic processes are thus seen to be the constituent means of behavior which is endued with

---

* *Democracy and Education* (New York, 1916), p. v.

† "Body and Mind," *Philosophy and Civilization* (New York, 1931), pp. 301–302.

‡ *Ibid.*, pp. 302–303.

purpose and meaning, animate with affection, and informed by recollection and foresight.*

On this view the *body* is fundamentally a way of referring to the means and conditional features of actions that have intended consequences.

The study of human behavior thus requires a unification of these points of view. The focus is on "a kind of behavior in which outcomes of the past and outlook on the future are incorporated; with something longitudinal and not something cross-sectionally lateral." † The "longitudinal" dimension is the historical and autobiographical, purposive course, the distinctly "mental" aspect of action. This cannot occur without but must not be equated with the lateral cross-sections of organic structures of reflexes and reactions to stimuli. Some theories have made specific reactions to a specific stimulus the whole unit of behavior; all other behavior is treated as compounded of these units. Behavior is then regarded as going on "inside" the organism, and consciousness, the emotional and intellectual qualities of behavior, is then treated as either fictional or reducible to physicochemical properties. But for Dewey the original unit of behavior is "action in which the entire organism is involved" and the mechanism of reflexes is a special development occurring within the whole of behavior. On this view also the environment is not a place within which behavior occurs, but rather is a genuine part and contributary condition of behavior. The environment is not where but how behavior goes on. Indeed fish swim *in* water; but it is how water is a function of that behavior which is the significant environmental feature. Stimuli are not external objects to which organisms respond, but how certain environing conditions become incorporated into action. What determines any particular thing to be a stimulus is relative to the action of an organism: whatever evokes an adaptive response and use in the course of living behavior is a stimulus. But then it is the condition of the total state of an organism at a given time, its needs and the behavior engaged in, that endow certain traits and objects with the function of a stimulus. Stimuli are not *given*, they *become* so as they enter into the whole act of behavior; they are not isolated occurrences like events of sensory excitation and reaction which, as events, happen but do not lead further into complete acts of behavior. The sequential order of behavior cannot be explained by a "reflex arc" of separated stimulus, central activity, and motor response. The arc is a thesis of a "disjointed psychology," Dewey argues, and it cannot account for the actual circuit of developing behavior. For Dewey, the stimulus is the earlier phase of coordinated serial behavior and the response is the later part.

> Normal behavior development is thus a circuit of which the earlier or "open" phase is the tension of various elements of organic energy, while the final and "closed" phase is the institution of integrated interaction of organism and environment.*

Stimulus constitutes response and response reconstitutes or reconstructs the stimulus. The whole coordinated act of behavior is a cumulative development of contributary acts, and it is completed in the reconstructed unification of experience.

Dewey's "Reflex Arc Concept" (1896, see XIII) is a classic statement of the above ideas and the theory of the *act* or coordinated circuit of behavior. It foreshadows the same more general analysis of intelligent action in "The Pattern of Inquiry" of Dewey's Logic (1938, see XVI).

I have sketched Dewey's theory of action above because of the central place it has in his writing and thinking. In each of the selections one can find Dewey giving explicit expression to or working out the consequences of these leading ideas in illumining and proposing solutions to different kinds of philosophic problems.

There is another part of Dewey's pragmatism—or "instrumentalism" as he preferred to call it—that deserves our attention. In his description of Instrumentalism Dewey says one concern is with "how thought functions in the experimental determination of future consequences." Here is the precise equivalent of Peirce's conception of the purposive nature of thought, of the "inseparable connection between rational cognition and rational purpose," and it serves the same theoretical end: the unification of knowledge and ideals of conduct. Indeed, for Dewey, as for Peirce, knowledge is essentially an act of valuation. This was not an attempt to reduce ethics to science, or moral

* *Logic: The Theory of Inquiry* (New York, 1938), p. 31.

judgment to the allegedly purely intellectual, nor to derive *ought* from *is*. It is rather to show how scientific method or inquiry in its very execution of selective interpretation of the possibilities of experience, of directing observation and anticipating possible outcomes, of modifying, qualifying, and controlling its respective subject matters so as to bring action to a specific issue is a paradigm of moral conduct.

Like Peirce, Dewey construed inquiry as a process by which "open" and doubtful situations become ordered and settled. The chapter, "The Pattern of Inquiry" (see XVI) describes the stages of this transition from indeterminate to unified situation. The outcome of inquiry is knowledge. But since inquiry is the "controlled transformation" of an initially indeterminate situation, it produces an existential change in and of situations. This is Dewey's version of the "practical character" of knowing, of how thought and its objects are cooperative in instituting changes in the world. The means of this change include not only the present and working conceptual and observational instruments of inquiry but environing conditions and human agents with their organic and cultural inheritances of past experience, habits, dispositions, language, and purposes (the whole of the "longitudinal" discussed in the above paragraphs). All these are constituents in the changing situation and directive of its transformation.

With this idea of the active transformational character of inquiry, Dewey advanced his theory of *truth* as "warranted assertion." It is inquiry that warrants an assertion, and it is the assertion warranted by inquiry that resolves or "answers" the problematic situation that gave rise to inquiry. A warranted assertion is to a problematic situation as an answer is to a question. The answerable resolves the questionable, but the questionable determines the relevance and adequacy of the answer. Dewey spoke of *truth* as the "successful" and "satisfactory" outcome of inquiry. However, "successful" and "satisfactory" like "doubtful" do not refer to interior personal states; these have reference to objective traits of *situations*: "*We* are doubtful because the situation is inherently doubtful."

Since, for Dewey, all reflective judgment involves an *evaluation* of a situation with respect to its outcome and to future action, inquiry is, as we noticed above, ultimately an evaluative procedure. As a way of transforming situations and reconstructing experience, inquiry has a like function and common pattern, whether the experience in question is "moral" or "scientific." The role of inquiry is clear in this description of a moral situation:

> A moral situation is one in which judgment and choice are required antecedently to overt action. The practical meaning of the situation—that is to say the action needed to satisfy it—is not self-evident. It has to be searched for. There are conflicting desires and alternative apparent goods. What is needed is to find the right course of action, the right good. Hence inquiry is exacted. . . . This inquiry is intelligence. . . .
>
> *Moral* goods and ends exist only when something has to be done. The fact that something has to be done proves that there are deficiencies, evils in the existent situation. . . . Consequently the good of the situation has to be discovered, projected and attained on the basis of the exact defect and trouble to be rectified. . . .
>
> The process of growth, of improvement and progress, rather than the static outcome and result, becomes the significant thing. Not health as an end fixed once for all, but the needed improvement in health—a continual process—is the end and good. The end is no longer a terminus or limit to be reached. It is the active process of transforming the existent situation. Not perfection as a final goal, but the ever-enduring process of perfecting, maturing, refining is the aim of living. Honesty, industry, temperance, justice, like health, wealth, and learning, are not goods to be possessed as they would be if they expressed fixed ends to be attained. They are directions of change in the quality of experience. Growth itself is the only moral "end." *

The above point of view and the problem of the relation between knowledge and moral conduct—the crucially needed application of intelligent experimental method in forming judgments about values—is carefully explored by Dewey in "The Construction of Good" (XV, below).

Since, for Dewey, inquiry is a condition of human growth and the attainment of goods, since it is the exercise of intelligently directed changes in and reconstructions of experience, it is the essence of progressive social life. As a communal and cooperative means of directing growth and the renewal of values, inquiry took on a religious significance for Dewey. There are links between Peirce's view of the community of scientific inquirers ever approximating

---

* *Reconstruction in Philosophy* (New York, 1920), pp. 163–164, 169, 177.

to truth and Dewey's conception of democracy as a self-corrective process of persuasion, discussion, and the free play of intelligence. Entirely consistent with his more technical enunciation of the nature of inquiry and action, Dewey gave profound and sometimes eloquent expression to the ideal of democracy.

> Democracy is belief in the ability of human experience to generate the aims and methods by which further experience will grow in ordered richness. . . . Democracy is the faith that the process of experience is more important than any special result attained, so that special results achieved are of ultimate value only as they are used to enrich and order the ongoing process. Since the process of experience is capable of being educative, faith in democracy is all one with faith in experience and education. . . .
>
> Democracy as compared with other ways of life is the sole way of living which believes wholeheartedly in the process of experience as end and as means; as that which is capable of generating the science which is the sole dependable authority for the direction of further experience and which releases emotions, needs, and desires so as to call into being the things that have not existed in the past. . . . Since it is one that can have no end till experience itself comes to an end, the task of democracy is forever that of creation of a freer and more human experience in which all share and to which all contribute.*

More than the other pragmatists, he saw and carefully stated the extensive social implications and moral consequences of pragmatism. His conception of democracy forms one of the major contributions to social philosophy in our time. Dewey was the uncommonly able philosophic spokesman for the common man.

---

* From an address delivered by Dewey at a celebration of his eightieth birthday: "Democracy as a Moral Ideal." Printed in *The Philosopher of the Common Man* (New York, 1940). Reprinted in *John Dewey, His Contribution to the American Tradition*, Irwin Edman, ed. (New York, 1955), pp. 308–315; for the above, pp. 314–315.

XIII. The Unit of Behavior (The Reflex Arc Concept in Psychology)*

That the greater demand for a unifying principle and controlling working hypothesis in psychology should come at just the time when all generalizations and classifications are most questioned and questionable is natural enough. It is the very accumulation of discrete facts creating the demand for unification which breaks down previous lines of classification. The material is too great in mass and too varied in style to fit into existing pigeonholes, and the cabinets of science break of their own dead weight. The idea of the reflex arc has upon the whole come nearer to meeting this demand for a general working hypothesis than has any other single concept. It being admitted that the sensory-motor apparatus represents both the unit of nerve structure and the type of nerve function, the image of this relationship passed over into psychology and became an organizing principle to hold together the multiplicity of fact.

In criticizing this conception it is not intended to make a plea for the principles of explanation and classification which the reflex arc idea has replaced; but, on the contrary, to show that they are not sufficiently displaced, and that in the idea of the sensory-motor circuit, conceptions of the nature of sensation and of action derived from the nominally displaced psychology are still in control.

The older dualism between sensation and idea is repeated in the current dualism of peripheral and central structures and functions; the older dualism of body and

* Originally from *The Psychological Review*, vol. III (1896). For the complete source see p. 376, below.

soul finds a distinct echo in the current dualism of stimulus and response. Instead of interpreting the character of sensation, idea, and action from their place and function in the sensory-motor circuit, we still incline to interpret the latter from our preconceived and preformulated ideas of rigid distinctions between sensations, thoughts, and acts. The sensory stimulus is one thing, the central activity, standing for the idea, is another thing, and the motor discharge, standing for the act proper, is a third. As a result, the reflex arc is not a comprehensive, or organic unity, but a patchwork of disjointed parts, a mechanical conjunction of unallied processes. What is needed is that the principle underlying the idea of the reflex arc as the fundamental unit shall be consistently employed to determine the values of its constructive factors. More specifically, what is wanted is that sensory stimulus, central connections, and motor responses shall not be viewed as separate and complete entities in themselves, but as divisions of labor, functioning factors, within the single concrete whole, now designated the reflex arc.

But what can we properly *term* that which is not sensation-followed-by-idea-followed-by-movement, but which is, as it were, the mental organism of which sensation, idea, and movement are the chief organs? Stated on the physiological side, this more inclusive process may most conveniently be termed coordination. This is the essence of the facts held together by and subsumed under the reflex arc concept. Let us take, for our example, the familiar child-candle instance (James, *Psychology,* vol. I, p. 25). The ordinary interpretation would say the sensation of light is a stimulus to the grasping as a response, the burn resulting is a stimulus to withdrawing the hand as response and so on. No doubt this is a rough, practical way of representing the seeming course of events. But when we ask for its psychological adequacy, the case is quite different. Upon analysis, we find that we *begin*, not with a sensory stimulus, but with a sensory-motor coordination, the optical-ocular, and that in a certain sense it is the movement which is primary, and the sensation which is secondary, the movement of body, head, and eye muscles determining the quality of what is experienced. In other words, the real beginning is with the *act* of seeing; it is looking, and not a sensation of light. The sensory quale gives the value of the act, just as the movement furnishes its mechanism and control, but both sensation and movement lie inside, not outside the act.

Now if this act, the seeing, stimulates another act, the reaching, it is because both of these acts fall within a larger coordination; because seeing and grasping have been so often bound together to reinforce each other, to help each other out, that each may be considered practically a subordinate member of a bigger coordination. More specifically, the ability of the hand to do its work will depend, either directly or indirectly, upon its control, as well as its stimulation, by the act of vision. If the light did not inhibit as well as excite the reaching, the latter would be purely indeterminate, it would be for anything or nothing, not for the particular object seen. The reaching, in turn, must both stimulate and control the seeing. The eye must be kept upon the candle if the arm is to do its work; let it wander, and the arm takes up another task. In other words, we now have an enlarged and transformed coordination; the act is seeing no less than before, but it is now seeing-for-reaching purposes. There is still a sensory-motor circuit—one with more content or value, not a substitution of a motor response for a sensory stimulus.*

Now take the affair at its next stage, that in which the child gets burned. It is hardly necessary to point out again that this is also a sensory-motor coordination and not a mere sensation. It is worth while, however, to note especially the fact that it is simply the completion, or fulfillment, of the previous eye-arm-hand coordination and not an entirely new occurrence. Only because the heat-pain quale enters into the same circuit of experience with the optical-ocular and muscular quales, does the child learn from the experience and get the ability to avoid the experience in the future.

More technically stated, the so-called response is not merely to the stimulus; it is, so to speak, *into* it. The burn is the original seeing, the original optical-ocular experience, enlarged and transformed in its value. It is no longer mere seeing; it is seeing-of-a-light-that-means-pain-when-contact occurs. The ordinary reflex arc theory proceeds upon the more or less tacit assumption that the outcome of the response is a totally new experience; that it is, say, the substitution of a burn sensation for a light sensation

---

* See *The Psychological Review* (May, 1896), p. 253, for an excellent statement and illustration, by Messrs. Angell and Moore, of this mutuality of stimulation.

through the intervention of motion. The fact is that the sole meaning of the intervening movement is to maintain, reinforce or transform (as the case may be) the original quale; we do not have the replacing of one sort of experience by another, but the development or, as it seems convenient to term it, the mediation of an experience. The seeing, in a word, remains to control the reaching, and is, in turn, interpreted by the burning.*

The discussion up to this point may be summarized by saying that the reflex arc idea, as commonly employed, is defective, first, in that it assumes sensory stimulus and motor reponse as distinct mental existences, while in reality they are always inside a coordination and have their significance purely from the part played in maintaining or reconstructing the coordination; and secondly, in assuming that the quale of experience which precedes the "motor" phase and that which succeeds it are two different states, instead of the last being always the first reconstituted, the motor phase coming in only for the sake of such mediation. The result is that the reflex arc idea leaves us with a disjointed psychology, whether viewed from the standpoint of development in the individual or the race, or from that of the analysis of the mature consciousness. As to the former, in its failure to see that the "arc" of which it talks is actually a *circuit,* a continual reconstruction, it breaks continuity and leaves us nothing but a series of jerks, the origin of each jerk to be sought outside the process of experience itself in either an external pressure of "environment," or else in an unaccountable spontaneous variation from within the "soul" or the "organism." † As to the latter, failing to see the unity of activity, no matter how much it may prate of unity, still leaves us with sensation or peripheral stimulus; idea, or central process (the equivalent of attention); and motor response, or act, as three

* See, for a further statement of mediation, my *Syllabus of Ethics,* [Ann Arbor, 1894], p. 15.

† It is not too much to say that the whole controversy in biology regarding the source of variation, represented by Weismann and Spencer respectively, arises from beginning with stimulus or response instead of with the coordination with reference to which stimulus and response are functional divisions of labor. The same may be said, on the psychological side, of the controversy between the Wundtian "apperceptionists" and their opponents. Each has a *disjectum membrum* of the same organic whole, whichever is selected being an arbitrary matter of personal taste.

disconnected existences, having to be somehow adjusted to each other, whether through the intervention of an extraexperimental soul, or by mechanical push and pull.

Before proceeding to a consideration of the general meaning for psychology of the summary, it may be well to give another descriptive analysis, as the value of the statement depends entirely upon the universality of its range of application. For such an instance we may conveniently take Baldwin's analysis of the reactive consciousness. In this there are, he says (*Feeling and Will*, p. 60), "three elements corresponding to the three elements of the nervous arc. First, the receiving consciousness, the stimulus —say a loud, unexpected noise; second, the attention involuntarily drawn, the registering element; and, third, the muscular reaction following upon the sound—say flight from fancied danger." Now, in the first place, such an analysis is incomplete; it ignores the status prior to hearing the sound. Of course, if this status is irrelevant to what happens afterwards, such ignoring is quite legitimate. But is it irrelevant either to the quantity or to the quality of the stimulus?

If one is reading a book, if one is hunting, if one is watching in a dark place on a lonely night, if one is performing a chemical experiment, in each case, the noise has a very different mental value; it is a different experience. In any case, what precedes the "stimulus" is a whole act, a sensory-motor coordination. What is more to the point, the "stimulus" emerges out of this coordination; it is born from it as its matrix; it represents as it were an escape from it. I might here fall back upon authority, and refer to the widely accepted sensation continuum theory, according to which the sound cannot be absolutely *ex abrupto* from the outside, but is simply a shifting of focus of emphasis, a redistribution of tensions within a former act; and declare that unless the hearing activity had been present to some extent in the prior coordination, it would be impossible for it now to come to prominence in consciousness. And such a reference would be only an amplification of what has already been said concerning the way in which the prior activity influences the value of the sound sensation. Or, we might point to cases of hypnotism, monoidealism, and absentmindedness, like that of Archimedes, as evidences that if the previous coordination is such as rigidly to lock the door, the auditory disturbance will knock in vain for admission, so that the auditory activity must already have one foot over the threshold if it is ever to gain admittance.

But it will be more satisfactory, probably, to refer to the biological side of the case, and point out that as the ear activity has been evolved on account of the advantage gained by the whole organism, it must stand in the strictest histological and physiological connection with the eye, or hand, or leg, or whatever other organ has been the overt center of action. It is absolutely impossible to think of the eye center as monopolizing consciousness and the ear apparatus as wholly quiescent. What happens is a certain relative prominence and subsidence as between the various organs which maintain the organic equilibrium.

Furthermore, the sound is not a mere stimulus, or mere sensation; it again is an act, that of hearing. Muscular response as well as sensory stimulus is involved; that is, there is a certain definite motor apparatus involved in hearing just as much as there is in subsequent running away. The movement and posture of the head, the tension of the ear muscles, are required for the "reception" of the sound. It is just as true to say that the sensation of sound arises from a motor response as that the running away is a response to the sound. This may be brought out by reference to the fact that Professor Baldwin, in the passage quoted, has inverted the real order as between his first and second elements. We do not have first a sound and then activity of attention, unless sound is taken as mere nervous shock or physical event, not as conscious quality. The conscious sensation of sound depends upon the motor response having already taken place; or, in terms of the previous statement (if stimulus is used as a conscious fact, and not as a mere physical event), it is the motor response or attention which develops the original nervous shock into the stimulus to another act. Once more, the final "element," the running away, is not merely motor, but is sensory-motor, having its sensor value and its muscular mechanism. It is also a coordination. And, finally, this sensory-motor coordination is not a new act, supervening upon what preceded. Just as the "response" is necessary to constitute the stimulus to determine it as sound and as *this* kind of sound—of wild beast or robber—so the sound experience must persist as a value in the running, to keep it up, to control it. No one thinks that the motor reaction involved in the running is a separate, disconnected event, but neither is it to be regarded as merely reaction to the sound. It occurs to change the sound, or more exactly, to develop the suggested experiences which make the sound really significant. The movement, whatever it may be, has its meaning wholly determined by reference to the hearing of the sound. It *is* that experience mediated.* What we have is a circuit, not an arc or broken segment of a circle. This circuit is more truly termed organic than reflex, because the motor response determines the stimulus, just as truly as sensory stimulus determines movement. Indeed, the movement is only for the sake of determining the stimulus, of fixing what kind of stimulus it is, of interpreting it.

I hope it will not appear that I am introducing needless refinements and distinctions into what, it may be urged, is after all an undoubted fact, that movement as response follows sensation as stimulus. It is not a question of making the account of the process more complicated, though it is always wise to beware of that false simplicity which is attained by leaving out of account a large part of the problem. It is a question of finding out what stimulus or sensation, what movement and response mean; a question of seeing that they mean distinctions of flexible function only, not of fixed existence; that one and the same occurrence plays either or both parts, according to the shift of interest; and that because of this functional distinction and relationship, the supposed problem of the adjustment of one to the other, whether by superior force in the stimulus or an agency *ad hoc* in the center or the soul, is a purely self-created problem.

We may see the disjointed character of the present theory by calling to mind that it is impossible to apply the phrase "sensory-motor" to the occurrence as a simple phrase of description; it has validity only as a term of interpretation, only, that is, as defining various functions exercised. In terms of description, the whole process may be

---

* In other words, every reaction is of the same type as that which Professor Baldwin ascribes to imitation alone, viz., circular. Imitation is simply that particular form of the circuit in which the "response" lends itself to comparatively unchanged maintenance of the prior experience. I say comparatively unchanged, for so far as this maintenance means additional control over the experience, it is being physically changed, becoming more distinct. It is safe to suppose, moreover, that "repetition" is kept up only so long as this growth or mediation goes on. There is a new-in-the-old, if it is only the new sense of power.

sensory or it may be motor, but it cannot be sensory-motor. The "stimulus," the excitation of the nerve ending and of the sensory nerve, the central change, are just as much, or just as little, motion as are the events taking place in the motor nerve and the muscles. It is one uninterrupted, continuous redistribution of mass in motion. And there is nothing in the process, from the standpoint of description, which entitles us to call this reflex. It is redistribution pure and simple; as much so as the burning of a log, or the falling of a house or the movement of the wind. In the physical process, as physical, there is nothing which can be set off as stimulus, nothing which reacts, nothing which is response. There is just a change in the system of tensions.

The same sort of thing is true when we describe the process purely from the psychical side. It is now all sensation, all sensory quale; the motion, as psychically described, is just as much sensation as is sound or light or burn. Take the withdrawing of the hand from the candle flame as example. What we have is a certain visual-heat-pain-muscular quale, transformed into another visual-touch-muscular quale—the flame now being visible only at a distance, or not at all, the touch sensation being altered, etc. If we symbolize the original visual quale by v, the temperature by h, the accompanying muscular sensation by m', the whole experience may be stated as vhm-vhm-vhm'; m being the quale of withdrawing, m' the sense of the status after the withdrawal. The motion is now not a certain kind of existence; it is a sort of sensory experience interpreted, just as is candle flame, or burn from candle flame. All are on a par.

But, in spite of all this, it will be urged, there is a distinction between stimulus and response, between sensation and motion. Precisely, but we ought now to be in a condition to ask of what nature is the distinction, instead of taking it for granted as a distinction somehow lying in the existence of the facts themselves.

If the previous descriptive analysis has made obvious the need of reconsideration of the reflex arc idea, and the nest of difficulties and assumptions in the apparently simple statement, it is now time to undertake an explanatory analysis. The fact is that stimulus and response are not distinctions of existence, but teleological distinctions, that is, distinctions of function, or part played, with reference to reaching or maintaining an end. With respect to this teleological process, two stages should be discriminated, as their confusion is one cause of the confusion attending the whole matter. In one stage, the relation represents an organization of means with reference to a comprehensive end. It represents an accomplished adaptation. Such is the case in all well developed instincts, as when we say that the contact of eggs is a stimulus to the hen to set; or the sight of corn a stimulus to peck; such also is the case with all thoroughly formed habits, as when the contact with the floor stimulates walking. In these instances there is no question of consciousness of stimulus *as* stimulus, of response *as* response. There is simply a continuously ordered sequence of acts, all adapted in themselves and in the order of their sequence, to reach a certain objective, end, the reproduction of the species, the preservation of life, locomotion to a certain place. The end has got thoroughly organized into the means. In calling one stimulus, another response we mean nothing more than that an orderly sequence of acts is taking place. The same sort of statement might be made equally well with reference to the succession of changes in a plant, so far as these are considered with reference to their adaptation to, say, producing seed. It is equally applicable to the series of events in the circulation of the blood, or the sequence of acts occurring in a self-binding reaper.*

Cases of organization which already attained, we may say, positively, that it is only the assumed common reference to an inclusive end which makes either member off as stimulus or response, that apart from such reference we have only antecedent and consequent; † in other words, the distinction is one of interpretation. Negatively, it must be pointed out that it is not legitimate to carry over, without change, exactly the same order of considerations to cases where it is a question of *conscious* stimulation and response. We may, in this stage, regard, if we please, stimulus and response each as an entire act, having an individuality of its own, subject even here to the qualification that

---

* To avoid misapprehension, I would say that I am not raising the question as to how far this teleology is real in any one of these cases; real or unreal, my point holds equally well. It is only when we regard the sequence of acts *as if* they were adapted to reach some end that it occurs to us to speak of one as stimulus and the other as response. Otherwise, we look at them as *mere* succession.

† Whether, even in such a determination, there is still not a reference to a more latent kind of an end is, of course, left open.

individuality means not an entirely independent whole, but a division of labor as regards maintaining or reaching an end. But in any case, it is an *act*, a sensory-motor coordination, which stimulates the response, itself in turn sensory-motor, not a sensation which stimulates a movement. Hence the illegitimacy of identifying, as is so often done, cases of organized instincts or habits with the so-called reflex arc or of transferring, without modification, considerations valid of this serial coordination of acts to the sensation-movement case.

The fallacy that arises when this is done is virtually the psychological or historical fallacy. A set of considerations which hold good only because of a completed process, is read into the content of the process which conditions this completed result. A state of things characterizing an outcome is regarded as a true description of the events which led up to this outcome; when, as a matter of fact, if this outcome had already been in existence, there would have been no necessity for the process. Or, to make the application to the case in hand, considerations valid of an attained organization or coordination, the orderly sequence of minor acts in a comprehensive coordination, are used to describe a process, viz., the distinction of mere sensation as stimulus and of mere movement as response, which takes place only because such an attained organization is no longer at hand, but is in process of constitution. Neither mere sensation, nor mere movement, can ever be either stimulus or response; only an act can be that; the *sensation* as stimulus means the lack of and search for such an objective stimulus, or orderly placing of an act; just as mere movement as response means the lack of and search for the right act to complete a desired coordination.

A recurrence to our example will make these formulas clearer. As long as the seeing is an unbroken act, which is as experienced no more mere sensation than it is mere motion (though the onlooker or psychological observer can interpret it into sensation and movement), it is in no sense the sensation which stimulates the reaching; we have, as already sufficiently indicated, only the serial steps in a coordination of *acts*. But now take a child who, upon reaching for bright light (that is, exercising the seeing-reaching coordination), has sometimes had a delightful exercise, sometimes found something good to eat, and sometimes burned himself. *Now the response is not only uncertain, but the stimulus is equally uncertain; one is uncertain only in so far as the other is.* The real problem may be equally well stated as either to discover the right stimulus, to constitute the stimulus, or to discover, to constitute, the response. The question of whether to reach or to abstain from reaching is the question what sort of bright light have we here? Is it the one which means playing with one's hands, eating milk, or burning one's fingers? The stimulus must be constituted for the response to occur. Now it is at precisely this juncture and because of it that the distinction of sensation as stimulus and motion as response arises.

The conscious sensation of a stimulus is not a thing or existence by itself; it is that phase of a coordination requiring attention because, by reason of the conflict within the coordination, it is uncertain how to complete it. Uncertainty as to the next act, whether to reach or not, gives the motive to examining the act. The end to follow is, in this sense, the stimulus. It furnishes the motivation to attend to what has just taken place; to define it more carefully. From this point of view the discovery of the stimulus is the "response" to possible movement as "stimulus." We must have an anticipatory sensation, an image, of the movements that may occur, together with their respective values, before attention will go to the seeing to break it up as a sensation of light, and of light of this particular kind. It is the initiated activities of reaching, which, inhibited by the conflict in the coordination, turn round, as it were, upon the seeing, and hold it from passing over into further act until its quality is determined. Just here the act as objective stimulus becomes transformed into sensation as *possible,* or conscious, stimulus. Just here, also, motion as conscious response emerges.

In other words, sensation as stimulus does not mean any particular psychical *existence.* It means simply a function, and it will have its value shift according to the special work requiring to be done. At one moment the various activities of reaching and withdrawing will be the sensation, because they are that phase of activity which sets the problem, or creates the demand for the next act. At the next moment the previous act of seeing will furnish the sensation, being, in turn, that phase of activity which sets the pace upon which depends further action. Generalized, sensation as stimulus is always that phase of activity requiring to be defined in order that a coordination may be completed. What the sensation will be in particular at a given time, therefore, will depend entirely upon the way in which an activity is being directed. It has no fixed quality of its own. The search for the stimulus is the search for exact conditions of action; that is, for the state of things which decides how a beginning coordination should be completed.

Similarly, motion, as response, has only a functional value. It is whatever will serve to complete the disintegrating coordination. Just as the discovery of the sensation marks the establishing of the problem, so the constitution of the response marks the solution of this problem. At one time, holding the eye fixed upon the seeing and thus bringing out a certain quale of light is the response, because that is the particular act called for just then; at another time, the movement of the arm away from the light is response. There is nothing in itself which may be labeled response. That one certain set of sensory qualities should be marked off by themselves as "motion" and put in antithesis to such sensory qualities as those of color, sound and contact, as legitimate claimants to the title of sensation, is wholly inexplicable unless we keep the difference of function in view. It is the eye and ear sensations which fix for us the problem; which report to us the conditions which have to be met if the coordination is to be successfully completed; and just the moment we need to know about our movements to get an adequate report, just that moment, motion miraculously (from the ordinary standpoint) ceases to be motion and becomes "muscular sensation." On the other hand, take the change in values of experience, the transformation of sensory quales. Whether this change will or will not be interpreted as movement, whether or not any consciousness of movement will arise, will depend upon whether this change is satisfactory, whether or not it is regarded as a harmonious development of a coordination, or whether the change is regarded simply as a means in solving a problem, an instrument in reaching a more satisfactory coordination. So long as our experience runs smoothly we are no more conscious of motion as motion than we are of this or that color or sound by itself.

To sum up: the distinction of sensation and movement as stimulus and response respectively is not a distinction which can be regarded as descriptive of anything which holds of psychical events or physical existences as such.

The only events to which the terms stimulus and response can be descriptively applied are minor acts serving by their respective positions the maintenance of some organized coordination. The conscious stimulus or sensation, and the conscious response or motion, have a special genesis or motivation, and a special end or function. The reflex arc theory, by neglecting, by abstracting form, this genesis and this function gives us one disjointed part of a process as if it were the whole. It gives us literally an arc, instead of the circuit; and not giving us the circuit of which it is an arc, does not enable us to place, to center, the arc. This arc, again, falls apart into two separate existences having to be either mechanically, or externally, adjusted to each other.

The circuit is a coordination, some of whose members have come into conflict with each other. It is the temporary disintegration and need of reconstruction which occasions, which affords the genesis of, the conscious distinction into sensory stimulus on one side and motor response on the other. The stimulus is that phase of the forming coordination which represents the conditions which have to be met in bringing it to a successful issue; the response is that phase of one and the same forming coordination which gives the key to meeting these conditions, which serves as instrument in effecting the successful coordination. They are therefore strictly correlative and contemporaneous. The stimulus is something to be discovered; to be made out; if the activity affords its own adequate stimulation, there is no stimulus save in the objective sense already referred to. As soon as it is adequately determined, then and only then is the response also complete. Attainment of either, means that the coordination has completed itself. Moreover, it is the motor response which assists in discovering and constituting the stimulus. It is the holding of the movement at a certain stage which creates the sensation, which throws it into relief.

It is the coordination which unifies that which the reflex arc concept gives us only in disjointed fragments. It is the circuit within which fall distinctions of stimulus and response as functional phases of its own mediation or completion. The point of this story is in its application; but the application of it to the question of the nature of mental development, to the distinction between sensational and rational consciousness, and to the nature of judgment must be deferred to a more favorable opportunity.

XIV The Practical Character
of Reality*

. . . Why should the idea that knowledge makes a difference to and in things be antecedently objectionable? If one is already committed to a belief that Reality is neatly and finally tied up in a packet without loose ends, unfinished issues, or new departures, one would object to knowledge making a difference just as one would object to any other impertinent obtruder. But if one believes that the world itself is in transformation, why should the notion that knowledge is the most important mode of its modification and the only organ of its guidance be *a priori* obnoxious?

There is, I think, no answer save that the theory of knowledge has been systematically built up on the notion of a static universe, so that even those perfectly free to feel the lessons of physics and biology concerning moving energy and evolution, and of history concerning the constant transformation of man's affairs (science included), retain an unquestioning belief in a theory of knowledge which is out of any possible harmony with their own theory of the matters to be known. Modern epistemology, having created the idea that the way to frame right conceptions is to analyze knowledge, has strengthened this view. For it at once leads to the view that realities must themselves have a theoretic and intellectual complexion—not a practical one. This view is naturally congenial to idealists; but that realists should so readily play in to the hands of idealists by asserting what, on the basis of a formal theory of knowledge, realities must be, instead of accepting the guidance of things in divining what knowledge *is,* is an anomaly so striking as to support the view that the notion of static

* Originally in *Essays, Philosophical and Psychological in Honor of William James* (New York, 1908). For the complete source see p. 377, below.

reality has taken its last stand in ideas about knowledge. Take, for example, the most striking, because the extreme case—knowledge of a past event. It is absurd to suppose that knowledge makes a difference to the final or appropriate content of knowledge: to the subject matter which fulfils the requirements of knowing. In this case, it would get in its own way and trip itself up in endless regress. But it seems the very superstition of intellectualism to suppose that this fact about knowledge can decide what is the nature of that reference to the past which, when rightly made, is final. No doctrine about knowledge can hinder the belief—if there be sufficient specific evidence for it—that what we know as past may be something which has *irretrievably* undergone just the difference which knowledge makes.

Now arguments against pragmatism—by which I mean the doctrine that reality possesses practical character and that this character is most efficaciously expressed in the function of intelligence *—seem to fall blandly into this fallacy. They assume that to hold that knowledge makes a difference in existences is equivalent to holding that it makes a difference in the object *to be* known, thus defeating its own purpose; witness that the reality which is the appropriate object of knowledge in a given case may be precisely a reality in which knowing has succeeded in making the needed difference. This question is not one to be settled by manipulation of the concept of knowledge, nor by dialectic discussion of its essence or nature. It is a question of facts, a question of what knowing exists as in the scheme of existence. If things undergo change without thereby ceasing to be real, there can be no *formal* bar to knowing being one specific kind of change in things, nor to its test being found in the successful carrying into effect of the kind of change intended. If knowing be a change in a reality, then the more knowing reveals this change, the more transparent, the more adequate, it is. And if all exis-

---

* This definition, in the present state of discussion, is an arbitrary or personal one. The text does not mean that "pragmatism" is currently used exclusively in this sense; obviously there are other senses. It does not mean it is the sense in which it *ought* to be used. I have no wish to legislate either for language or for philosophy. But it marks the sense in which *is* is used in this paper; and the pragmatic movement is still so loose and variable that I judge one has a right to fix his own meaning, provided he serves notice and adheres to it.

tences are in transition, then the knowledge which treats
them as if they were something of which knowledge is a
kodak fixation is just the kind of knowledge which refracts
and perverts them. And by the same token a knowing
which actively participates in a change in the way to effect
it in the needed fashion would be the type of knowing
which is valid. If reality be itself in transition—and this
doctrine originated not with the objectionable pragmatist
but with the physicist and naturalist and historian—then
the doctrine that knowledge *is* reality making a particular
and specified sort of change in itself seems to have the
best chance at maintaining a theory of knowing which is
in wholesome touch with the genuine and valid.

ii

If the ground be cleared of *a priori* objections, and if it be
evident that pragmatism cannot be disposed of by any formal or dialectic manipulations of "knowledge" or "truth,"
but only by showing that some specific things are not of
the sort claimed, we may consider some common sense
affiliations of pragmatism. Common sense regards intelligence as having a purpose, and knowledge as amounting
to something. I once heard a physicist, quite innocent of
the pragmatic controversy, remark that the knowledge of
a mechanic or farmer was what the Yankee calls gumption—acknowledgment of things in their belongings and
uses, and that to his mind natural science was gumption
on a larger scale: the convenient cataloguing and arranging of a whole lot of things with reference to their most
efficacious services. Popularly, good judgment is judgment
as to the relative values of things: good sense is horse
sense, ability to take hold of things right end up, to fit an
instrument to an obstacle, to select resources apt for a task.
To be reasonable is to recognize things in their office as obstacles and as resources. Intelligence, in its ordinary use, is a
practical term; ability to size up matters with respect to the
needs and possibilities of the various situations in which
one is called to do something; capacity to envisage things
in terms of the adjustments and adaptations they make possible or hinder. One objective test of the presence or ab-

sence of intelligence is influence upon behavior. No capacity to make adjustments means no intelligence; conduct evincing management of complex and novel conditions means a high degree of reason. Such conditions at least suggest that a reality-to-be-known, a reality which is the appropriate subject-matter of knowledge is reality-of-use-and-inuse, direct or indirect, and that a reality which is not in any sort of use, or bearing upon use, may go hang, *so far as knowledge is concerned.*

No one, I suppose, would deny that knowledge *issues* in some action which changes things to some extent— be the action only a more deliberate maintenance of a course of conduct already instinctively entered upon. When I see a sign on the street corner I can turn or go on, knowing what I am about. The perceptions of the scientist need have no such overt or "utilitarian" uses, but surely after them he behaves differently, as an inquirer if in no other way; and the cumulative effect of such changes finally modifies the overt action of the ordinary man. That knowing, *after the event,* makes a difference of this sort, few I suppose would deny: if that were all pragmatism means, it would perhaps be accepted as a harmless truism. But there is a further question of fact: just how is the "consequent" action related to the "precedent" knowledge? When *is* "after the event"? What degree of continuity exists? Is the difference between knowing and acting intelligently one of kind or simply one of dominant quality? How does a thing, if it is not already in change in the knowing, manage to issue at its term in action? Moreover, do not the changes actively effected constitute the whole *import* of the knowledge, and hence its final measure and test of validity? If it merely *happens* that knowing when it is done with passes into some action, by what miracle is the subsequent action so pat to the situation? Is it not rather true that the "knowledge" is instituted and framed in anticipation of the consequent issue, and, in the degree in which it is wise and prudent, is held open to revision during it? Certainly the moralist (one might quote, for example, Goethe, Carlyle, and Mazzini) and the common man often agree that full knowledge, adequate assurance of reality is found only in the issue which fulfills ideas; that we have to do a doctrine to *know* its truth; otherwise it is only dogma or doctrinaire program. Experimental science is a recognition that no idea is entitled to be termed knowledge till it has passed into such overt manipulation of physical conditions as constructs the object to which the idea refers. If one could get rid of one's traditional logical theories and set to work afresh to frame a theory of knowledge on the basis of the procedure of the common man, the moralist, and the experimentalist, would it be the forced or the natural procedure to say that the realities which we *know,* which we are sure of, are precisely those realities that have taken shape in and through the active procedures of knowing?

I turn to another type of consideration. Certainly one of the most genuine problems of modern life is the reconciliation of the scientific view of the universe with the claims of the moral life. Are judgments in terms of the redistribution of matter in motion (or some other closed formula) alone valid? Or are accounts of the universe in terms of possibility and desirability, of initiative and responsibility, also valid? There is no occasion to expatiate on the importance of the moral life, nor upon the supreme importance of intelligence within the moral life. But there does seem to be occasion for asking how moral judgments—judgments of the would and should—relate themselves to the world of scientific knowledge. To frame a theory of knowledge which makes it necessary to deny the validity of moral ideas, or else to refer them to some other and separate kind of universe from that of common sense and science, is both provincial and arbitrary. The pragmatist has at least tried to face, and not to dodge, the question of how it is that moral and scientific "knowledge" can both hold of one and the same world. And whatever the difficulties in his proffered solution, the conception that scientific judgments are to be assimilated to moral is closer to common sense than is the theory that validity is to be denied to moral judgments because they do not square with a preconceived theory of the nature of the world to which scientific judgments must refer. And all moral judgments are about changes to be made.

iii

I turn to one affiliation of the pragmatic theory with the results of recent science. The necessity, for the occurrence of an event in the way of knowledge, of an organism which reacts or behaves in a specific way, would seem to be as well established as any specific proposition. It is a peculiar fact, a fact fit to stir curiosity, that the rational function seems to be intercalated in a scheme of practical adjustments. The parts and members of the organism are certainly not there primarily for pure intellection or for theoretic contemplation. The brain, the last physical organ of thought, is a part of the same practical machinery for bringing about adaptation of the environment to the life requirements of the organism, to which belong legs and hand and eye. That the brain frees organic behavior from complete servitude to immediate physical conditions, that it makes possible the liberation of energy for remote and ever expanding ends is, indeed, a precious fact, but not one which removes the brain from the category of organic devices of behavior.* That the organ of thinking, of knowledge, was at least originally an organ of conduct, few, I imagine, will deny. And even if we try to believe that the cognitive function has supervened as a different operation, it is difficult to believe that the transfiguration has been so radical that knowing has lost all traces of its connection with vital impulse. But unless we so assume, have we any alternatives except to hold that this continual presence of vital impulse is a disturbing and refracting factor, which forever prevents knowledge from reaching its own aim; or else that a certain promoting, a certain carrying forward of the vital impulse, importing certain differences in things, *is* the aim of knowledge?

The problem cannot be evaded—save ostrich-wise—by saying that such considerations are "merely genetic," or

---

* It is interesting to note how the metaphysical puzzles regarding "parallelism," "interaction," "automatism," the relation of "consciousness" to "body," evaporate when one ceases isolating the brain into a peculiar physical substrate of mind at large, and treats it simply as one portion of the body which is the instrumentality of adaptive behavior.

"psychological," having to do only with the origin and natural history of knowing. For the point is that the organic reaction, the behavior of the organism, affects the *content* of awareness. The subject matter of all awareness is thing-related-to-organism—related as stimulus direct or indirect or as material of response, present or remote, ulterior or achieved.

No one—so far as I know—denies this with respect to the perceptual field of awareness. Pains, pleasures, hunger, and thirst, all "secondary" qualities, involve inextricably the "interaction" of organism and environment. The perceptual field is distributed and arranged as the possible field of selective reactions of the organism at its center. Up and down, far and near, before and behind, right and left, hard and soft (as well as white and black, bass and alto), involve reference to a center of behavior.

This material has so long been the stock in trade of both idealistic arguments and proclamations of the agnóstic "relativity" of knowledge that philosophers have grown aweary of listening. But even this lethargy might be quickened by a moderate hospitality to the pragmatic interpretation. That red, or far and near, or hard and soft, or big and little, involves a relation between organism and environment is no more an argument for idealism than is the fact that water involves a relation between hydrogen and oxygen.* It is, however, an argument for the ultimately practical value of these distinctions—that they are *differences* made in what things would have been without organic behavior—differences made not by "consciousness" or "mind," but by the organism as the active center of a system of activities. Moreover, the whole agnostic sting of the doctrine of "relativity" lies in the assumption that the ideal or aim of knowledge is to repeat or copy a prior existence—in which case, of course, the making of contemporaneous differences by the organism in the very fact of awareness would get in the way and forever hinder the knowledge function from the fulfillment of its proper end. Knowledge, awareness, in this case suffers from an impediment which no surgery can better. But if the aim of knowing be precisely to make *certain* differences in an environment, to carry on to *favorable issue*, by the readjustment

* I owe this illustration to my colleague, Dr. Montague.

of the organism, certain changes going on indifferently in the environment, then the fact that the changes of the organism enter pervasively into the subject matter of awareness is no restriction or perversion of knowledge, but part of the fulfillment of its office.

The only question would then be whether *proper* reactions take place. The whole agnostic, positivistic controversy is flanked by a single move. The issue is no longer an ideally necessary but actually impossible copying, *versus* an improper but unavoidable modification of reality through organic inhibitions and stimulations: but it is the right, the economical, the effective, and, if one may venture, the useful and satisfactory reaction *versus* the wasteful, the enslaving, the misleading, and the confusing reaction. The presence of organic response, influencing and modifying every content, every subject matter of awareness, is the undoubted fact. But the significant thing is the *way* organic behavior enters in—the *way* it influences and modifies. We assign very different values to different types of "knowledge"—or subject matters involving organic attitudes and operations. Some are only guesses, opinions, suspicious characters; others are "knowledge" in the honorific and eulogistic sense—science; some turn out mistakes, blunders, errors. Whence and how this discrimination of quality in what is taken at its own time to be good knowledge? Why and how is the content of some "knowledge" genuine-knowing and of other mis-knowing? Awareness is itself a blanket term, covering, in the same bed, delusion, doubt, confusion, ambiguity, and definition, organization, logical conclusiveness assured by evidence and reason. Any naturalistic or realistic theory is committed to the idea that all of these terms bear impartially the same relation to things considered as sheer existence. What we must have in any case is the same existences—the same in kind —only differently arranged or linked up. But why then the tremendous difference in value? And if the unnaturalist, the nonrealist, says the difference is one of existential kind, made by the working here malign, there benign, of "consciousness," "psychical" operations and states, upon the existences which are the direct subject matter of knowledge, there is still the problem of discriminating the conditions and nature of the respective beneficent and malicious interventions of the peculiar "existence" labeled consciousness.* The realness of error, ambiguity, doubt and guess poses a problem. It is a problem which has perplexed philosophy so long and has led to so many speculative adventures, that it would seem worth while, were it only for the sake of variety, to listen to the pragmatic solution according to which it is the business of the organic adaptation involved in all knowing to make a *certain* difference in reality, but *not* to make any old or casual difference. The right, the true and good, difference is that which carries out satisfactorily the specific purpose for the sake of which knowing occurs. All manufactures are the product of an activity, but it does not follow that all manufactures are equally good. And so all "knowledges" are differences made in things by knowing, but some differences are not calculated or wanted in the knowing, and hence are disturbers and interlopers when they come—while others fulfill the intent of the knowing, being in harmony with the consistent behavior of the organism and reinforcing and enlarging its function. A mistake is literally a mishandling; a doubt is a temporary suspense and vacillation of reactions; and ambiguity is the tension of alternative but incompatible modes of responsive treatment; an inquiry is a tentative and retrievable (because intraorganic) mode of activity, entered upon prior to launching upon a knowledge which is public, ineluctable—without anchors to windward—since it has taken physical effect through overt action.

It is practically all one to say that the norm of honorable knowing is to make no difference in *its* object, and that its aim is to attain and buttress a specific kind of difference in reality. Knowing fails in its business if it makes a change in its *own* object—that is a mistake; but its own object is none the less a prior existence changed in a certain way. Nor is this a play upon the two senses—end and subject matter—of "object." The organism has its appropriate functions. To maintain, to expand, adequate functioning is its business. This functioning does not occur *in vacuo*. It involves cooperative and readjusted changes in the cosmic medium. Hence the appropriate subject matter of awareness is not reality at large, a metaphysical heaven to be mimeographed at many removes upon a badly con-

* Of course on the theory I am interested in expounding, the so-called action of "consciousness" means simply the organic releases in the way of behavior which are the conditions of awareness, and which also modify its content.

structed mental carbon paper which yields at best only fragmentary, blurred, and erroneous copies. Its proper and legitimate object is that relationship of organism and environment in which functioning is most amply and effectively attained; or by which, in case of obstruction and consequent needed experimentation, its later eventual free course is most facilitated. As for the reality, metaphysical reality *at large,* it may, so far as awareness is concerned, go to its own place.

For ordinary purposes, that is for practical purposes, the truth and the realness of things are synonymous. We are all children who say "really and truly." A reality which is taken in organic response so as to lead to subsequent reactions that are off the track and aside from the mark, while it is, existentially speaking, perfectly real, is not *good* reality. It lacks the hallmark of value. Since it is a certain *kind* of object which we want, one which will be as favorable as possible to a consistent and liberal or growing functioning, it is this kind, the *true* kind, which for us monopolizes the title of reality. Pragmatically, teleologically, this identification of truth and "reality" is sound and reasonable: rationalistically, it leads to the notion of the duplicate versions of reality, one absolute and static because exhausted; the other phenomenal and kept continually on the jump because otherwise its own inherent nothingness would lead to its total annihilation. Since it is only genuine or sincere things, things which are good for what they lay claim to in the way of consequences, which we want or are after, *morally* they alone are "real."

iv

So far we have been dealing with awareness as a fact—a fact there like any fact—and have been concerned to show that the subject matter of awareness is, in any case, things in process of change; and in such change that the knowing function takes a hand in trying to guide it or steer it, so that *some* (and *not* other) consequences accrue. But what about the awareness itself? What happens when it is made the subject matter of awareness? What sort of a thing is it? It is, I submit, mere sophistication (futile at that), to argue either that we cannot become aware of awareness without involving ourselves in an endless regress, or that whenever we are aware of anything we are thereby necessarily aware of awareness once for all, so that it has no character save a purely formal and empty one. Taken concretely, awareness is an event with certain specifiable conditions. We may indeed be aware of it formally, as a bare fact, just as we may be cognizant of an explosion without knowing anything of its nature. But we may also be aware of it in a curious and analytic spirit, undertaking to study it in detail. This inquiry, like any other inquiry, proceeds by determining conditions and consequences. Here awareness is a characteristic fact, presenting to inquiry its own characteristic earmarks, and a valid knowledge of awareness is the same sort of thing as valid knowledge of the spectrum or of a trotting horse; it proceeds generically in the same way and must satisfy the same generic tests.

What, then, is awareness found to be? The following answer, dogmatically summary in form, involves positive difficulties, and glides over many points where our ignorance is still too great. But it represents a general trend of scientific inquiry, carried on, I hardly need say, on its own merits without respect to the pragmatic controversy. Awareness means *attention,* and attention means a crisis of some sort in an existent situation; a forking of the roads of some material, a tendency to go this way and that. It represents something the matter, something out of gear, or in some way menaced, insecure, problematical and strained. This state of tension, of ambiguous indications, projects, and tendencies, is not merely in the "mind," it is nothing merely emotional. It is in the facts of the situation as transitive facts; the emotional or "subjective" disturbance is just a part of the larger disturbance. And if, employing the *language* of psychology, we say that attention is a phenomenon of conflicting habits, being the process of resolving this conflict by finding an act which functions all the factors concerned, this language does not make the facts "merely psychological"—whatever that means.* The habits are as biologic as they are "personal," and as cosmic as they are biologic. They are the total order of

---

* What does it mean? Does the objectivity of fact disappear when the biologist gives it a biological statement? Why not object to his conclusions on the ground that they are "merely" biological?

things expressed in one way; just as a physical or chemical phenomenon is the same order expressed in another way. The statement in terms of conflict and readjustment of habits is at most one way of locating the disturbance in *things;* it furnishes no substitute for, or rival of, reality, and no "psychical" duplication.

If this be true, then awareness, even in its most perplexed and confused state, that of maximum doubt and precariousness of subject matter, means things entering, *via* the particular thing known as organism, into a peculiar condition of differential—or additive—change. How can we refuse to raise and consider the question of how things in this condition are related to the prior state which emerges into it, and to the subsequent state of things into which it issues? *

Suppose the case to be awareness of a chair. Suppose that this awareness comes only when there is some problematic affair with which the chair is in some way—in whatever degree of remoteness—concerned. It may be a wonder whether it is a chair at all; or whether it is strong enough to stand on; or where I shall put it; or whether it is worth what I paid for it; or, as not infrequently happens, the situation involved in uncertainty may be some philosophic matter in which the perception of the chair is cited as evidence or illustration. (Humorously enough, awareness of it may even be cited in the course of a philosophic argument intended to show that awareness has nothing to do with situations of incompleteness and ambiguity.) Now what of the change the chair undergoes in entering this way into a situation of perplexed inquiry? Is this any part of the genuiness of that chair with which we are concerned? If not, where is the change found? In something totally different called "consciousness"? In that case how can the operations of inquiry, of observation and memory and reflection, ever have any assurance of getting referred back to the *right* object? Positively the presump-

---

* It is this question *of the relation to one another of different successive states of things* which the pragmatic method substitutes for the epistemological inquiry of how one sort of existence, purely mental, temporal but not spatial, immaterial, made up of sublimated gaseous consciousness, can get beyond itself and have valid reference to a totally different kind of existence—spatial and extended; and how it can receive impressions from the latter, etc.—all the questions which constitute that species of confirmed intellectual lockjaw called epistemology.

tion is that the *chair-of-which-we-are-speaking is* the chair *of-which-we-are-speaking;* it is the *same* thing that is out there which is also involved in the doubtful situation. Moreover, the reference to "consciousness" as the exclusive locus of the doubt only repeats the problem, for "consciousness," by the theory under consideration, means, after all, only the chair *as* concerned in the problematical situation. The *physical* chair remains unchanged, you say. Surely, if, as is altogether likely, what is *meant by* physical is precisely *that part* of the chair as object of total awareness which remains unaffected, for certain possible purposes, by entering for certain other actual purposes into the situation of awareness. But how can we segregate, *antecedently* to experimental inquiry, the "physical" chair from the chair which is now the object to be known; into what contradictions do we fall when we attempt to define the object of one awareness not in its own terms, but in terms of a selected type of object which is the appropriate subject-matter of some other cognizance!

But awareness means inquiry as well as doubt—there are the negative and positive, the retrospective and the prospective relationships of the thing. This means a genuinely *additive* quality—one of readjustment in prior things.* I know the dialectic argument that nothing can assume a new relation, because in order to do so it must already be completely related—when it comes from an absolutist I can understand why he holds it, even if I cannot understand the idea itself. But apart from this conceptual reasoning we must follow the lead of our subject matter; and when we find a thing assuming new relations in the process of inquiry, must accept the fact, and frame our theory of things and of knowing to include it, not assert that it is impossible because we already have a theory of knowledge which precludes it. In inquiry, the existence which has become doubtful always undergoes experimental reconstruction. This may be largely imaginative or "speculative." We may view certain things *as if* placed under varying conditions, and consider what then happens to them. But such differences are really transformative as far as they go— and besides, such inquiries never reach conclusions finally

---

* We have arrived here, upon a more analytic platform, at the point made earlier concerning the fact that knowing *issues* in action which changes things.

justifiable. In important and persistent inquiry, we insist upon something in the way of actual physical making—be it only a diagram. In other words, *science,* or knowing in its honorific sense, is experimental, involving physical construction. We insist upon something being *done about* it, that we may see how the idea when carried into effect comports with the other things through which our activities are hedged in and released. To avoid this conclusion by saying that knowing makes no difference in the "truth," but merely is the preliminary exercise which discovers it, is that old friend whose acquaintance we have repeatedly made in this discussion: the fallacy of confusing an existence anteceding knowing with the object which terminates and fulfills it. For knowing to make a difference in its own final term is gross self-stultification; it is none the less so when the aim of knowing is precisely to guide things straight up to this term. When "truth" means the accomplished introduction of certain new differences into conditions, why be foolish enough to introduce other differences, which are not wanted since they are irrelevant and misleading?

Were it not for the teachings of sad experience, it would not be necessary to add that the change in environment made by knowing is not a total or miraculous change. Transformation, readjustment, reconstruction, all imply prior existences: existences which have characters and behaviors of their own which must be accepted, consulted, humored, manipulated or made light of, in all kinds of differing ways in the different contexts of different problems. Making a difference in reality does not mean making any more difference than we find by experimentation can be made under the given conditions—even though we may still hope for different fortune another time under other circumstances. Still less does it mean making a thing into an unreality, though the pragmatist is sometimes criticized as if any change in reality must be a change into nonreality. There are difficulties, indeed, both dialectic, and real or practical, in the fact of change—in the fact that only a permanent can change and that change is alteration of a permanent. But till we enjoin botanists and chemists from referring to changes and transformations in their subject matter on the ground that for anything to change means for it to part with its reality, we may as well permit the logician to make similar references.

v

Sub specie æternitatis? or *sub specie generationis?* I am
susceptible to the esthetic charm of the former ideal—who
is not? There are moments of relaxation: there are moments when the demand for peace, to be let alone and re-
lieved from the continual claim of the world in which we
live that we be up and doing something about it, seems ir-
resistible; when the responsibilities imposed by living in a
moving universe seem intolerable. We contemplate with
equal mind the thought of the eternal sleep. But, after all,
this is a matter in which reality and not the philosopher is
the court of final jurisdiction. Outside of philosophy, the
question seems fairly settled; in science, in poetry, in social organization, in religion—wherever religion is not
hopelessly at the mercy of a Frankenstein philosophy
which it originally called into being to be its own slave.
Under such circumstances there is danger that the philosophy which tries to escape the form of generation by taking
refuge under the form of eternity will only come under
the form of a bygone generation. To try to escape from
the snares and pitfalls of time by recourse to traditional
problems and interests:—rather than that let the dead
bury their own dead. Better it is for philosophy to err in
active participation in the living struggles and issues of its
own age and times than to maintain an immune monastic
impeccability, without relevancy and bearing in the gener-
ating ideas of its contemporary present. In the one case, it
will be respected, as we respect all virtue that attests its
sincerity by sharing in the perplexities and failures, as well
as in the joys and triumphs, of endeavor. In the other
case, it bids fair to share the fate of whatever preserves its
gentility, but not its activity, in descent from better days;
namely, to be snugly ensconced in the consciousness of its
own respectability.

XV. The Construction of Good*

We saw at the outset of our discussion that insecurity generates the quest for certainty. Consequences issue from every experience, and they are the source of our interest in what is present. Absence of arts of regulation diverted the search for security into irrelevant modes of practice, into rite and cult; thought was devoted to discovery of omens rather than of signs of what is to occur. Gradually there was differentiation of two realms, one higher, consisting of the powers which determine human destiny in all important affairs. With this religion was concerned. The other consisted of the prosaic matters in which man relied upon his own skill and his matter-of-fact insight. Philosophy inherited the idea of this division. Meanwhile in Greece many of the arts had attained a state of development which raised them above a merely routine state; there were intimations of measure, order and regularity in materials dealt with which give intimations of underlying rationality. Because of the growth of mathematics, there arose also the ideal of a purely rational knowledge, intrinsically solid and worthy and the means by which the intimations of rationality within changing phenomena could be comprehended within science. For the intellectual class the stay and consolation, the warrant of certainty, provided by religion was henceforth found in intellectual demonstration of the reality of the objects of an ideal realm.

With the expansion of Christianity, ethicoreligious traits came to dominate the purely rational ones. The ultimate authoritative standards for regulation of the dispositions and purposes of the human will were fused with those which satisfied the demands for necessary and universal truth. The authority of ultimate Being was, moreover, rep-

* From *The Quest for Certainty* (New York, 1929). For the specific source, see pp. 376–377, below.

resented on earth by the Church; that which in its nature transcended intellect was made known by a revelation of which the Church was the interpreter and guardian. The system endured for centuries. While it endured, it provided an integration of belief and conduct for the western world. Unity of thought and practice extended down to every detail of the management of life; efficacy of its operaation did not depend upon thought. It was guaranteed by the most powerful and authoritative of all social institutions.

Its seemingly solid foundation was, however, undermined by the conclusions of modern science. They effected, both in themselves and even more in the new interests and activities they generated, a breach between what man is concerned with here and now and the faith concerning ultimate reality which, in determining his ultimate and eternal destiny, had previously given regulation to his present life. The problem of restoring integration and cooperation between man's beliefs about the world in which he lives and his beliefs about the values and purposes that should direct his conduct is the deepest problem of modern life. It is the problem of any philosophy that is not isolated from that life.

The attention which has been given to the fact that in its experimental procedure science has surrendered the separation between knowing and doing has its source in the fact that there is now provided within a limited, specialized and technical field the possibility and earnest, as far as theory is concerned, of effecting the needed integration in the wider field of collective human experience. Philosophy is called upon to be the theory of the practice, through ideas sufficiently definite to be operative in experimental endeavor, by which the integration may be made secure in actual experience. Its central problem is the relation that exists between the beliefs about the nature of things due to natural science to beliefs about values—using that word to designate whatever is taken to have rightful authority in the direction of conduct. A philosophy which should take up this problem is struck first of all by the fact that beliefs about values are pretty much in the position in which beliefs about nature were before the scientific revolution. There is either a basic distrust of the capacity of experience to develop its own regulative standards, and an appeal to what philosophers call eternal values, in order to ensure regulation of belief and action; or there is acceptance of enjoyments actually experienced irrespective of the method or operation by which they are brought into existence. Complete bifurcation between rationalistic method and an empirical method has its final and most deeply human significance in the ways in which good and bad are thought of and acted for and upon.

As far as technical philosophy reflects this situation, there is division of theories of values into two kinds. On the one hand, goods and evils, in every region of life, as they are concretely experienced, are regarded as characteristic of an inferior order of Being—intrinsically inferior. Just because they are things of human experience, their worth must be estimated by reference to standards and ideals derived from ultimate reality. Their defects and perversion are attributed to the same fact; they are to be corrected and controlled through adoption of methods of conduct derived from loyalty to the requirements of Supreme Being. This philosophic formulation gets actuality and force from the fact that it is a rendering of the beliefs of men in general as far as they have come under the influence of institutional religion. Just as rational conceptions were once superimposed upon observed and temporal phenomena, so eternal values are superimposed upon experienced goods. In one case as in the other, the alternative is supposed to be confusion and lawlessness. Philosophers suppose these eternal values are known by reason; the mass of persons that they are divinely revealed.

Nevertheless, with the expansion of secular interests, temporal values have enormously multiplied; they absorb more and more attention and energy. The sense of transcendent values has become enfeebled; instead of permeating all things in life, it is more and more restricted to special times and acts. The authority of the church to declare and impose divine will and purpose has narrowed. Whatever men say and profess, their tendency in the presence of actual evils is to resort to natural and empirical means to remedy them. But in formal belief, the old doctrine of the inherently disturbed and unworthy character of the goods and standards of ordinary experience persists. This divergence between what men do and what they nominally profess is closely connected with the confusions and conflicts of modern thought.

It is not meant to assert that no attempts have been

made to replace the older theory regarding the authority of immutable and transcendent values by conceptions more congruous with the practices of daily life. The contrary is the case. The utilitarian theory, to take one instance, has had great power. The idealistic school is the only one in contemporary philosophies, with the exception of one form of neorealism, that makes much of the notion of a reality which is all one with ultimate moral and religious values. But this school is also the one most concerned with the conservation of "spiritual" life. Equally significant is the fact that empirical theories retain the notion that thought and judgment are concerned with values that are experienced independently of them. For these theories, emotional satisfactions occupy the same place that sensations hold in traditional empiricism. Values are constituted by liking and enjoyment; to be enjoyed and to be a value are two names for one and the same fact. Since science has extruded values from its objects, these empirical theories do everything possible to emphasize their purely subjective character of value. A psychological theory of desire and liking is supposed to cover the whole ground of the theory of values; in it, immediate feeling is the counterpart of immediate sensation.

I shall not object to this empirical theory as far as it connects the theory of values with concrete experiences of desire and satisfaction. The idea that there is such a connection is the only way known to me by which the pallid remoteness of the rationalistic theory and the only too glaring presence of the institutional theory of transcendental values can be escaped. The objection is that the theory in question holds down value to objects *antecedently* enjoyed, apart from reference to the method by which they come into existence; it takes enjoyments which are causal because unregulated by intelligent operations to be values in and of themselves. Operational thinking needs to be applied to the judgment of values just as it has now finally been applied in conceptions of physical objects. Experimental empiricism in the field of ideas of good and bad is demanded to meet the conditions of the present situation.

The scientific revolution came about when material of direct and uncontrolled experience was taken as problematic; as supplying material to be transformed by reflective operations into known objects. The contrast between experienced and known objects was found to be a temporal one; namely, one between empirical subject matters which were had or "given" prior to the acts of experimental variation and redisposition and those which succeeded these acts and issued from them. The notion of an act whether of sense or thought which supplied a valid measure of thought in immediate knowledge was discredited. Consequences of operations became the important thing. The suggestion almost imperatively follows that escape from the defects of transcendental absolutism is not to be had by setting up as values enjoyments that happen anyhow, but in defining value by enjoyments which are the consequences of intelligent action. Without the intervention of thought, enjoyments are not values but problematic goods, becoming values when they reissue in a changed form from intelligent behavior. The fundamental trouble with the current empirical theory of values is that it merely formulates and justifies the socially prevailing habit of regulation of these enjoyments. This issue involves nothing less than the problem of the directed reconstruction of economic, political and religious institutions.

There was seemingly a paradox involved in the notion that if we turned our backs upon the immediately perceived qualities of things, we should be enabled to form valid conceptions of objects, and that these conceptions could be used to bring about a more secure and more significant experience of them. But the method terminated in disclosing the connections or interactions upon which perceived objects, viewed as events, depend. Formal analogy suggests that we regard our direct and original experience of things liked and enjoyed as only *possibilities* of values to be achieved; that enjoyment becomes a value when we discover the relations upon which its presence depends. Such a causal and operational definition gives only a conception of a value, not a value itself. But the utilization of the conception in action results in an object having secure and significant value.

The formal statement may be given concrete content by pointing to the difference between the enjoyed and the enjoyable, the desired and the desirable, the satis*fying* and the satis*factory*. To say that something is enjoyed is to make a statement about a fact, something already in existence; it is not to judge the value of that fact. There is no difference between such a proposition and one which says that something is sweet or sour, red or black. It is just correct or incorrect and that is the end of the matter. But to call an object a value is to assert that it satisfies or fulfills certain conditions. Function and status in meeting conditions is a different matter from bare existence. The fact that something is desired only raises the *question* of its desirability; it does not settle it. Only a child in the degree of his immaturity thinks to settle the question of desirability by reiterated proclamation: "I want it, I want it, I want it." What is objected to in the current empirical theory of values is not connection of them with desire and enjoyment but failure to distinguish between enjoyments of radically different sorts. There are many common expressions in which the difference of the two kinds is clearly recognized. Take for example the difference between the ideas of "satisfying" and "satisfactory." To say that something satisfies is to report something as an isolated finality. To assert that it is satis*factory* is to define it in its connections and interactions. The fact that it pleases or is immediately congenial poses a problem to judgment. How shall the satisfaction be rated? Is it a value or is it not? Is it something to be prized and cherished, *to be* enjoyed? Not stern moralists alone but everyday experience informs us that finding satisfaction in a thing may be a warning, a summons to be on the lookout for consequences. To declare something satis*factory* is to assert that it meets specifiable conditions. It is, in effect, a judgment that the thing "will do." It involves a prediction; it contemplates a future in which the thing will continue to serve; it *will* do. It asserts a consequence the thing will actively institute; it will *do*. That it is satisfying is the content of a proposition of fact; that it is satisfactory is a judgment, an estimate, an appraisal. It denotes an attitude *to be* taken, that of striving to perpetuate and to make secure.

It is worth notice that besides the instances given, there are many other recognitions in ordinary speech of the distinction. The endings "able," "worthy," and "ful" are cases in point. Noted and notable, noteworthy; remarked and remarkable; advised and advisable; wondered at and wonderful; pleasing and beautiful; loved and lovable; blamed and blameable, blameworthy; objected to and objectionable; esteemed and estimable; admired and admirable; shamed and shameful; honored and honorable; approved and approvable; worthy of approbation, etc. The multiplication of words adds nothing to the force of the distinction. But it aids in conveying a sense of the fundamental character of the distinction; of the difference between mere report of an already existent fact and judgment as to the importance and need of bringing a fact into existence; or, if it is already there, of sustaining it in existence. The latter is a genuine practical judgment, and marks the only type of judgment that has to do with the direction of action. Whether or no we reserve the term "value" for the latter, (as seems to me proper) is a minor matter; that the distinction be acknowledged as the key to understanding the relation of values to the direction of conduct is the important thing.

This element of direction by an idea of value applies to science as well as anywhere else. For in every scientific undertaking, there is passed a constant succession of estimates; such as "it is worth treating these facts as data or evidence; it is advisable to try this experiment; to make that observation; to entertain such and such a hypothesis; to perform this calculation," etc.

The word "taste" has perhaps got too completely associated with arbitrary liking to express the nature of judgments of value. But if the word be used in the sense of an appreciation at once cultivated and active, one may say that the formation of taste is the chief matter wherever values enter in, whether intellectual, esthetic or moral. Relatively immediate judgments, which we call tact or to which we give the name of intuition, do not precede reflective inquiry, but are the funded products of much thoughtful experience. Expertness of taste is at once the result and the reward of constant exercise of thinking. Instead of there being no disputing about tastes, they are the one thing worth disputing about, if by "dispute" is signified discussion involving reflective inquiry. Taste, if we use the word in its best sense, is the outcome of experience brought cumulatively to bear on the intelligent appreciation of the real worth of likings and enjoyments. There is nothing in which a person so completely reveals himself as in the things which he judges enjoyable and desirable. Such judgments are the sole alternative to the domination of belief by impulse, chance, blind habit and self-interest. The formation of a cultivated and effectively operative good judgment or taste with respect to what is esthetically admirable, intellectually acceptable and morally approvable is the supreme task set to human beings by the incidents of experience.

Propositions about what is or has been liked are of instrumental value in reaching judgments of value, in as far as the conditions and consequences of the thing liked are thought about. In themselves they make no claims; they put forth no demand upon subsequent attitudes and acts; they profess no authority to direct. If one likes a thing he likes it; that *is* a point about which there can be no dispute:—although it is not so easy to state just *what* is liked as is frequently assumed. A judgment about what is *to be* desired and enjoyed is, on the other hand, a claim on future action; it possesses *de jure* and not merely *de facto* quality. It is a matter of frequent experience that likings and enjoyments are of all kinds, and that many are such as reflective judgments condemn. By way of self-justification and "rationalization," an enjoyment creates a tendency to assert that the thing enjoyed is a value. This assertion of validity adds authority to the fact. It is a decision that the object has a right to exist and hence a claim upon action to further its existence.

The analogy between the status of the theory of values and the theory of ideas about natural objects before the rise of experimental inquiry may be carried further. The sensationalistic theory of the origin and test of thought evoked, by way of reaction, the transcendental theory of *a priori* ideas. For it failed utterly to account for objective connection, order and regularity in objects observed. Similarly, any doctrine that identifies the mere fact of being liked with the value of the object liked so fails to give direction to conduct when direction is needed that it automatically calls forth the assertion that there are values eternally in Being that are the standards of all judgments and the obligatory ends of all action. Without the introduction of operational thinking, we oscillate between a theory that, in order to save the objectivity of judgments of values, isolates them from experience and nature, and a theory that, in order to save their concrete and human significance, reduces them to mere statements about our own feelings.

Not even the most devoted adherents of the notion that enjoyment and value are equivalent facts would venture to assert that because we have once liked a thing we should go on liking it; they are compelled to introduce the idea that *some* tastes are to be cultivated. Logically, there is no ground for introducing the idea of cultivation; liking is liking, and one is as good as another. If enjoyments *are* values, the judgment of value cannot regulate the form which liking takes; it cannot regulate its own conditions. Desire and purpose, and hence action, are left without guidance, although the question of regulation of their formation is the supreme problem of practical life. Values (to sum up) may be connected inherently with liking, and yet not with *every* liking but only with those that judgment has approved, after examination of the relation upon which the object liked depends. A casual liking is one that happens without knowledge of how it occurs nor to what effect. The difference between it and one which is sought because of a judgment that it is worth having and is to be striven for, makes just the difference between enjoyments which are accidental and enjoyments that have value and hence a claim upon our attitude and conduct.

In any case, the alternative rationalistic theory does not afford the guidance for the sake of which eternal and immutable norms are appealed to. The scientist finds no help in determining the probable truth of some proposed theory by comparing it with a standard of absolute truth and immutable being. He has to rely upon definite operations undertaken under definite conditions—upon method. We can hardly imagine an architect getting aid in the construction of a building from an ideal at large, though we can understand his framing an ideal on the basis of knowledge of actual conditions and needs. Nor does the ideal of perfect beauty in antecedent Being give direction to a painter in producing a particular work of art. In morals, absolute perfection does not seem to be more than a generalized hypostatization of the recognition that there is a good to be sought, an obligation to be met—both being concrete matters. Nor is the defect in this respect merely negative. An examination of history would reveal, I am confident, that these general and remote schemes of value actually obtain a content definite enough and near enough to concrete situations as to afford guidance in action only by consecrating some institution or dogma already having social currency. Concreteness is gained, but it is by protecting from inquiry some accepted standard which perhaps is outworn and in need of criticism.

When theories of values do not afford intellectual assistance in framing ideas and beliefs about values that are adequate to direct action, the gap must be filled by other means. If intelligent method is lacking, prejudice, the pressure of immediate circumstance, self-interest and class interest, traditional customs, institutions of accidental historic origin, are *not* lacking, and they tend to take the place of intelligence. Thus we are led to our main proposition: *Judgments about values are judgments about the conditions and the results of experienced objects; judgments about that which should regulate the formation of our desires, affections and enjoyments.* For whatever decides their formation will determine the main course of our conduct, personal and social.

If it sounds strange to hear that we should frame our judgments as to what has value by considering the connections in existence of what we like and enjoy, the reply is not far to seek. As long as we do not engage in this inquiry enjoyments (values if we choose to apply that term) are casual; they are given by "nature," not constructed by art. Like natural objects in their qualitative existence, they at most only supply material for elaboration in rational discourse. A *feeling* of good or excellence is as far removed from goodness in fact as a feeling that objects are intellectually thus and so is removed from their being actually so. To recognize that the truth of natural objects can be reached only by the greatest care in selecting and arranging directed operations, and then to suppose that values can be truly determined by the mere fact of liking seems to leave us in an incredible position. All the serious perplexities of life come back to the genuine difficulty of forming a judgment as to the values of the situation; they come back to a conflict of goods. Only dogmatism can suppose that serious moral conflict is between something clearly bad and something known to be good, and that uncertainty lies wholly in the will of the one choosing. Most conflicts of importance are conflicts between things which are or have been satisfying, not between good and evil. And to suppose that we can make a hierarchical table of values at large once for all, a kind of catalogue in which they are arranged in an order of ascending or descending worth, is to indulge in a gloss on our inability to frame intelligent judgments in the concrete. Or else it is to dignify customary choice and prejudice by a title of honor.

The alternative to definition, classification and systematization of satisfactions just as they happen to occur is judgment of them by means of the relations under which they occur. If we know the conditions under which the act of liking, of desire and enjoyment, takes place, we are in a position to know what are the consequences of that act. The difference between the desired and the desirable, admired and the admirable, becomes effective at just this point. Consider the difference between the proposition "That thing has been eaten," and the judgment "That thing is edible." The former statement involves no knowledge of any relation except the one stated; while we are able to judge of the edibility of anything only when we have a knowledge of its interactions with other things sufficient to enable us to foresee its probable effects when it is taken into the organism and produces effects there.

To assume that anything can be known in isolation from its connections with other things is to identify knowing with merely having some object before perception or in feeling, and is thus to lose the key to the traits that distinguish an object as known. It is futile, even silly, to suppose that some quality that is directly present constitutes the whole of the thing presenting the quality. It does not do so when the quality is that of being hot or fluid or heavy, and it does not when the quality is that of giving pleasure, or being enjoyed. Such qualities are, once more, effects, ends in the sense of closing termini of processes involving causal connections. They are something to be investigated, challenges to inquiry and judgment. The more connections and interactions we ascertain, the more we *know* the object in question. Thinking is search for these connections. Heat experienced as a consequence of directed operations has a meaning quite different from the heat that is casually experienced without knowledge of how it came about. The same is true of enjoyments. Enjoyments that issue from conduct directed by insight into relations have a meaning and a validity due to the way in which they are experienced. Such enjoyments are not repented of; they generate no aftertaste of bitterness. Even in the midst of direct enjoyment, there is a sense of validity, of authorization, which intensifies the enjoyment. There is solicitude for perpetuation of the *object* having value which is radically different from mere anxiety to perpetuate the *feeling* of enjoyment.

Such statements as we have been making are therefore,

far from implying that there are values apart from things actually enjoyed as good. To find a thing enjoy*able* is, so to say, a *plus* enjoyment. We saw that it was foolish to treat the scientific object as a rival to or substitute for the perceived object, since the former is intermediate between uncertain and settled situations and those experienced under conditions of greater control. In the same way, judgment of the value of an object to be experienced is instrumental to appreciation of it when it is realized. But the notion that every object that happens to satisfy has an equal claim with every other to be a value is like supposing that every object of perception has the same cognitive force as every other. There is no knowledge without perception; but objects perceived are *known* only when they are determined as consequences of connective operations. There is no value except where there is satisfaction, but there have to be certain conditions fulfilled to transform a satisfaction into a value.

The time will come when it will be found passing strange that we of this age should take such pains to control by every means at command the formation of ideas of physical things, even those most remote from human concern, and yet are content with haphazard beliefs about the qualities of objects that regulate our deepest interests; that we are scrupulous as to methods of forming ideas of natural objects, and either dogmatic or else driven by immediate conditions in framing those about values. There is, by implication, if not explicitly, a prevalent notion that values are already well known and that all which is lacking is the will to cultivate them in the order of their worth. In fact the most profound lack is not the will to act upon goods already known but the will to know what they are.

It is not a dream that it is possible to exercise some degree of regulation of the occurrence of enjoyments which are of value. Realization of the possibility is exemplified, for example, in the technologies and arts of industrial life —that is, up to a definite limit. Men desired heat, light, and speed of transit and of communication beyond what nature provides of itself. These things have been attained not by lauding the enjoyment of these things and preaching their desirability, but by study of the conditions of their manifestation. Knowledge of relations having been obtained, ability to produce followed, and enjoyment ensued as a matter of course. It is, however, an old story that enjoyment of these things as goods is no warrant of their bringing only good in their train. As Plato was given to pointing out, the physician may know to heal and the orator to persuade, but the ulterior knowledge of whether it is better for a man to be healed or to be persuaded to the orator's opinion remains unsettled. Here there appears the split between what are traditionally and conventionally called the values of the baser arts and the higher values of the truly personal and humane arts.

With respect to the former, there is no assumption that they can be had and enjoyed without definite operative knowledge. With respect to them it is also clear that the degree in which we value them is measurable by the pains taken to control the conditions of their occurrence. With respect to the latter, it is assumed that no one who is honest can be in doubt what they are; that by revelation, or conscience, or the instruction of others, or immediate feeling, they are clear beyond question. And instead of action in their behalf being taken to be a measure of the extent in which things *are* values to us, it is assumed that the difficulty is to persuade men to act upon what they already know to be good. Knowledge of conditions and consequences is regarded as wholly indifferent to judging what is of serious value, though it is useful in a prudential way in trying to actualize it. In consequence, the existence of values that are by common consent of a secondary and technical sort are under a fair degree of control, while those denominated supreme and imperative are subject to all the winds of impulse, custom and arbitrary authority.

This distinction between higher and lower types of value is itself something to be looked into. Why should there be a sharp division made between some goods as physical and material and others as ideal and "spiritual"? The question touches the whole dualism of the material and the ideal at its root. To denominate anything "matter" or "material" is not in truth to disparage it. It is, if the designation is correctly applied, a way of indicating that the thing in question is a condition or means of the existence of something else. And disparagement of effective means is practically synonymous with disregard of the things that are termed, in eulogistic fashion, ideal and spiritual. For the latter terms if they have any concrete application at all signify something which is a desirable consummation of conditions, a cherished fulfillment of means. The sharp separation between material and ideal good thus deprives the latter of the underpinning of effective support while it opens the way for treating things which should be employed as means as ends in themselves. For since men cannot after all live without some measure of possession of such matters as health and wealth, the latter things will be viewed as values and ends in isolation unless they are treated as integral constituents of the goods that are deemed supreme and final.

The relations that determine the occurrence of what human beings experience, especially when social connections are taken into account, are indefinitely wider and more complex than those that determine the events termed physical; the latter are the outcome of definite selective operations. This is the reason why we know something about remote objects like the stars better than we know significantly characteristic things about our own bodies and minds. We forget the infinite number of things we do not know about the stars, or rather that what we call a star is itself the product of the elimination, enforced and deliberate, of most of the traits that belong to an actual existence. The amount of knowledge we possess about stars would not seem very great or very important if it were carried over to human beings and exhausted our knowledge of them. It is inevitable that genuine knowledge of man and society should lag far behind physical knowledge.

But this difference is not a ground for making a sharp division between the two, nor does it account for the fact that we make so little use of the experimental method of forming our ideas and beliefs about the concerns of man in his characteristic social relations. For this separation religions and philosophies must admit some responsibility. They have erected a distinction between a narrower scope of relations and a wider and fuller one into a difference of kind, naming one kind material, and the other mental and moral. They have charged themselves gratuitously with the office of diffusing belief in the necessity of the division, and with instilling contempt for the material as something inferior in kind in its intrinsic nature and worth. Formal philosophies undergo evaporation of their technical solid contents; in a thinner and more viable form they find their way into the minds of those who know nothing of their original forms. When these diffuse and, so to say, airy emanations recrystallize in the popular mind they form a hard deposit of opinion that alters slowly and with great difficulty. What difference would it actually make in the arts of conduct, personal and social, if the experimental theory were adopted not as a mere theory, but as a part of the working equipment of habitual attitudes on the part of everyone? It would be impossible, even were time given, to answer the question in adequate detail, just as men could not foretell in advance the consequences for knowledge of adopting the experimental method. It is the nature of the method that it has to be tried. But there are generic lines of difference which, within the limits of time at disposal, may be sketched.

Change from forming ideas and judgments of value on the basis of conformity to antecedent objects, to constructing enjoyable objects directed by knowledge of consequences, is a change from looking to the past to looking to the future. I do not for a moment suppose that the experiences of the past, personal and social, are of no importance. For without them we should not be able to frame any ideas whatever of the conditions under which objects are enjoyed nor any estimate of the consequences of esteeming and liking them. But past experiences are significant in giving us intellectual instrumentalities of judging just these points. They are tools, not finalities. Reflection upon what we have liked and have enjoyed is a necessity. But it tells us nothing about the *value* of these things until enjoyments are themselves reflectively controlled, or, until, as they now recalled, we form the best judgment possible about what led us to like this sort of thing and what has issued from the fact that we liked it.

We are not, then, to get away from enjoyments experienced in the past and from recall of them, but from the notion that they are the arbiters of things to be further enjoyed. At present, the arbiter is found in the past, although there are many ways of interpreting what in the past is authoritative. Nominally, the most influential conception doubtless is that of a revelation once had or a perfect life once lived. Reliance upon precedent, upon institutions created in the past, especially in law, upon rules of morals that have come to us through unexamined customs, upon uncriticized tradition, are other forms of dependence. It is not for a moment suggested that we can get away from customs and established institutions. A mere break would doubtless result simply in chaos. But there is no danger of such a break. Mankind is too inertly conservative both by constitution and by education to give the idea of this danger actuality. What there is genuine danger of is that the force of new conditions will produce disruption externally and mechanically: this is an ever present danger. The prospect is increased, not mitigated, by that conservatism which insists upon the adequacy of old standards to meet new conditions. What is needed is intelligent examination of the consequences that are actually effected by inherited institutions and customs, in order that there may be intelligent consideration of the ways in which they are to be intentionally modified in behalf of generation of different consequences.

This is the significant meaning of transfer of experimental method from the technical field of physical experience to the wider field of human life. We trust the method in forming our beliefs about things not directly connected with human life. In effect, we distrust it in moral, political and economic affairs. In the fine arts, there are many signs of a change. In the past, such a change has often been an omen and precursor of changes in other human attitudes. But, generally speaking, the idea of actively adopting experimental method in social affairs, in the matters deemed of most enduring and ultimate worth, strikes most persons as a surrender of all standards and regulative authority. But in principle, experimental method does not signify random and aimless action; it implies direction by ideas and knowledge. The question at issue is a practical one. Are there in existence the ideas and the knowledge that permit experimental method to be effectively used in social interests and affairs?

Where will regulation come from if we surrender familiar and traditionally prized values as our directive standards? Very largely from the findings of the natural sciences. For one of the effects of the separation drawn between knowledge and action is to deprive scientific knowledge of its proper service as a guide of conduct—except once more in those technological fields which have been degraded to an inferior rank. Of course, the complexity of the conditions upon which objects of human and liberal value depend is a great obstacle, and it would be too optimistic to say that we have as yet enough knowledge of the scientific type to enable us to regulate our judgments of value very extensively. But we have more knowledge than we try to put to use, and until we try more systematically we shall not know what are the important gaps in our sciences judged from the point of view of their moral and humane use.

For moralists usually draw a sharp line between the field of the natural sciences and the conduct that is regarded as moral. But a moral that frames its judgments of value on the basis of consequences must depend in a most intimate manner upon the conclusions of science. For the knowledge of the relations between changes which enable us to connect things as antecedents and consequences *is* science. The narrow scope which moralists often give to morals, their isolation of some conduct as virtuous and vicious from other large ranges of conduct, those having to do with health and vigor, business, education, with all the affairs in which desires and affection are implicated, is perpetuated by this habit of exclusion of the subject matter of natural science from a role in formation of moral standards and ideals. The same attitude operates in the other direction to keep natural science a technical specialty, and it works unconsciously to encourage its use exclusively in regions where it can be turned to personal and class advantage, as in war and trade.

Another great difference to be made by carrying the experimental habit into all matter of practice is that it cuts the roots of what is often called subjectivism, but which is better termed egoism. The subjective attitude is much more widespread than would be inferred from the philosophies which have that label attached. It is as rampant in realistic philosophies as in any others, sometimes even more so, although disguised from those who hold these philosophies under the cover of reverence of and enjoyment of ultimate values. For the implication of placing the standard of thought and knowledge in antecedent existence is that our thought makes no difference in what is significantly real. It then affects only our own attitude toward it.

This constant throwing of emphasis back upon a change made in ourselves instead of one made in the world in which we live seems to me the essence of what is objectionable in "subjectivism." Its taint hangs about even Platonic realism with its insistent evangelical dwelling upon the change made within the mind by contemplation of the realm of essence, and its depreciation of action as transient and all but sordid—a concession to the necessities of organic existence. All the theories which put conversion "of the eye of the soul" in the place of a conversion of natural and social objects that modifies goods actually experienced, is a retreat and escape from existence—and this retraction into self is, once more, the heart of subjective egoisms. The typical example is perhaps the otherworldliness found in religions whose chief concern is with the salvation of the personal soul. But otherworldliness is found as well in estheticism and in all seclusion within ivory towers.

It is not in the least implied that change in personal attitudes, in the disposition of the "subject," is not of great importance. Such change, on the contrary, is involved in any attempt to modify the conditions of the environment. But there is a radical difference between a change in the self that is cultivated and valued as an end, and one that is a means to alteration, through action, of objective conditions. The Aristotelian-medieval conviction that highest bliss is found in contemplative possession of ultimate Being presents an ideal attractive to some types of mind; it sets forth a refined sort of enjoyment. It is a doctrine congenial to minds that despair of the effort involved in creation of a better world of daily experience. It is, apart from theological attachments, a doctrine sure to recur when social conditions are so troubled as to make actual endeavor seem hopeless. But the subjectivism so externally marked in modern thought as compared with ancient is either a development of the old doctrine under new conditions or is of merely technical import. The medieval version of the doctrine at least had the active support of a great social institution by means of which man could be brought into the state of mind that prepared him for ultimate enjoyment of eternal Being. It had a certain solidity and depth which is lacking in modern theories that would attain the result by merely emotional or speculative procedures, or by any means not demanding a change in objective existence so as to render objects of value more empirically secure.

The nature in detail of the revolution that would be wrought by carrying into the region of values the principle now embodied in scientific practice cannot be told; to attempt it would violate the fundamental idea that we know only after we have acted and in consequences of the outcome of action. But it would surely effect a transfer of attention and energy from the subjective to the objective. Men would think of themselves as agents not as ends; ends would be found in experienced enjoyment of the fruits of a transforming activity. In as far as the subjectivity of modern thought represents a discovery of the part played by personal responses, organic and acquired, in the causal production of the qualities and values of objects, it marks the possibility of a decisive gain. It puts us in possession of some of the conditions that control the occurrence of experienced objects, and thereby it supplies us with an instrument of regulation. There is something querulous in the sweeping denial that things as experienced, as perceived and enjoyed, in any way depend upon interaction with human selves. The error of doctrines that have exploited the part played by personal and subjective reactions in determining what is perceived and enjoyed lies either in exaggerating this factor of constitution into the sole condition—as happens in subjective idealism—or else in treating it as a finality instead of, as with all knowledge, an instrument in direction of further action.

A third significant change that would issue from carrying over experimental method from physics to man concerns the import of standards, principles, rules. With the transfer, these, and all tenets and creeds about good and goods, would be recognized to be hypotheses. Instead of being rigidly fixed, they would be treated as intellectual instruments to be tested and confirmed—and altered—through consequences effected by acting upon them. They would lose all pretense of finality—the ulterior source of dogmatism. It is both astonishing and depressing that so much of the energy of mankind has gone into fighting for (with weapons of the flesh as well as of the spirit) the truth of creeds, religious, moral, and political, as distinct from what has gone into effort to try creeds by putting them to the test of acting upon them. The change would do away with the intolerance and fanaticism that attend the notion that beliefs and judgments are capable of inherent truth and authority; inherent in the sense of being independent of what they lead to when used as directive principles. The transformation does not imply merely that men are responsible for acting upon what they profess to believe; that is an old doctrine. It goes much further. Any belief as such is tentative, hypothetical; it is not just to be acted upon, but is to be *framed* with reference to its office as a guide to action. Consequently, it should be the last thing in the world to be picked up casually and then clung to rigidly. When it is apprehended as a tool and only a tool, an instrumentality of direction, the same scrupulous attention will go to its formation as now goes into the making of instruments of precision in technical fields. Men, instead of being proud of accepting and asserting beliefs and "principles" on the ground of loyalty, will be as ashamed of that procedure as they would now be to confess their assent to a scientific theory out of reverence for Newton or Helmholz or whomever, without regard to evidence.

If one stops to consider the matter, is there not something strange in the fact that men should consider loyalty to "laws," principles, standards, ideals to be an inherent virtue, accounted unto them for righteousness? It is as if they were making up for some secret sense of weakness by rigidity and intensity of insistent attachment. A moral law, like a law in physics, is not something to swear by and stick to at all hazards; it is a formula of the way to respond when specified conditions present themselves. Its soundness and pertinence are tested by what happens when it is acted upon. Its claim or authority rests finally upon the imperativeness of the situation that has to be dealt with, not upon its own intrinsic nature—as any tool achieves dignity in the measure of needs served by it. The idea that adherence to standards external to experienced objects is the only alternative to confusion and lawlessness was once held in science. But knowledge became steadily progressive when it was abandoned, and clues and tests found within concrete acts and objects were employed. The test of consequences is more exacting than that afforded by fixed general rules. In addition, it secures constant development, for when new acts are tried new results are experienced, while the lauded immutability of eternal ideals and norms is in itself a denial of the possibility of development and improvement.

The various modifications that would result from adoption in social and humane subjects of the experimental way of thinking are perhaps summed up in saying that it would place *method and means* upon the level of importance that has, in the past, been imputed exclusively to ends. Means have been regarded as menial, and the useful as the servile. Means have been treated as poor relations to be endured, but not inherently welcome. The very meaning of the word "ideals" is significant of the divorce which has obtained between means and ends. "Ideals" are thought to be remote and inaccessible of attainment; they are too high and fine to be sullied by realization. They serve vaguely to arouse "aspiration," but they do not evoke and direct strivings for embodiment in actual existence. They hover in an indefinite way over the actual scene; they are expiring ghosts of a once significant kingdom of divine reality whose rule penetrated to every detail of life.

It is impossible to form a just estimate of the paralysis of effort that has been produced by indifference to means. Logically, it is truistic that lack of consideration for means signifies that so-called ends are not taken seriously. It is as if one professed devotion to painting pictures conjoined with contempt for canvas, brush and paints; or love of music on condition that no instruments, whether the voice or something external, be used to make sounds. The good workman in the arts is known by his respect for his tools and by his interest in perfecting his technique. The glorification in the arts of ends at the expense of means would be taken to be a sign of complete insincerity or even insanity. Ends separated from means are either sentimental indulgences or if they happen to exist are merely accidental. The ineffectiveness in action of "ideals" is due precisely to the supposition that means and ends are not on exactly the same level with respect to the attention and care they demand.

It is, however, much easier to point out the formal contradiction implied in ideals that are professed without equal regard for the instruments and techniques of their realization, than it is to appreciate the concrete ways in which belief in their separation has found its way into life and borne corrupt and poisonous fruits. The separation marks the form in which the traditional divorce of theory and practice has expressed itself in actual life. It accounts for the relative impotency of arts concerned with enduring human welfare. Sentimental attachment and subjective eulogy take the place of action. For there is no art without tools and instrumental agencies. But it also explains the fact that in actual behavior, energies devoted to matters nominally thought to be inferior, material and sordid, engross attention and interest. After a polite and pious deference has been paid to "ideals," men feel free to devote themselves to matters which are more immediate and pressing.

It is usual to condemn the amount of attention paid by people in general to material ease, comfort, wealth, and success gained by competition, on the ground that they give to mere means the attention that ought to be given to ends, or that they have taken for ends things which in reality are only means. Criticisms of the place which economic interest and action occupy in present life are full of complaints that men allow lower aims to usurp the place that belongs to higher and ideal values. The final source of the trouble is, however, that moral and spiritual "leaders" have propagated the notion that ideal ends may be cultivated in isolation from "material" means, as if means and material were not synonymous. While they condemn men for giving to means the thought and energy that ought to go to ends, the condemnation should go to them. For they have not taught their followers to think of material and economic activities as *really* means. They have been unwilling to frame their conception of the values that should be regulative of human conduct on the basis of the actual conditions and operations by which alone values can be actualized.

Practical needs are imminent; with the mass of mankind they are imperative. Moreover, speaking generally, men are formed to act rather than to theorize. Since the ideal ends are so remotely and accidentally connected with immediate and urgent conditions that need attention, after lip service is given to them, men naturally devote themselves to the latter. If a bird in the hand is worth two in a neighboring bush, an actuality in hand is worth, for the direction of conduct, many ideals that are so remote as to be invisible and inaccessible. Men hoist the banner of the ideal, and then march in the direction that concrete conditions suggest and reward.

Deliberate insincerity and hypocrisy are rare. But the notion that action and sentiment are inherently unified in the constitution of human nature has nothing to justify it. Integration is something to be achieved. Division of attitudes and responses, compartmentalizing of interests, is easily acquired. It goes deep just because the acquisition is unconscious, a matter of habitual adaptation to conditions. Theory separated from concrete doing and making is empty and futile; practice then becomes an immediate seizure of opportunities and enjoyments which conditions afford without the direction which theory—knowledge and ideas—has power to supply. The problem of the relation of theory and practice is not a problem of theory alone; it is that, but it is also the most practical problem of life. For it is the question of how intelligence may inform action, and how action may bear the fruit of increased insight into meaning: a clear view of the values that are worth while and of the means by which they are to be made secure in experienced objects. Construction of ideals in general and their sentimental glorification are easy; the responsibilities both of studious thought and of action are shirked. Persons having the advantage of positions of leisure and who find pleasure in abstract theorizing—a most delightful indulgence to those to whom it appeals—have a large measure of liability for a cultivated diffusion of ideals and aims that are separated from the conditions which are the means of actualization. Then other persons who find themselves in positions of social power and authority readily claim to be the bearers and defenders of ideal ends in church and state. They then use the prestige and authority their representative capacity as guardians of the highest ends confers on them to cover actions taken in behalf of the harshest and narrowest of material ends.

The present state of industrial life seems to give a fair index of the existing separation of means and ends. Isolation of economics from ideal ends, whether of morals or of organized social life, was proclaimed by Aristotle. Certain things, he said, are conditions of a worthy life, personal and social, but are not constituents of it. The economic life of man, concerned with satisfaction of wants, is of this nature. Men have wants and they must be satisfied. But they are only prerequisites of a good life, not intrinsic elements in it. Most philosophers have not been so frank nor perhaps so logical. But upon the whole, economics has been treated as on a lower level than either morals or politics. Yet the life which men, women, and children actually lead, the opportunities open to them, the values they are capable of enjoying, their education, their share in all the things of art and science, are mainly determined by economic conditions. Hence we can hardly expect a moral system which ignores economic conditions to be other than remote and empty.

Industrial life is correspondingly brutalized by failure to equate it as the means by which social and cultural values are realized. That the economic life, thus exiled from the pale of higher values, takes revenge by declaring that it is the only social reality, and by means of the doctrine of materialistic determination of institutions and conduct in all fields, denies to deliberate morals and politics any share of causal regulation, is not surprising.

When economists were told that their subject matter was merely material, they naturally thought they could be "scientific" only by excluding all reference to distinctively human values. Material wants, efforts to satisfy them, even the scientifically regulated technologies highly developed in industrial activity, are then taken to form a complete and closed field. If any reference to social ends and values is introduced it is by way of an external addition, mainly hortatory. That economic life largely determines the conditions under which mankind has access to concrete values may be recognized or it may not be. In either case, the notion that it is the means to be utilized in order to secure significant values as the common and shared possession of mankind is alien and inoperative. To many persons, the idea that the ends professed by morals are impotent save as they are connected with the working machinery of economic life seems like deflowering the purity of moral values and obligations.

The social and moral effects of the separation of theory and practice have been merely hinted at. They are so manifold and so pervasive that an adequate consideration of them would involve nothing less than a survey of the whole field of morals, economics, and politics. It cannot be justly stated that these effects are in fact direct consequences of the quest for certainty by thought and knowledge isolated from action. For, as we have seen, this quest was itself a reflex product of actual conditions. But it may be truly asserted that this quest, undertaken in religion and philosophy, has had results which have reinforced the conditions which originally brought it about. Moreover, search for safety and consolation amid the perils of life by means other than intelligent action, by feeling and thought alone, began when actual means of control were lacking, when arts were undeveloped. It had then a relative historic justification that is now lacking. The primary problem for thinking which lays claim to be philosophic in its breadth and depth is to assist in bringing about a reconstruction of all beliefs rooted in a basic separation of knowledge and action; to develop a system of operative ideas congruous with present knowledge and with present facilities of control over natural events and energies.

We have noted more than once how modern philosophy has been absorbed in the problem of affecting an adjustment between the conclusions of natural science and the beliefs and values that have authority in the direction of life. The genuine and poignant issue does not reside where philosophers for the most part have placed it. It does not consist in accommodation to each other of two realms, one physical and the other ideal and spiritual, nor in the reconciliation of the "categories" of theoretical and practical reason. It is found in that isolation of executive means and ideal interests which has grown up under the influence of the separation of theory and practice. For this, by nature, involves the separation of the material and the spiritual. Its solution, therefore, can be found only in action wherein the phenomena of material and economic life are equated with the purposes that command the loyalties of affection and purpose, and in which ends and ideals are framed in terms of the possibilities of actually experienced situations. But while the solution cannot be found in "thought" alone, it can be furthered by thinking which is operative—which frames and defines ideas in terms of what may be done, and which uses the conclusions of science as instrumentalities. William James was well within the bounds of moderation when he said that looking forward instead of backward, looking to what the world and life might become instead of to what they have been, is an alteration in the "seat of authority."

It was incidentally remarked earlier in our discussion that the serious defect in the current empirical philosophy of values, the one which identifies them with things actually enjoyed irrespective of the conditions upon which they depend, is that it formulates and in so far consecrates the conditions of our present social experience. Throughout these chapters, primary attention has perforce been given to the methods and statements of philosophic theories. But these statements are technical and specialized in formulation only. In origin, content and import they are reflections of some condition or some phase of concrete human experience. Just as the theory of the separation of theory and practice has a practical origin and a momentous practical consequence, so the empirical theory that values are identical with whatever men actually enjoy, no matter how or what, formulates an aspect, and an undesirable one, of the present social situation.

For while our discussion has given more attention to the other type of philosophical doctrine, that which holds that regulative and authoritative standards are found in transcendent eternal values, it has not passed in silence over the fact that actually the greater part of the activities of the greater number of human beings is spent in effort to seize upon and hold onto such enjoyments as the actual scene permits. Their energies and their enjoyments are controlled in fact, but they are controlled by external conditions rather than by intelligent judgment and endeavor. If philosophies have any influence over the thoughts and acts of men, it is a serious matter that the most widely held empirical theory should in effect justify this state of things by identifying values with the objects of any interest as such. As long as the only theories of value placed before us for intellectual assent alternate between sending us to a realm of eternal and fixed values and sending us to enjoyments such as actually obtain, the formulation, even as only a theory, of an experimental empiricism which finds values to be identical with goods that are the fruit of intelligently directed activity has its measure of practical significance.

XVI. The Pattern of Inquiry*

The first chapter set forth the fundamental thesis of this volume: logical forms accrue to subject matter when the latter is subjected to controlled inquiry. It also set forth some of the implications of this thesis for the nature of logical theory. The second and third chapters stated the independent grounds, biological and cultural, for holding that logic is a theory of experiential naturalistic subject matter. The first of the next two chapters developed the theme with reference to the relations of the logic of common sense and science, while the second discussed Aristotelian logic as the organized formulation of the language of Greek life, when that language is regarded as the expression of the meanings of Greek culture and of the significance attributed to various forms of natural existence. It was held throughout these chapters that inquiry, in spite of the diverse subjects to which it applies, and the consequent diversity of its special techniques has a common structure or pattern: that this common structure is applied both in common sense and science, although because of the nature of the problems with which they are concerned, the emphasis upon the factors involved varies widely in the two modes. We now come to the consideration of the common pattern.

The fact that new formal properties accrue to subject matter in virtue of its subjection to certain types of operation is familiar to us in certain fields, even though the idea corresponding to this fact is unfamiliar in logic. Two outstanding instances are provided by art and law. In music, the dance, painting, sculpture, literature, and the other fine arts, subject matters of everyday experience are *trans-formed* by the development of forms which render certain

* Chapter VI of *Logic: The Theory of Inquiry* (New York: 1938). For the specific source see p. 377, below.

products of doing and making objects of fine art. The materials of legal regulations are transactions occurring in the ordinary activities of human beings and groups of human beings; transactions of a sort that are engaged in apart from law. As certain aspects and phases of these transactions are legally formalized, conceptions such as misdemeanor, crime, torts, contracts, and so on arise. These formal conceptions arise out of the ordinary transactions; they are not imposed upon them from on high or from any external and *a priori* source. But when they are formed they are also *formative;* they regulate the proper conduct of the activities out of which they develop.

All of these formal legal conceptions are operational in nature. They formulate and define *ways* of operation on the part of those engaged in the transactions into which a number of persons or groups enter as "parties," and the ways of operation followed by those who have jurisdiction in deciding whether established forms have been complied with, together with the existential consequences of failure of observation. The forms in question are not fixed and eternal. They change, though as a rule too slowly, with changes in the habitual transactions in which individuals and groups engage and the changes that occur in the consequences of these transactions. However hypothetical may be the conception that *logical* forms accrue to existential materials in virtue of the control exercised over inquiries in order that they may fulfill their end, the conception is descriptive of something that verifiably exists. The development of forms in consequence of operations is an established fact in some fields; it is not invented *ad hoc* in relation to logical forms.

The existence of inquiries is not a matter of doubt. They enter into every area of life and into every aspect of every area. In everyday living, men examine; they turn things over intellectually; they infer and judge as "naturally" as they reap and sow, produce and exchange commodities. As a mode of conduct, inquiry is as accessible to objective study as are these other modes of behavior. Because of the intimate and decisive way in which inquiry and its conclusions enter into the management of all affairs of life, no study of the latter is adequate save as it is noted how they are affected by the methods and instruments of inquiry that currently obtain. Quite apart, then, from the particular hypothesis about logical forms that is put forth, study of the objective facts of inquiry is a matter of tremendous import, practically and intellectually. These materials provide the theory of logical forms with a subject matter that is not only objective but is objective in a fashion that enables logic to avoid the three mistakes most characteristic of its history.

1. In virtue of its concern with objectively observable subject matter by reference to which reflective conclusions can be tried and tested, dependence upon subjective and "mentalistic" states and processes is eliminated.

2. The distinctive existence and nature of forms is acknowledged. Logic is not compelled, as historic "empirical" logic felt compelled to do, to reduce logical forms to mere transcripts of the empirical materials that antecede the existence of the former. Just as art forms and legal forms are capable of independent discussion and development, so are logical forms, even though the "independence" in question is intermediate, not final and complete. As in the case of these other forms, they originate *out of* experiential material, and when constituted introduce new ways of operating with prior materials, which ways modify the material out of which they develop.

3. Logical theory is liberated from the unobservable, transcendental and "intuitional."

When methods and results of inquiry are studied as objective data, the distinction that has often been drawn between noting and reporting the ways in which men *do* think, and prescribing the ways in which they *ought* to think, takes on a very different interpretation from that usually given. The usual interpretation is in terms of the difference between the psychological and the logical, the latter consisting of "norms" provided from some source wholly outside of and independent of "experience."

The way in which men *do* "think" denotes, as it is *here* interpreted, simply the ways in which men at a given time carry on their inquiries. So far as it is used to register a difference from the ways in which they *ought* to think, it denotes a difference like that between good and bad farming or good and bad medical practice.* Men think in ways they should not when they follow methods of inquiry that

* Cf. pp. V and X of Introduction. [i.e., *Logic: The Theory of Inquiry*, New York, 1938.]

experience of past inquiries shows are not competent to reach the intended end of the inquiries in question.

Everybody knows that today there are in vogue methods of farming generally followed in the past which compare very unfavorably in their results with those obtained by practices that have already been introduced and tested. When an expert tells a farmer he *should* do thus and so, he is not setting up for a bad farmer an ideal drawn from the blue. He is instructing him in methods that have been tried and that have proved successful in procuring results. In a similar way we are able to contrast various kinds of inquiry that are in use or that have been used in respect to their economy and efficiency in reaching warranted conclusions. We know that some methods of inquiry are better than others in just the same way in which we know that some methods of surgery, farming, road making, navigating, or whatnot are better than others. It does not follow in any of these cases that the "better" methods are ideally perfect, or that they are regulative or "normative" because of conformity to some absolute form. They are the methods which experience up to the present time shows to be the best methods available for achieving certain results, while abstraction of these methods does supply a (relative) norm or standard for further undertakings.

The search for the pattern of inquiry is, accordingly, not one instituted in the dark or at large. It is checked and controlled by knowledge of the kinds of inquiry that have and that have not worked; methods which, as was pointed out earlier, can be so compared as to yield reasoned or rational conclusions. For, through comparison-contrast, we ascertain *how and why* certain means and agencies have provided warrantably assertible conclusions, while others have not and *cannot* do so in the sense in which "cannot" expresses an intrinsic incompatibility between means used and consequences attained.

We may now ask: What is the *definition* of Inquiry? That is, what is the most highly generalized conception of inquiry which can be justifiably formulated? The definition that will be expanded, directly in the present chapter and indirectly in the following chapters, is as follows: *Inquiry is the controlled or directed transformation of an indeterminate situation into one that is so determinate in its constit-*

*uent distinctions and relations as to convert the elements
of the original situation into a unified whole.*＊

The original indeterminate situation is not only "open"
to inquiry, but it is open in the sense that its constituents
do not hang together. The determinate situation on the
other hand, *qua* outcome of inquiry, is a closed and, as it
were, finished situation or "universe of experience." "Controlled or directed" in the above formula refers to the fact
that inquiry is competent in any given case in the degree
in which the operations involved in it actually do terminate in the establishment of an objectively unified existential situation. In the intermediate course of transition and
transformation of the indeterminate situation, *dis*course
through use of symbols is employed as means. In received
logical terminology, propositions, or terms and the relations between them, are intrinsically involved.

I. *The Antecedent Conditions of Inquiry: The Indeterminate Situation.* Inquiry and questioning, up to a certain point,
are synonymous terms. We inquire when we question; and
we inquire when we seek for whatever will provide an
answer to a question asked. Thus it is of the very nature of
the indeterminate situation which evokes inquiry to be *questionable;* or, in terms of actuality instead of potentiality, to
be uncertain, unsettled, disturbed. The peculiar quality of
what pervades the given materials, constituting them a situation, is not just uncertainty at large; it is a unique
doubtfulness which makes that situation to be just and
only the situation it is. It is this unique quality that not
only evokes the particular inquiry engaged in but that ex-
ercises control over its special procedures. Otherwise, one
good procedure in inquiry would be as likely to occur and
to be effective as any other. Unless a situation is uniquely
qualified in its very indeterminateness, there is a condition
of complete panic; response to it takes the form of blind
and wild overt activities. Stating the matter from the personal side, we have "lost our heads." A variety of names
serves to characterize indeterminate situations. They are
disturbed, troubled, ambiguous, confused, full of conflicting tendencies, obscure, etc.

It is the *situation* that has these traits. *We* are doubtful
because the situation is inherently doubtful. Personal states

＊ The word "situation" is to be understood in the sense already expounded.

of doubt that are not evoked by and are not relative to some existential situation are pathological; when they are extreme they constitute the mania of doubting. Consequently, situations that are disturbed and troubled, confused or obscure, cannot be straightened out, cleared up and put in order, by manipulation of our personal states of mind. The attempt to settle them by such manipulations involves what psychiatrists call "withdrawal from reality." Such an attempt is pathological as far as it goes, and when it goes far it is the source of some form of actual insanity. The habit of disposing of the doubtful as if it belonged only to *us* rather than to the existential situation in which we are caught and implicated is an inheritance from subjectivistic psychology. The biological antecedent conditions of an unsettled situation are involved in that state of imbalance in organic-environmental interactions which has already been described. Restoration of integration can be effected, in one case as in the other, only by operations which actually modify existing conditions, not by merely "mental" processes.

It is, accordingly, a mistake to suppose that a situation is doubtful only in a "subjective" sense. The notion that in actual existence everything is completely determinate has been rendered questionable by the progress of physical science itself. Even if it had not been, complete determination would not hold of existences as an *environment*. For Nature is an environment only as it is involved in interaction with an organism, or self, or whatever name be used.*

Every such interaction is a temporal process, not a momentary cross-sectional occurrence. The situation in which it occurs is indeterminate, therefore, with respect to its *issue.* If we call it *confused,* then it is meant that its outcome cannot be anticipated. It is called *obscure* when its course of movement permits of final consequences that cannot be clearly made out. It is called *conflicting* when it tends to evoke discordant responses. Even where existential conditions unqualifiedly determinate in and of them-

---

* Except of course a purely mentalistic name, like *consciousness.* The alleged problem of "interactionism" versus automatism, parallelism, etc., is a problem (and an insoluble one) because of the assumption involved in its statement—the assumption, namely, that the interaction in question is with something mental instead of with biological-cultural human beings.

selves, they are indeterminate in *significance:* that is, in what they import and portend in their interaction with the organism. The organic responses that enter into the production of the state of affairs that is temporally later and sequential are just as existential as are environing conditions.

The immediate *locus* of the problem concerns, then, what kind of responses the organism shall make. It concerns the interaction of organic responses and environing conditions in their movement toward an existential issue. It is a commonplace that in any troubled state of affairs *things* will come out differently according to what is done. The farmer won't get grain unless he plants and tills; the general will win or lose the battle according to the way he conducts it, and so on. Neither the grain nor the tilling, neither the outcome of the battle nor the conduct of it, are "mental" events. Organic interaction becomes inquiry when existential consequences are anticipated; when environing conditions are examined with reference to their *potentialities;* and when responsive activities are selected and ordered with reference to actualization of some of the potentialities, rather than others, in a final existential situation. Resolution of the indeterminate situation is active and operational. If the inquiry is adequately directed, the final issue is the unified situation that has been mentioned.

II. *Institution of a Problem.* The unsettled or indeterminate situation might have been called a *problematic* situation. This name would have been, however, proleptic and anticipatory. The indeterminate situation becomes problematic in the very process of being subjected to inquiry. The indeterminate situation comes into existence from existential causes, just as does, say, the organic imbalance of hunger. There is nothing intellectual or cognitive in the existence of such situations, although they are the necessary condition of cognitive operations or inquiry. In themselves they are precognitive. The first result of evocation of inquiry is that the situation is taken, adjudged, to be problematic. To see that a situation requires inquiry is the initial step in inquiry.*

---

* If by "two-valued logic" is meant a logic that regards "true and false" as the sole logical values, then such a logic is necessarily so truncated that clearness and consistency in logical doctrine are impossible. Being the matter of a problem is a primary logical property.

Qualification of a situation as problematic does not, however, carry inquiry far. It is but an initial step in institution of a problem. A problem is not a task to be performed which a person puts upon himself or that is placed upon him by others—like a so-called arithmetical "problem" in school work. A problem represents the partial transformation by inquiry of a problematic situation into a determinate situation. It is a familiar and significant saying that a problem well put is half solved. To find out *what* the problem and problems are which a problematic situation presents to be inquired into is to be well along in inquiry. To mistake the problem involved is to cause subsequent inquiry to be irrelevant or to go astray. Without a problem, there is blind groping in the dark. The way in which the problem is conceived decides what specific suggestions are entertained and which are dismissed; what data are selected and which rejected; it is the criterion for relevancy and irrelevancy of hypotheses and conceptual structures. On the other hand, to set up a problem that does not grow out of an actual situation is to start on a course of dead work, nonetheless dead because the work is "busy work." Problems that are self-set are mere excuses for seeming to do something intellectual, something that has the semblance but not the substance of scientific activity.

III. *The Determination of a Problem Solution.* Statement of a problematic situation in terms of a problem has no meaning save as the problem instituted has, in the very terms of its statement, reference to a possible solution. Just because a problem well stated is on its way to solution, the determining of a genuine problem is a *progressive* inquiry; the cases in which a problem and its probable solution flash upon an inquirer are cases where much prior ingestion and digestion have occurred. If we assume, prematurely, that the problem involved is definite and clear, subsequent inquiry proceeds on the wrong track. Hence the question arises: How is the formation of a genuine problem so controlled that further inquiries will move toward a solution?

The first step in answering this question is to recognize that no situation which is *completely* indeterminate can possibly be converted into a problem having definite constituents. The first step then is to search out the *constituents* of a given situation which, as constituents, are settled.

When an alarm of fire is sounded in a crowded assembly hall, there is much that is indeterminate as regards the activities that may produce a favorable issue. One may get out safely or one may be trampled and burned. The fire is characterized, however, by some settled traits. It is, for example, located *somewhere*. Then the aisles and exits are at fixed places. Since they are settled or determinate in *existence*, the first step in institution of a problem is to settle them in *observation*. There are other factors which, while they are not as temporally and spatially fixed, are yet observable constituents; for example, the behavior and movements of other members of the audience. All of these observed conditions taken together constitute "the facts of the case." They constitute the terms of the problem, because they are conditions that must be reckoned with or taken account of in any relevant solution that is proposed.

A *possible* relevant solution is then suggested by the determination of factual conditions which are secured by observation. The possible solution presents itself, therefore, as an *idea,* just as the terms of the problem (which are facts) are instituted by observation. Ideas are anticipated consequences (forecasts) of what will happen when certain operations are executed under and with respect to observed conditions.* Observation of facts and suggested meanings or ideas arise and develop in correspondence with each other. The more the facts of the case come to light in consequence of being subjected to observation, the clearer and more pertinent become the conceptions of the way the problem constituted by these facts is to be dealt with. On the other side, the clearer the idea, the more definite, as a truism, become the operations of observation and of execution that must be performed in order to resolve the situation.

An idea is first of all an anticipation of something that may happen; it marks a *possibility*. When it is said, as it

---

* The theory of *ideas* that has been held in psychology and epistemology since the time of Locke's successors is completely irrelevant and obstructive in logical theory. For in treating them as copies of perceptions or "impressions," it ignores the prospective and anticipatory character that defines *being* an idea. Failure to define ideas functionally, in the reference they have to a solution of a problem, is one reason they have been treated as merely "mental." The notion, on the other hand, that ideas are fantasies is a derivative. Fantasies arise when the function an idea performs is ruled out when it is entertained and developed.

sometimes is, that science is *prediction*, the anticipation that constitutes every idea an idea is grounded in a set of controlled observations and of regulated conceptual ways of interpreting them. Because inquiry is a progressive determination of a problem and its possible solution, ideas differ in grade according to the stage of inquiry reached. At first, save in highly familiar matters, they are vague. They occur at first simply as suggestions; suggestions just spring up, flash upon us, occur to us. They may then become stimuli to direct an overt activity but they have as yet no logical status. Every idea originates as a suggestion, but not every suggestion is an idea. The suggestion becomes an idea when it is examined with reference to its functional fitness; its capacity as a means of resolving the given situation.

This examination takes the form of reasoning, as a result of which we are able to appraise better than we were at the outset, the pertinency and weight of the meaning now entertained with respect to its functional capacity. But the final test of its possession of these properties is determined when it actually functions—that is, when it is put into operation so as to institute by means of observations facts not previously observed, and is then used to organize them with other facts into a coherent whole.

Because suggestions and ideas are of that which is not present in given existence, the meanings which they involve must be embodied in some symbol. Without some kind of symbol, no idea; a meaning that is completely disembodied cannot be entertained or used. Since an existence (which *is* an existence) is the support and vehicle of a meaning and is a symbol instead of a merely physical existence only in this respect, embodied meanings or ideas are capable of objective survey and development. To "look at an idea" is not a mere literary figure of speech.

"Suggestions" have received scant courtesy in logical theory. It is true that when they just "pop into our heads," because of the workings of the psychophysical organism, they are not logical. But they are both the conditions and the primary stuff of logical ideas. The traditional empiristic theory reduced them, as has already been pointed out, to mental copies of physical things and assumed that they were *per se* identical with ideas. Consequently it ignored the function of ideas in directing observation and in ascertaining relevant facts. The rationalistic school, on the other hand, saw clearly that "facts" apart from ideas are trivial, that they acquire import and significance only in relation to ideas. But at the same time it failed to attend to the operative and functional nature of the latter. Hence, it treated ideas as equivalent to the ultimate structure of "Reality." The Kantian formula that apart from each other "perceptions are blind and conceptions empty" marks a profound logical insight. The insight, however, was radically distorted because perceptual and conceptual contents were supposed to originate from different sources and thus required a third activity, that of synthetic understanding, to bring them together. In logical fact, perceptual and conceptual materials are instituted in functional correlativity with each other, in such a manner that the former locates and describes the problem while the latter represents a possible method of solution. Both are determinations in and by inquiry of the original problematic situation whose pervasive quality controls their institution and their contents. Both are finally checked by their capacity to work together to introduce a resolved unified situation. As distinctions they represent logical divisions of labor.

IV. *Reasoning.* The necessity of developing the meaning contents of ideas in their relations to óne another has been incidentally noted. This process, operating with symbols (constituting propositions) is reasoning in the sense of ratiocination or rational discourse.* When a suggested meaning is immediately accepted, inquiry is cut short. Hence the conclusion reached is not grounded, even if it happens to be correct. The check upon immediate acceptance is the examination of the meaning as a meaning. This examination consists in noting what the meaning in question implies in relation to other meanings in the system of which it is a member, the formulated relation constituting a proposition. If such and such a relation of meanings is accepted, then we are committed to such and such other relations of meanings because of their membership in the same system. Through a series of intermediate meanings, a meaning is finally reached which is more clearly *relevant* to the problem in hand than the originally suggested idea. It indicates operations which can be performed to test its

---

* "Reasoning" is sometimes used to designate *inference* as well as ratiocination. When so used in logic the tendency is to identify inference and implication and thereby seriously to confuse logical theory.

applicability, whereas the original idea is usually too vague to determine crucial operations. In other words, the idea or meaning when developed in discourse directs the activities which, when executed, provide needed evidential material.

The point made can be most readily appreciated in connection with scientific reasoning. An hypothesis, once suggested and entertained, is developed in relation to other conceptual structures until it receives a form in which it can instigate and direct an experiment that will disclose precisely those conditions which have the maximum possible force in determining whether the hypothesis should be accepted or rejected. Or it may be that the experiment will indicate what modifications are required in the hypothesis so that it may be applicable, i.e., suited to interpret and organize the facts of the case. In many familiar situations, the meaning that is most relevant has been settled because of the eventuations of experiments in prior cases so that it is applicable almost immediately upon its occurrence. But, indirectly, if not directly, an idea or suggestion that is not developed in terms of the constellation of meanings to which it belongs can lead only to overt response. Since the latter terminates inquiry, there is then no adequate inquiry into the meaning that is used to settle the given situation, and the conclusion is in so far logically ungrounded.

V. *The Operational Character of Facts' Meanings.* It was stated that the observed facts of the case and the ideational contents expressed in ideas are related to each other, as, respectively, a clarification of the problem involved and the proposal of some possible solution; that they are, accordingly, functional divisions in the work of inquiry. Observed facts in their office of locating and describing the problem are existential; ideational subject matter is nonexistential. How, then, do they cooperate with each other in the resolution of an existential situation? The problem is insoluble save as it is recognized that both observed facts and entertained ideas are operational. Ideas are operational in that they instigate and direct further operations of observation; they are proposals and plans for acting upon existing conditions to bring new facts to light and to organize all the selected facts into a coherent whole.

What is meant by calling facts operational? Upon the negative side what is meant is that they are not self-sufficient and complete in themselves. They are selected and described, as we have seen, for a purpose, namely statement of the problem involved in such a way that its material both indicates a meaning relevant to resolution of the difficulty and serves to test its worth and validity. In regulated inquiry facts are selected and arranged with the express intent of fulfilling this office. They are not merely *results* of operations of observation which are executed with the aid of bodily organs and auxiliary instruments of art, but they are the particular facts and kinds of facts that will link up with one another in the definite ways that are required to produce a definite end. Those not found to connect with others in furtherance of this end are dropped and others are sought for. Being functional, they are necessarily operational. Their function is to serve as evidence and their evidential quality is judged on the basis of their capacity to form an ordered whole in response to operations prescribed by the ideas they occasion and support. If "the facts of the case" were final and complete in themselves, if they did not have a special operative force in resolution of the problematic situation, they could not serve as evidence.

The operative force of facts is apparent when we consider that no fact in isolation has evidential potency. Facts are evidential and are tests of an idea in so far as they are capable of being organized with one another. The organization can be achieved only as they *interact* with one another. When the problematic situation is such as to require extensive inquiries to effect its resolution, a series of interactions intervenes. Some observed facts point to an idea that stands for a possible solution. This idea evokes more observations. Some of the newly observed facts link up with those previously observed and are such as to rule out other observed things with respect to their evidential function. The new order of facts suggests a modified idea (or hypothesis) which occasions new observations whose result again determines a new order of facts, and so on until the existing order is both unified and complete. In the course of this serial process, the ideas that represent possible solutions are tested or "proved."

Meantime, the orders of fact, which present themselves in consequence of the experimental observations the ideas call out and direct, are *trial* facts. They are provisional. They are "facts" if they are observed by sound organs and techniques. But they are not on that account the *facts of the case.* They are tested or "proved" with respect to their evidential function just as much as ideas (hypotheses) are tested with reference to their power to exercise the function of resolution. The operative force of both ideas and facts is thus practically recognized in the degree in which they are connected with *experiment*. Naming them "operational" is but a theoretical recognition of what is involved when inquiry satisfies the conditions imposed by the necessity for experiment.

I recur, in this connection, to what has been said about the necessity for symbols in inquiry. It is obvious, on the face of matters, that a possible mode of solution must be carried in symbolic form since it is a possibility, not an assured present existence. Observed facts, on the other hand, are existentially present. It might seem therefore, that symbols are not required for refering to them. But if they are not carried and treated by means of symbols, they lose their provisional character, and in losing this character they are categorically asserted and inquiry comes to an end. The carrying on of inquiry requires that the facts be taken as *re*presentative and not just as *pre*-sented. This demand is met by formulating them in propositions—that is, by means of symbols. Unless they are so represented they relapse into the total qualitative situation.

VI. *Common Sense and Scientific Inquiry.* The discussion up to this point has proceeded in general terms which recognize no distinction between common sense and scientific inquiry. We have now reached a point where the community of pattern in these two distinctive modes of inquiry should receive explicit attention. It was said in earlier chapters that the difference between them resides in their respective subject matters, not in their basic logical forms and relations; that the difference in subject matters is due to the difference in the problems respectively involved; and, finally, that this difference sets up a difference in the ends or objective consequences they are concerned to achieve. Because common sense problems and inquiries have to do with the interactions into which living creatures enter in connection with environing conditions in order to establish objects of use and enjoyment, the symbols employed are those which have been determined in the habitual culture of a group. They form a system but the system is practical rather than intellectual. It is constituted by the traditions, occupations, techniques, interests, and established institutions of the group. The meanings that compose it are carried in the common everyday language of communication between members of the group. The meanings involved in this common language system determine what individuals of the group may and may not do in relation to physical objects and in relations to one another. They regulate *what* can be used and enjoyed and *how* use and enjoyment shall occur.

Because the symbol-meaning systems involved are connected directly with cultural life activities and are related to each other in virtue of this connection, the specific meanings which are present have reference to the specific and limited environing conditions under which the group lives. Only those things of the environment that are taken, according to custom and tradition, as having connection with and bearing upon this life, enter into the meaning system. There is no such thing as disinterested intellectual concern with either physical or social matters. For, until the rise of science, there were no problems of common sense that called for such inquiry. Disinterestedness existed practically in the demand that group interests and concerns be put above private needs and interests. But there was no intellectual disinterestedness beyond the activities, interests, and concerns of the group. In other words, there was no science as such, although, as was earlier pointed out, there did exist information and techniques which were available for the purposes of scientific inquiry and out of which the latter subsequently grew.

In scientific inquiry, then, meanings are related to one another on the ground of their character *as* meanings, freed from direct reference to the concerns of a limited group. Their intellectual abstractness is a product of this liberation, just as the "concrete" is practically identified by directness of connection with environmental interactions. Consequently a new language, a new system of symbols related together on a new basis, comes into existence, and in this new language semantic coherence, as such, is the controlling consideration. To repeat what has already been said, connection with problems of use and enjoyment is the source of the dominant role of qualities, sensible and moral, and of ends in common sense.

In science, since meanings are determined on the ground of their relation as meanings to one another, *relations* become the objects of inquiry and qualities are relegated to a secondary status, playing a part only as far as they assist in institution of relations. They are subordinate because they have an instrumental office, instead of being themselves, as in pre-scientific common sense, the matters of final importance. The enduring hold of common sense is testified to historically by the long time it took before it was seen that scientific objects are strictly relational. First tertiary qualities were eliminated; it was recognized that moral qualities are not agencies in determining the structure of nature. Then secondary qualities, the wet-dry, hot-cold, light-heavy, which were the explanatory principles of physical phenomena in Greek science, were ejected. But so-called primary qualities took their place, as with Newton and the Lockian formulation of Newtonian existential postulates. It was not until the threshold of our time was reached that scientific inquires perceived that their own problems and methods required an interpretation of "primary qualities" in terms of relations, such as position, motion, and temporal span. In the structure of distinctively scientific objects these relations are indifferent to qualities.

The foregoing is intended to indicate that the different objectives of common sense and of scientific inquiry demand different subject matters and that this difference in subject matters is not incompatible with the existence of a common pattern in both types. There are, of course, secondary logical forms which reflect the distinction of properties involved in the change from qualitative and teleological subject matter to nonqualitative and nonteleological relations. But they occur and operate within the described community of pattern. They are explicable, and explicable only, on the ground of the distinctive problems generated by scientific subject matter. The independence of scientific objects from limited and fairly direct reference to the environment as a factor in activities of use and enjoyment, is equivalent, as has already been intimated, to their *abstract* character. It is also equivalent to their *general* character in the sense in which the generalizations of science are different from the generalizations with which common sense is familiar. The generality of *all* scientific subject matter as such means that it is freed from restriction to conditions which present themselves at particular times and places. Their reference is to *any* set of time and place conditions —a statement which is not to be confused with the doctrine that they have no reference to actual existential occasions. Reference to time-place of existence is necessarily involved, but it is reference to whatever set of existences fulfils the general relations laid down in and by the constitution of the scientific object.*

Summary. Since a number of points have been discussed, it will be well to round up conclusions reached about them in a summary statement of the structure of the common pattern of inquiry. Inquiry is the directed or controlled transformation of an indeterminate situation into a determinately unified one. The transition is achieved by means of operations of two kinds which are in functional correspondence with each other. One kind of operations deals with ideational or conceptual subject matter. This subject matter stands for possible ways and ends of resolution. It anticipates a solution, and is marked off from fancy because, or, in so far as, it becomes operative in instigation and direction of new observations yielding new factual material. The other kind of operations is made up of activities involving the techniques and organs of observation. Since these operations are existential they modify the prior existential situation, bring into high relief conditions previously obscure, and relegate to the background other aspects that were at the outset conspicuous. The ground and criterion of the execution of this work of emphasis, selection, and arrangement is to delimit the problem in such a way that existential material may be provided with which to test the ideas that represent possible modes of solution. Symbols, defining terms and propositions, are necessarily required in order to retain and carry forward both ideational and existential subject matters in order that they may serve their proper functions in the control of inquiry. Otherwise the problem is taken to be closed and inquiry ceases.

One fundamentally important phase of the transformation of the situation which constitutes inquiry is central in the treatment of judgment and its functions. The transformation is existential and hence temporal. The precognitive

---

* The consequences that follow are directly related to the statement in Ch. IV [i.e., *Logic: The Theory of Inquiry*] that the elimination of qualities and ends is intermediate; that, in fact, the construction of purely relational objects has enormously liberated and expanded commonsense uses and enjoyments by conferring control over production of qualities, by enabling new ends to be realistically instituted, and by providing competent means for achieving them.

unsettled situation can be settled only by modification of its constituents. Experimental operations change existing conditions. Reasoning, as such, can provide means for effecting the change of conditions but by itself cannot effect it. Only execution of existential operations directed by an idea in which ratiocination terminates can bring about the reordering of environing conditions required to produce a settled and unified situation. Since this principle also applies to the meanings that are elaborated in science, the experimental production and rearrangement of physical conditions involved in natural science is further evidence of the unity of the pattern of inquiry. The temporal quality of inquiry means, then, something quite other than that the process of inquiry takes time. It means that the objective subject matter of inquiry undergoes temporal modification.

Terminological. Were it not that knowledge is related to inquiry as a product to the operations by which it is produced, no distinctions requiring special differentiating designations would exist. Material would merely be a matter of knowledge or of ignorance and error; that would be all that could be said. The content of any given proposition would have the values "true" and "false" as final and exclusive attributes. But if knowledge is related to inquiry as its warrantably assertible product, and if inquiry is progressive and temporal, then the material inquired into reveals distinctive properties which need to be designated by distinctive names. As *undergoing* inquiry, the material has a different logical import from that which it has as the *outcome* of inquiry. In its first capacity and status, it will be called by the general name *subject matter.* When it is necessary to refer to subject matter in the context of either observation or ideation, the name *content* will be used, and, particularly on account of its *representative* character, content of propositions.

The name *objects* will be reserved for subject matter so far as it has been produced and ordered in settled form by means of inquiry; proleptically, objects are the *objectives* of inquiry. The apparent ambiguity of using "objects" for this purpose (since the word is regularly applied to things that are observed or thought of) is only apparent. For things exist *as* objects for us only as they have been previously determined as outcomes of inquiries. When used in carrying on new inquiries in new problematic situations, they are known as objects in virtue of prior inquiries which warrant their assertibility. In the new situation, they are *means* of attaining knowledge of something else. In the strict sense, they are part of the *contents* of inquiry as the word content was defined above. But retrospectively (that is, as products of prior determination in inquiry) they are objects.

George Herbert Mead

INTRODUCTION

George Herbert Mead (1862–1931) was born in South Hadley, Massachusetts. His father was a minister and later Professor of Homiletics at Oberlin Theological Seminary, Ohio. Mead attended Oberlin and graduated in 1879. For a time he worked as a school teacher and also as a surveyer. In 1887 he entered Harvard where he studied primarily under Royce and James and from which he graduated in 1888. After Harvard he spent some years in the Universities of Berlin and Leipzig studying philosophy and psychology.

When Mead returned to the United States he began teaching at the University of Michigan. There from 1891 to 1894, he was a colleague and became a close friend of Dewey with whom he moved to the University of Chicago in 1894. Although he did not publish extensively, at Chicago Mead became famous as a teacher; his course in Social Psychology drew students from many fields of study.

Mead's major philosophic work combined pragmatism with social psychology. He made the most ambitious and comprehensive attempt of the pragmatists to set forth a theory of mind and behavior. Many of his publications were specific contributions to various developing aspects of this theory. Central to this concern was to determine the genesis and phases of the formation of the Self, or the "minded individual." Mind, consciousness, selfhood, do not come to us *ex nihilo* nor at birth. These are acquisitions that are won and made to emerge in the course of an elaborate process of development. The matrix of that process, Mead argued, is social, and the fundamental feature here is elborated in his theory of the "social act." He described his position as "social behaviorism": His theory of the act has many affinities with Dewey's conception of the act as the unit of behavior (see XIII above) and his theory of inquiry (XVI above). Dewey described Mead as "a seminal mind of the very first order" and "the most original mind in philosophy in America of the last generation." He added, "I dislike to think of what my own thinking might have been were it not for the seminal ideas which I derived from him."

For Mead, a *social act* occurs at its simplest level when the behavior of one individual serves to elicit a response from another individual. The overt phase of the act takes place in gestures. There are simple acts such as one bird calling and another responding, or animals growling and baring their teeth at one another. Gestures function as stimuli to performed reactions among individuals. As he points out in the first paragraphs of the paper that follows, "gesture" is used in a large sense to include a wide range of different kinds of physical expressions and standardized or "appropriate" responses.

An important transition from simple acts to "conversations of gestures" occurs when acts undergo modification in the light of responses beginning to take place; when the character of the act is modified by the kind of responses it calls out. In these cases the acting individual is responding to his own action as other individuals respond—or would respond—and readjusting his action accordingly. Here is the basis of consciousness of meaning. For Mead, consciousness is a kind of literal *reflection,* a responding to our own gestures. This is aptly illustrated in the organized game. Thus consider A and B playing the game of tag. A is "it" and must try to catch B. B runs, dodging, and feinting in attempting to elude A. In pursuit, A responds to B's attempts to elude him by anticipating B's feints and consequently modifying some of his actions; he may also make a feinting gesture, or simulate fatigue or confusion. In the game A and B play roles, but much of their skill consists in their ability to exchange roles. A is a skillful pursuer because he knows the technique of the pursued. A's action is continuously modified both by what B does and by A's ability to assume B's role (to respond *as* B to his own actions); knowing what he *might* do *if* he were B. Here knowledge is directed to certain hypothetical conditions and the control of future possibilities; and these future conditions enter in turn to control present activity. "We are conscious when what we are going to do is controlling what we are doing." The complexity of the acting of the game is a function of the abilities of A and B to assume reciprocal roles and to readjust the courses of their respective acts as the respective responses are called forth. Tag has a grimmer counterpart in the hunt; there is a similar pattern of behavior engaged in by the hunter and his quarry. Certain structural features of this pattern carry over into other diverse forms of behavior such as an actor practicing a role (with his mirror he is able to assume the role of the other, the critical audience, thus modifying his delivery and performance by responding as others would) or our learning our language. And it is in language, in the acquisition of vocal gestures especially, that mind and self emerge. For no other form of gesturing is so finely conducive to enabling one to respond to his own act—that is, responding to what one is saying and one's manner of saying it as others would respond. There is a reflexive feature to vocal gestures that is like the actor's mirror; we are enabled to hear and respond to ourselves, and we are able to take the part of others, and respond as others would, to what we are saying. Our vocal gesturing, our conversations, will go through modifications and readjustments accordingly. In social situations these forms of act become increasingly complex; we not only respond to ourselves as others respond, in modifying our conduct we are responding to how we respond to our own conduct.

The social *act* then, for Mead, is essentially a reconstruction of experience, a working out of purposes and attitudes among individuals. In the social act one becomes a "social self," an object to one's self and a self-observer and responder. There arises, then, as Mead explains in "The Social Self" (below, XVIII), an "I" and "me." There is the empirical self, the "me" whom I and others respond to and observe. "The me is a reply to a man's own talk," the field of inner experience. The "I" is that other self. The "me" is an object of consciousness, the "I" is not. But the "I" is always presupposed. The "process of replying to one's own talk, implies an 'I' behind the scenes who answers to gestures, the symbols, that arise in consciousness."*

* *Mead, Selected Writings*, Andrew J. Reck, ed. (New York, 1964), p. 141.

As Mead says:

> The "I" is the response of the organism to the attitudes of the others which one himself assumes. The attitudes of the others constitute the organized "me," and then one reacts toward that as an "I." *

Mead's pragmatism infuses and guides his analyses of the act and the conscious self. With Peirce and Dewey he viewed thought and action as arising in conditions where conduct has become blocked and perplexed. Truth, he said, "is synonymous with the solution of the problem." The test of truth

> is the ability to act where action was formerly estopped. . . .
> Truth expresses a relationship between the judgment and reality . . . the relationship lies between the reconstruction, which enables conduct to continue, and the reality within which conduct advances.†

Judgment, as the solution of the problem restricting conduct, issues in a reinterpretation of meanings and reconstruction of the conditions that stopped action. In this Mead agrees with Dewey's theory of inquiry (see p. 316, above). While he recognized a place for disinterested theorizing, Mead regarded the function and test of thought to be its contribution to the release of action and continuance of conduct and the organization of the self in specific situations. Ultimately, the function of intelligence is to render the world "favorable for conduct." In this, observed Mead, scientific knowledge and the evolutionary process coincide.

* *Mind, Self and Society* (Chicago, 1934), p. 175.
† "A Pragmatic Theory of Truth," *University of California Publications in Philosophy*, XI (1929). Reprinted in Andrew J. Reck, *Selected Writings*, pp. 320–344. For the above, pp. 328, 338.

XVII. Social Consciousness and the Consciousness of Meaning*

In an earlier publication† I have supported the position that gestures in their original forms are the first overt phases in social acts, a social act being one in which one individual serves in his action as a stimulus to a response from another individual. The adaptation of these individuals to each other implies that their conduct calls out appropriate and valuable responses from each other. Such adjustment on the part of each form to the action of the other naturally leads to the direction of the action of the one form by the earliest phases of the conduct of the other. The more perfect the adaptation of the conduct of a social form the more readily it would be able to determine its actions by the first indications of an act in another form. From such a situation there follows a peculiar importance attaching to these earlier stages of social acts, serving as they do to mediate the appropriate responses of other forms in the same group. The earlier stages in social acts involve all the beginnings of hostility, wooing, and parental care, all the control of the sense organs which precede the overt conduct directed by the sense organ, the attitudes of the body expressing readiness to act and the direction which the act will take, and finally the vasomotor preparations for action, such as the flushing of the blood vessels, the change in the rhythm of breathing and the ex-

* *The Psychological Bulletin,* VII (1910). For the specific source see p. 377, below.

† *The Psychological Bulletin,* VI (1909), p. 401.

plosive sounds which accompany the change in the breathing rhythm and circulation.

All of these early stages in animal reaction are of supreme importance as stimuli to social forms—i.e., forms whose lives are conditioned by the conduct of other forms —and must become in the process of evolution peculiarly effective as stimuli, or, put the other way around, social forms must become peculiarly sensitive to these earliest overt phases in social acts. The import which these early stages in social acts have is a sufficient explanation for their preservation even though some of them may have lost their original function in the social act. The gesture as the beginning of a social activity has become provocative of a certain response on the part of another form. It serves in wooing and quarreling to produce a summation of stimuli for reproductive and hostile reactions. This interplay of preliminary and preparatory processes even in the conduct of animal forms lower than man places the animals *en rapport* with each other, and leads in wooing, quarreling, and animal play to relatively independent activities that answer to human intercourse.

There exists thus a field of conduct even among animals below man, which in its nature may be classed as gesture. It consists of the beginnings of those actions which call out instinctive responses from other forms. And these beginnings of acts call out responses which lead to readjustments of acts which have been commenced, and these readjustments lead to still other beginnings of response which again call out still other readjustments. Thus there is a conversation of gesture, a field of palaver within the social conduct of animals. Again the movements which constitute this field of conduct are themselves not the complete acts which they start out to become. They are the glance of the eye that is the beginning of the spring or the flight, the attitude of body with which the spring or flight commences, the growl, or cry, or snarl with which the respiration adjusts itself to oncoming struggle, and they all change with the answering attitudes, glances of the eye, growls and snarls which are the beginnings of the actions which they themselves arouse.

Back of these manifestations lie the emotions which the checking of the acts inevitably arouse. Fear, anger, lust of hunger and sex, all the gamut of emotions arise back of the activities of fighting, and feeding, and reproduction, because these activities are for the moment stopped in the process of readjustment. While these gestures thus reveal emotion to the observer their function is not that of revealing or expressing emotion. While the very checking of activity and readiness, straining to adjust oneself to indications of action on the part of the other individual, imply excess of energy seeking outlet, the setting free of surplus energy is not the function of the gesture. Nor yet is it an adequate explanation to find in the gesture the psychophysical counterpart of the emotional consciousness. The first function of the gesture is the mutual adjustment of changing social response to changing social stimulation, when stimulation and response are to be found in the first overt phases of the social acts.

I desire in this paper to emphasize and elaborate the position taken earlier that only in the relation of this mutual adjustment of social stimulation and response to the activities which they ultimately mediate, can the consciousness of meaning arise.

It is the assumption of the author that the consciousness of meaning consists mainly in a consciousness of attitude, on the part of the individual, over against the object to which he is about to react. The feeling of attitude represents the coordination between the process of stimulation and that of response when this is properly mediated. The feelings of readiness to take up or read a book, to spring over a ditch, to hurl a stone, are the stuff out of which arises a sense of the meaning of the book, the ditch, the stone. Professor Royce has perhaps given the most simple and convincing statement of the doctrine, in his *Psychology*.

It is important to thus identify the sense of meaning with the consciousness of response or readiness to respond, because such an identification throws some light on the conditions under which the sense of meaning can arise. The power of distinguishing clearly the different elements in contents of consciousness belongs peculiarly to the field of stimulation and its imagery. Such sharp distinction of contents is not characteristic of the consciousness of response.

Vision with its assimilated imagery of contact sensation readily distinguishes the form, shadings. and colors of a rock and can mark the different areas of color and brightness, the changing curve of line and plane, but the tendencies to react to each of these different stimulations lie back in a field into which we can only indirectly introduce clear distinctions of content. We may detect a tendency of the eye to follow the curving line and to arrest its movement with its breaks in the contour. We may catch the finger in a readiness to follow a like path, or we may be unable to analyze out these contents, and these are but a minimal fraction of the responses which are indicated in our sense of familiarity with the boulder.

The motor imagery which lies in the background of the sensuous discriminations is notably difficult to detect, and even when consciously aroused, to differentiate into clearly distinguishable parts. This difficulty in presenting the contents of response—either in terms of the attitude of body, the position of the limbs, feel of contracting muscles, or in terms of the memory of past responses—indicates that these contents, at least in their analyzed elements, are of negligible importance in the economy of immediate conduct. On the contrary, conduct is controlled by recognized differences in the field of stimulation. It is the difference in the visual or auditory or tactual experience which results in changed response. It is the failure to secure a difference in these fields that leads to renewed effort. We are conscious of muscular strain to some degree, but attention follows the changing objects about us that register the success or failure of the activity. It is further true that the more perfect the adjustment between the stimulation and response within the act the less conscious are we of the response itself. Of incomplete adjustment we are aware as awkwardness of movement and uncontrolled reactions. Perfection of adjustment leaves us with only the recognition of the sensuous characteristics of the objects about, and we have only the attitude of familiarity to record the readiness to make a thousand responses to distinctions of vision, sound, and feel that lie in our field of stimulation. Yet the meaning of these distinctions in sense experience must lie in the relation of the stimulation to the response.

The recurrence in memory of the past experience is the content that is commonly supposed to mediate this consciousness of meaning. The burnt child avoids the fire. Something to be shunned has become to him the most important element of the fascinating flame, and it is the *consequence* of the response that is supposed to give the child the all-important content. The recurrence of the imagery of the past disaster insures the avoidance of the flame. Does it give the child a consciousness that this is the meaning of the fire? There is wide difference between merging the memory of the past experience with the present sensuous stimulation leading to the withdrawal of the child's hand, and a consciousness that hot fire *means* withdrawal. In the first case an immediate content of sensation assimilates a content of imagery that ensures a certain response. This assimilation in no sense guarantees a consciousness of a distinguishable meaning. As indicated above the more complete the assimilation the less conscious are we of the actual content of response. That with which we are most familiar is least likely to be distinguished in direct conduct in terms of meaning. That this familiarity is still a guarantee that upon demand we can give a meaning illustrates the point I desire to make, that the bringing into consciousness of a meaning content is an act which must in every instance be distinguished from the mere consciousness of stimulation resulting in response. To see one's hat may at once lead to picking it up and putting it on. This sureness and immediacy of action is not the same as the consciousness that it is his hat. In fact it is essential to the economy of our conduct that the connection between stimulation and response should become habitual and should sink below the threshold of consciousness. Furthermore if the relation between stimulation and response is to appear as the meaning of the object—if the characters of the stimulation are to be referred to the appropriate characters in response, we find ourselves before the difficulty presented above. There is in our response so little content which can be distinguished and related to the characters in the content of stimulation. There is the leaping flame which means to the child a plaything, there is heat which means a burn. In this case the results of the past responses are related to characters in the content of stimulation—movement means plaything, heat means burn. Still the meaning of plaything is playing and the meaning of burn is drawing back the hand. The association of these contents with the dancing flame does not enable the child to present to himself the playing or hurried withdrawal. It simply gives other contents, other stimulation values to his immediate experience. The association of one content with another content is not the symbolism of meaning. In the consciousness of meaning the symbol and that which is symbolized—the thing and what it means—must be presented separately. Association of contents of stimulation tends to become a complete merging and loss of distinction. And these contents of imagery which are merged are not the attitudes, the feels of readiness to act which lie back of our consciousness of meaning. The general habit of reacting to objects of a certain class, such as a book, must be got before the mind's eye before a recognition of the meaning of a book can appear. No amount of enrichment of the sensuous content of the book through the eye, hand or memory image will bring this habitual generalized attitude into consciousness. Unquestionably these enrichments furnish us with more cues for setting off this habitual reaction. But this is their entire function, to act as cues to habitual reactions, not to appear as symbols of these reactions, as separate contents. The facility of habitual conduct forbids such separation between the stimulation cue and the response. The more perfect the habit the less possibility would there be that the content which serves to stimulate could serve directly as the symbol of the response, could bring out separately and relate to itself the reaction for which it is responsible. If the fact be simple, consisting only in well-organized stimulation and response, there cannot be found in its mechanism the occasion for the appearance of the consciousness of meaning. The perfection of adjustment between these two parts of the act leaves no opening for the distinction between characteristic and its meaning, and without such a distinction, involved in the process of relation, there can be no recognition of meaning. Furthermore the contents in consciousness which answer to the meaning of objects are our generalized habitual responses to them. These contents are the consciousness of attitudes, of muscular tensions and the feels of readiness to act in presence of certain stimulations. There is nothing in the economy of the act itself which tends to being these contents above the threshold, nor distinguish them as separable elements in a process of relation, such as is implied in the consciousness of meaning.

The foregoing analysis has considered only the act made perfect in habit. This act is of course the basis of the consciousness of meaning. Meaning is a statement of the relation between the characteristics in the sensuous stimulation and the responses which they call out. While therefore there is nothing in the mechanism of the act which brings this relation itself to consciousness the consciousness of the relation rests upon the perfection of the act.

If the occasion for the consciousness of meaning is not found in the habitual act may it not be found in the conflict of acts? The same psychology that states meaning in terms of the attitudes which are the registrations in consciousness of habits of reaction is wont to find in conflicting activities occasion for reflective consciousness. Thinking for this psychology is always the solution of a problem. It would then be consonant with this point of view to find in conflicting activities just that conscious distinction between the characteristic in the stimulation and the attitude of response which is the prerequisite of the consciousness of meaning. For example, a man is in doubt whether the clouds and wind mean rain or fair weather. His inclination to walk abroad, and his inclination to seek shelter are in conflict. This conflict is precisely the situation which brings sharply into consciousness the characteristics of sky and atmosphere which are signs of fair and of foul weather. A certain direction of the wind and dampness in the air are so merged in experience with the imagery of rainy weather that one instinctively draws back from expeditions far from shelter, while a still unclouded sky arouses the inclinations to wander abroad. Does this conflict which must emphasize the opposing characteristics of the morning heavens also lead to that relation of the characteristics to response which is implied in the consciousness of meaning? A legitimate guide in seeking an answer to this question will be found in the direction of attention; and attention under such conditions is directed toward the differences in the characteristics of weather, and not toward the feels of attitude which reveal our habits of response. The man so situated studies the heavens, sniffs the air, detects a thickening of the sky which would otherwise have passed unnoticed, but does not immediately become conscious that rain means his habit of withdrawing from its inclemency, nor is he impelled to define to himself fair weather in terms of far-ranging expeditions. The connections are of course there, but the conflict of tendencies directs the attention not to these connections but toward the sharper definition of the objects which constitute the stimulation.

In the field of gesture, on the other hand, the interplay

of social conduct turns upon changes of attitude, upon signs of response. In themselves these signs of response become simply other stimulations to which the individual replies by means of other responses and do not at first seem to present a situation essentially different from that of the man hesitating before the uncertainties of the morning sky. The difference is found, however, in the fact that we are conscious of interpreting the gestures of others by our own responses or tendencies to respond. We awaken to the hostility of our neighbors' attitudes by the arising tendency to attack or assume the attitude of defense. We become aware of the direction of another's line of march by our tendencies to step to one side or the other.

During the whole process of interaction with others we are analyzing their oncoming acts by our instinctive responses to their changes of posture and other indications of developing social acts. We have seen that the ground for this lies in the fact that social conduct must be continually readjusted after it has already commenced, because the individuals to whose conduct our own answers, are themselves constantly varying their conduct as our responses become evident. Thus our adjustments to their changing reactions take place, by a process of analysis of our own responses to their stimulations. In these social situations appear not only conflicting acts with the increased definition of elements in the stimulation, but also a consciousness of one's own attitude as an interpretation of the meaning of the social stimulus. We are conscious of our attitudes because they are responsible for the changes in the conduct of other individuals. A man's reaction toward weather conditions has no influence upon the weather itself. It is of importance for the success of his conduct that he should be conscious not of his own attitudes, of his own habits of response, but of the signs of rain or fair weather. Successful social conduct brings one into a field within which a consciousness of one's own attitudes helps toward the control of the conduct of others.

In the field of social conduct, attention is indeed directed toward the stimulation existing in the overt actions and preparations for action on the part of others, but the response to these indications of conduct leads to change in this conduct. The very attention given to stimulation may throw one's attention back upon the attitude he will assume toward the challenging attitude in another, since this attitude will change the stimulation. To make the two situations somewhat more specific we may compare the state of consciousness of a man running through a forest or over broken ground, with that of a man face to face with a number of enemies. The first is constantly faced by problems requiring rapid solution, problems of the pace he can keep up, and the direction he should take in the midst of the crowded obstacles to his progress. He responds instantaneously to indications of distance, of contour, and of resistance by rapid movements toward which as attitudes he has not the slightest temptation to turn his attention.

The second is subject to the same type of stimulation. He must act instantaneously and judge as quickly the characters of the stimulations to which he must respond. His situation however differs in this, that the attitudes he assumes to meet an anticipated blow may lead his opponent to change the attack, and he must, if he is to survive, be aware of this value. His own gesture thus interprets his opponent's attitude and must be held in consciousness as changing the situation to which he must respond. In a word, within social conduct the feels of one's own responses become the natural objects of attention, since they interpret first of all attitudes of others which have called them out, in the second place, because they give the material in which one can state his own value as a stimulus to the conduct of others. Thus we find here the opportunity and the means for analyzing and bringing to consciousness our responses, our habits of conduct as distinguished from the stimulations that call them out. The opportunity is found in the import of the response in determining the conduct of others. The means are our gestures as they appear in the feel of our own attitudes and movements, which are the beginnings of social reactions.

I may refer in closing to the accepted doctrine that language, in which our meanings almost exclusively arise in consciousness, is but a form—a highly specialized form—of gesture, and to the other important fact that in these presentations of others' attitudes and our own we have the material out of which selves are constructed, and to the fact that consciousness of meaning is so intimately bound up with self-consciousness.

Thus the consciousness of meaning at least at this stage is a consciousness of one's own attitudes of response as they answer to, control, and interpret the gestures of others. The elements in this consciousness are first of all a social situation, i.e., stimulation by another's act with tendencies to respond revealing themselves in our own reactions, these tendencies and the stimulations which call them out mutually influencing each other; secondly, the consciousness of this value of one's own gesture in terms of the change in the gesture of the other form, i.e., one is conscious of the relation between the stimulation and the response; thirdly, the terms in which this relation appears in consciousness, i.e., the feel of one's own attitude arising spontaneously to meet the gesture of the other, then the imagery of the change in the gesture of the other which would answer this expression, which again would arouse the tendency to respond in still different fashion. It must remain for a later paper to analyze the process of language in these terms, and to indicate the fundamental character of this consciousness of meaning in the consciousness of self, and finally to present the process of thought itself as such a play of gesture between selves, even when those selves are a part of our inner self-consciousness.

XVIII. The Social Self*

Recognizing that the self cannot appear in consciousness as an "I," that it is always an object, i.e., a "me," I wish to suggest an answer to the question, What is involved in the self being an object? The first answer may be that an object involves a subject. Stated in other words, that a "me" is inconceivable without an "I." And to this reply must be made that such an "I" is a presupposition, but never a presentation of conscious experience, for the moment it is presented it has passed into the objective case, presuming, if you like, an "I" that observes—but an "I" that can disclose himself only by ceasing to be the subject for whom the object "me" exists. It is, of course, not the Hegelism of a self that becomes another to himself in which I am interested, but the nature of the self as revealed by introspection and subject to our factual analysis. This analysis does reveal, then, in a memory process an attitude of observing oneself in which both the observer and the observed appear. To be concrete, one remembers asking himself how he could undertake to do this, that, or the other, chiding himself for his shortcomings or pluming himself upon his achievements. Thus, in the reintegrated self of the moment passed, one finds both a subject and an object, but it is a subject that is now an object of observation, and has the same nature as the object self whom we present as in intercourse with those about us. In quite the same fashion we remember the questions, admonitions, and approvals addressed to our fellows. But the subject attitude which we instinctively take can be presented only as something experienced—as we can be conscious of our acts only through the sensory processes set up after the act has begun.

* *The Journal of Philosophy, Psychology, and Scientific Methods*, X (1913). For the specific source see p. 377, below.

The contents of this presented subject, who thus has become an object in being presented, but which still distinguish him as the subject of the passed experience from the "me" whom he addressed, are those images which initiated the conversation and the motor sensations which accompany the expression, plus the organic sensations the response of the whole system to the activity initiated. In a word, just those contents which go to make up the self which is distinguished from the others whom he addresses. The self appearing as "I" is the memory image of the self who acted toward himself and is the same self who acts toward other selves.

On the other hand, the stuff that goes to make up the "me" whom the "I" addresses and whom he observes is the experience which is induced by this action of the "I." If the "I" speaks, the "me" hears. If the "I" strikes, the "me" feels the blow. Here again the "me" consciousness is of the same character as that which arises from the action of the other upon him. That is, it is only as the individual finds himself acting with reference to himself as he acts towards others, that he becomes a subject to himself rather than an object, and only as he is affected by his own social conduct in the manner in which he is affected by that of others, that he becomes an object to his own social conduct.

The differences in our memory presentations of the "I" and the "me" are those of the memory images of the initiated social conduct and those of the sensory responses thereto.

It is needless, in view of the analysis of Baldwin, of Royce, and of Cooley and many others, to do more than indicate that these reactions arise earlier in our social conduct with others than in introspective self-consciousness, i.e., that the infant consciously calls the attention of others before he calls his own attention by affecting himself and that he is consciously affected by others before he is conscious of being affected by himself.

The "I" of introspection is the self which enters into social relations with other selves. It is not the "I" that is implied in the fact that one presents himself as a "me." And the "me" of introspection is the same "me" that is the object of the social conduct of others. One presents himself as acting toward others—in this presentation he is presented in indirect discourse as the subject of the action and is still an object—and the subject of this presentation can never appear immediately in conscious experience. It is the same self who is presented as observing himself, and he affects himself just insofar and only insofar as he can address himself by the means of social stimulation which affect others. The "me" whom he addresses is the "me," therefore, that is similarly affected by the social conduct of those about him.

This statement of the introspective situation, however, seems to overlook a more or less constant feature of our consciousness, and that is that running current of awareness of what we do which is distinguishable from the consciousness of the field of stimulation, whether that field be without or within. It is this "awareness" which has led many to assume that it is the nature of the self to be conscious both of subject and of object—to be subject of action toward an object world and at the same time to be directly conscious of. this subject as subject—"Thinking its nonexistence* along with whatever else it thinks." Now, as Professor James pointed out, this consciousness is more logically conceived of as sciousness—the thinker being an implication rather than a content, while the "me" is but a bit of object content within the stream of sciousness. However, this logical statement does not do justice to the findings of consciousness. Besides the actual stimulations and

* [Reference to James' *Principles of Psychology* (New York, 1890), vol. I, p. 304 would indicate that Mead evidently meant "own existence" in repeating James' quotation from the Scottish metaphysician, James F. Ferrier. For this, and James' use of the term "sciousness" the passage from *Psychology* is as follows:

> . . . this *condition* of the experience is not one of the *things experienced* at the moment; this knowing is not immediately *known*. It is only known in subsequent reflection. Instead, then, of the stream of thought being one of *con*-sciousness, "thinking its own existence along with whatever else it thinks," (as Ferrier says) it might be better called a stream of *Sciousness* pure and simple, thinking objects of some of which it makes what it calls a "Me," and only aware of its "pure" Self in an abstract, hypothetic or conceptual way. Each "section" of the stream would then be a bit of sciousness or knowledge of this sort, including and contemplating its "me" and its "not-me" as objects which work out their drama together, but not yet including or contemplating its own subjective being. The sciousness in question would be the *Thinker,* and the existence of this thinker would be given to us rather as a logical postulate than as that direct inner perception of spiritual activity which we naturally believe ourselves to have.]

responses and the memory images of these, within which lie perforce the organic sensations and responses which make up the "me," there accompanies a large part of our conscious experience, indeed all that we call self-conscious, an inner response to what we may be doing, saying, or thinking. At the back of our heads we are a large part of the time more or less clearly conscious of our own replies to the remarks made to others, of innervations which would lead to attitudes and gestures answering our gestures and attitudes towards others.

The observer who accompanies all our self-conscious conduct is then not the actual "I" who is responsible for the conduct in *propria persona*—he is rather the response which one makes to his own conduct. The confusion of this response of ours, following upon our social stimulations of others with the implied subject of our action, is the psychological ground for the assumption that the self can be directly conscious of itself as acting and acted upon. The actual situation is this: The self acts with reference to others and is immediately conscious of the objects about it. In memory it also redintegrates the self acting as well as the others acted upon. But besides these contents, the action with reference to the others calls out responses in the individual himself—there is then another "me" criticizing, approving, and suggesting, and consciously planning, i.e., the reflective self.

It is not to all our conduct toward the objective world that we thus respond. Where we are intensely preoccupied with the objective world, this accompanying awareness disappears. We have to recall the experience to become aware that we have been involved as selves, to produce the self-consciousness which is a constituent part of a large part of our experience. As I have indicated elsewhere, the mechanism for this reply to our own social stimulation of others follows as a natural result from the fact that the very sounds, gestures, especially vocal gestures, which man makes in addressing others, call out or tend to call out responses from himself. He cannot hear himself speak without assuming in a measure the attitude which he would have assumed if he had been addressed in the same words by others.

The self which consciously stands over against other selves thus becomes an object, an other to himself, through the very fact that he hears himself talk, and replies. The mechanism of introspection is therefore given in the social attitude which man necessarily assumes toward himself, and the mechanism of thought, insofar as thought uses symbols which are used in social intercourse, is but an inner conversation.

Now it is just this combination of the remembered self which acts and exists over against other selves with the inner response to his action which is essential to the self-conscious ego—the self in the full meaning of the term—although neither phase of self-consciousness, insofar as it appears as an object of our experience, is a subject.

It is also to be noted that this response to the social conduct of the self may be in the role of another—we present his arguments in imagination and do it with his intonations and gestures and even perhaps with his facial expression. In this way we play the roles of all our group; indeed, it is only insofar as we do this that they become part of our social environment—to be aware of another self as a self implies that we have played his role or that of another with whose type we identify him for purposes of intercourse. The inner response to our reaction to others is therefore as varied as is our social environment. Not that we assume the roles of others toward ourselves because we are subject to a mere imitative instinct, but because in responding to ourselves we are in the nature of the case taking the attitude of another than the self that is directly acting, and into this reaction there naturally flows the memory images of the responses of those about us, the memory images of those responses of others which were in answer to like actions. Thus the child can think about his conduct as good or bad only as he reacts to his own acts in the remembered words of his parents. Until this process has been developed into the abstract process of thought, self-consciousness remains dramatic, and the self which is a fusion of the remembered actor and this accompanying chorus is somewhat loosely organized and very clearly social. Later the inner stage changes into the forum and workshop of thought. The features and intonations of the dramatis personae fade out and the emphasis falls upon the meaning of the inner speech, the imagery becomes merely the barely necessary cues. But the mechanism remains social, and at any moment the process may become personal.

It is fair to say that the modern western world has lately

done much of its thinking in the form of the novel, while earlier the drama was a more effective but equally social mechanism of self-consciousness. And, in passing, I may refer to that need of filling out the bare spokesman of abstract thought, which even the most abstruse thinker feels, in seeking his audience. The import of this for religious self-consciousness is obvious.

There is one further implication of this nature of the self to which I wish to call attention. It is the manner of its reconstruction. I wish especially to refer to it, because the point is of importance in the psychology of ethics.

As a mere organization of habit the self is not self-conscious. It is this self which we refer to as character. When, however, an essential problem appears, there is some disintegration in this organization, and different tendencies appear in reflective thought as different voices in conflict with each other. In a sense the old self has disintegrated, and out of the moral process a new self arises. The specific question I wish to ask is whether the new self appears together with the new object or end. There is of course a reciprocal relation between the self and its object, the one implies the other and the interests and evaluations of the self answer exactly to the content and values of the object. On the other hand, the consciousness of the new object, its values and meaning, seems to come earlier to consciousness than the new self that answers to the new object.

The man who has come to realize a new human value is more immediately aware of the new object in his conduct than of himself and his manner of reaction to it. This is due to the fact to which reference has already been made that direct attention goes first to the object. When the self becomes an object, it appears in memory, and the attitude which it implies has already been taken. In fact, to distract attention from the object to the self implies just that lack of objectivity which we criticize not only in the moral agent, but in the scientist.

Assuming as I do the essentially social character of the ethical end, we find in moral reflection a conflict in which certain values find a spokesman in the old self or a dominant part of the old self, while other values answering to other tendencies and impulses arise in opposition and find other spokesmen to present their cases. To leave the field to the values represented by the old self is exactly what we term selfishness. The justification for the term is found in the habitual character of conduct with reference to these values. Attention is not claimed by the object and shifts to the subjective field where the affective responses are identified with the old self. The result is that we state the other conflicting ends in subjective terms of other selves and the moral problem seems to take on the form of the sacrifice either of the self or of the others.

Where, however, the problem is objectively considered, although the conflict is a social one, it should not resolve itself into a struggle between selves, but into such a reconstruction of the situation that different and enlarged and more adequate personalities may emerge. Attention should be centered on the objective social field.

In the reflective analysis, the old self should enter upon the same terms with the selves whose roles are assumed, and the test of the reconstruction is found in the fact that all the personal interests are adequately recognized in a new social situation. The new self that answers to this new situation can appear in consciousness only after this new situation has been realized and accepted. The new self cannot enter into the field as the determining factor because he is consciously present only after the new end has been formulated and accepted. The old self may enter only as an element over against the other personal interests involved. If he is the dominant factor it must be in defiance of the other selves whose interests are at stake. As the old self he is defined by his conflict with the others that assert themselves in his reflective analysis.

Solution is reached by the construction of a new world harmonizing the conflicting interests into which enters the new self.

The process is in its logic identical with the abandonment of the old theory with which the scientist has identified himself, his refusal to grant this old attitude any further weight than may be given to the other conflicting observations and hypotheses. Only when a successful hypothesis, which overcomes the conflicts, has been formulated and accepted, may the scientist again identify himself with this hypothesis as his own, and maintain it *contra mundum*. He may not state the scientific problem and solution in terms of his old personality. He may name his new hypothesis after himself and realize his enlarged scientific personality in its triumph.

The fundamental difference between the scientific and

moral solution of a problem lies in the fact that the moral problem deals with concrete personal interests, in which the whole self is reconstructed in its relation to the other selves whose relations are essential to its personality. The growth of the self arises out of a partial disintegration—the appearance of the different interests in the forum of reflection, the reconstruction of the social world, and the consequent appearance of the new self that answers to the new object.

Clarence Irving Lewis

INTRODUCTION

Clarence Irving Lewis (1883–1964) was born in Stoneham, Massachusetts. He graduated from Harvard in 1906, and after receiving his doctorate in 1910, taught at the Universities of Colorado and California. He returned to Harvard in 1920. For many years he offered a famous course on Kant's *Critique of Pure Reason*. Indeed the philosophy of Kant and certain technical problems that Lewis found in it were a formative source of his theory of the pragmatic *a priori*. He was Edgar Peirce Professor of Philosophy at Harvard until his retirement in 1953.

Lewis' writings were devoted to logic, the theory of knowledge, and ethics. His *Survey of Symbolic Logic* (1918) was an important historical survey of the development of systems in and features of modern logic (up to 1916). This was amplified further in *Symbolic Logic* (1932, with C. H. Langford). Lewis' theory of knowledge and his "conceptualistic pragmatism" was set forth in *Mind and the World Order* (1929). The position was developed more fully and included an analysis of value in *An Analysis of Knowledge and Valuation* (1947). Two later works of an ethical nature were *The Ground and Nature of Right* (1955) and *Our Social Inheritance* (1957).

Lewis' analysis of knowledge and especially his discussions of the modes of meaning and judgment have occasioned much recent critical philosophizing on the nature of meaning and the structure of knowledge.

It was Lewis' teacher at Harvard, Josiah Royce, who encouraged him to study formal logic. Royce regarded logic as a valuable instrument for investigating and expressing types and abstract systems of order. He had become interested in working out an inclusive system of order within which numerous other special systems would have a place. This was the formal structure of his system of philosophical Idealism. Lewis carried on Royce's interest in investigating logical systems; in his own important studies of the logical features and the central roles played by the modal concepts, *possibility* and *necessity*, in the formulation and analysis of knowledge, Lewis continued some of the work of Peirce.

Royce had also developed a theory of "absolute pragmatism," which undoubtedly influenced Lewis. Royce argued that "our whole interpretation of experience is determined, in a sense akin to that which Kant defined, by certain modes of our own activity." These "modes of activity" issue in the categories, the methods, and the concepts of scientific knowledge which we use in defining and judging reality. Royce also interpreted these "modes" as products of will—as postulates we make in order to satisfy certain human needs. One such postulate is the existence of "the external world"; for the world is "no fixed *datum* to which we are bound to submit," wrote Royce, but something we will to have and need to believe in. Here was another contribution to the purposive nature of thought. Peirce wrote of Royce that "his insistence on the element of purpose in intellectual concepts is essentially the pragmatic position." Peirce, James, and Royce were agreed on the teleological formation and direction of conceptual activity. This is basic to Lewis' conception of the pragmatic *a priori*.

The following paper, which was amplified by Lewis in *Mind and the World Order*, is a fundamental and concentrated statement of his "conceptualistic pragmatism." For Lewis, the mind contributes order to experience. Classification, categories, and definition are the means by which we render experience intelligible. The given, the brute fact of experience, comes to us "unalterable" as it will; but *how* given experience is taken is to some extent an "uncompelled initiative of mind." These initiatives, the *a priori* element in knowledge, function as the stipulations and principles by which we organize inquiries and systems of knowledge. How we classify and order experience, since not dictated by experience itself but rather our attitude toward it, is not subject to refutation or test by matters of fact. The *a priori* is "true, no matter what." But how we order experience is subject to considerations of social efficacy and working purposes and needs.

The interpretation of experience must always be in terms of categories . . . and concepts which the mind itself determines. There may be alternative conceptual systems, giving rise to alternative descriptions of experience, which are equally objective and equally valid. . . . When this is so, choice will be determined . . . on pragmatic grounds.*

Here Lewis' thought takes a distinctly un-kantian departure from the initial Kantian thesis that it is the mind that brings order to experience (see the Introduction, above, pp. 16-17). Tradition had long taught that Reason issuing in logically necessary and universal categories, human purposes and needs, and the special character of experience were three widely separate domains. Lewis argues for the fact of existing interrelationships and the theoretically fruitful suggestion that philosophical explanation of any one of these domains will be incomplete if it does not take into account the other two.

* *Mind and the World Order* (New York, 1929), p. 271.

XIX. A Pragmatic Conception of the *A Priori.* *

The conception of the *a priori* points two problems which are perennial in philosophy; the part played in knowledge by the mind itself, and the possibility of "necessary truth" or of knowledge "independent of experience." But traditional conceptions of the *a priori* have proved untenable. That the mind approaches the flux of immediacy with some godlike foreknowledge of principles which are legislative for experience, that there is any natural light or any innate ideas, it is no longer possible to believe.

Nor shall we find the clue to the *a priori* in any compulsion of the mind to incontrovertible truth or any peculiar kind of demonstration which establishes first principles. All truth lays upon the rational mind the same compulsion to belief; as Mr. Bosanquet has pointed out, this character belongs to all propositions or judgments once their truth is established.

The difficulties of the conception are due, I believe, to two mistakes: whatever is *a priori* is necessary, but we have misconstrued the relation of necessary truth to mind. And the *a priori* is independent of experience, but in so taking it, we have misunderstood its relation to empirical fact. What is *a priori* is necessary truth not because it compels the mind's acceptance, but precisely because it does not. It is given experience, brute fact, the *a posteriori* element in knowledge which the mind must accept willy-nilly. The *a priori* represents an attitude in some sense freely taken, a stipulation of the mind itself, and a stipulation which might be made in some other way if it suited

* The Journal of Philosophy, XX (1923), pp. 169–177.

our bent or need. Such truth is necessary as opposed to contingent, not as opposed to voluntary. And the *a priori* is independent of experience not because it prescribes a form which the data of sense must fit, or anticipates some preestablished harmony of experience with the mind, but precisely because it prescribes nothing to experience. That is *a priori* which is true, *no matter what*. What it anticipates is not the given, but our attitude toward it: it concerns the uncompelled initiative of mind or, as Josiah Royce would say, our categorical ways of acting.

The traditional example of the *a priori par excellence* is the laws of logic. These can not be derived from experience since they must first be taken for granted in order to prove them. They make explicit our general modes of classification. And they impose upon experience no real limitation. Sometimes we are asked to tremble before the specter of the "alogical," in order that we may thereafter rejoice that we are saved from this by the dependence of reality upon mind. But the "alogical" is pure bogey, a word without a meaning. What kind of experience could defy the principle that everything must either be or not be, that nothing can both be and not be, or that if x is y and y is z, then x is z? If anything imaginable or unimaginable could violate such laws, then the ever-present fact of change would do it every day. The laws of logic are purely formal; they forbid nothing but what concerns the use of terms and the corresponding modes of classification and analysis. The law of contradiction tells us that nothing can be both white and not-white, but it does not and can not tell us whether black is not-white, or soft or square is not-white. To discover *what contradicts what* we must always consult the character of experience. Similarly the law of the excluded middle formulates our decision that whatever is not designated by a certain term shall be designated by its negative. It declares our purpose to make, for every term, a complete dichotomy of experience, instead—as we might choose—of classifying on the basis of a tripartite division into opposites (as black and white) and the middle ground between the two. Our rejection of such tripartite division represents only our penchant for simplicity.

Further laws of logic are of similar significance. They are principles of procedure, the parliamentary rules of intelligent thought and speech. Such laws are independent of experience because they impose no limitations whatever upon it. They are legislative because they are addressed to ourselves—because definition, classification, and inference represent no operations of the objective world, but only our own categorical attitudes of mind.

And further, the ultimate criteria of the laws of logic are pragmatic. Those who suppose that there is, for example, *a* logic which everyone would agree to if he understood it and understood himself, are more optimistic than those versed in the history of logical discussion have a right to be. The fact is that there are several logics, markedly different, each self-consistent in its own terms and such that whoever, using it, avoids false premises, will never reach a false conclusion. Mr. Russell, for example, bases *his* logic on an implication relation such that if twenty sentences be cut from a newspaper and put in a hat, and then two of these be drawn at random, one of them will certainly imply the other, and it is an even bet that the implication will be mutual. Yet upon a foundation so remote from ordinary modes of inference the whole structure of *Principia Mathematica* is built. This logic— and there are others even more strange—is utterly consistent and the results of it entirely valid. Over and above all questions of consistency, there are issues of logic which cannot be determined—nay, can not even be argued—except on pragmatic grounds of conformity to human bent and intellectual convenience. That we have been blind to this fact, itself reflects traditional errors in the conception of the *a priori*.

We may note in passing one less important illustration of the *a priori*—the proposition "true by definition." Definitions and their immediate consequences, analytic propositions generally, are necessarily true, true under all possible circumstances. Definition is legislative because it is in some sense arbitrary. Not only is the meaning assigned to words more or less a matter of choice—that consideration is relatively trivial—but the manner in which the precise classifications which definition embodies shall be effected, is something not dictated by experience. If experience were other than it is, the definition and its corresponding classification might be inconvenient, fantastic, or useless, but it could not be false. Mind makes classifications and determines meanings; in so doing it creates the *a priori* truth of analytic judgments. But that the manner of this creation responds to pragmatic considerations, is so obvious that it hardly needs pointing out.

If the illustrations so far given seem trivial or verbal, that impression may be corrected by turning to the place which the *a priori* has in mathematics and in natural science. Arithmetic, for example, depends *in toto* upon the operation of counting or correlating, a procedure which can be carried out at will in any world containing identifiable things—even identifiable ideas—regardless of the further characters of experience. Mill challenged this *a priori* character of arithmetic. He asked us to suppose a demon sufficiently powerful and maleficent so that every time two things were brought together with two other things, this demon should always introduce a fifth. The implication which he supposed to follow is that under such circumstances $2 + 2 = 5$ would be a universal law of arithmetic. But Mill was quite mistaken. In such a world we should be obliged to become a little clearer than is usual about the distinction between arithmetic and physics, that is all. If two black marbles were put in the same urn with two white ones, the demon could take his choice of colors, but it would be evident that there were more black marbles or more white ones than were put in. The same would be true of all objects in any wise identifiable. We should simply find ourselves in the presence of an extraordinary physical law, which we should recognize as universal in our world, that whenever two things were brought into proximity with two others, an additional and similar thing was always created by the process. Mill's world would be physically most extraordinary. The world's work would be enormously facilitated if hats or locomotives or tons of coal could be thus multiplied by anyone possessed originally of two pairs. But the laws of mathematics would remain unaltered. It is because this is true that arithmetic is *a priori*. Its laws prevent *nothing;* they are compatible with anything which happens or could conceivably happen in nature. They would be true in any possible world. Mathematical addition is not a physical transformation. Physical changes which result in an increase or decrease of the countable things involved are matters of everyday occurrence. Such physical processes present us with phenomena in which the purely mathematical has to be separated out by abstraction. Those laws and those laws only have necessary truth which we are prepared to maintain, no matter what. It is because we shall always separate out that part of the phenomenon not in conformity with arithmetic and designate it by some other category—physical change, chemical reaction, optical illusion—that arithmetic is *a priori*.

The *a priori* element in science and in natural law is greater than might be supposed. In the first place, all science is based upon definitive concepts. The formulation of these concepts is, indeed, a matter determined by the commerce between our intellectual or our pragmatic interests and the nature of experience. Definition is classification. The scientific search is for such classification as will make it possible to correlate appearance and behavior, to discover law, to penetrate to the "essential nature" of things in order that behavior may become predictable. In other words, if definition is unsuccessful, as early scientific definitions mostly have been, it is because the classification thus set up corresponds with no natural cleavage and does not correlate with any important uniformity of behavior. A name itself must represent *some* uniformity in experience or it names nothing. What does not repeat itself or recur in intelligible fashion is not a thing. Where the definitive uniformity is a clue to other uniformities, we have successful scientific definition. Other definitions can not be said to be false; they are merely useless. In scientific classification the search is, thus, for *things worth naming*. But the naming, classifying, defining activity is essentially prior to investigation. We can not interrogate experience in general. Until our meaning is definite and our classification correspondingly exact, experience can not conceivably answer our questions.

In the second place, the fundamental laws of any science—or those treated as fundamental—are *a priori* because they formulate just such definitive concepts or categorical tests by which alone investigation becomes possible. If the lightning strikes the railroad track at two places, *A* and *B*, how shall we tell whether these events are simultaneous? "We . . . require a definition of simultaneity such that this definition supplies us with the method by means of which . . . we can decide whether or not both the lightning strokes occurred simultaneously. As long as this requirement is not satisfied, I allow myself to be deceived as a physicist (and of course the same applies if I am not a physicist), when I imagine that I am able to attach a meaning to the statement of simultaneity. . . .

"After thinking the matter over for some time you then offer the following suggestion with which to test simultaneity. By measuring along the rails, the connecting line $A-B$ should be measured up and an observer placed at the midpoint M of the distance $A-B$. This observer should be supplied with an arrangement (e.g., two mirrors inclined at 90 degrees) which allows him visually to observe both places A and B at the same time. If the observer perceives the two flashes at the same time, then they are simultaneous.

"I am very pleased with this suggestion, but for all that I can not regard the matter as quite settled, because I feel constrained to raise the following objection: 'Your definition would certainly be right, if I only knew that the light by means of which the observer at M perceives the lightning flashes travels along the length $A-M$ with the same velocity as along the length $B-M$. But an examination of this supposition would only be possible if we already had at our disposal the means of measuring time. It would thus appear as though we were moving here in a logical circle.'

"After further consideration you cast a somewhat disdainful glance at me—and rightly so—and you declare: 'I maintain my previous definition nevertheless, because in reality it assumes absolutely nothing about light. There is only *one* demand to be made of the definition of simultaneity, namely, that in every real case it must supply us with an empirical decision as to whether or not the conception which has to be defined is fulfilled. That light requires the same time to traverse the path $A-M$ as for the path $B-M$ is in reality *neither a supposition nor a hypothesis* about the physical nature of light, but a *stipulation* which I can make of my own free will in order to arrive at a definition of simultaneity.' . . . We are thus led also to a definition of 'time' in physics." *

As this example from the theory of relativity well illustrates, we can not even ask the questions which discovered law would answer until we have first by *a priori* stipulation formulated definitive criteria. Such concepts are not verbal definitions, nor classifications merely; they are themselves laws which prescribe a certain uniformity of

---

* Einstein, *Relativity*, pp. 26–28: italics are the author's.

behavior to whatever is thus named. Such definitive laws are *a priori;* only so can we enter upon the investigation by which further laws are sought. Yet it should also be pointed out that such *a priori* laws are subject to abandonment if the structure which is built upon them does not succeed in simplifying our interpretation of phenomena. If, in the illustration given, the relation "simultaneous with," as defined, should not prove transitive—if event A should prove simultaneous with B, and B with C, but not A with C—this definition would certainly be rejected.

And thirdly, there is that *a priori* element in science—as in other human affairs—which constitutes the criteria of the real as opposed to the unreal in experience. An object itself is a uniformity. Failure to behave in certain categorical ways marks it as unreal. Uniformities of the type called "natural law" are the clues to reality and unreality. A mouse which disappears where no hole is, is no real mouse; a landscape which recedes as we approach is but illusion. As the queen remarked in the episode of the wishing carpet, "If this were real, then it would be a miracle. But miracles do not happen. Therefore I shall wake presently." That the uniformities of natural law are the only reliable criteria of the real is inescapable. But such a criterion is *ipso facto a priori.* No conceivable experience could dictate the alteration of a law so long as failure to obey that law marked the content of experience as unreal.

This is one of the puzzles of empiricism. We deal with experience: what any reality may be which underlies experience, we have to learn. What we desire to discover is natural law, the formulation of those uniformities which obtain amongst the real. But experience as it comes to us contains not only the real but all the content of illusion, dream, hallucination and mistake. The *given* contains both real and unreal, confusingly intermingled. If we ask for uniformities of this unsorted experience, we shall not find them. Laws which characterize all experience, of real and unreal both, are nonexistent and would in any case be worthless. What we seek are the uniformities of the *real;* but *until we have such laws, we cannot sift experience and segregate the real.*

The obvious solution is that the enrichment of experience, the separation of the real from the illusory or meaningless, and the formulation of natural law, all grow up together. If the criteria of the real are *a priori,* that is not to say that no conceivable character of experience would lead to alteration of them. For example, spirits cannot be photographed. But if photographs of spiritistic phenomena, taken under properly guarded conditions, should become sufficiently frequent, this *a priori* dictum would be called in question. What we should do would be to redefine our terms. Whether "spook" was spirit or matter, whether the definition of "spirit" or of "matter" should be changed; all this would constitute one interrelated problem. We should reopen together the question of definition or classification, of criteria for this sort of real, and of natural law. And the solution of one of these would mean the solution of all. Nothing could *force* a redefinition of spirit or of matter. A sufficiently fundamental relation to human bent, to human interests, would guarantee continuance unaltered even in the face of unintelligible and baffling experiences. In such problems, the mind finds itself uncompelled save by its own purposes and needs. I *may* categorize experience as I will; but *what* categorical distinctions will best serve my interests and objectify my own intelligence? What the mixed and troubled experience shall be—that is beyond me. But what I shall do with it—that is my own question, when the character of experience is sufficiently before me. I am coerced only by my own need to understand.

It would indeed be inappropriate to characterize as *a priori* a law which we are wholly prepared to alter in the light of further experience, even though in an isolated case we should discard as illusory any experience which failed to conform. But the crux of the situation lies in this; beyond such principles as those of logic, which we seem fully prepared to maintain no matter what, there must be further and more particular criteria of the real prior to any investigation of nature whatever. We can not even interrogate experience without a network of categories and definitive concepts. And we must further be prepared to say what experimental findings will answer what questions, there is no question which experience could answer at all. Thus the most fundamental laws in any category—or those which we regard as most fundamental—are *a priori,* even though continued failure to render experience intelligible in such terms might result eventually in the abandonment of that category altogether. Matters so comparatively small as the behavior of Mercury and of starlight passing the sun's limb may, if there be persistent failure to bring them within the field of previously accepted modes of explanation, result in the abandonment of the independent categories of space and time. But without the definitions, fundamental principles, and tests, of the type which constitute such categories, no experience whatever could prove or disprove anything. And to that mind which should find independent space and time absolutely necessary conceptions, no possible experiment could prove the principles of relativity. "There must be some error in the experimental findings, or some law not yet discovered," represents an attitude which can never be rendered impossible. And the only sense in which it could be proved unreasonable would be the pragmatic one of comparison with another method of categorical analysis which more successfully reduced all such experience to order and law.

At the bottom of all science and all knowledge are categories and definitive concepts which represent fundamental habits of thought and deep-lying attitudes which the human mind has taken in the light of its total experience. But a new and wider experience may bring about some alteration of these attitudes, even though by themselves they dictate nothing as to the content of experience, and no experience can conceivably prove them invalid.

Perhaps some will object to this conception on the ground that only such principles should be designated *a priori* as the human mind *must* maintain, no matter what; that if, for example, it is shown possible to arrive at a consistent doctrine of physics in terms of relativity, even by the most arduous reconstruction of our fundamental notions, then the present conceptions are by that fact shown not to be *a priori*. Such objection is especially likely from those who would conceive the *a priori* in terms of an absolute mind or an absolutely universal human nature. We should readily agree that a decision by popular approval or a congress of scientists or anything short of such a test as would bring to bear the full weight of human capacity and interest, would be ill-considered as having to do with the *a priori*. But we wish to emphasize two facts: first, that in the field of those conceptions and principles which have altered in human history, there are those which could neither be proved nor disproved by any experience, but represent the uncompelled initiative of human thought— that without this uncompelled initiative no growth of science, nor any science at all, would be conceivable. And second, that the difference between such conceptions as are, for example, concerned in the decision of relativity versus absolute space and time, and those more permanent attitudes such as are vested in the laws of logic, is only a difference of degree. The dividing line between the *a priori* and the *a posteriori* is that between principles and definitive concepts which *can* be maintained in the face of all experience and those genuinely empirical generalizations which *might* be proven flatly false. The thought which both rationalism and empiricism have missed is that there are principles, representing the initiative of mind, which impose upon experience no limitations whatever, but that such conceptions are still subject to alteration on pragmatic grounds when the expanding boundaries of experience reveal their infelicity as intellectual instruments.

Neither human experience nor the human mind has a character which is universal, fixed, and absolute. "The human mind" does not exist at all save in the sense that all humans are very much alike in fundamental respects, and that the language habit and the enormously important exchange of ideas has greatly increased our likeness in those respects which are here in question. Our categories and definitions are peculiarly social products, reached in the light of experiences which have much in common, and beaten out, like other pathways, by the coincidence of human purposes and the exigencies of human cooperation. Concerning the *a priori* there need be neither universal agreement nor complete historical continuity. Conceptions, such as those of logic, which are least likely to be affected by the opening of new ranges of experience, represent the most stable of our categories; but none of them is beyond the possibility of alteration.

Mind contributes to experience the element of order of classification, categories, and definition. Without such, experience would be unintelligible. Our knowledge of the validity of these is simply consciousness of our own fundamental ways of acting and our own intellectual intent. Without this element, knowledge is impossible, and it is here that whatever truths are necessary and independent of experience must be found. But the commerce between our categorical ways of acting, our pragmatic interests, and the particular character of experience is closer than we have realized. No explanation of any one of these can be complete without consideration of the other two.

Pragmatism has sometimes been charged with oscillating between two contrary notions; the one, that experience is "through and through malleable to our purpose," the other, that facts are "hard" and uncreated by the mind. We here offer a mediating conception: through all our knowledge runs the element of the *a priori*, which is indeed malleable to our purpose and responsive to our need. But throughout, there is also that other element of experience which is "hard," "independent," and unalterable to our will.

SOURCES of the SELECTIONS

I. John Dewey. "The Development of American Pragmatism." Originally *"La Développement du Pragmatisme Américain,"* *Revue de Métaphysique et de Morale*, XXIX (1922), pp. 411–430. English translation in *Studies in the History of Ideas*. New York: Columbia University Press, 1925, Vol. II, pp. 352–377. Reprinted in *Philosophy and Civilization*. New York: Minton, Balch and Co., 1931, pp. 13–35.

II. Charles Sanders Peirce. "Definition and Description of Pragmatism."
(i) "Definition of Pragmatic and Pragmatism." From "Pragmatic and Pragmatism," J. M. Baldwin, ed. *Dictionary of Philosophy and Psychology*. New York: Macmillan Co., 1902, Vol. II, pp. 321–322. In Charles Hartshorne and Paul Weiss, eds. *Collected Papers of Charles Sanders Peirce*. Cambridge: Harvard University Press, 1934, Vol. V, pp. 1–3. Notes other than those in square brackets and all subtitles in this and selections ii and iii below, are those of the editors of the *Collected Papers*.
(ii) "The Architectonic Construction of Pragmatism." From ms. c. 1905. *Collected Papers*, Vol. V, pp. 3–6.
(iii) "Historical Affinities and Genesis." From ms. c. 1906. *Collected Papers*, Vol. V, pp. 6–9; 317–320.

III. Charles Sanders Peirce. "The Fixation of Belief," *Popular Science Monthly*, 12 (1877), pp. 1–15. The first of six papers in a series called "Illustrations of the Logic of Science." In this and the two following papers minor changes in punctuation and notes in square brackets have been added by the editor of the present volume.

IV. Charles Sanders Peirce. "How To Make Our Ideas Clear," *Popular Science Monthly*, 12 (1878), pp. 286–302. The second paper in the series "Illustrations of the Logic of Science."

V. Charles Sanders Peirce. "What Pragmatism Is," *The Monist*, 15 (1905), pp. 161–181.

VI. William James. "An Interview: Pragmatism—What It Is,"

The New York Times (November 3, 1907). The interview was by Edwin Bjorkman.

VII. William James. "Selections from *The Principles of Psychology*": New York: Henry Holt and Co., 1890. 2 vols.

    (i) "Habit," Vol. I, pp. 104–109; 121–122.

    (ii) "Two Kinds of Knowledge: Knowledge of Acquaintance and Knowledge-About," Vol. I, pp. 221–223.

    (iii) "The Stream of Thought," Vol. I, pp. 239–243; 249–251; 258–261.

    (iv) "The Self," Vol. I, pp. 319–320; 324–325; 400–401.

    (v) "Note: Body as the Center of Self," *A Pluralistic Universe*. New York: Longmans, Green, and Co., 1909, p. 380*n*.

    (vi) "Discrimination and Comparison," *The Principles of Psychology*, Vol. I, pp. 487–489.

    (vii) "Belief and Perception of Reality," Vol. II, pp. 283–298; 307–309; 311–312.

    (viii) "Emotion," Vol. II, pp. 449–452; 478–479.

    (ix) "Action and Will," Vol. II, pp. 528–535.

VIII. William James. "The Will to Believe," *New World*, 5 (1896), pp. 327–347. Reprinted in *The Will to Believe and Other Essays in Popular Philosophy*. New York: Longmans, Green, and Co., 1896, pp. 1–31.

IX. William James. "What Pragmatism Means," *Pragmatism: A New Name for Some Old Ways of Thinking*. New York: Longmans, Green, and Co., 1907, pp. 43–81.

X. William James. "Pragmatism's Conception of Truth," *Pragmatism*. New York: Longmans, Green, and Co., 1907, pp. 197–236.

XI. William James. "The Tigers in India," *The Meaning of Truth: A Sequel to "Pragmatism."* New York: Longmans, Green, and Co., 1909, pp. 43–50.

XII. William James. "The Meaning of the Word Truth." Remarks at the Cornell meeting of the American Philosophical Association, 1907. Reprinted in *The Meaning of Truth*. New York: Longmans, Green, and Co., 1909, pp. 217–220.

XIII. John Dewey. "The Unit of Behavior." Originally "The Reflex Arc Concept in Psychology," *The Psychological Review*, III (1896), pp. 357–370. Reprinted with some revisions as "The Unit of Behavior," *Philosophy and Civilization*. New York: Minton, Balch and Co., 1934, pp. 233–248. The selection in the present volume is the reprinted version.

XIV. John Dewey. "The Practical Character of Reality." Originally "Does Reality Possess Practical Character?" in *Essays, Philosophical and Psychological, in Honor of William James*. New York: Longmans, Green, and Co., 1908. Reprinted as "The Practical Character of Reality," *Philosophy and Civilization*. New York: Minton, Balch and Co., 1934, pp. 36–55.

XV. John Dewey. "The Construction of Good," *The Quest for Certainty.* New York: Minton, Balch and Co., 1929, pp. 254–286.

XVI. John Dewey. "The Pattern of Inquiry," Ch. VI of *Logic: The Theory of Inquiry.* New York: Henry Holt and Co., 1938, pp. 101–119.

XVII. George Herbert Mead. "Social Consciousness and the Consciousness of Meaning," *The Psychological Bulletin,* VII (1910), pp. 397–405. Reprinted in Andrew Reck, ed. *Selected Writings of George Herbert Mead.* New York: The Bobbs-Merrill Co., Inc., 1964, pp. 123–133.

XVIII. George Herbert Mead. "The Social Self," *The Journal of Philosophy, Psychology, and Scientific Methods,* X (1913), pp. 374–380. Reprinted in Andrew J. Reck, ed. *Selected Writings,* pp. 142–149.

XIX. Clarence Irving Lewis. "A Pragmatic Conception of the A Priori," *The Journal of Philosophy,* XX (1923), pp. 169–177.

SELECTED BIBLIOGRAPHY

GENERAL WORKS ON PRAGMATISM

Ayer, A. J. *The Origins of Pragmatism.* San Francisco: Freeman, Cooper & Company, 1968.

Eames, S. Morris. *Pragmatic Naturalism.* Carbondale: Southern Illinois University Press, 1977.

Hook, Sidney. *Pragmatism and the Tragic Sense of Life.* New York: Basic Books, Inc., 1974.

Mills, C. W. *Sociology and Pragmatism.* Irving L. Horowitz, ed. New York: Oxford University Press, 1969.

Morris, Charles, *The Pragmatic Movement in American Philosophy.* New York: George Braziller, 1970.

Rucker, Darnell. *The Chicago Pragmatists.* Minneapolis: University of Minnesota Press, 1969.

Scheffler, Israel. *Four Pragmatists: A Critical Introduction to Peirce, James, Mead, and Dewey.* New Jersey: Humanities Press, 1974.

Smith, John. *Purpose and Thought: The Meaning of Pragmatism.* New Haven: Yale University Press, 1978.

Thayer, H. S. *Meaning and Action: A Critical History of Pragmatism.* Indianapolis, Indiana: Hackett Publishing Company, 1981.

————. "Pragmatism." In the *Encyclopædia Britannica.* Fifteenth Edition. Vol. 14. Chicago: Encyclopaedia Britannica, Inc., 1974, 725-744.

White, Morton. *Pragmatism and the American Mind.* New York: Oxford University Press, 1973.

Wiener, Philip P. *Evolution and the Founders of Pragmatisn.* Cambridge, Mass.: Harvard University Press, 1949.

Note on Texts. The best editions of the writings of James and Dewey are the recent publication of carefully edited and reliable texts. On James: *The Works of William James,* Frederick Burkhardt, General Editor, Cambridge, Mass.: Harvard University Press, 1975 —. Ten volumes to date. On Dewey: *The Early Works, The Middle Works, The Later Works.* Jo Ann Boydston, Editor, Carbondale, Ill.: Southern Illinois University Press, 1969 —. Sixteen volumes to date. A new edition of Peirce's writings is forthcoming, under Max. H. Fisch's direction, from Indiana University Press.

WORKS BY PEIRCE

Charles S. PEIRCE. *Collected Papers of Charles Sanders Peirce.* 8 vols. Vols.I–VI, C. Hartshorn and P. Weiss, eds. Vols.VII–VIII, A. W. Burks, ed. Cambridge, Mass.: Harvard University Press, 1931–1958.

Buchler, Justus, ed. *The Philosophy of Peirce: Selected Writings.* New York: Harcourt, Brace & Company, 1940.

Eisele, Carolyn, ed. *New Elements of Mathematics by Charles S. Peirce.* 4 vols. The Hague: Mouton & Co.: New Jersey: The Humanities Press, 1976.

Hardwick, Charles S., ed. *Semantics and Significance: The Correspondence between Charles S. Peirce and Victoria Lady Welby.* Bloomington, Indiana University Press, 1977.

Ketner, Kenneth L., and James E. Cook, eds. *Charles Sanders Peirce: Contributions to THE NATION.* 3 vols. Lubbock, Texas: Texas Tech Press, 1975–1979.

Wiener, Philip P., ed. *Charles S. Peirce: Selected Writings.* New York: Dover Publications, 1966.

WORKS ABOUT PEIRCE

Almeder, Robert. *The Philosophy of Charles S. Peirce.* Totowa, New Jersey: Roman and Littlefield, 1980.

Buchler, Justus. *Charles Peirce's Empiricism.* New York: Harcourt, Brace, 1939.

Fisch, Max H. "A Chronicle of Pragmaticism, 1865–1879," *The Monist,* XLVIII (1964), 441–66.

Gallie, W. B. *Peirce and Pragmatism.* London: Penguin Books, 1952.

Murphy, Murray G. *The Development of Peirce's Philosophy.* Cambridge, Mass.: Harvard University Press, 1961.

Peirce commemorative issue of the *Journal of Philosophy, Psychology and Scientific Methods,* XII (1916).

Rescher, Nicholas. *Peirce's Philosophy of Science.* South Bend, Indiana: University of Notre Dame Press, 1978.

Skagestad, Peter. *The Road of Inquiry:* Charles Peirce's Pragmatic Realism. New York: Columbia University Press, 1981.

WORKS BY JAMES

"Remarks on Spencer's Definition of Mind as Correspondence," *Journal of Speculative Philosophy,* XII (1878), 1–18. Reprinted in *Essays in Philosophy.* Cambridge, Mass.: Harvard University Press, 1978.

The Principles of Psychology. 3 vols. Cambridge, Mass.: Harvard University Press, 1981.

The Will to Believe and Other Essays in Popular Philosophy. Cambridge, Mass.: Harvard University Press, 1979.

The Varieties of Religious Experience. New York: Longmans, Green and Co., 1902.

Pragmatism: A New Name for Some Old Ways of Thinking. Cambridge, Mass.: Harvard University Press, 1975.

The Meaning of Truth, A Sequel to 'Pragmatism.' Cambridge, Mass.: Harvard University Press, 1975.

A Pluralistic Universe. Cambridge, Mass.: Harvard University Press, 1977.

Essays in Radical Empiricism. Cambridge, Mass.: Harvard University Press, 1976.

Letters of William James. Henry James, ed. 2 vols. Boston: The Atlantic Monthly Press, 1920.

The Writings of William James. John J. McDermott, ed. Chicago: University of Chicago Press, 1977.

WORKS ABOUT JAMES

Allen, Gay W. *William James, A Biography.* New York: The Viking Press, 1967.

Corti, Walter Robert, ed. *The Philosophy of William James.* Hamburg: Felix Meiner Verlag, 1976.

Matthiessen, F. O. *The James Family.* New York: Alfred A. Knopf, 1947.

Perry, R. B. *The Thought and Character of William James.* 2 vols. Boston: Little, Brown and Co., 1936.

WORKS BY DEWEY

"The Reflex Arc Concept in Psychology." See selection XIII of this volume. Reprinted in *The Early Works,* vol. 5. Carbondale, Ill.: Southern Illinois University Press, 1972.

"Logical Conditions of a Scientific Treatment of Morality," in University of Chicago, The Decennial Publications, first series. Chicago: The University of Chicago Press, 1903. 3, 115–39. Reprinted in *The Middle Works,* vol. 3. Carbondale, Ill.: Southern Illinois University Press, 1977.

How We Think. The Middle Works, vol. 6. Carbondale, Ill.: Southern Illinois University Press, 1978.

Democracy and Education. The Middle Works, vol. 9. Carbondale, Ill.: Southern Illinois University Press, 1980.

Essays in Experimental Logic. Chicago: University of Chicago Press, 1916.

Reconstruction in Philosophy. New York: Henry Holt and Co., 1920. Reprinted with new Introduction, New York: Mentor Books, 1950.

Human Nature and Conduct. New York: Henry Holt and Co., 1922.

Experience and Nature. The Later Works, vol. 1. Carbondale, Ill.: Southern Illinois University Press, 1981.

The Quest for Certainty. New York: Minton, Balch and Co., 1930.

Philosophy and Civilization. New York: Minton, Balch and Co., 1931.

Art as Experience. New York: Minton, Balch and Co., 1934.

Logic: The Theory of Inquiry. New York: Henry Holt and Co., 1938.

Theory of Valuation. International Encyclopedia of Unified Science, Vol. II. No. 4. Chicago: University Press, 1939.

Problems of Men. New York: Philosophical Library, 1946.

John Dewey on Experience, Nature and Freedom. Richard J. Bernstein, ed. New York: The Bobbs-Merrill Co., 1955.

John Dewey, Lectures in China, 1919-1920. Robert W. Clopton and Ou Tsuin-chen, eds. and trans. Honolulu: University of Hawaii Press, 1973.

The Philosophy of John Dewey. John J. McDermott, ed. 2 vols. New York: G. P. Putnam's Sons, 1973.

WORKS ABOUT DEWEY

Bernstein, Richard J. *John Dewey.* New York: Washington Square Press, 1967.

Boydston, Jo Ann, ed. *Guide to the Works of John Dewey.* Carbondale, Ill.: Southern Illinois University Press, 1972.

Geiger, G. R. *John Dewey in Perspective.* New York: Oxford University Press, 1958.

Dykhuizen, George. *The Life and Mind of John Dewey.* Carbondale, Ill.: Southern Illinois University Press, 1873.

Hook, Sidney. *John Dewey: An Intellectual Portrait.* The John Day Co., 1939.

Schilpp, Paul Arthur, ed. *The Philosophy of John Dewey.* The Library of Living Philosophers. Vol. I. Evanston and Chicago: Northwestern University Press, 1939.

White, Morton. *The Origin of Dewey's Instrumentalism.* New York: Columbia University Press, 1943.

WORKS BY MEAD

The Philosophy of the Present. Introduction by Arthur E. Murphy, ed. Chicago: Open Court, 1932.

Mind, Self, and Society. Introduction by Charles W. Morris, ed. Chicago: University of Chicago Press, 1934.

The Philosophy of the Act. Introduction by Charles W. Morris, ed. Chicago: University of Chicago Press, 1938.

Selected Writings. Andrew J. Reck, ed. New York: Bobbs -Merrill Co., 1964.

WORKS ABOUT MEAD

Corti, Walter R., ed. *The Philosophy of George Herbert Mead.* Felix Meiner Verlag, 1973.

Miller, David L. *George Herbert Mead: Self, Language, and the World.* Austin: University of Texas Press, 1973.

WORKS BY LEWIS

"A Pragmatic Conception of the A Priori." See selection XIX of this volume. Reprinted in *Collected Papers.*

"The Pragmatic Element in Knowledge." *University of California Publications in Philosophy,* Vol. XI, No. 3, pp. 205–227. Berkeley: University of California Press, 1926. Reprinted in *Collected Papers.*

Mind and the World Order. New York: Charles Scribner's Sons, 1929.

An Analysis of Knowledge and Valuation. La Salle, Ill.: Open Court, 1946.

Our Social Inheritance. Bloomington: Indiana University Press, 1957.

Collected Papers of Clarence Irving Lewis. John D. Goheen and John L. Mothershead, Jr., eds. Stanford, California: Stanford University Press, 1970.

WORKS ABOUT LEWIS

C. I. Lewis Commemorative Symposium. *Journal of Philosophy* LXI (1964).

Rosenthal, Sandra B. *The Pragmatic A Priori: A Study in the Epistemology of C. I. Lewis.* St. Louis, Missouri: Warren H. Green, Inc. 1976.

Schilpp, Paul Arthur, ed. *The Philosophy of C. I. Lewis.* The Library of Living Philosophers. La Salle, Ill.: The Open Court Publishing Co., 1968.